Professor S. B. Chrimes is Head of the Department of History and Acting Head of the Department of Welsh History at University College, Cardiff, in the University of Wales. His previous books include *English Constitutional Ideas in the Fifteenth Century*; *An Introduction to the Administrative History of Mediaeval England*; and *Lancastrians, Yorkists and Henry VII*.

Henry VII by Pietro Torrigiano. Believed to be *c.* 1508–9
(*Victoria and Albert Museum*)

HENRY VII

S. B. Chrimes

Professor of History in the University of Wales,
at University College, Cardiff

EYRE METHUEN

LONDON

First published 1972

© *1972 S. B. Chrimes*
Printed in Great Britain for
Eyre Methuen Ltd
11 New Fetter Lane, London EC4P 4EE
by Butler and Tanner Ltd, Frome and London

SBN *413 28590 1*

CONTENTS

APPENDICES

ILLUSTRATIONS

Acknowledgements and thanks for permission to reproduce the plates are due to the Victoria and Albert Museum for the frontispiece; to the Trustees of the British Museum for plates 1a and 7a; to Areofilms Ltd for plate 1b; to the Master and Fellows, St John's College, Cambridge, for plate 3a; to the Dean and Chapter of Westminster for plates 3b, 6c, 14b and 16; to the Bodleian Library, Oxford, for plate 4a; to the British Museum (photography Richard Du Cane) for plates 4b and 10; to Giraudon for plates 5 and 11c; to Malvern Priory Church and Mrs L. F. Hamand for plates 6a, 12a and 14a; to the Mansell Collection for plates 6b and 12c; to the Public Record Office for plates 7b, 7c, 8 and 9; to Lt-Col J. W. Stirling for plate 11a; to the National Portrait Gallery for plates 12, 12b, 13a and 13b; and to Hofmann and Freeman, antiquarian booksellers, for plate 15. Plates 11b, 13c and 13d appear by gracious permission of Her Majesty the Queen.

Plates 2a and 2b are from the *Churchbook of St Mary the Virgin, Tenby* by Edward Laws, and plate 11a is from Hester Chapman's *The sisters of Henry VIII.*

Maps 2, 5 and 6 are from *England under the Tudors* by A. D. Innes; Maps 1 and 4 are from *An historical atlas of Wales* and are reproduced here by kind permission of the author, William Rees; and Map 3 is from *History of parliament, 1439–1509*, by J. C. Wedgwood, reproduced here by kind permission of George Philip & Son Ltd.

All the maps were redrawn by M. Verity.

PREFACE

This book is not to be regarded as primarily a biography, since little evidence exists for the more personal and intimate side of Henry's life, half of which was spent in more or less obscure circumstances before he became king. Very few letters of a personal as distinct from a formal or official nature survive; direct reports of his spoken words are scarce; descriptions of him by contemporaries are brief and scanty. The greater part of our views about him must be formed by inferences from what he did as king and what was done by others in his name or with his countenance.

Nor is this book intended to be a history of England during his reign. It might perhaps best be described as a study of the impact of Henry Tudor upon the government of England. It seeks to analyse and assess Henry's actions and policies as king, as the man in whom supreme executive power, and therefore ultimate responsibility, was vested.

For some three hundred years the common understanding of Henry VII's reign was almost wholly derived from Francis Bacon's classic *History of the reign of King Henry VII*, which appeared in 1622. Historians continued to be profoundly influenced by what Bacon had written until far into the present century. This is not surprising, for there was no other study of comparable magnitude until the late nineteenth century. Bacon's powerful intellect and seductive prose style commended his work to generations of his readers. But it was far from being, as some students seem to have assumed, a primary source. Its splendidly-turned phrases and striking appraisals were no substitute for research. The delusion that Bacon had said all that need be said about Henry VII was shattered by a distinguished German scholar, Wilhelm Busch, as long ago as 1892, whose volume on *King Henry VII* was published in English three years later. Busch's work carried forward the formidable task of subjecting the materials for the reign as a whole to the scrutiny of critical historical scholarship, and brought into account far more material than Bacon used or knew existed. Busch's work was recommended to English readers by James Gairdner, whose indefatigable labours as editor of records had helped to make it possible, but whose valuable even if tentative and concise study of *Henry VII* published in 1889 was thereby largely superseded.

In the twentieth century, especially during the last few decades, great advances have been made in our knowledge of the administrative, parliamentary, and financial history of the second half of the fifteenth century, and it has become possible to give a greater measure of realism to our understanding of Henry VII's reign than would have seemed feasible fifty years ago. Many scholars have contributed to this advance. It would be invidious to single out individuals here, but all of them, I hope, figure in the footnotes and bibliographical list below.

There remain many dark places in our knowledge of the realities of Henry VII's regime. Much that we should like to know we shall never know, for lack of evidence. But there are still masses of record material in the Public Record Office and elsewhere that have not even begun to be studied. Much arduous research will be needed, as well as further detailed study of known material, before we can hope to be as well informed as we might be.

The present work therefore is to be regarded as a report—an interim report—on the existing state of knowledge on these matters. I have sought to put the materials available in print into perspective whilst maintaining, I hope, a due sense of proportion. It may seem to some readers that in places too little or too much has been presented. Certainly I have tried to omit trivialities, points of merely antiquarian interest, and hackneyed anecdotes. But elsewhere I have not hesitated to supply more detail than has commonly been done. Thus, to take one example, it seems to me to be futile to try to assess the importance or otherwise of the parliamentary legislation of the reign by mentioning only the very few well-known enactments without specifically mentioning the far more numerous items of less significance. The risk of tediousness in such a procedure is less than the risk of misrepresentation. Similarly, some detail is necessary in considering finance, a vital theme that cannot be understood in generalities alone. Nor have I thought it wise to interlard my chapters with premature characterizations of the monarch himself. I have preferred to analyse what he did before trying to estimate what manner of man he was, a theme mainly reserved for the Epilogue.

My greatest debt is to those whose works I cite. I owe much to the resources of the Library of University College, Cardiff, and the patient indulgence of many members of its staff. I am grateful to the General Editor of the English Monarchs series, Professor David Douglas, for his initial encouragement and interest. I cordially acknowledge more than common indebtedness to the members of the staff of Eyre Methuen, especially to Miss M. I. Weir for her expertise as copy editor and to Miss Ann Mansbridge for her zeal in the collection of illustrations, as well as to many nameless ones without whom no book can be produced.

S. B. CHRIMES

University College,
Cardiff
July 1972

ABBREVIATIONS

Arch. Camb.	*Archaeologia Cambrensis*
B.I.H.R.	*Bulletin of the Institute of Historical Research*
Bull. J.R.L.	*Bulletin of John Rylands Library*
C.C.R.	*Calendar of Close Rolls, Henry VII*, I, *1485–1500*; II, *1500–9*
Cal. Papal Reg.	*Entries in the papal registers relating to Great Britain and Ireland*, XIV, *1484–92*, ed. J. A. Twemlow
C.P.R.	*Calendar of Patent Rolls, Henry VII*, I, *1485–94*; II, *1494–1509*
Cal. S.P. Spanish	*Calendar of state papers, etc. relating to negotiations between England and Spain*, ed. G. A. Bergenroth, I, *1485–1509*
Cal. S.P. Venetian	*Calendar of state papers relating to English affairs, in the archives of Venice, etc.*, I, *1202–1509*, ed. R. Brown
D.N.B.	*Dictionary of national biography*
E.E.T.S.	Early English Text Society
E.H.R.	*English Historical Review*
Foedera	*Foedera, conventiones, litterae, etc.*, ed. T. Rymer, ed. of 1704–35
G.E.C.	*The complete peerage*, G. E. Cokayne, rev. ed.
H.J.	*Historical Journal*
J. Eccles. Hist.	*Journal of Ecclesiastical History*
L. & P.	*Letters and papers illustrative of the reigns of Richard III and Henry VII*, ed. J. Gairdner, 2 vols (Rolls Series)
L.Q.R.	*Law Quarterly Review*
Materials	*Materials for a history of the reign of Henry VII*, ed. W. Campbell, 2 vols (Rolls Series)
Memorials	*Memorials of King Henry VII*, ed. J. Gairdner (Rolls Series)
P.V.	Polydore Vergil, *Anglica historia*, ed. D. Hay (Camden Society), 3rd ser., LXXIV; or ed. H. Ellis, old ser., XXIX

R.P.	*Rotuli parliamentorum*
S.R.	*Statutes of the realm* (Record Commission)
S.S.	Selden Society
T.R.H.S.	*Transactions of the Royal Historical Society*
W.H.R.	*Welsh History Review*
Y.B.	*Year Books,* or *Les reports des cases,* ed. of 1679

PART I

The Establishment of the Dynasty

Chapter 1

TO THE BATTLE OF BOSWORTH

The Welshness of Henry Tudor can easily be, and often is, exaggerated. His father, Edmund of Hadham, earl of Richmond, was by descent partly English, French and Welsh; his mother, Margaret Beaufort, was English; his grandfather Owen Tudor was indeed wholly Welsh, but his grandmother Catherine of Valois was partly French and partly Bavarian in ancestry. It is true that Henry was brought up for the first fourteen years of his life (1457 to 1471) in Wales and during these years may not have even visited England more than once at most. But there is no evidence one way or the other that he ever spoke or understood Welsh, and the next fourteen years before he came to the throne he spent for the most part in Brittany and for a short time at the end in France. He owed much, perhaps everything, in his final progress towards Bosworth, to either Welsh support or at least Welsh abstention from opposition in the crucial days of August 1485. He could and did make some political capital out of his Welsh ancestry, and on occasion flaunted the red dragon banner of Cadwallader, used the red dragon along with his favoured white greyhound as the supporters of his royal shield of arms, and appointed a Rouge Dragon pursuivant; but there is no evidence that he regarded himself as primarily a Welshman or did very much for Wales after he had ascended the throne of England. His partial Welsh descent could not, of course, in any event lend strength to his actual claim to the throne, which, in so far as it depended upon hereditary questions, rested entirely upon his descent from Edward III through the Beauforts and their progenitor John of Gaunt, duke of Lancasters.

But to contemporary Welsh bards and prophets, Henry did, naturally, appear to be the new Messiah. The bardic hopes and visions which had at one time been inspired, on the basis of the Mortimer connection, firstly by Richard, duke of York, and then by Edward IV, could be more positively transferred to and focused upon the descendants of Owen ap Meredith ap Tudor; at first, but not for long, upon Edmund, earl of Richmond, then upon his brother Jasper, earl of Pembroke, and finally with more promising prospects, upon the former's son and the latter's nephew, Henry Tudor.[1]

[1] For a summary of this matter, *see* S. Anglo, 'The British history in early Tudor propaganda', *Bull. J.R.L.*, 44 (1961), 17–48.

Henry was first and foremost a statecraftsman, who was prepared to use any material or sentiments that might strengthen his own position as king. Among these materials was his Welsh descent, and this was used to harness the sentiments of Wales, but could hardly at any time have enhanced his prestige among the English. Nor is there any evidence that he took any very keen interest in his own Welsh ancestry. It is probably a delusion to suppose that after his accession he appointed a commission to enquire into his lineage.[1] The fact was that his Welsh ancestry, though no doubt endearing him to Welsh supporters, was not such that he could afford as king to boast about. Whatever his remoter Welsh forbears may have been (and there is no reason to suppose that they were in any way remarkable), his more immediate ancestors had ruined themselves by throwing in their lot with Owain Glyndŵr, whose prolonged and disastrous rebellion against the first of the Lancastrian kings could hardly be brought into the limelight by one whose sole hope of attaining to the Crown depended upon his claim to be the rightful heir of the House of Lancaster itself.

In the first half of the thirteenth century, Henry's forbears had been reasonably prosperous.[2] The most important of them, Ednyfed Fychan, had been seneschal of Gwynedd, and before his death in 1246 had served both Llewyllyn the Great and his son David, and received substantial grants in Anglesey, Caernarvonshire, and the future Cardiganshire and Carmarthenshire. His sons Goronwy and Tudur maintained the family position into the fourteenth century, mainly by supporting the Crown; and the great-grandson and heir of the former, Tudur ap Goronwy, continued the process. But his five sons were first cousins of Owain Glyndŵr himself, and this circumstance proved to be the source of calamity to the family. Three of these sons are known to have been at one time in the service of Richard II, and this fact, as well as their kinship, may have induced the surviving brothers to have sided with Glyndŵr against Richard II's displacer, Henry IV. The consequence in due course was execution for one of the brothers, and the forfeiture of all the lands of the survivors. The heir of the eldest of them, Goronwy, eventually recovered the Penmynydd estates, but his family, the senior line, fell into complete obscurity in the following centuries, a position from which they were in no way rescued by their eventually

---

[1] S. Anglo, loc. cit. 24–5.

[2] For what follows, see D. Williams, 'The family of Henry VII', *History Today*, IV (1954), 77–84; Glyn Roberts, 'Wyrion Eden', *Trans. Anglesey Antiquarian Society* (1951), 34–72; E. Owen, 'The decline of the Tudors of Penmynydd, Mon.', ibid. (1934), 46–60; (1935), 80–9.

royal kinsman. Obscurity in his own lifetime seems likewise to have been the fate of the youngest of the brothers, Meredith (Maredudd), and would doubtless have been the fate of the whole family, but for the activities of his son Owen, who, like the young sons of some of the other rebels, was provided for by Henry V, and was taken as a page in or near his own household. Little, indeed, could Henry V have imagined that this Owen ap Meredith ap Tudor would in later years be taken in marriage by his own widow Catherine of Valois, daughter of Charles VI of France and of Queen Isabella (Wittelsbach), and that their grandson would become Henry VII of England.[1]

How and when the first moves were made which led on to this extraordinary turn of events remain unknown. Owen's career in the royal entourage is shrouded in obscurity. There is no evidence that he was at Agincourt, or ever knighted.[2] He is said to have become a member of the retinue of Sir Walter Hungerford in France in 1420,[3] and this may have been a circumstance of crucial importance in the long run. Presumably, Owen was as yet too young to have done more than participate in a very modest capacity in the life of the court. Henry V married Catherine of Valois, then aged about nineteen years, on 2 June 1420. By 1 September 1422 she had become a widow. In the government of England during the minority of her son Henry VI, born on 21 December 1421, she was to have no part, and very little share in the upbringing of her son.[4]

[1] The validity of the marriage of Catherine and Owen, and the legitimacy of their children, were not questioned at the time. *See* T. Artemus Jones, 'Owen Tudor's marriage', *Bull. Bd. of Celtic Studies*, XI (1943), 142–9; there are numerous mistakes in this article, but its main conclusion, that in fact there was no statute of 1428 or 1430 or any other year forbidding marriage with the Queen Dowager, is firmly established. The erroneous assertions frequently made to the contrary spring from unsupported statements by Sir Edward Coke, *Institutes. See* also p. 6, fn. 4 below.

[2] T. Artemus Jones, loc. cit. 106.

[3] H. T. Evans, *Wales and the Wars of the Roses* (1915), 47, cited A. D. Carr, 'Welshmen and the Hundred Years War', *W.H.R.*, 4 (1960), 1 and 37.

[4] *See* generally, references in Agnes Strickland, *Lives of the queens of England*, 2nd ed. (1841), III. The assertion by K. Vickers, *Humphrey, duke of Gloucester* (1907), that Gloucester had induced the council to forbid the marriage Catherine wished to make with Edmund Beaufort, earl (1441) and marquis (1442) of Dorset, duke of Somerset (1447), killed at St Albans (1455), rests upon the story given under the year 1438 in the anonymous chronicle known as Giles's chronicle. The story is interesting but in the absence of any corroboration can hardly be taken as authentic. If the story is true, the question must arise as to the date at which it occurred. Edmund Beaufort (b. *c.* 1406) was made count of Mortain before 25 February 1427. He actually married Eleanor Beauchamp, widow of Thomas, eighth earl of Ros (d. 18 August 1430) without the king's licence, for which he received a pardon (7 March 1438), and a papal dispensation (27 January 1445) (*see* G.E.C. and *D.N.B.*).

Nothing at all is known for certain, although there are many legends, about the process whereby Owen came into the service and intimate favour of the Queen Dowager. But Sir Walter Hungerford, later first Baron Hungerford, was one of the executors of Henry V's will, a councillor, and from 1424 to 1426 steward of Henry VI's Household,[1] and it may well be that the Hungerford connection, if there was one, was the channel through which Owen was brought to Catherine's notice. Nor is there any valid evidence as to what happened between Catherine and Owen, except that at some stage they were canonically married and begot at least three sons and one daughter, whose legitimacy was never contested at the time.[2] There is likewise no evidence that anyone outside their own immediate circle knew of these facts until just before or after Catherine's death on 3 January 1437. Whether or not the grant to Owen in 1432 of substantial exemption from the restrictions placed on Welshmen by statute (2 Henry IV) had any connection with his marriage with Catherine, must remain a matter of surmise since we do not know the date of that event. It is quite probable that this grant (which other Welshmen had obtained) would have been secured before he ventured upon matrimony with the Queen Dowager, but at any rate, from 1432 onwards Owen was officially regarded '*sicut verus anglicus ligeus*' ('as if he were a true English subject'), and was legally restrained only from becoming a citizen or burgess of a city or borough or an officer or minister of the king in any city, borough, or market town.[3]

There is no reason to doubt that Catherine and Owen were lawfully married, that is, canonically by a priest. The law of matrimony was, of course, wholly a matter for the Church, and we may well doubt whether an act of parliament, if there had been a relevant one, could have prevented or defeated a marriage canonically sanctioned, though such an act might impose penalties on the parties. The allegation that an act was passed in 1428 or 1430 expressly to prohibit marriage with the Queen Dowager, has been shown to be false.[4] It is true that an

---

[1] Walter Hungerford, 1378–1449, several times a member of parliament in the early Lancastrian period, fought at Agincourt, commanded the naval expedition at Harfleur in 1416, and became a distinguished soldier, diplomat, and administrator. In addition he was treasurer, 1426–32, and was summoned to parliament by writ as a baron from January 1426 onwards.

[2] Sir James Ramsay's reference to the marriage, 'if such the connexion really was' (*Lancaster and York*, I (1892), 496), has no validity.

[3] *R.P.*, IV, 415. Owen himself petitioned the commons for this grant, but without any specific reference to matrimonial rights. *C.P.R.*, 429–36, 212.

[4] The allegation made originally by Sir Edward Coke, *First Institute* (1629), 133b, that an act of 8 Henry VI, and *Second Institute*, 18, an act of 6 Henry VI, was made prohibiting marriage with the Queen Dowager without the king's licence, followed in

ordinante[1] was promulgated by the Prince of Wales's Council at Chester early in the century as part of the 'penal laws' against Welshmen, purporting to forbid marriage between Welsh and English persons, but it can hardly be supposed, even if this ordinance had any relevance to the case, that Catherine of Valois could have been deemed an English woman for this purpose, if indeed such an ordinance could be applied to the Queen Dowager at all, and in any event Owen's grant of 1432 certainly took him out of any such restriction. It may well have been, however, that in marrying the Queen Dowager without the king's consent, Owen violated the normal usages of feudal society and exposed himself to the possibility of a substantial financial penalty, though Catherine could scarcely have been considered an heiress in the usual feudal sense of the term. But at the time whenever exactly the wedding was, Henry VI could not have been more than a young boy, and even the most austere upholders of social conventions could hardly have expected a royal mother, in the circumstances, to have asked permission from her own boy-son to contract a *mésalliance*; furthermore, Owen himself would not have had sufficient resources of his own to pay any considerable fine. The king's displeasure was about the worst that he need expect when the facts became known, at any rate from such a generally benign monarch as Henry VI, and displeasure was what he received. When Henry VI learnt of the marriage, probably just before his mother's death on 3 January 1437, he himself was sixteen years of age, and the protectorate had lapsed for some six years. As he was to be declared of full age within a year, he could scarcely have been very pleased at the news. It took even his benevolent and charitable disposition some years to extend much favour to his half-brothers or any favour to their father Owen.

There is no reason to suppose that Catherine's removal to Bermondsey Abbey during 1436 was caused by any other circumstance than her illness, the nature of which is not disclosed, but which, according to her own will, was long and grievous. It is probable that the king visited her there, and certainly he gave her as a New Year's gift a jewelled golden

---

Cotton's *Abridgement of parliamentary records* (1657), 589, was accepted by Nicolas, op. cit. xvii, fn. 2, who, however, explained the fact that no such act had ever been found in the rolls of parliament or the statute rolls by asserting that the original membrane on the rolls had been torn off and the other membranes renumbered. T. Artemus Jones, with the assistance of a Public Record Office official, demonstrated (loc. cit.) that this story of fraudulent alterations in the rolls is wholly imaginary.

[1] The allegation that a general prohibition on intermarriage between Welsh and English was a statutory prohibition has been examined and shown to be false by J. Gwynfor Jones, 'The supposed prohibition of intermarriage in 1401' (forthcoming).

crucifix, and most likely it was at this time that he was informed of the facts about the marriage. Catherine's will makes no reference to her second husband or to her children by him, but requests Henry VI to be her executor with power to depute, and, in vague terms only trusts him to see to 'the tender and favourable fulfilling of my intent'.[1] These words imply that she had previously spoken with him and can reasonably be taken to allude to her intent regarding either her husband or children, or both. But what the intent was we do not know.

It seems to be impossible to reconstruct with any assurance what exactly happened to Owen during the years following the revelation of his relations with Catherine. But it is clear that the King's Council committed the two elder sons of the marriage, Edmund ap Meredith ap Tydier and Jasper ap Meredith ap Tydier (as they were called at this stage), to the care of Catherine de la Pole, sister of the earl of Suffolk, abbess of Barking, from 27 July 1437, and eventually paid her for her services up until at least 31 October 1440.[2] But the boys were not knighted until 15 December 1449 nor created earls until 23 November 1452.[3] Suggestions as to the dates of birth of these boys are guesswork, but the comparatively late date of their knighthoods does suggest that the commonly proposed dates of 1430 and 1431, respectively, are too early, unless the honours were unusually delayed, and may tend to confirm the theory that the marriage did not occur before 1432.

Information as to the fate of Owen Tudor at this period is scanty, and depends largely upon two papers printed by Sir Harris Nicolas in what he called *The proceedings and ordinances of the Privy Council*.[4]

---

[1] For what follows, *see* generally, Agnes Strickland, op. cit. III, 159. Agnes Strickland provides the fullest account of Catherine's life, though where not documented it has to be read with caution. She was probably right in saying that for thirteen years after Henry V's death, no public document tells of Catherine's activities, but she went beyond her evidence in describing Owen Tudor as 'a hardy predatory soldier'. Extracts from Catherine's will are printed, ibid. 166–7, from B.M. MS. Cott. Tiberius E. viii, fo. 221. It is notable that Cardinal Beaufort and Humphrey, duke of Gloucester, were also to be executors. The relevant passage in the will reads, 'And I trust fully and am right sure that, among all creatures earthly, ye best may and will best tender and favour my will in ordaining for my soul and body, in seeing that my debts be paid and my servants guerdoned, and in tender and favourable fulfilling of mine intent.' Catherine's body was conveyed to St Katherine's by the Tower, then on to St Paul's, and eventually to the Lady chapel in Westminster Abbey, where Henry VI later built her tomb.

[2] *Foedera*, X, 828.   [3] G.E.C., sub-tit. Richmond.

[4] These papers are somewhat obscure in themselves, and their meaning was misunderstood by Nicolas, whose garbled account as set out in his Preface has been too closely followed by later writers. *See* below, Appendix A, 'Owen Tudor and the Privy Council'.

Two facts stand out from these documents. One is that Owen is expressly stated to have been in ward, i.e. in prison, at the date of the documents, viz, 15 July 1437. The second is that no reason for his detention is given in the first of these documents, and only very vague allusions to it are made in the second. There is no reference to the marriage, but a passing allusion is made to the king's mother 'with whom Oweyn Tidir dwelt' – the sole known mention of the matter in any official document of the time. These documents do not record any passage between Owen and the council on 15 July 1437, although reference is made to a passage which had previously occurred, but they do record consideration by the council of the question whether an arrest of Owen that had recently been made was lawful in view of a verbal safe-conduct that had previously been accorded to him. It is clear that the council was concerned to try to establish the legality of this arrest, without stating the reason for it. The arrest was made, it is stated, 'at the suit of the party', in prejudice of whose rights by common law and statute the king's grant could not take effect unless the circumstances were covered by a statutory exception, which was not the case. Owen could not have the advantage of a safe-conduct twice, and the council therefore advised the king that the recent arrest had been lawful, and the duke of Gloucester asked for and was granted a declaration under the Great Seal to this effect.

At some stage in the following months, Owen escaped from Newgate,[1] for on 24 March 1438 the council ordered 20 marks to be paid to Lord Beaumont for his services in guarding Owen, who had recently escaped from Newgate, had been arrested and conveyed to him; and Beaumont by the king's command had brought him to the council and delivered him to the earl of Suffolk, constable of Wallingford Castle, together with the priest and servant who had assisted his escape. Owen was then handed over to the sheriffs of London and recommitted to Newgate. The sum of £89 found on the priest was sent to the treasurer and

---

[1] The earliest known contemporary chronicle reference to the marriage and to the escape from Newgate is contained in *A chronicle of London*, ed. Tyrrell and Nicolas (1827), 123, which was discovered in 1823 among the archives of the City of London. The reference is cryptic, and is inserted in the annal for the sixteenth year of the reign, i.e. 1 September 1437 to 31 August 1438. 'This same yere on Oweyn, no man of birthe nother of lyflode, brak out of Newgate ayens nyght at serchynge tyme, thorough helpe of his prest, and wente his way hurtynge foule his kepere; but at the laste, blessyd be God, he was taken ayeyn; the whiche Oweyn hadde prevyley wedded the quene Katerine, and had ijj or iiij chyldren be here, unwetyng the comoun peple tyl that sche were ded and beryed.' It is noticeable that no causal connection between the wedding and the imprisonment is hinted at here.

chamberlains of the Treasury.[1] Where this considerable sum of money
came from and why it was so confiscated are unanswerable questions,
but the surmise must be that the source had been Catherine's privy purse.
There is no indication here of the dates when Owen had escaped, or when
he was recaptured, except that the escape was said to have been recent
when Lord Beaumont was reimbursed. But there is no evidence at all
that he escaped from Newgate *twice*.[2]

On 14 July 1438 an order was sent by the council to the constable of
Windsor Castle to receive Owen ap Meredith ap Tider, who would be
delivered to him on the king's behalf, and to keep him in custody.[3]
Removal from Newgate to Windsor Castle was no doubt an improvement in fortunes and a step towards rehabilitation. On 29 July 1438
the sheriffs of London were pardoned for having 'allowed' the escape.[4]
On 15 July 1439 Sir Thomas Stanley was issued by the king with an

[1] *Foedera*, X, 685–6. Lord Beaumont (born *c.* 1417), sixth baron, was created the
first English viscount in 1440, had a distinguished career in the French wars, and at
court, became constable of England in 1450, and was killed at the battle of Northampton, 1460. The councillors ordering the payment met in 'the secret room of our lord
cardinal', and were Cardinal Beaufort, John Stafford, bishop of Bath and Wells,
chancellor; William de la Pole, earl of Suffolk, Ralph, Lord Cromwell, treasurer;
Lord Hungerford, and John Stourton.

[2] The error appears to spring from Nicolas, loc. cit. xix and fn. 3, although he
realized that there is extant only one relevant pardon to the sheriffs of London, and he
was naturally unable to say whether this related to the 'first or second' escape.
Nicolas followed the story in the versions by Stow and Hall, who derived their information from Polydore Vergil, whose account of Owen Tudor is astonishingly terse.
After the death of Catherine, he tells us, 'Owen was twice committed to ward [New-
gate is not mentioned] by the duke of Gloucester because he had been so presump-
tuous as by marriage with the young queen to intermix his blood with the noble race of
kings, and in the end was beheaded.' This version clearly skates over very thin ice.
Neither commitment was by the duke of Gloucester personally; the reason given for
the committal is unconvincing, since even Gloucester could hardly imprison a man
for mere presumption, and the beheading was, of course, in quite other circumstances
and nearly twenty-five years later. Polydore Vergil's glossing over of the story of
Owen Tudor, written years after Owen's grandson had come to the throne, is rather
surprising, even though he naturally had to write very cautiously. He could not resist
a criticism of Catherine, but eulogized Owen. 'This woman,' he said, 'after the death
of her husband . . . being but young in years and thereby of less discretion to judge
what was decent for her estate, married one Owen Tyder, a gentleman of Wales,
adorned with wonderful gifts of body and minde, who derived his pedigree from
Cadwalleder, the last king of the Britons.' The references to Vergil are cited from
the English version, ed. Ellis, Camden Soc., XXIX (1844), 62, which is in agreement
on this passage with the Basle edition (1534), 481, but ill accords with the contemporary London chronicler's dismissal of Owen as a 'no man of birthe nother of
lyflod', cited above, p. 9, fn. 1.

[3] *C.C.R.*, *Henry VI*, III, 155.

[4] *Foedera*, X, 709–10; and *C.P.R.*, *Henry VI*, III, 182.

order to allow Owen Meredith esquire to go freely, although he had
'for particular causes' lately been committed by the king to custody
until further order.[1] The reason for his release was that he had found
security in Chancery to appear in person before the King and Council
on the morrow of St Martin's day (12 November) or earlier to answer
'what should be laid before him, and for his good behaviour towards
the king and his people', but until he had done so, he was not to be
allowed to go to Wales, the Marches, or parts adjacent to Wales. On
16 July Owen ap Meredith esquire gave a general release of all personal
actions to John de Stanley, John Piker, and eight other persons.[2] A
memorandum of mainprise under penalty of £200 was made in
Chancery on 17 July by William Wolf of Coton in Suffolk and nine
others that Owen would appear in person before the King and Council
by the due date, and this memorandum was vacated by writ of Privy
Seal to the chancellor on 1 January 1440, as Owen had fulfilled the
requirement.[3] On 10 November 1439 a general pardon was granted to
Owen for all offences committed before 10 October, but the nature of
these offences is not stated.[4]

Whatever offences the government regarded Owen as having committed or likely to commit – his temporary exclusion from Wales
suggests that political repercussions springing from his family's former
involvement in the Glyndnŵr rebellion were feared – from now on he
became respectable. In 1441 he appears as a witness to a charter by
which one Robert Banastre made a grant of land to no less a person
than Humphrey, duke of Gloucester.[5] In 1442 he shared with four
others in a grant of a holding in Lambeth made by Robert Ashwell,
alias Lancaster, son of John, late king of Arms.[6] In 1459 he was
commissioned, along with his own son Jasper, to arrest certain male-
factors.[7] On 19 December 1459 he was granted by the king an annuity
of £100 from the estates confiscated from John, Lord Clinton.[8] On 5
February 1460 he was granted the office of parker of the King's Parks
in parts of Denbighshire, to hold by himself or his deputies, with the
usual wages, fees, and profits.[9] At long last Owen ap Meredith ap Tider
had become unequivocally Owen Tudor esquire.[10] But the battle of

---

[1] *C.C.R.*, III, 225.   [2] ibid. 283.   [3] ibid. 285.
[4] ibid. 344.   [5] ibid. 474.   [6] ibid. IV, 78.
[7] *C.P.R.*, VI, 494.   [8] ibid. 532; and *C.C.R.*, VI, 405.   [9] *C.P.R.*, VI, 547.
[10] The allegation often made that Owen at some time adopted as his patronymic
not his father's name but his grandfather's appears to be a delusion. It seems that it
was the Crown that made the choice for him. The references given above indicate
that for many years he was variously designated in letters patent or close as Owen ap
Meredith ap Tudur, Owen Meredith, Owen ap Meredith, Owen ap Tuder (1438,

Mortimer's Cross – a severe Lancastrian defeat – was but a twelve-month ahead, and fighting then as a soldier for Lancaster, Owen was captured and beheaded during the first days of February 1461.[1]

Of the four children (if that was the number) of Catherine and Owen, only two, Edmund and Jasper survived to make any impact on subsequent events.[2] The ultimate destinies of these two sons differed greatly. Both were taken into favour by Henry VI, and were created earls of Richmond and of Pembroke, respectively, in 1452, but Edmund lived barely four years after that, whereas Jasper lived on until 1495, the strenuous and enterprising protagonist of the Lancastrian cause, and the stalwart champion and protector of his nephew – Edmund's son Henry.[3]

Edmund's comparatively short life, terminated by natural causes in his early twenties, showed no particular distinction, and is notable

---

Foedera, X, 709; *C.P.R.*, III, 182). He called himself Owen ap Meredith in his petition to the commons in 1432; his sons were at first called Edmund or Jasper ap Meredith ap Tydier, and in the creating of their earldoms in 1452 no patronymic at all was used. His general pardon in 1439 was made out to Owen Meredith, but from 1459 his designation became Owen Tuder esquire. It was thus that in time we acquired a Tudor instead of a Meredith dynasty.

[1] The chronicler's dates for this event vary from 1 February to 3 February. The battle was fought between Edward, earl of March, and Jasper Tudor, earl of Pembroke, James Butler, earl of Wiltshire, and other Lancastrian supporters, at Mortimer's Cross near Wigmore. Pembroke and Wiltshire escaped the rout, but Owen was among those who were pursued to Hereford, and he and others were captured and beheaded in the market place there. The chronicle attributed to William Gregory, mayor of London, 1451–2, which was contemporary at this time, gives a vivid account of the final scene in Owen's career.

'And in that jornay was Owyn Tetyr i-take and brought unto Herforde este, an he was be heddyde at the market place, and hys hedde sette a-pone the hygh-eyste gryce of the market crosse, and a madde woman kembyd hys here and wysche a way the blode of hys face, and she gate candellys and sette a-boote hym bren-nynge, moo then a C. Thys Owyne Tytyr was fadyr unto the Erle of Pembroke, and hadde weddyd Quene Kateryn, Kyng Harry the VI ys modyr, wenyng and trustyng all eway that he shulde not be hedyd tylle he sawe the axe and the blocke, and wherin that he was in hys dobelet he trustyd on pardon and grace tylle the coler of hys redde vellvet dobbelet was rypped of. Then he sayde, "That hede shalle ly on the stocke that was wonte to ly on Quene Kateryn's lappe," and put hys herte and mynde holy unto God, and fulle mekely toke hys dethe.' (*Chronicle of William Gregory, skinner*, ed. J. Gairdner, *The historical collections of a citizen of London in the fifteenth century*, Camden Soc., new ser. XVII (1876), 211.

[2] Accounts differ somewhat as to particulars of the children, but probably Polydore Vergil's statement (op. cit. 62) is reliable. He states definitely that a third son became a Benedictine monk and died young, and that there was a daughter who became a nun.

[3] On the careers of Edmund and Jasper generally, *see* G.E.C., sub.-tits, Richmond and Pembroke, and references therein. Polydore Vergil, op. cit., supplies many details. For valuable detailed information on the lives of Owen Tudor, his two sons

mainly because of his marriage to Margaret Beaufort. He was created earl of Richmond and given the honour, county, and lordship of Richmond in 1452, as well as other lands and minor offices. He and Jasper were also given in 1452 the marriage and custody of Margaret Beaufort and of her deceased father's lands.[1] The grant of such rights in respect of so important an heiress as Margaret was a matter of great moment, and Henry VI can scarcely have made it without some expectation that the collateral lines would become entwined, although there were difficulties to be overcome. For the fact was that Margaret had already been married, even though only nominally, to John de la Pole, heir of the first duke of Suffolk. Moreover, as recently as 18 August 1450, a papal dispensation had been obtained to allow the couple to remain in marriage although it had been contracted in ignorance of the fact that they were within the prohibited degrees of relationship. The couple, however, were but infants, and at some stage the marriage was dissolved. John de la Pole eventually married Elizabeth, the sister of the future Edward IV, and the way had been cleared for Edmund to marry his ward, which he did in 1455. Edmund is known to have been fighting in Wales in early 1456, but whether his death from illness on 3 November 1456, probably at Carmarthen Castle, was caused by this activity, is not known. He was buried at the Greyfriars, Carmarthen, and in 1536 his body was removed to St David's Cathedral. Some three months after his death, his widow Margaret, still not quite fourteen years of age, gave birth, in Pembroke Castle, to their son Henry, on 28 January 1457.[2]

Pembroke Castle had become the stronghold of her brother-in-law Jasper, who from this time on began his life-long task of protecting and furthering the fortunes of his nephew. Jasper had already fought at the battle of St Albans in 1455, and been appointed constable of several Welsh castles, but his own fortunes and power to safeguard Margaret and her infant son were soon to suffer severely as the political and military circumstances changed. He took part in the Lancastrian

---

Edmund and Jasper, and of Henry Tudor before Bosworth, *see* Roger S. Thomas, 'The political career, estates, and connection of Jasper Tudor, earl of Richmond and duke of Bedford, d. 1495', unpublished Ph.D. thesis (University of Wales, Swansea, 1971), *passim*.

[1] Margaret was the only daughter and heiress of John Beaufort III, duke of Somerset (who had died in 1444), and his wife Margaret Beauchamp of Bletso. She was thus a great-great-grand-daughter of Edward III.

[2] Busch, *England under the Tudors*, I, *King Henry VII*, (London, 1895), 12; and 319, n. 2, rightly prefers 28 January as the date to the confused assertions of Bernard André, *Vita*; cf. J. Gairdner, *Henry VII*, 3.

triumph at Ludlow in 1459, and captured Denbigh Castle in early 1460, only to be among the defeated at Mortimer's Cross in early February 1461. Unlike his father Owen, he evaded capture, but after the accession of Edward IV on 4 March could not prevent the surrender of Pembroke Castle, along with Margaret and her son, to the Yorkist forces under William Lord Herbert of Raglan, on 30 September, nor avoid his own attainder and the forfeiture of his honours and lands on 4 November.[1]

For Jasper there followed many years as a landless fugitive, seeking in desperation a restoration of the Lancastrian fortunes. In October 1462 he made a landing in Northumberland with Margaret of Anjou, and he was besieged in Bamborough Castle, which he was obliged to surrender on 21 December. Edward IV apparently would not promise to restore him to his estates, but allowed him to retire to Scotland under safe-conduct. Thereafter Jasper withdrew to Brittany and France.

The king of France, Louis XI, recognized him as a cousin germane (i.e. first cousin once removed) and made him a member of his House-hold.[2] He conferred with Sir John Fortescue, the exiled chief justice, at Rouen, probably on 13 June 1464.[3] In 1468 he sailed from Honfleur on 24 June with three ships and about fifty men, made an incursion into Wales near Harlech, and captured Denbigh Castle again, but only to be routed by Lord Herbert, and forced to retire again to France. His great opportunity seemed to have come with the apparently successful *revanche* resulting from the extraordinary alliance between Louis XI and Margaret of Anjou and the earl of Warwick, aimed at and procuring the restoration of Henry VI in 1470. Jasper was appoin-ted by Queen Margaret and Prince Edward, along with George, duke of Clarence, and the earls of Warwick and Oxford, to release Henry VI and to carry on the government in his name. The enterprise was temporarily successful and the Readeption of Henry VI in fact occurred (3 October 1470 to 11 April 1471). Jasper shared in the restoration of Lancaster, and soon travelled down to Pembroke, sought out Henry of Richmond and, we are told, took him to London and presented him to Henry VI.[4] He returned to Wales at an early date and presumably took

---

[1] For valuable detail, *see* D. H. Thomas, 'The Herberts of Raglan as supporters of the House of York in the second half of the fifteenth century', unpublished M.A. thesis (University of Wales, Cardiff, 1968).

[2] Morice, *Preuves*, III, col. 87, pp. 266–7.

[3] Fortescue, *De laudibus legum Anglie*, ed. S. B. Chrimes (1942), lxvi, lxxiii.

[4] P.V., op. cit. 135. The visit to London may well have occurred, but we may doubt whether Henry VI was moved to prophecy when he gazed upon the boy Henry, although this story also appears in André, *Vita*, 14.

Henry back with him. On 30 January 1471 he was commissioned with others to array Welsh forces.[1] But the Lancastrian triumph was short-lived. The battle of Barnet was fought and lost on 14 April, and that of Tewkesbury on 4 May. Jasper had not succeeded in joining up his Welsh forces in time to support Queen Margaret and the other Lancastrian lords on that fatal field, and on hearing the news of the disaster he returned at once to Chepstow with his nephew and thence to Pembroke, where they found themselves briefly besieged,[2] but were not prevented from fleeing to Tenby. There they received help[3] and were able to escape by sea. The intention was to go to France, but, probably because of a storm, in fact they landed at Le Conquet in Brittany, where they were promptly apprehended by officers of Duke Francis II, who took them into his protection.

The first fourteen years of Henry of Richmond's life remain largely obscure, even though enough is known to show that it was somewhat chequered. We can presume that as a baby he lived peacefully enough with his mother Margaret at Pembroke Castle, under at least the nominal protection of Jasper, who was not in residence there himself, as we have seen, for much of this period. When the castle surrendered to Lord Herbert on 30 September 1461, Henry's circumstances and prospects took on an entirely different colour. By early February 1462 his custody and marriage had been sold for £1,000 to Lord Herbert,[4] and in August he was deprived of the honour of Richmond.[5] There can be little doubt that he was soon parted from his mother, who at an uncertain date before 1464 married Henry Stafford, the second son of Humphrey, first duke of Buckingham. But Stafford died on 4 October 1471, and Margaret married Thomas Lord Stanley before October

---

[1] *Foedera*, XI, 680.

[2] The siege was laid by Morgan Thomas, sent by Edward IV for the purpose, but on the eighth day Morgan's brother David, a friend of Jasper's, raised the siege and made the escape possible. P.V., op. cit. 115.

[3] Help is said to have been provided by Thomas White, merchant and mayor of Tenby, who is alleged to have owned the ship. For particulars and illustrations of the interesting tomb effigies of Thomas White and his son John, *see* E. Laws and E. H. Edwards, *Church book of St Mary the Virgin, Tenby* (1907), 14, 71-4, 193. Information, without very much evidence but with a good deal of imaginary reconstruction, is supplied by W. Dane Russell, 'The Lady Beaufort and King Henry VII', *Arch. Camb.*, XVL (6th ser., 1916), 189-221, 301-40.

[4] *C.P.R., 1461-7*, 114.

[5] ibid. 197. The honour was transferred briefly to Richard, duke of Gloucester, and then in September to George, duke of Clarence, and on his death in 1478 to Gloucester again (*see* G.E.C.).

1473.[1] She can hardly have seen very much of her son during these years except perhaps briefly during the Readeption of Henry VI. The young Henry passed into the household of Lord Herbert. William Herbert had become prominent as a Yorkist supporter in Wales, and had been appointed a king's councillor and chief justice in South Wales in 1461. His summons as a baron to parliament in July 1461 made him the first of the Welsh gentry to enter the peerage of England. He was created a knight of the Garter in 1462.[2] The town, castle, and lordship of Pembroke, along with a number of other lordships, with profits thereof from the previous 4 March, had been granted to Herbert on 3 February 1462,[3] and we can assume that Henry continued to live there for a time at least, under the care of Herbert's wife Ann, but at some time he was certainly living at the Herbert stronghold of Raglan.[4] There is no evidence that he went outside Wales at all at this period, or at any period until the flight to Brittany in 1471, except perhaps for the visit to London with Jasper during the Readeption. In the Herbert household, therefore, Henry was nurtured and given, we may assume, the training appropriate to his birth and descent, and as befitted a boy whom Lord Herbert intended to make in time his own son-in-law by marrying him to his daughter Maud. Good tutors were said to have been provided for him, and it seems as though his quick capacity for learning and his intelligence made a distinct impression on his mentors.[5] It seemed,

[1] See G.E.C., sub.-tit. Richmond.
[2] See D. H. Thomas, op. cit.
[3] C.P.R., 1461–7, 114.
[4] André, Vita, 12, states that Henry was born in Pembroke Castle, and that he spent his early youth in various places in Wales. A manuscript history of the Herbert family (Cardiff MS. 5. 7, Herbertorum prosapia, fo. 47) specifically states that the said Lord Henry (who was afterwards King Henry VII) remained with the said countess at Raglan and that his education was entrusted to her. Polydore Vergil, whose allusions to Henry's early youth are very sparse, states that when Jasper returned to Wales after the Readeption he found Henry 'not fully ten years old' (actually he was nearly fourteen) 'kept as a prisoner, but honourably brought up with the wife of William Herbert' (loc. cit. 134). Bernard André also says of him, 'Educationis locus illi pro aeris et corporis salubritate ut infantibus assolet esse principus, varius in Wallia ac multiplex fuit, usque adeo anni temporibus variis pro tuenda ita exigentibus. Et quia in tenella aetate saepe valetudinarius fuit, tenero a suis nutritoribus educabatur, viris alioquin probis atque prudentioribus' (ibid. 12–13). Whether this passage obliges us to believe that Henry was 'troubled by ill health in his early years', as R. B. Wernham, Before the Armada (1966), 27, infers, is perhaps open to some doubt.
[5] André also says that one of his tutors was Andreas Scotus, an Oxford teacher who told André, 'numquam tantae celeritatis illa aetate capacem doctrinae puerum se audivisse'. The other tutor was Edward Haseley, later dean of Warwick (Leland, Itinerary, ed. Lucy Toulman Smith, II, 42, 151). Busch, loc. cit. 12, assumes that these tutors were

1a. Sir William Herbert, later Lord Herbert and earl of Pembroke, and his wife Ann Devereux, kneeling before Edward IV, *c.* 1461–2 (*John Lydgate, Troy Book, B.M. Royal MS. 18. D. II, fo. 6*)

1b. Pembroke Castle

2a and b. Thomas White (d. 1482) and his son John (d. *c.* 1498), merchants and mayors of the town of Tenby (*tomb effigies in the Church of St Mary the Virgin, Tenby*)

therefore, that Henry would grow up with and eventually marry into this prominent Yorkist family, and follow a career under the favour of Edward IV. The further advancement of Lord Herbert, signalized by the grant to him in September 1468 of Jasper's forfeited earldom of Pembroke,[1] was terminated by his death after Edgecote in July 1469. Henry, so far as we know, continued as before, at Raglan, but the Herbert prospects could never again be the same, and in any event the resurgence of the Lancastrians at the Readeption of Henry VI put an entirely different complexion upon Henry's position. The Yorkist associations he had were quickly severed; once more his uncle Jasper took possession of him, and he doubtless for a time regained his mother's attention.[2] But the collapse of the Lancastrian restoration brought him to Tenby harbour, to flight and exile for the second fourteen years of his life.

Jasper and his nephew, with the help of Thomas White, the mayor, set sail in a barque from Tenby, on 2 June,[3] intending to go to France, to seek refuge presumably at the court of Louis XI, who, having been largely responsible for the restoration of Henry VI, might be expected to receive the refugees, if not with enthusiasm, at least with consideration and calculation. If this had occurred, there can be little doubt that they would have been sacrificed to Edward IV at the time of the Treaty of Picquigny in 1475. Fortunately for them, adverse winds landed them in Brittany,[4] and they were duly received into the protection of Duke Francis II. There they were destined to stay for thirteen years. For the most part these years were placid enough for the refugees, apart from some episodes springing from the efforts of Edward IV or Richard III to extract them from their refuge; we are left to our imaginations to reconstruct how Henry and his uncle employed their

---

provided by his uncle, but since Henry ceased to be in Jasper's care at the age of about four and a half years, this could scarcely have been the case, and the tutors must have been provided by Lord Herbert. Haseley was in later years given an annuity of £10 for services in Henry's 'tender age' (*C.P.R.*, 1485–94, 332). *See* also A. B. Emden, *Biographical register of the University of Oxford before 1500*, sub.-tit. Scot and Haseley.

[1] *C. Charter Rolls*, VI, 225.

[2] The conferences between Margaret Beaufort and Jasper reported by André, op. cit. 15–17, in which they proposed to send Henry abroad, must be purely imaginary, since the political and military reasons for their eventual flight are not mentioned at all.

[3] André, op. cit. 17.

[4] Both André, ibid. and P.V., (ed. Ellis), 158, clearly imply that the arrival in Brittany was due to chance, and make no reference to the often alleged but little supported assertion that the cause was the treachery of a Breton master.

H — B

prolonged leisure, and we do not know who their companions were, until late in the period.

Edward IV apparently 'took very grievously'[1] the news of their courteous reception by Duke Francis. The problem confronting Edward IV was sufficiently common knowledge to be mentioned by 28 September in a letter sent by Sir John Paston in London to his brother in Norwich.[2] Edward IV's first efforts at persuading the duke to surrender up his guests, which cannot be exactly dated, were unavailing. This offer of large rewards for the delivery of Henry and Jasper did not shake the duke from his promises to them, but he did undertake to guard them so that they could do no harm to Edward IV. A renewal of the offer seems merely to have increased the duke's sense of the value of his guests and to determine him to make sure that they would not escape. He thereupon deprived them of their English servants and put Bretons to wait upon them and guard them, and separated the two. This deprivation of English company and separation of uncle and nephew was doubtless disagreeable enough, but worse was to follow. The relative strengths of Edward IV and Duke Francis underwent a change detrimental to Brittany after the invasion of France by Edward IV and his coming to favourable terms with Louis XI in the Treaty of Picquigny in August 1475. Edward IV renewed his efforts to get hold of Henry, 'the only imp now left of Henry VI's brood', and apparently succeeded in persuading Duke Francis that all he intended was to marry him off, presumably to one of his own daughters, so as to settle the dynastic question. Henry, therefore, was packed off with the English emissaries to St Malo *en route* to England. Henry, we are told, realized only too well that he was being conveyed to his death, and through 'agony of mind' fell by the way into a fever (or pretended he had). Only the timely intervention of John Chenlet, a favourite counsellor of the duke's, who induced Francis II to understand that Henry's fate was likely to be something quite different from that suggested by Edward IV's ambassadors, saved Henry. The duke's treasurer, Peter Landois, was sent post-haste to St Malo, where he distracted the ambassadors whilst causing Henry to be removed to a safe sanctuary in the town, and they were forced to return to England empty handed except for assurances that Henry would be safely guarded. These assurances were kept, and

[1] P.V., ibid.

[2] *Paston Letters*, III, No. 676, p. 17. 'Alsso it is seyde that the Erle of Pembroke is taken on to Brettayn; and men saye that the Kynge schall have delyvere off hym hastely, and som seye that the Kynge of France woll se hym saffe, and schall sett hym at lyberte ageyn.'

no further attempts to obtain his surrender appear to have been made during Edward IV's lifetime.[1]

After Edward IV's death, however, the restraints that had been put upon Henry and Jasper were removed.[2] Duke Francis had little to fear from Richard III, and clearly hoped to use the valuable pawns he possessed to extract further advantages for himself. By the time Richard III had achieved his usurpation, incarcerated or otherwise disposed of his nephews Edward V and Richard, duke of York, he could very ill afford to allow Henry to roam freely and to form the nucleus of plots against him. For it was essentially the circumstances of Richard III's usurpation that brought to Henry a totally unexpected change of prospects and a potential opportunity such as could never have arisen but for the premature death of Edward IV and the removal of his two sons. Richard III could not achieve the Crown himself without converting Henry of Richmond from being an obscure and hopeless exile into a potent rival to himself. Even so, the initiative came, not from Henry, who as yet was in no position to initiate anything very much, but from interested parties at home, who saw for the first time how the hitherto at best latent potentiality of Henry as a claimant to the Crown might be converted into reality.

Richard III had scarcely been on the throne a month before he sought to establish friendly relations with Duke Francis. In July 1483 he sent his confidential agent Thomas Hutton, 'a man of pregnant wit', to Brittany ostensibly to negotiate with a view to settling in a conference the maritime disputes that had disturbed relations between the kingdom and the duchy. The formal instructions given to Hutton made no reference to the question of Henry's position,[3] but it is evident from the instructions that Francis issued to George de Mainbier on 26 August that the question was raised, even if perhaps somewhat obliquely. At any rate Francis called attention to Louis XI's pressure upon him to hand over Henry to him; he had made great offers and even threatened

---

[1] P.V. (ed. Ellis), 158–9, 164–7, has the most detailed account of these matters. Cora L. Scofield, *Edward IV*, II, 19–29, 32, n. 3, 166, 172–3, adds some particulars, mainly by citations from MS. sources. She thus states that in the early part of 1475; Henry was a prisoner at Elven, and Jasper at Josselin, and that in October 1476 Henry was at Vannes in the custody of Vincent de la Landelle, and that Jasper was also there in November in charge of Bertrand du Parc (citing *Compte de François Avignon, Le grand collection MS. français*, 6982, fo. 326 (Paris, Bibliothèque Nationale), cf. Roger S. Thomas, op. cit. 226–9).

[2] P.V. (ed. Ellis), 191–216. Vergil furnishes a detailed account of these events, but provides very few precise dates.

[3] *L. & P.*, I, 22.

war to achieve his purpose. This was indeed a bogey with which to try to frighten Richard III into meeting the duke's demands, which were not modestly stated. Francis roundly declared that he must have military help to prevent Louis XI's threats from being realized, otherwise he might be obliged to surrender Henry. He wanted four thousand archers to be supplied within a month of such a request, paid by Richard III for six months, and two or three thousand more within another month, at the duke's expense, if required. If Richard III would agree, then Francis would be willing 'to await the fortune of war' rather than deliver up Henry.[1]

But Louis XI died on 30 August 1483, and any urgent threat from France died with him. Nor was Richard III in a position to contemplate military assistance to Brittany for any purpose. Before long he was under the necessity of using whatever forces he could procure for more immediate purposes at home.

What exactly it was that moved Henry Stafford, second duke of Buckingham, to rebel against the man whom he had played so great a part in putting on the throne only a few months earlier is likely to remain conjectural. His recent dispute with Richard III over the Hereford inheritance, and Richard III's wounding but suggestive taunt that he might next claim the usurped rights of the House of Lancaster, as reported by Polydore Vergil, are hardly likely in themselves to have provoked Buckingham to so extreme a course, though they may well have contributed to his resolve. Buckingham may conceivably have played a double game with Richard from the start, and set him up only with the intention of toppling him over as opportunity served. He may well have thought of himself as a possible successor to Richard III, at least for a time. Whether he himself conceived the idea of working for the succession of Henry of Richmond (as Polydore Vergil says), or whether the idea was planted in his head by others, remains unknowable. The part played by John Morton, bishop of Ely since 1478, who had aroused the suspicions of Richard III and been committed to Buckingham's custody at Brecon Castle, remains speculative.[2] Whatever Buckingham's precise process of mind may have been, there can

---

[1] *L. & P.*, I 37–41.

[2] The accounts given by Polydore Vergil and Sir Thomas More on this episode differ greatly. Vergil affirms that Buckingham told Morton of his intent regarding Henry (op. cit. 194), but More magnifies Morton's part into that of instigator of the rebellion, apparently intended at first to be in Buckingham's favour, but his text breaks off at this point (*The history of Richard III*, ed. R. S. Sylvester (Yale ed., 1963), 91–3). Vergil, however, concedes that the common report ran otherwise, and had it that Buckingham intended to substitute himself for Richard III.

be little doubt that the chief spinner of plots so far as Henry's future was concerned, was his own mother, Margaret Beaufort. But neither Buckingham's intent nor Margaret's schemes could have made much headway, unless it could at the least be plausibly rumoured that the princes in the Tower were already dead. No conspiracy to replace Richard III by Buckingham or Henry of Richmond could succeed if any chance remained of restoring either of the sons of Edward IV to what everyone believed to be their rightful place. The appropriate rumours were certainly forthcoming by early October, but whether or not these rumours were based upon fact it is impossible to say.[1]

Although up to this point Henry himself had made no overt move to advance his pretensions – he was scarcely in a position to do so – it is hardly necessary to believe that he was unaware that his ancestors the Beauforts had been legitimated by act of parliament in the time of Richard II, whilst Buckingham did know of it.[2] Whilst Henry himself may have been too young when in Wales to have acquainted himself with the matter, it is impossible to doubt that Jasper would have been fully informed of it and had had plenty of opportunity to pass on to his nephew all relevant information. But there is no reason at all to suppose that Henry at any time had any grounds for doubting the legitimacy of his mother's family since 1397. Whether he was also aware of Henry IV's insertion of the words *excepta dignitate regali* (the royal dignity excepted) in his confirmation of Richard II's act of legitimation, is perhaps more doubtful, but his ignoring of it later on does not mean that he was unaware of it. If he did know of it, he may well have rejected the notion that such an exception could have any validity.

At any rate, if the terms of Richard III's act of attainder passed in his parliament are to be believed, Buckingham had got himself at some stage to the point of writing to Henry of Richmond inciting him to participate in a rebellion.[3] The complicated web of intrigue that had been going on to make such an invitation possible is partially known to us.

It would seem, if Vergil is to be believed, as he probably is in this

---

[1] *See* below, p. 23.

[2] Busch, op. cit. 13, makes the assertion categorically, following the more guarded suggestion of Gairdner, *L. & P.*, II, xxx, who had no positive grounds for it.

[3] *R.P.*, VI, 245. Gairdner, *Richard III*, 130; followed by Busch, op. cit. 13, is in error in saying that Buckingham wrote to Henry on 24 September informing him that a general rising would occur on 18 October and inviting him to invade at the same time. The Rolls merely say that Buckingham wrote to Henry at various times, and that Henry set out from Brittany on 19 October (probably a mistake for 18 October, as no previous reference is made to 19 October).

matter, that the ladies concerned, Margaret Beaufort and Queen Elizabeth Woodville, were concocting a scheme before Buckingham had got so far as to focus on Henry of Richmond as the rival to Richard III. When Buckingham had won over Morton (if that is the correct phrase to use), the latter sent a message to Margaret to send down to Brecon her steward Reginald Bray (of whom we shall hear a great deal more later on) to confer with the duke. But in the meantime Margaret had laid the foundation of a plot. After the death of Edward IV's children was known or believed to have occurred she contemplated the future and evidently perceived an altogether new prospect for her son Henry (whom she had not seen for some twelve years, and very little at all since he was about five years of age), and confided her ideas to her Welsh-born physician named Lewis, who happened very conveniently to be also physician to Queen Elizabeth, then still in sanctuary in Westminster Abbey, and who therefore could readily act as a go-between. Lewis was sent to the queen and disclosed a plot which he pretended at that stage was of his own devising. The scheme was that the Woodville interest should support Henry as rival claimant to the crown on the understanding that he would promise to marry one of Elizabeth's daughters when he became king. Queen Elizabeth agreed with the project and sent Lewis to Margaret to tell her that she would procure all her friends to take Henry's part if he would swear to marry her eldest daughter Elizabeth, or, if she should die, her younger daughter Cecily. Margaret, thus sustained in her scheme, appointed Bray to be her chief agent in the business and entrusted him with the dangerous task of seeking recruits to the conspiracy. Within a few days he succeeded in gathering in and putting on oath a number of substantial gentlemen.[1] Margaret herself took into her employment and confidence Christopher Urswick, 'an honest, approved, and serviceable priest' recommended by Lewis, and intended to send him with messages to Henry in Brittany. But before he could leave, she was apprised of Buckingham's design, and at once stopped Urswick from leaving, and instead sent Hugh Conway to Henry with a 'good great sum of money' and an exhortation to arrange to go to Wales and participate in an insurrection. Richard Guildford also sent out Thomas Romney from Kent. Unless Henry had already received messages from Buckingham, the arrival of these emissaries must have brought to him the first definite information of the nucleus of a plot to put him on the throne instead of Richard III, and at once his prospects changed radically.

[1] Cont. Croyland (ed. Fulmer), 567–8.

He could now hasten to the duke of Brittany and invite his practical help in starting an expedition. Without the duke's aid Henry's chances of raising a force for invasion would have been forlorn indeed. But the duke, notwithstanding the pressure that Richard III had been putting upon him, readily agreed and promised help. Henry thereupon sent Conway and Romney back to England to give notice of his intention to come himself to warn his friends to await his arrival. In the meantime the organization of the conspiracy, in which Morton took the chief part, proceeded apace, and many likely supporters were alerted by secret messages. Perhaps the organization was none too efficient; the messages may not always have been kept as secret as they should have been; and the coordination of plans insufficiently strict. At any rate, Richard III got to know that Buckingham was up to something, and in the event a rising in Kent may have erupted prematurely.

Richard III, to gain time and resources and better knowledge of the location of the danger, dissembled and sent a courteous letter to Buckingham, inviting him to come to court. The duke feigned illness and refrained from putting his head into the noose; a more threatening letter from Richard III was equally unavailing, and Buckingham pressed on with his plans. Important adherents of the cause showed their hands and raised up armed forces: Thomas, marquis of Dorset, Queen Elizabeth's eldest son by her first marriage, in Yorkshire; Edward Courtenay and Peter Courtenay, bishop of Exeter, in Devonshire; and Richard Guildford, with others, in Kent.

Whether the risings in several different regions[1] were insufficiently coordinated, or whether in the home counties the risings were more or less popular and spontaneous and induced by a feeling of anxiety on behalf of the princes in the Tower, or by a proposal to rescue Edward IV's daughters from sanctuary and get them into safety abroad lest the princes should disappear altogether, or whether all the significant risings occurred on the same day, 18 October, as the later act of attainder against the chief rebels clearly stated,[2] must remain uncertain. Certainly the act asserts that Buckingham was in treasonable communication with

[1] The main centres of the rising are clearly revealed by the acts of attainder of 1484. They were Brecon, and Maidstone, Rochester, and Gravesend in Kent, Guildford in Surrey, Newbury in Berks., Salisbury, and Exeter. *See* below, Appendix C.

[2] *R.P.*, VI, 245–50. The adoption of the same date for the treasonable acts in the several regions may be formal and conventional only and fixed as a uniform date for the forfeiture of all the attainted, but this evidence is difficult to ignore, especially as we have to rely largely upon the information contained in the act for any details as to what happened. *See* below, Appendix C.

Henry and Jasper by 24 September, but also refers vaguely to such communications 'many times before and after'.

It is clear that when he was at Lincoln Richard III learnt of Buckingham's intentions well before 12 October, as is shown beyond doubt by his letter[1] to John Russell, bishop of Lincoln, the chancellor, requiring him in view of the latter's ill-health to send him the Great Seal, with such of the staff of Chancery as might be thought necessary. But the chancellor did not act on this instruction until 11 a.m. on Thursday, 16 October, and Richard did not receive the seal until noon on Sunday, 19 October, in the 'king's chamber in the hospice of the Angel at Grantham'. The king retained the seal in his own custody until 26 November, when after using it for the sealing of writs, commissions, etc., he returned it to the chancellor in the Star Chamber at Westminster.[2]

This delay of a week before Richard III got hold of the Great Seal may help to explain the slowness with which he took overt action to mobilize men and resources against the rebellions, and no doubt he was uncertain as to where he could strike most effectively.[3] Apparently he decided to concentrate his own forces against Buckingham, and with that end in view marched towards Salisbury as a likely strategic centre. Even so, little seems to have emerged under the Great Seal until 23 October. On that day, whilst at Leicester, he ordered by word of mouth a commission of array to be issued to Francis, Viscount Lovel, the chamberlain, to resist Buckingham,[4] and also sent a command to the sheriffs of a number of southern and western counties and the mayors of some towns therein to issue a proclamation denouncing the marquis of Dorset and a number of other persons who had risen to support Buckingham.[5] The total omission from this proclamation of any refer-

---

[1] Printed in H. Ellis, *Original Letters* (1827), 2nd ser., I, 159–60.

[2] *C.C.R., 1476–85*, No. 1170; *Foedera*, XII, 189.

[3] But the words of Vergil in this context must not be overlooked. King Richard he describes as 'a man much to be feared for circumspection and celerity' (op. cit. 200).

[4] *C.P.R., 1476–85*, 370. On the next day Ralph Assheton, vice-chamberlain of England, was likewise ordered to proceed against certain persons guilty of *lèse majesté* (ibid. 368).

[5] The command was sent to the sheriffs of Devon, Cornwall, Shropshire, Wiltshire, Somerset and Dorset, Staffordshire, Oxford and Berkshire, Surrey and Sussex, Kent, Middlesex, Herefordshire, Gloucestershire, and Southamptonshire; and to the officials of London, Bristol, Coventry, Bath, Southampton, Devizes, New Sarum and Bridgwater; and the warden of the Cinque ports (ibid. 371). The contents of part of the proclamation, made in English, is very curious (printed in *Foedera*, XII, 204–5). It is not easy to see why Richard III should have prefaced such a proclamation with a

ence to Henry of Richmond strongly suggests that at this date Richard III had no knowledge of the extent of the plot, unless the ommission was deliberate policy, made to avoid publicity for the threat from overseas.

Other commissions to raise forces in Wales, Kent, Sussex, the western shires and Wiltshire were issued during the next few days and weeks.[1] But no doubt Richard had taken other steps to frustrate Buckingham, whose rebellion, as it turned out, collapsed with little or no manifest fighting.[2] On the Welsh side of Brecon, Sir Thomas Vaughan of Tretower had been alerted to watch the surrounding country and eventually captured Brecon Castle itself.[3] Humphrey Stafford destroyed some of the bridges into England, and guarded the rest of the approaches. Buckingham, 'a sore and hard-dealing man',[4] was far from popular among his Welsh tenants, who showed little desire to rise in support, and deserted him as soon as possible. Unfavourable weather and the flooding of the rivers which needed to be crossed to get into England, contributed to the fiasco. Buckingham at the crucial time was at Weobley in Herefordshire, the residence of Walter Devereux, Lord Ferrers, along with Morton and other advisers, and finding himself in a position of extreme difficulty, decided to flee and to go into hiding at once. His refuge with a servant of his, Humphrey Bannister, whom he trusted, proved to be short-lived;[5] he was captured, taken to Salisbury,

---

rambling moral homily, and have alleged that the marquis of Dorset was living in adultery with Jane Shore. The persons denounced as assisting 'his great rebel and traitor the duke of Buckingham', and the bishops of Ely and Salisbury, were Dorset, Sir William Noreys, Sir William Knevet, Sir Thomas Bourchier of Barnes, Sir George Brown, knights; John Cheyney, John Noreis, Walter Hungerford, John Russle, and John Harecourt of Stainton. The rewards for the capture of any of these were fixed on a sliding scale: £1,000 or £100 in land for the duke; 1,000 marks or 100 marks in land for the marquis or bishops; 50 marks or £40 in land for any of the rest.

[1] e.g. *C.P.R.*, ibid. 370–1.

[2] *Cont. Croyland chron.*, 568–70; P.V. (ed. Ellis), 198–201.

[3] T. B. Pugh, *The marcher lordship of South Wales, 1415–1536* (1963), 240–1. Mr Pugh points out that Sir Thomas Vaughan's father had been executed by Jasper Tudor at Chepstow in 1471, and that no Welshman was listed among the ninety-seven supporters of Buckingham in the act of attainder in 1484, whereas twenty-two men of South Wales were rewarded with annuities by Richard III. He is of the opinion that the plot to make Henry Tudor king attracted no support among the gentry of South Wales in 1483.

[4] P.V. (ed. Ellis), 200.

[5] His capture may not have been caused by his betrayal by Bannister, 'for fear or money', as Vergil, op. cit. 201, suggests. The Croyland chronicler says that the discovery was caused by noticing a greater quantity of provisions than usual being carried to a poor man's house (op. cit. 492).

questioned, and beheaded in the market place on 2 November, without the meeting with Richard III which he 'sorely desired'. What he wished to say to him we shall never know, but before long Henry had emerged from and returned to Brittany, where he was now or soon to be joined by a number of refugees, important recruits to his cause from thenceforward.[1]

Henry's blandishments of Francis, duke of Brittany, had evoked some aid from him, not perhaps very much, but sufficient if Vergil is to be believed, to enable him to set out on 10 October (the later attainder says 19 October), with five thousand men and fifteen ships.[2] He was certainly given 10,000 golden crowns by the duke, at about this period.[3] His expedition, however, proved to be a total failure. Adverse weather scattered his ships and drove some of them back to Normandy or Brittany. Henry's own ship, and apparently only one other, tossed all night, arrived very early in the morning, in calmer weather, at the south coast; whether off Plymouth, as the act of attainder subsequently said, or off Poole, as Vergil had it, is unascertainable. Henry, in either case, it is said, seeing the shore guarded, forbade any landing until the remainder of his ships should come together, but sent a boat to investigate the soldiers on the shore. Notwithstanding their efforts at beguiling

---

[1] P.V., op. cit. 200, states that the flight of Buckingham dismayed his associates, and all fled, some without hope of safety, others to sanctuary or 'the wilderness', or tried to sail overseas, of whom a large part reached Brittany. See below, Appendix B, 'Henry's companions in exile'. Vergil also says that about the same time John Morton, Christopher Urswick, John Halwell, Edward Peningham (described as chief captain of the army), and many others escaped into Flanders.

[2] The exact date of Henry's sailing cannot be determined. Vergil clearly says 6 ides of October, i.e. 10 October; and the act of attainder, 19 October. Both of these dates appear to be far too early, but there is no means at present of ascertaining the date. The Croyland chronicler says that Henry anchored off Plymouth, at a time when Richard III was still at Exeter (8 November and on for about a week, and where he heard of the death of Henry, duke of Buckingham, i.e. on or after 2 November). Some useful details are supplied in B. A. Pocquet du Haut-Jussé, *François II duc de Bretagne et l'Angleterre, 1458–1488* (Paris, 1929), 176. It was not, according to Vergil, until after he had returned to Brittany that he learnt of Buckingham's death on 2 November. The number of ships and men that Vergil says formed the expedition is probably exaggerated. G.E.C., sub.-tit. Richmond, may well be right in suggesting that Henry had intended to land at Plymouth but was diverted by conditions to Poole.

[3] Henry acknowledged a loan of 10,000 crowns from the duke, on 31 October (B.M. Add. MSS 19, 398, fo. 33). On 22 November, at Nantes, the duke instructed his auditors to allow to Giles Thomas, the treasurer of his exchequer, if he should require it, the sum of 10,000 crowns of gold which he had delivered by command to the lord of Richmond (*L. & P.*, I, 54). It does not follow, as P. M. Kendall, *Richard III*, 482–3, assumes, that these were two different transactions.

the boat's crew, by trying to persuade them that they had come from the duke of Buckingham, who they said was on his way with an army, Richard III's soldiers failed to entrap the invaders. Henry declined the invitation, and seeing none of his other ships, hoisted sail and returned to Normandy, where he waited three days on shore, and then decided to march with part of his followers on foot to Brittany. He sought permission from Charles VIII of France to traverse Normandy, and received not only permission, but messages of goodwill and money to defray his expenses. When he arrived in Brittany, he first heard the news that Buckingham was dead. This depressing information was soon offset by the more hopeful intelligence that the marquis of Dorset and a number of other fugitives had already reached Vannes waiting to join him. He then rightly believed that his cause, instead of being ruined, was now strengthened. He sent for the refugees to meet him at Rennes. They, relieved to learn that Henry had escaped Richard III's clutches, hastened to join him. After rejoicings and prolonged deliberations, on Christmas day, 1483 they all met in the cathedral and ratified all agreements by plighting their troth. Henry then promised that as soon as he became king, he would marry Elizabeth, Edward IV's eldest daughter; whereupon the assembled company swore homage to him as if he were king already. Henry lost no time in appealing once again to the duke of Brittany for more help and money, saying that what he had previously received had been spent on his recent expedition, and promising faithful repayment later on. The duke's calculation of the chances enabled him to agree.[1]

But for those who had taken part in the abortive rising at home, there was to be less rejoicing. The writs of summons to Richard III's first parliament had been issued about 25 September, to meet at Westminster on 6 November, but had been cancelled on the day Buckingham was beheaded, and fresh writs were issued on 9 December, to meet at Westminster on 23 January 1484. The postponement, necessitated by the occurrence of the rebellion, certainly served to give time *inter alia* for very lengthy bills of attainder to be prepared. The day of reckoning had come for those rebels who still survived.

By the time the parliament was dissolved on 22 February, four bills of attainder had been passed, penalizing one hundred and four persons.[2] Among these were Henry of Richmond himself, his uncle Jasper, and his mother Margaret Beaufort, as well as John Morton, bishop of Ely,

---

[1] P.V., op. cit. 201–4.
[2] *See* below, Appendix C, 'The attainders of January to February 1484'.

Lionel Woodville, bishop of Salisbury, and Peter Courtenay, bishop of Exeter, and also Thomas Grey, marquis of Dorset, and certain others who were successful in fleeing in time and who either had already or were soon to join Henry abroad.[1] How many of the total number attainted actually suffered the death penalty is unknown.[2] A few were subsequently pardoned, and the more important people were either not in the realm at the time of the attainder or were able to escape in time. The chief schemer on behalf of Henry – his mother Margaret – was available, but was spared the 'great punishment of attainder' and suffered only the forfeiture of her titles and estates, the latter of which were transferred to her husband Thomas, Lord Stanley,[3] with reversion to the king and his heirs. The comparative leniency with which Richard III treated Margaret Beaufort is remarkable. As a means of conciliating Lord Stanley no doubt the measure commended itself, even though at the last it proved to be unavailing. The 'good care and trust' which Richard III stated he had in him would not hold him when, on Bosworth field, Stanley saw a chance to make himself the stepfather of a king.

Henry of Richmond's expedition, supported and financed as it had been by Duke Francis, abortive and ineffective as it had proved to be, naturally did not improve relations between England and Brittany. But some time elapsed before Richard III could again bring pressure to bear upon the duchy to surrender Henry's person. The events of November 1483 brought in a phase of acute maritime friction between the two countries, and Richard III sought, it seems, to penalize Brittany by encouraging naval hostilities against Breton ships and ports.[4] When that phase should be concluded, the time would return for a further effort to secure Henry.

In the meantime Richard III aimed at undermining the potential strength of Henry's position. Before the parliament was over it seems Richard III assembled nearly all the lords spiritual and temporal and caused them to take an oath of adherence to his son Prince Edward should anything untoward happen to himself.[5] But this effort at securing the succession was frustrated by Edward's death, probably on 9 April.

---

[1] *See* below, Appendix B.

[2] In addition to Buckingham, Vergil (op. cit.) states that Richard III executed Sir George Brown, Sir Roger Clifford, Sir Thomas Seintlegh, Thomas Romney, Robert Clifford, and 'divers others, even of his own household'.

[3] According to Vergil (op. cit. 204), Stanley was himself in danger, and was interrogated by the council, who found him guiltless of the conspiracy, but ordered him to remove his wife's servants, and to keep her so straitly that she could not pass any messages to her son or her friends nor practise against the king; all of which was done.

[4] *See* Kendall, op. cit. 278–9.   [5] *Crovland chronicle*, 572.

Before that event Richard III had played another card, and had come to terms with the dowager Queen Elizabeth. He persuaded her to come out of sanctuary with her daughters, and made promises for their welfare in writing under sign manual, 1 March.[1] This agreement meant, so far as Henry was concerned, that the daughters might not be available should the time come for him to fulfil the oath to marry one of them that he had solemnly taken at Rennes on Christmas day; and that Queen Elizabeth might try to induce her son, the marquis of Dorset, to desert Henry and his cause. The first of these dangers did not, as it turned out, materialize, but the second up to a point did.[2]

Richard III's preoccupation at home and the ill will and friction between England and Brittany appear to have delayed any overt action on his part to obtain the surrender of Henry's person until after June 1484. It was necessary first to come to a pacification with Brittany. On 8 June an agreement was reached to abstain from hostilities from 1 July until the following April, and on 26 June Richard III agreed to supply Brittany with a thousand archers for use in the defence of the duchy.[3] Whether or not the matter was broached in some secret negotiations, the scheme arranged with Peter Landois, the treasurer of Brittany, who was the effective head of the government of the duchy during a period when Duke Francis was incapacitated, must presumably have been concocted at about this time. Landois apparently succumbed to Richard III's blandishments, not because of any hostility he felt towards Henry, but because by gaining the king of England's support he hoped to strengthen his own position vis-à-vis the Breton nobility, among whom he was highly unpopular. Being for the time in control, he agreed to surrender the person of Henry.[4]

How it was that John Morton who had fled to Flanders got wind of this plot and was able to send warning to Henry remains a mystery, but this signal service, which must be understood as equivalent to saving Henry's freedom and life and all that depended thereon, was one that Henry could never forget and could not fail to endear Morton to him should he become king. Morton entrusted the message to Christopher

[1] The text of the letter is printed in Gairdner, *Richard III*, 165–6, from Ellis, *Original letters*, 2nd ser., I, 149.

[2] *See* below, p. 38.

[3] *Foedera*, XII, 226 and 229; and *C.P.R.*, 517, 547. Polydore Vergil, who seldom mentions any precise dates, cannot be relied upon for the chronology of this phase. He appears, for example, to suppose that Richard III's agreement with Queen Elizabeth occurred in 1485, after Henry had escaped to France, but this is untenable.

[4] For this and the immediately following episodes, P.V., op. cit., is the only detailed source of information.

Urswick, Margaret Beaufort's confidential agent, who had recently joined Morton in Flanders, and advised Henry, then at Vannes, to escape into France. On receipt of this message, Henry at once sent Urswick to the French court to gain permission to enter France, which was readily obtained.

There then followed the extraordinary sequence of events which enabled Henry to escape in the nick of time. Henry devised a stratagem which brought him and many of his party to safety. He arranged to send the 'English nobility' who were with him to call upon the duke, at that time residing near the borders of Anjou, ostensibly to plead Henry's private cause with him, but secretly told his uncle Jasper, who was to lead the mission, to take the whole party over into France when they approached the frontier. This they did, and Henry himself, a day or two later, accompanied by only five servants, pretended to set out to pay a visit to a friend at a neighbouring manor. No one suspected him of any ulterior design as a large number of English were left in Vannes. But after journeying for about five miles, he withdrew into a wood, changed into a serving man's clothes, and followed one of his own servants, who guided him with the maximum speed into Anjou, where he joined his advance party. Landois had intended to seize him four days later but on learning of his flight, he sent out troops in all directions to find him, and he had scarcely been an hour in Anjou before some of them reached the border. When the news of Henry's arrival reached the French Council of Regency, orders were issued on 11 October for the honourable reception and escort of him and his party, and financial provision was made for immediate necessities.[1] A valuable prize had come into France's possession,[2] even though it would take time to decide how it could be put to the most profitable use.

The Englishmen left in Vannes, said to number about three hundred, were now in jeopardy and feared for their safety. But Duke Francis recovered from his incapacity at the right moment, and learning of these events, was enraged at Peter Landois's scheme and, shocked by the episode, sent to Vannes for Edward Poynings and Edward Wood-ville to come to him. He gave them money to defray the costs involved and told them to conduct all the English party to Henry in France.

---

[1] See *Procès-verbaux des séances du Conseil de Régence du roi Charles VIII*, August 1484 to January 1485, ed. A. Bernier (Paris, 1836); *Coll. de Docs. Inédits*, 128, 129, 164, 168.

[2] e.g. A. Dupuy, *Histoire de la réunion de la Bretagne á la France* (1880), II, 46, '*Henri Tudor etáit pour le gouvernement français un précieux auxiliare contre Richard III*'. M. Dupuy appears to give an inaccurate paraphrase (ibid. 46) of the council minutes cited above.

Henry was naturally overjoyed at this handsome treatment, and returned thanks to the duke with promises of requital in future.

But the turn of events, unpredictable to Henry as yet, was destined to make it more difficult for him to requite the favours shown to him. For from now on his fortunes and prospects depended entirely upon what degree of goodwill and support he' could get from the government of France, and that in its turn depended on the extent to which Henry could be used as a pawn in the unfolding crisis in the relations between France and Brittany. This was the all-important question, and Henry could have had very little, indeed, so far as can be seen, no chance of the necessary amount of support, unless the regency government of France saw a feasible opportunity for using Henry's aspirations and pretensions as a means of embarrassing Richard III of England and preventing him from going to the aid of Brittany in the forthcoming struggle with that last of the independent duchies of France. The circumstances which in fact made such an opportunity possible were peculiar and complicated, but require some consideration, for without them Henry Tudor's fate might well have been that of a penurious exile for the rest of his life.

Richard III had been crowned king on 26 June 1483, and Louis XI died on 30 August that year. The succession in France of Charles VIII, Louis XI's only son, at the age of thirteen, changed the face of international politics at once, gave rise to a regency government in France, and brought into the foreground the problem of the fate of Brittany in the predictable event of the death of Duke Francis II without male heir. That France, in these circumstances, would seek by all possible means to acquire the duchy, was obvious to all; equally obviously neither England nor the Austrian Hapsburg archduke, Maximilian, then regent of the Netherlands for his son Philip, could view such an aggrandizement of France and such change in the international balance, without grave concern and apprehension. What was not predictable was the fact that the policies of the minority Council of Regency in France would be virtually directed for some years by that remarkable young stateswoman, the eldest child of Louis XI, Anne of Beaujeu, who at the age of twenty-two now became the dominating figure in the government of France, ruling her young and somewhat wayward brother Charles VIII, pulling the strings in the council through her husband Pierre de Bourbon, lord of Beaujeu and heir to the duchy of Bourbon, and setting her impress upon the course of French politics and government for ten years. She was, as has been justly said, '*vrây image en tout du son père*', but without his cruelty, hypocrisy, and cunning. It was a cardinal objective

of her policy to ensure that Brittany in due course should become part
of the kingdom of France. It followed that if Henry Tudor could be
used to contribute to that end, then he would be so used.[1]

Only two days before the death of Louis XI, Duke Francis of Brittany
instructed his envoy George de Mainbier to negotiate with Richard III
with a view to securing his support against France in the coming struggle.
Ostensibly in reply to Richard III's overtures made to the duke as
early as July, the ducal envoy was to raise matters of wider import than
those mentioned in Richard III's instructions to his ambassador, Dr
Thomas Hutton.[2] De Mainbier was to apprise Richard III that Louis
XI had several times since the death of Edward IV requested the duke
to deliver to him the person of Henry Tudor, and had made great offers
to that end, which the duke had refused to accept, lest by doing so he
should injure his own friends. But now Francis feared that Louis XI
would make war upon him, so that he might be compelled to surrender
Henry. To avoid such a regrettable necessity, he now sought military
aid from Richard, without, however, offering to yield Henry into
Richard's hands.[3]

Richard III, however, did not at this stage comply with Francis's
proposals, and later in the year came the duke's support for Henry's
abortive expedition to England in connection with Buckingham's
rebellion. Naturally, Richard III did not view the Breton share in this
enterprise with any favour, but he was able to persuade Landois to
agree to surrender Henry. Landois's compliance, although dictated
partly by a desire to strengthen his own position, nevertheless was also
partly inspired as a means of getting support for Brittany in the menacing situation in which it now found itself. A number of Breton lords
were now in a state of rebellion, and had appealed to the Beaujeu
regime to come to their aid, with a view both to procuring the downfall of Landois and to coercing the duke into revising his policies. In
this situation, Landois not only sought to win over Richard III, but
also sought to enter into negotiations with Archduke Maximilian and
took the drastic, and in the long run, disastrous step of trusting Louis,
duke of Orléans (the future Louis XII), chaffering and malcontent as
he was with the French regime, to come to the aid of Duke Francis.

[1] For the regency of Anne of Beaujeu generally, *see* the valuable detailed account in
J. S. C. Bridge, *A history of France from the death of Louis XI*, I, *Reign of Charles VIII:
regency of Anne of Beaujeu* (1921), esp. pp. 28, 112–31, and refs. therein; *see* also P.
Pelicier, *Essai sur le gouvernement de la dame de Beaujeu, 1483–91* (Chartres, 1882); and
Dupuy, op. cit.

[2] *L. & P.*, I, 22–3.   [3] ibid. I, 37–43, 54.

Louis of Orléans's intervention in Brittany further bedevilled Franco-Breton relations, but before long helped to determine the attitude of the Beaujeu regime towards Henry Tudor, after his providential escape into France.

Very soon after that event, the Archduke Maximilian sought to take advantage of the possibilities of embarrassing France by aiding Brittany, and sent an embassy to Richard III, fortified with instructions of enormous length.[1] Richard III had previously expressed his willingness for Maximilian to mediate between himself and the duke of Brittany if the latter would surrender the English refugees. Maximilian was now eager for an alliance with England, and his envoy was to explain to Richard III the intricacies of the archduke's policy, with a view to persuading Richard to join in hostilities against France, which Richard could do best by going to the aid of the duke of Brittany. If Richard complained of what had taken place in Brittany regarding the person of Henry and the other fugitives, both when they were in Brittany and since they had left it, the best thing would be for negotiations to take place, and if the duke of Brittany were content to 'leave the party' of the earl (of Richmond) and no longer support him, then Maximilian would act as the duke's pledge and surety.

Whether any substantial threat to France would have materialized from these plots may be doubted, but in the circumstances Henry's unexpected flight into France was a not unwelcome event. No hasty decisions, however, could be reached, for the regime for many months had its hands full with domestic as well as foreign politics. The regime had to establish itself firmly, and in the process was obliged to call the States-General which met on 15 January 1484 and lasted in session until 13 March.[2] However, because the Beaujeu regime wished to avoid the Orléanist influences predominant in the Paris region, the seat of the government was moved temporarily to Montargis, an obscure small town in the diocese of Sens, and it happened to be at this place that Henry, who was there attending the French court, received news

[1] ibid. II, 3–51.

[2] See Bridge, op. cit. 54–102. It was at the opening of this assembly that the chancellor, Guillaume de Rochefort, was able to contrast loyalty to the Crown in France with the different state of affairs recently displayed in England, and to give point to his homily by referring to what had happened in England after Edward IV's death, how his children had been murdered, how the crown was transferred to the assassin by the goodwill of the nation. This appears to be the earliest overt accusation of Richard III as the murderer of the princes. The source of this allegation was Dominic Mancini, who had just completed his *De occupatione regni Anglie per Ricardum tercium*, at Beaugency in early December 1483. See C. A. G. Armstrong's edition, 15; and for discussion, P. M. Kendall, *Richard III* (1958), 395–6.

that not only encouraged him, but must also have considerably improved his not very impressive stock in French estimates.

When the rest of his following from Brittany joined him, Henry sought an interview with Charles VIII, then at Angers. Henry now, it seems, adopted the posture of rightful claimant to the throne of England – as indeed he must if he were to gain active support – and talked of his 'nobility' and their call to him to 'return' to his kingdom, and of their abhorrence of the tyranny of Richard III. Charles VIII, or the regime through him, vaguely promised and showed goodwill, but could not take any rash actions at this stage. The court moved on to Montargis, and later to Paris, taking Henry with them. Some twelve months were to elapse before Henry found himself in a position to take any positive steps to stage a second expedition.[1]

But whilst still at Montargis, Henry unexpectedly had good reason to be, as Vergil said, 'ravished with joy'. For he gained as a recruit to his party no less a person than John de Vere, thirteenth earl of Oxford, who, after ten years' confinement in Hammes Castle, suddenly escaped and joined Henry, bringing with him such valuable additional supporters as James Blunt, the captain of Hammes Castle, and Sir John Fortescue, the gentleman porter of Calais.[2] The acquisition of so experienced a soldier and faithful Lancastrian as De Vere was very solid grounds for joy, for, as Henry perceived, many of his existing supporters had sided with Edward IV in the past and had come over because of the turn of events in England, but De Vere had never submitted to the Yorkists, and was an experienced man to whom he might 'safely commit all things'. With such a recruit, Henry might indeed 'begin to hope better of his affairs'.

He continued to press his suit with Charles VIII's council and while at Paris further recruits joined him; some who came over from England, and some who were studying in Paris, presumably at the university. Among the latter was a certain man 'of excellent wit and learned', by name Richard Fox, whom Henry at once received into his 'privy

[1] It does not seem possible at present to ascertain the exact date on which the French government decided to enable Henry to start active preparations. Possibly further investigation into the French archives may give a clue.

[2] John de Vere, thirteenth earl of Oxford (1442–1512), had been allowed to succeed to his father the twelfth earl, who was beheaded by Edward IV in 1461 for treason. He eventually fled to the continent and took part in the Readeption of Henry VI, and was appointed constable of England. He commanded the Lancastrian left wing at Barnet, escaped and fled to Scotland, and later France. He engaged in privateering and seized St Michael's Mount, September 1473. He was there beseiged for some months but was obliged to surrender. He was imprisoned in Hammes Castle, and attainted in 1475.

council'. For the rest of his long life, Fox was destined to remain at the centre of Tudor affairs, and to grow great in that service.[1]

Henry's potentiality as a rival to Richard III thus grew, slowly, but ominously, and as the months passed, Richard III's apprehensions became more intense. Well they might, for no sooner had he come to his agreement with Queen Elizabeth than his own dynastic hopes received a shattering blow. His only son and heir apparent Prince Edward died about 9 April 1484, aged eleven. There would be no hope for Richard III of having an heir apparent of even this age for many years, and still less hope when his wife Queen Ann also died, on 16 March 1485. Doubtless in these circumstances Richard's thoughts turned in the direction of making a second marriage and also of preventing any of Edward IV's daughters from marrying Henry of Richmond at a future date. It does not follow that he seriously supposed that these two thoughts could be fused into one thought, by himself marrying the eldest or any of the daughters, still less that the demise of his own queen was induced by any action of his own. The possible coalescence of all these thoughts into one gave an opportunity for rumour and propaganda that was not lost on his opponents at the time and later on. But the probabilities of the matter are all to the contrary. Richard III's agreement with Queen Elizabeth was reached before his son died, and a year before his wife died, and cannot have been reached with the contingencies of their deaths in mind. When Queen Ann had died, his thoughts may have turned in the direction of Edward IV's daughter Elizabeth, but such a project was a non-starter, since Richard's title to the throne itself depended upon his own declaration of the bastardy of Edward IV's children, and he could hardly have strengthened his position by marrying a 'bastard' niece, even if it were possible to make a canonically valid marriage out of such a project. The fact was that by April 1485 Richard had reached a dynastic impasse; he married no one and did not, as he might easily have done, cause any of his surviving nieces to be married so as to prevent Henry's policy from ever being fulfilled.[2] All that he could do, as the months passed, was to take such military precautions against Henry as he could. As early as 7 December

[1] Richard Fox became keeper of the Privy Seal, 24 February 1487, and remained in that office until 1516, becoming also bishop of Exeter, 1487–92, of Bath and Wells, 1492–4, of Durham, 1494–1501, of Winchester, 1501–28.

[2] None of Edward IV's seven daughters was married by August 1485. (1) The eldest, Elizabeth (b. 11 February 1465, d. 11 February 1503), was to marry Henry VII on 18 January 1486; (2) Mary (b. 1467, d. 23 May 1482); (3) Cecily (b. 1467, d. 24 August 1507) married, first, John, first Viscount Welles, between 25 November 1487 and 1 June 1488; second, Thomas Kymber in 1503; (4) Margaret (b. 9 April

1484, he publicly announced the danger, and issued his first proclamation against Henry Tydder and others. Henry, the public were told, had taken upon him the name and title of royal estate, to which he had no shadow of right, had abandoned all claim to the crown of France, and present and former English possessions in France, as a means of furthering his ends, and all the king's subjects were commanded to be ready in their most defensible array to do his highness service in war when called upon.[1]

But it was another six months before a second proclamation in similar terms was issued, and eight months before the threat became actual.

The government of France was in no hurry, and indeed in no position to extend much practical help to Henry as yet. Many months of uncertainty were to elapse before vague promises were converted into material assistance. The fact was that the French court itself was in grave difficulties and unable to come to a decisive conclusion on the

---

1472, d. in July); (5) Anne (b. 2 November 1475) married, 4 February 1495, Thomas Howard II, later earl of Surrey and third duke of Norfolk, and died 23 November 1511; (6) Katherine (b. 1479) married, October 1495, Sir William Courtenay, later earl of Devon, and died 15 November 1527; (7) Bridget, a nun at Dartford (b. 1480, d. 1517). The marriage of Henry VII's eldest sister-in-law to Viscount Welles is explained by the fact that John Welles was Henry's uncle of the half-blood. John's father, Lionel, sixth baron Welles, had married, c. 1447, as his second wife, Margaret, baroness Beauchamp of Bletso, the widow of John Beaufort, first duke of Somerset and mother of Margaret Beaufort, Henry's mother. Lionel Welles was killed at Towton, 1461, and his son and heir Richard, the seventh baron, was beheaded in 1470; likewise Richard's son and heir Robert, the eighth baron. The attainder of these two prevented John, Lionel's second youngest son, from succeeding to the barony; a pardon in 1478 did not prevent him from participating in Buckingham's rebellion in 1483, after which he avoided the penalties of attainder by escaping to Brittany, where he joined Henry of Richmond. Henry knighted him on 7 August 1485; he was recognized as Baron Welles on the reversal of his attainder in 1485, and was created viscount before 1 September 1487, and given substantial grants. He died s.m.p. 9 February 1498. Ann his only daughter and heiress died soon after her father, when the title became extinct. See G.E.C., fn. 103. Presumably Henry VII in agreeing to this not very distinguished marriage for his eldest sister-in-law sought both to reward his half-uncle for his loyalty and to play for safety.

[1] The proclamation which Richard III issued on 7 December 1484 exists in a copy contained in B.M. MS. Harl. 433, fo. 273b, and was reissued in almost identical terms on 23 June 1485. The latter issue was printed by Fenn in his edition of the *Paston letters*, apparently from the copy addressed to the sheriff of Kent, and also is imperfectly contained in MS. Harl. 437, fo. 230b, printed by Ellis, *Original letters*, 2nd ser., I, 162. J. Gairdner, *Paston letters*, III, No. 883, gives the 23 June version collated with the texts of the two Harl. MSS, and the Fenn edition. It is notable that the proclamation of 7 December 1484 included the name of Thomas, marquis of Dorset, dropped from that of 23 June 1485.

question as to whether it would or would not give assistance to Henry's project for overthrowing Richard III. Even when the decision was reached to allow and help Henry to start an expedition, the help given was not, it seems, on anything but a very modest scale. No doubt the French government did not view the enterprise as much more than a diversion to hamper Richard III from giving aid to Brittany, and could scarcely have imagined that Henry would achieve the full measure of success that he did. Moreover, if the expedition had not been prepared and launched when it was, the chances are that a little later on, when French policy achieved its more immediate ends in Brittany and had little to fear from Richard III's possible intervention, no help at all would have been forthcoming for Henry. At the very time when Henry was completing his preparation and was about to set out, French intervention in Brittany with the connivance of the rebel Breton lords procured the downfall and death of Peter Landois on 19 July 1485. On 7 August Henry was to land in Milford Haven; on 9 August, the government of Charles VIII signed the Treaty of Bourges with Duke Francis II, bringing hostilities with Brittany to an end for the time being. Whatever hopes recalcitrant Bretons may still have entertained for help from Richard III were, as it turned out, to be dashed by the battle of Bosworth. In the space of little more than a month, the destinies of France, Brittany, and England for some time to come were given a decisive twist.[1]

But as the early months of 1485 wore on, Henry's own position suffered setbacks. He was able, indeed, to make a show of consolidating his prestige by effectively preventing Richard III from recovering his grip upon Hammes Castle.[2] Richard III, when he heard of the flight from there of the earl of Oxford and its captain John Blunt, sent a substantial part of the garrison of Calais to recover Hammes. Those still in the castle defended it and sent for aid from Henry's party. Henry therefore dispatched the earl of Oxford and a force to relieve the besieged. Thomas Brandon with thirty men succeeded in entering the castle and reinforced its defence with such effect that the besiegers allowed the garrison to depart freely, and the whole force left to join Henry in Paris. Richard III at this stage appears to have discounted

[1] For the course of events in Brittany, see Bridge, op. cit., esp. 120–31. Further information is obtainable in A. Dupuy, *Histoire de la réunion de la Bretagne á la France* (Paris, 1880), II, 41–6. Dupuy went so far as to say (ibid. 79) that the fall of Landois was fatal to Richard III and the duke of Orléans (who was forced to submit after the Treaty of Bourges). But Henry's preparations must have been far advanced well before Landois fell on 17 July.

[2] For what follows, Vergil, op. cit. 209–16, is the only detailed source.

the chances that Henry would be able to procure support from the French court sufficient to enable him to invade England; he relaxed his vigilance, withdrew his ships and soldiers from the stations they had taken up to ward off attack, and contented himself with keeping a watch on the likely coasts, especially in Wales; and organized a system of beacons to give warning of any future incursion.

But Richard's agreement with Queen Elizabeth bore some fruit, to Henry's embarrassment. Her eldest son, Thomas, marquis of Dorset, was persuaded to try to abandon Henry's cause; partly because of his estimate of Henry's chances, and partly because of Richard III's wiles. Thomas fled from Paris secretly by night, and hastened towards Flanders. This desertion by a man who was acquainted with all their plans greatly disturbed Henry and his party, and they at once sought permission from Charles VIII to arrest him. Permission was given and search parties were sent out. One of Henry's friends, Humphrey Cheyney, overtook the marquis at Compiègne and managed to persuade him to return to the fold. This disquieting episode contributed to hardening Henry's resolve that he must soon adventure all, lest others should seek to desert him and his opportunities be lost. He obtained a 'slender supply' from Charles VIII, borrowed from him and other private friends, and leaving behind as pledges the unreliable marquis and also John Bourchier, he set out for Rouen. Whilst he was busy organizing ships at the mouth of the Seine, more disturbing news reached him. Richard III's queen, Ann Neville, had died on 16 March, and the rumour (so we are told) was that Richard himself might seek to marry his niece Elizabeth, and that he had married off her sister Cecily to an obscure man of no reputation. The latter allegation was certainly false, and the former had no substance. But the rumour alarmed Henry greatly – it 'pinched him by the very stomach' (in Polydore Vergil's vivid phrase) – for if he could not himself eventually marry one of Edward IV's daughters, he feared that some of his friends would forsake him. He consulted a few of his party, and it was decided that in the circumstances it would be profitable to draw to the cause Walter Herbert, 'a man of authority among the Welsh' and the son of Henry's former guardian, and to raise the prospect of a marriage with Walter's sister.[1] The difficulty was to communicate any message.

---

[1] Walter Herbert was the second son of Henry of Richmond's former guardian, William Herbert, earl of Pembroke, and brother of William, the second earl, and subsequently earl of Huntingdon. Their sister Maud (designed for Henry himself originally) married, c. 1476, Henry Percy, eighth earl of Northumberland. Maud died 27 July 1485.

Messengers were sent to Henry Percy, earl of Northumberland, who had married Walter Herbert's other sister, Maud, but, no doubt fortunately as it turned out, none of the messengers was able to reach him.

From the reverse direction it was easier to receive messages, although presumably it was at about this time that Henry was writing in semi-regal style to some of his friends at home, warning them to be ready to support him when he arrived. A specimen of such a letter[1] reads as follows.

> Right trusty, worshipful, and honourable good friends, and our allies, I greet you well. Being given to understand your good devour and intent to advance me to the furtherance of my rightful claim due and lineal inheritance of the crown, and for the just depriving of that homicide and unnatural tyrant which now unjustly bears dominion over you, I give you to understand that no Christian heart can be more full of joy and gladness from the heart of me your poor exiled friend, who will, upon the instance of your sure advertise what powers ye will make ready and what captains and leaders you get to conduct, be prepared to pass over the sea with such forces as my friends here are preparing for me. And if you have such good speed and success as I wish, according to your desire, I shall ever be most forward to remember and wholly to requite this your great and most loving kindness in my just quarrel.
> Given under our Signet
>
> H.R.
>
> I pray you give credence to the messenger of that he shall impart to you.

Already some time previously, Thomas, Lord Stanley, his brother Sir William, Gilbert Talbot, and others had secretly conveyed messages of goodwill to Henry. Now from out of Wales, John Morgan sent word that Rhys ap Thomas and John Savage[2] were wholly on Henry's side, and that the faithful Reginald Bray had collected 'no small sum of money' with which to pay soldiers, and advised Henry to set out for Wales as soon as possible. Anxious to avoid any further delay, with all its risks and uncertainties, Henry finally sailed from the Seine with some two thousand men and a few ships, backed by a soft south wind, on Monday, 1 August.

---

[1] See Caroline A. Halstead, *Richard III* (1844), II, 566, from Harl. MS. 787, fo. 2; also Halliwell-Phillips, *Letters*, I, 161.

[2] John Morgan of Tredegar (d. 1504), after the accession of Henry VII became his first clerk of the parliament, dean of Windsor and a master in Chancery, received a number of church preferments, and in 1496 was appointed bishop of St David's. For Rhys ap Thomas, *see* p. 42, fn. 4. Sir John Savage, who had extensive influence in Cheshire and elsewhere, received large grants after Bosworth, was promoted K.G. in 1488, and was killed at the siege of Boulogne in 1492.

How many ships he had acquired, we do not know. As to men, he may have had a hard core of perhaps three to five hundred Englishmen who, as refugees, had joined his forces at one time or another in Brittany or France; but the bulk were such rabble as he had been able to recruit in Normandy,[1] captained by Philibert de Chandeé, a man who had some status in Brittany and who apparently had entertained Henry at an earlier stage of his exile.[2]

The expedition sailed, so far as we know, without incident, into Milford Haven, and landed at Mill Bay,[3] the first beach and cove round St Anne's Head, on the north side of the west haven, a little before sunset on Sunday, 7 August. Probably a small force was also landed near Angle immediately opposite on the other side of the haven, with a view to striking up to Pembroke Castle.[4]

Having landed, out of sight of Dale Point, Roads, and Castle, which he believed might be occupied against him, Henry and his forces marched up the hill and over the headland and took Dale Castle without

[1] Commynes, *Mémoires*, II, 234, says that Henry got from Charles VIII a good sum of money, and a few pieces of artillery. He also says that he had some five hundred Englishmen, and that he was able to pay the passage of only three or four thousand men. Elsewhere (loc. cit. 306) he says that Henry got a little money from the king, and procured some three thousand men out of Normandy '*et des plus meschantz que l'on peust trouver*'. Vergil, however, puts the total number of men at only two thousand (op. cit. 216). It is probable that the men brought the 'sweating sickness' with them but this disease was certainly known in England previously, as Thomas, Lord Stanley, according to the Croyland chronicle, told Richard III that he was suffering from it, as an excuse for not joining him a few days before Bosworth. There is some evidence that 'the sweat' or something like it, was known in York at an earlier date, and Stanley would have known that Richard III would have been obliged to recognize that if Stanley really had the sickness, he could not have gone to Nottingham when summoned. I am indebted to the late Sir Frederick Rees for showing me correspondence on this subject, dated September 1948, between himself and Professor J. F. D. Shrewsbury of Birmingham, which discloses most of the above facts.

[2] André, *Vita*, 25, calls him a strenuous and wise soldier. He was knighted by Henry on 7 August 1485, and was created by him earl of Bath on 6 January 1486, and given an annuity of 100 marks from Somerset and Dorset; and was called by him '*consanguineus noster*', but otherwise little is known of him in this country, and the earldom became extinct at his death at an unknown date. *See* G.E.C. He is described as 'of Savoy' in the list of knights referred to below, p. 42, fn. 1.

[3] The evidence for this conclusion the present author set out in *W.H.R.*, 2 (1964), 173–80. As long ago as 1916, Mr W. Dane Russell, 'The Lady Margaret Beaufort and King Henry VII', *Arch. Camb.*, XVI (6th ser., 1916), 303–4, perceived that Mill Bay was the most likely place of landing. Mr Russell, loc. cit. 336, however, is not convincing in arguing that the date of landing was on or about 1 August, as the Croyland chronicle has it. The weight of evidence supports Vergil's specific statement, and there was nothing impossible about the itinerary which resulted in the battle of Bosworth on 22 August.

[4] *See W.H.R.*, loc. cit. 177.

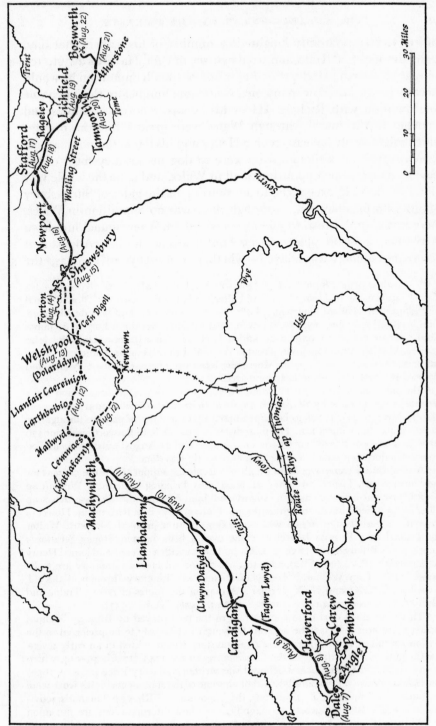

Map 1 Henry of Richmond's march to Bosworth, 1485

difficulty. He apparently knighted[1] a number of his leaders that day, spent the night at Dale and at dawn set out for Haverfordwest, ten miles to the north. All depended now on how much opposition he would meet in Wales, and how many men would join him before the inevitable confrontation with Richard III or his agents. The uncertainties and anxieties of the march through Wales were great.[2] But the disaster which might easily have overcome Henry and his forces did not happen. As it turned out, although fears were to dog his journey most of the way, he met with no opposition at all in Wales, and none the whole way to Bosworth itself, except the token shutting of the gates of Shrewsbury against him for one night. Although there was no opposition in Wales, there was no great rush to join forces with him. A few joined him from Pembroke, and from places *en route*,[3] but it was not until 12 August that his greatest anxiety was allayed – whether or not Rhys ap Thomas,[4] the

[1] J. Gairdner prints, *Richard III*, 363–5. Note VIII, from MS. Harl. 78, fo. 31, a list of the knights made by Henry before and after the battle of Bosworth. Those dubbed at landing were Edward Courtenay, later earl of Devonshire, Philibert de Chandée, John Welles, John Cheyney, David Owen, Edward Poynings, John Fortescue, James Blunt. At an uncertain date were added Richard Gyfford, John Halwell, John Ryseley, William Brandon, John Treury, William Tyler, Thomas Milbourne. After the battle, Gilbert Talbot, John Mortimer, Rhys ap Thomas, Robert Points, and Humphrey Stanley were similarly honoured.

[2] The only detailed source is Polydore Vergil, op. cit. A useful reconstruction of the probable route is made by William Rees, *An historical atlas of Wales* (1951), pl. 54 (*see* Map 1 above, p. 41). It has to be remembered that the dates of passage through the various places are conjectural. The total distance from Dale to Bosworth is about 176 miles, and to cover this distance between 8 August and 21 August must have entailed strenuous effort, but could be done and apparently was done.

[3] Arnold Butler came over from Pembroke to pledge support from the citizens for their former earl, Jasper, on 8 August, apparently bringing some men. William ap Griffith brought a few men on 9 August and John Morgan did likewise. Rhys ap Thomas, as stated above, brought substantial forces, as well as Richard ap Howel of Mostyn. Gilbert Talbot joined with some five hundred men at Newport. Walter Hungerford and Thomas Bourchier came over a little beyond Stoney Stratford; John Savage, Brian Sanford, Symon Digly and others with a choice band joined Henry at Tamworth (P.V. (ed. Ellis), 216–18). Discussions of Henry's itinerary are to be found in W. Tom Williams, 'Henry of Richmond's itinerary through Wales', *Y Cymmrodor*, XXIX; and H. N. Jarman, 'A map of the routes of Henry Tudor and Rhys ap Thomas through Wales in 1485', *Arch. Camb.*, XCII (1937).

[4] There is a good deal of uncertainty as to the part played by Rhys ap Thomas during these proceedings. The account by Vergil is generally to be preferred to the version contained in the anonymous family history which existed in an early seventeenth-century MS. printed in the *Cambrian register* for 1745 (1796), 49–144, which the late Professor Glyn Roberts believed was written by Henry Price (1590–c. 1659) (*see D.N.B.*, sub.-tit. Price family). Although some of the statements in this work were doubtless based upon family traditions, the importance of Rhys ap Thomas's activities before and after Bosworth is magnified, the best interpretations are put upon

leading Welsh figure in the region, would join or oppose him. Henry's promise to give him the 'lieutenancy' of Wales should he be successful, apparently sufficed to bring Rhys over to him, with a substantial force at Newtown. Rhys ap Thomas, the son of a substantial landholder in Wales, was born in 1449 and spent some of his youth with his father at the Burgundian court, from which he returned in 1467. For a time he had supported Lancaster but switched to Edward IV, who gave him some recognition and grants: and he ostensibly continued to support York in the person of Richard III. It is probable however that he was won over to Buckingham's scheme in 1483, even though he took no overt action. According to the family history[1] his tutor in early days had been none other than Lewis, the physician to Margaret Beaufort and Queen Elizabeth, and who was thus an excellent channel through which to win over Rhys. Through these means, and also through Morgan of Kidwelly, and John Morgan, later bishop, and others, not only was a personal quarrel between Rhys and Buckingham tided over, but Rhys was persuaded to espouse Henry's cause. Letters were exchanged between Rhys and Henry after Buckingham's death, and Henry probably had good reason to suppose that Rhys would come to his aid on arrival in Wales. But Richard III had grown suspicious of Rhys's reliability in 1483-4 and had extracted an oath of allegiance from him and demanded his young son as a hostage. Rhys confirmed his allegiance but declined to send his son because of his tender age of four to five years. Doubtless Rhys was obliged to move very cautiously, and we can

his motives and actions, and the whole is embroidered and sometimes confused, whilst legends are incorporated as facts. For valuable details, see J. M. Lloyd, 'The rise and fall of the House of Dinefwr (the Rhys family) 1430-1530', unpublished M.A. thesis (University of Wales, Cardiff, 1963). No doubt some promise of aggrandizement for Rhys was made as an inducement, but in fact Rhys's rewards were not to be very great, notwithstanding further services at Stoke, and elsewhere. He was appointed constable and steward of the lordship of Brecon, and chamberlain of South Wales, and steward of the lordship of Builth in November 1485 (Campbell, Materials, I, 105, 109), and was made a knight banneret after he captured Lord Audley at Blackheath in 1497, and was advanced to K.G. only in 1505. Presumably Henry never forgot the anxiety of his journey through Wales, which Rhys ap Thomas might have done much to allay (see article by Sir Frederick Rees in D.N.B.). J. G. Gairdner rightly pointed out (Richard III, 223-4) that the Morgan of Kidwelly who is reported in the family history to have participated in the early communications with Henry is not to be confused (as some historians continue to do) with the Morgan Kidwelly who was Richard III's attorney-general, who could not have acted in this way. Morgan of Kidwelly was of the same family as John Morgan and the Evan Morgan who is said to have 'oined Henry in Brittany after the Buckingham rebellion (Camb. Reg., 96).

[1] Camb. Reg., 83.

dismiss the family legend that he warmly welcomed Henry at Dale, and made speeches whilst Henry's French soldiers remained on board ship. Vergil specifically refers to the anxiety Henry felt on the march up to Shrewsbury, and there are no grounds for supposing that he met Rhys before the arrival at Newtown.

With the encouragement of Rhys's arrival Henry could continue the march into England with less apprehension, and reached Shrewsbury on 15 August. In the meantime he had sent secret messages to his mother Margaret, and Lord Stanley and his brother Sir William,[1] Lord Talbot, and others, intimating his intention to cross the Severn, penetrate into Shropshire, and, if possible, advance towards London. The replies he received at Shrewsbury were welcome so far as they were in cash, and at least hopeful in so far as they were promises that his friends would be ready to do their duty in time convenient. But the question very soon was – when exactly would the time be convenient?

He could not hope to win a major battle with Richard III unless he could obtain much stronger support than he had so far acquired, not even with the reinforcement of Gilbert Talbot, an uncle of the fourth earl of Shrewsbury of the Talbot line, with some five hundred men, which he received at Newport, probably on 15 August. Everything would depend on how far the Stanleys would commit themselves to his cause; only they could command large enough forces to turn the scale, and of Richard III's principal supporters, only they had shown any inclination to change sides. Without them, the hazards confronting Henry were daunting in the extreme. But the difficulties and dangers besetting the Stanleys were acute also. Lord Stanley's eldest son and heir was in Richard III's hands as a hostage, and there was every reason to suppose that the king could command ample forces with which to overwhelm the Stanleys on their own. The Stanleys, therefore, were compelled to move very warily.

At last, when Henry reached Stafford, probably on 17 August, Sir William Stanley with a small retinue made contact with him, had a short talk with him, and withdrew. What transpired between them we do not know, but presumably sufficient was said to enable Henry to continue the march forward, but it was disquieting enough to give him food for thought. With only twenty men with him, he lost contact with his forces marching on to Tamworth, and spent a very uneasy night as best he could, but was astute enough to pass off his dangerous adventure with a plausible and encouraging tale to his men, when he rejoined them in the morning. That day he was able to meet both the Stanleys at

[1] P.V. (ed. Ellis), 217–18.

Atherstone[1] and to take counsel with them as to the battle that could not be long delayed, for Richard III with the main body of his troops was now very near. But the Stanleys still did not openly join forces with him, and he had to take what comfort he could from the fact that John Savage and others with a 'choice band' did join him that evening. On Monday, 22 August, the issue was to be finally joined.

Richard III had taken up his quarters at Nottingham, probably from the middle of June, to await eventualities, being uncertain as to where Henry would make his landing. On 21 June he ordered the chancellor to reissue the proclamation against 'Henry Tydder and other rebels' which had been issued first on the previous 7 December, and this was done on 23 June.[2] Commissions of array were also sent out to many shires for the mustering of troops. He did not refuse permission to Thomas, Lord Stanley, steward of his Household, to depart to his estates, although he must have realized that such a request was highly suspicious, and would agree only on condition that Stanley's son George, Lord Strange, was sent for and obliged to act as his deputy whilst he should be away. A hostage was thus taken and given, but the event would show how effective this would be in restraining Stanley's actions.

As news of Henry's movements at the mouth of the Seine doubtless reached him, Richard III once again desired to have the Great Seal near him for all eventualities; he sent an instruction on 24 July to the chancellor in London to send it up to him, and received it on 1 August, the day on which Henry set sail. But it was not until 11 August that Richard III got word that Henry had made his landing on 7 August.[3] The king summoned the duke of Norfolk, the earl of Northumberland, Viscount Lovel, Sir John Brackenbury, and others to muster their forces and join him at Leicester. But notwithstanding the lateness with which he had received the vital news, Richard III did not himself move with any unseemly haste. Perhaps he assumed that Henry's puny

[1] The suggestion by K. B. McFarlane, in his review of *Cal. papal registers relating to Great Britain and Ireland*, XIV, *1484–92* (1960), in *E.H.R.*, LXXVIII (1963), 771–2, that Lord Stanley's assertion in connection with the dispensation proceedings for Henry VII's marriage with Elizabeth of York, that he had known Henry since 24 August, casts a doubt on the date of the Atherstone meeting, and the subsequent events, apparently followed by J. R. Lander, *The Wars of the Roses* (1965), 264, cannot be accepted as probable. It is inconceivable that Henry did not meet Lord Stanley until the second day after the battle, and it is preferable to suppose that Stanley's memory was consciously or unconsciously at fault in these proceedings, in which the accuracy of other person's memories is also open to doubt. *See* below, Appendix D.

[2] *See* above, p. 36.   [3] *See* above .p. 40.

forces would soon be crushed in Wales, by Rhys ap Thomas in the south, or by Sir William Stanley in the north. But just before he set out he received Lord Stanley's excuses for not obeying an instruction to return to Nottingham, and by the time his son Lord Strange had been interrogated, Richard could have perceived few grounds for further complacency. For Strange disclosed that his uncle Sir William and John Savage had secretly conspired to join Henry, even though his father, so he said, intended to continue to support the king, and offered to write to Lord Stanley to beg him to come at once with all his forces. Sir William Stanley and John Savage were forthwith proclaimed traitors.[1] Also before he left Nottingham, the gravest and most menacing news of all was brought to him. On the same date, 15 August, he learned that three days earlier Henry, unharmed and unmolested, had reached and entered Shrewsbury. All hopes that the threat would be confined to Wales, and Henry's career terminated there, were dashed. Further information indicated that the rebels had moved on to Stafford, and then apparently changed course to Lichfield, which Lord Stanley had evacuated three days earlier, and in the region of which Sir William Stanley was hovering. Decision could not be delayed any longer, and at last, on Friday, 19 August, Richard III moved and made for Leicester. By the night of Sunday, 21 August, all the forces of both sides were encamped in the vicinity of Ambien Hill, about four hundred feet high, set in Redmore plain, roughly midway between the villages of Shenton and Sutton Cheney, less than two miles south of Market Bosworth.

Many attempts have been made to reconstruct in detail what exactly happened at the battle of Bosworth, but mostly in vain. Plans of precise positions and movements on the field are necessarily conjectural, for no reliable contemporary account of them was written, or at any rate has survived, and the most likely description, that by Polydore Vergil, was composed some twenty years or more after the event. If his account, based upon what Henry and other surviving participants may have told him, can be accepted, some broad conclusions can be formulated, but later embroiderings and conjectural suggestions must be set aside as invalid if we are to avoid deluding ourselves into imagining that we know more about the realities of the event than we do, or are ever likely to do.[2]

[1] Cont. Croyland, 575.

[2] Recent attempts at reconstructing the battle include P. M. Kendall, Richard III (1955), 354–69, where the plan of battle on p. 363 probably represents the array of forces on the morning of 22 August as accurately as can be done. The plan on p. 362, purporting to show the position on the eve of the battle, is vitiated by assuming that

It is not certain, but most probable that early on Monday, 22 August
Richard III arrayed his forces along the top of Ambien Hill, with
archers in front under the command of John Howard, duke of Norfolk,
with himself and a choice force of men somewhere to the rearwards.
Probably still further to the rear Henry Percy, earl of Northumberland,
stood with his forces, but as Vergil does not mention him at all until he
surrendered without having struck a blow, it is difficult to be dogmatic
about his position. It is equally uncertain where exactly Thomas, Lord
Stanley, and his brother Sir William, and their forces were located, but
it would seem that the two forces were separate and positioned somewhat to the flanks of the main arena, but which one was to the right
and which to the left, cannot be ascertained for certain. But as Henry
sent a message before the battle to Lord Stanley to come and join him,
it can be assumed that he was readily accessible and in a position where
such a move would have been possible, and probably he was stationed
below the hill and to Henry's right flank. The brusque reply that
Henry received to the effect that he should put his own forces in order
and that Stanley would come with his army well appointed naturally
vexed and appalled him, for this attitude was not what he expected, and
is conclusive evidence that the Stanleys were determined to keep on the
winning side, whichever that might prove to be.

Henry's total force is put at scarcely five thousand, not counting 'the

Richard III's forces were located at Stapleton on 21 August, which cannot be proved
and also makes assumptions about the position at the time of other commanders'
forces. Albert Makinson gives an interesting account in 'The road to Bosworth field,
August 1485', *History Today*, XIII (1963), 239–49, but in the space available could
not cite authority for his reconstruction, and the plan of the battle on p. 241, although it places Richard III's camp at Sutton Cheney, not Stapleton, appears to
involve improbable complications in the moves during the battle. Both Professor
Kendall and Mr Makinson categorically dismiss Polydore Vergil's statement that
Henry marched with the marsh to his right and with the sun behind. Since we do not
know exactly how Henry approached the spot or at what time, we cannot repudiate
Vergil's plain assertion without definite proof to the contrary, which is not forthcoming. The best available account is still J. Gairdner, 'The battle of Bosworth',
Archaeologia, 2nd ser., V (1897), 159–78, with an excellent map of the terrain. Gairdner
examines the evidence with care, and gives cogent reasons for believing that it is not
necessary to reject Vergil's assertion, is critical of Hutton's chronology and unsupported statements, but is on unsafe ground, in accepting Hall's addition to Vergil's
story to the effect that Lord Stanley's forces actually joined in on Henry's side in the
early phase of the battle. He uses the evidence of the cannon balls on the west top of
Ambien Hill to show that Henry used cannon on the field, some of which he may have
brought with him from France, as Commynes said (*see* above, p. 40, fn. 1), but thought
that some were too large to have been conveyed rapidly on the march through Wales,
and suggests plausibly that these may have come from Tamworth Castle. A. L.
Rowse, *Bosworth field and the Wars of the Roses* (1966), has no independent value for the
battle.

Stanleyians', of whom about three thousand were 'at the battle' under Sir William. As there is no valid evidence that Lord Stanley and his forces took any active part in the battle, it is not surprising that until it was all over there is no further mention of him. Richard III's force we are told was twice as great as Henry's, but as we are not told whether 'the Stanleyians' or any part of them are to be included in this figure, we cannot calculate what the significance of this was.

Henry arrayed his forces so as to provide a slender vanguard, with a small number of archers in front, under the command of John de Vere, earl of Oxford, with a right wing under Gilbert Talbot and a left wing under John Savage. He himself followed, where exactly is not apparent, except that he 'trusted to the aid of Lord Stanley, with one troop of horsemen and a few footmen'. The only positive identification of location given by Vergil is that a marsh existed between the two hosts, that Henry deliberately passed this on the right hand, so that it would form a defensive terrain for his men (which of them is not stated) and so that he had the sun behind him. It is rash to argue, as some have done, that this relative position was impossible, and that therefore Vergil must have wrongly reported what he was told, especially as we do not know for certain how Henry approached the marsh, nor the hour at which he advanced.

When the rebels had passed the marsh, Richard III ordered an attack. The archers on both sides discharged their arrows, and also came to hand strokes. The earl of Oxford feared that too many of his men would be overwhelmed if they advanced too far and ordered that none of them should go ten feet further than the standards. This prudent order momentarily confused the king's forces, who suspected some sort of trap, and a lull in the fighting ensued, all the more because many of them were, it seems, not anxious to be too hotly engaged. The conflict of the vanguards, however, was renewed.

It was at this inconclusive stage that Richard III identified Henry of Richmond with his small personal force, and took his decision, fatal as it was to prove, immediately to spur forward with his choice band to attack Henry personally. What induced him to take such an impetuous and rash course can only be surmised, especially as action of this kind was scarcely in accord with his usual caution. It may, however, have been in accord with his other outstanding characteristic – calculation. He quickly calculated, we may suppose, that he was confronted with an opportunity to terminate the issue in his own favour before the equivocal inaction of the Stanleys and Northumberland turned into overt treason. He miscalculated only to the extent that he failed to reckon that any

3a. Lady Margaret Beaufort. Artist unknown, late sixteenth century (*St John's College, Cambridge*)

3b. Lady Margaret Beaufort, by Pietro Torrigiano, *c.* 1514 (*Westminster Abbey*)

4a. Introduction to the declaration of the king's title in the parliament of 1485, from a *Book of Statutes* privately compiled for Thomas Pigott, serjeant-at-law in 1503 (*Bodleian Library, Hatton MS. 10, fo. 336*)

4b. Gold medal struck to commemorate the wedding of Henry VII and Elizabeth of York on 18 January 1486 (*British Museum*)

delay in achieving his purpose would provide at any rate Sir William Stanley with a decisive opportunity for doing precisely that.

Richard III and his men were received by the small band surrounding Henry with great courage and met with stout resistance. Henry's standard was overthrown, and the standard bearer, William Brandon, and others were killed by Richard III, who also achieved the feat of overthrowing John Cheyney, a warrior of more than average size and stature. Henry, we are told – and the words are very revealing – bore the brunt longer than his own soldiers would have thought possible and who had begun to abandon hope. Long enough, indeed, to enable Sir William Stanley to decide that the crucial moment had come, to gallop with his men across from where they were, to intervene before it was too late, to cut down Richard III fighting manfully to the very end, and so to rescue Henry from the brink of utter disaster. In the meantime – whatever these words may mean exactly – the earl of Oxford put Norfolk's vanguard to flight; Norfolk himself had lost his life, and many were killed in the ensuing chase, and many fled the field. Whether as many as a thousand of Richard III's forces and as few as a hundred of Henry's were killed in the battle, as Vergil tells us, must remain problematical, but we would expect the former figure to be exaggerated and the latter underestimated.

For Henry of Richmond, so narrowly rescued from destruction, the outcome was a scene such as had never before been seen on the soil of England. His acclamation by the soldiers still on the field, their shouts of 'God save King Henry', and the symbolic placing on his head by Lord Stanley – no longer hesitating to show his hand – of the 'crown' of Richard III that had been found by someone somewhere among the spoils on the field,[1] brought his two years' conspiracy to a triumphant climax. The reign of the first Tudor had begun.

[1] As Dr Anglo justly remarks in 'The foundation of the Tudor dynasty', *Guildhall Miscellanea*, II (1960), 3, the story of the finding of the golden circlet worn by Richard III at Bosworth as the origin of the sign of the Tudor badge of the hawthorn and crown (J. Gairdner, *Richard III*, 244) is apocryphal. The Croyland chronicle and Polydore Vergil both say that the circlet was found amidst the spoils of the battle, and do not mention the hawthorn bush. Neither do Hall, Holinshed, Shakespeare, nor Bacon. There is no sixteenth-century authority for connecting the badge with Bosworth. Polydore Vergil states clearly that it was Lord Stanley who placed the crown on Henry's head. The suggestion, to be found in Hutton, op. cit., and elsewhere, that it may have been Sir William Stanley who did this, and that Bray had found it and brought it to Sir William, is not sufficiently supported to be credible. Even if the crown came into the hands of Sir William Stanley, it can hardly be supposed that he would have presumed to place it on Henry's head himself; he would have felt bound to hand it to his elder brother, the only peer not attainted on the victor's side (apart from Northumberland).

Chapter 2

ACCESSION, CORONATION, MARRIAGE, AND FAMILY

After the battle of Bosworth the reign of Henry VII had indeed begun in reality, but in pretence it had begun before that decisive event. Before Henry had left the continent, he had sent letters[1] under his signet initialled 'H. R.', and, when in his first parliament[2] the question arose of attainting 'Richard, late duke of Gloucester, calling and naming himself by usurpation King Richard III', and others, it was convenient to accuse them of having committed treason on 21 August against King Henry. For purposes of this kind, therefore, Henry was prepared to date his reign from 21 August, and some of the less recent historians and older works of reference were not wholly wrong in ascribing the earlier date rather than the later to the official commencement of the reign.[3]

Learned discussions on the subject of by what right Henry assumed the crown are largely otiose.[4] There is no evidence of much if any overt discussion at the time.[5] It was taken for granted that Henry was the male heir of the house of Lancaster through his mother Margaret Beaufort, whose own claims as heiress were ignored. The verdict of the God of battles had confirmed such hereditary right as existed, and acclamation on the field itself rounded off the traditional procedure for attainment of the throne. Thereafter there was nothing to impede Henry from proceeding to coronation in the normal forms, and there was nothing for his first parliament, when it met after the coronation, to do in this matter but to declare that the inheritance of the crowns of

---

[1] *See* above, p. 39; also printed in J. O. Halliwell-Phillips, *Letters*, I, 161–2.

[2] *See* below, p. 63.

[3] Thus, A. F. Pollard, 'The "*de facto*" act of Henry VII', *B.I.H.R.*, VII (1929), 3, was not justified in asserting that the common statement that Henry dated his reign and regnal years from 21 August instead of 22 August is not substantiated.

[4] The main points for consideration were outlined in Chrimes, *English constitutional ideas in the fifteenth century* (1936), 32–4, and references therein.

[5] The reference to this subject in the continuation of the *Croyland chronicle* (ed. Riley), 512, suggesting diversity of opinion, is hard to understand, because the allusions therein do not accord with the wording of the act of parliament setting out the king's title in most terse and guarded language.

England and France rested in the most royal person of Henry VII and the heirs of his body.[1]

Rapidity of decision and action had brought Henry successfully to the outcome of Bosworth, and speed characterized his first moves thereafter. The circular letter which Henry VII sent out very soon after the battle is of interest, not only for its good intentions, but for its assertion that Richard III was slain at a place called 'Sandeford'. The letter must have been sent very quickly, for the list of slain includes Thomas, earl of Surrey, and the fact that he had not been killed must have been revealed very soon. The text as printed reads as follows.

Henry, by the grace of God, king of England and of France, prince of Wales and lord of Ireland, strictly chargeth and commandeth, upon pain of death, that no manner of man rob or spoil no manner of commons coming from the field; but suffer them to pass home to their countries and dwelling places, with their horses and harness. And moreover, that no manner of man take upon him to go to no gentleman's place, neither in the county, nor within cities nor boroughs, nor pick no quarrels for old or new matters; but keep the king's peace, upon pain of hanging, etc.

And moreover, if there be any man offered to be robbed and spoiled of his goods, let him come to master Richard Borrow, the king's serjeant here, and he shall have a warrant for his body and his goods, until the time the king's pleasure be known.

And moreover, the king ascertaineth you, that Richard duke of Gloucester, lately called King Richard, was lately slain at a place called Sandeford, within the shire of Leicester, and there was laid openly, that every man might see and look upon him. And also there was slain upon the same field John, late duke of Norfolk, John, late earl of Lincoln, Thomas, late earl of Surrey, Francys Viscount Lovel, Sir Walter Deveres, Lord Ferrars, Richard Ratcliffe, knight, Robert Bracherly knight, with many other knights, squires, and gentlemen: on whose souls God have mercy.[2]

Even before he left Leicester *en route* for London, he dispatched Robert Willoughby to Sheriff Hutton in Yorkshire to secure the person of Edward, earl of Warwick, the fifteen-year-old son of George, duke of Clarence, and now heir of the house of York, and to remove him to the Tower of London, where he was destined to remain for the rest of his life. Out of the Tower was quickly brought Elizabeth of York, Henry's intended bride, and restored to her mother's custody, to await the turn of events.[3]

[1] *See* below, p. 62.

[2] A copy survives in the MS. archives of York, printed by J. O. Halliwell-Phillips, *Letters*, I (1846), 169–70.   [3] P.V. (ed. Hay), 2.

The City fathers soon set about receiving the victor with proper ceremony. The mayor made a suitable proclamation on 26 August, the
court of aldermen took precautions against unseemly activities that
might ensue, and by 3 September Henry was received at Shoreditch by
the representatives of the City, resplendently arrayed,[1] with trumpeters
sounding, and with Bernard André publicly reciting verses for the
occasion, and with other manifestations of popular joy. Proceeding at
once to St Paul's, Henry deposited three banners, presumably those
which had been used at Bosworth, one displaying the arms of St George,
one a red fiery dragon on white and green sarcenet, the third a banner
of Tarteron and Duncow.[2] After prayers and a *Te Deum*, he retired
to the palace of the bishop of London for a few days.

The problems that now confronted Henry must have been daunting.
The landless and penniless refugee, after fourteen years' exile and only
boyhood memories of Wales and one short visit at most to London to
guide him, with as yet no resources of his own, and little clothing even,[3]
no experience of government and administration, and no training as a
prince, found himself confronted at once with the whole burden of
kingship. What manner of man Henry had become at the age of twenty-
eight can only be surmised. He had not so far been at any time a person
of sufficient importance to attract much contemporary notice, and
almost all comment (other than Richard III's vituperation) that survives
was written after, mostly long after, his accession. It was therefore
highly coloured by what people came to know of him as king. Clearly
by August 1485 Henry had experienced the slings and arrows of
fortune which, if not exactly outrageous, had certainly been both
unusual and severely testing. His position during his boyhood in Wales
had been at best that of a favoured minor in the guardianship of a
political upstart who had prospered by hostility to the Lancastrian
family. Thereafter he had become an exile, for many years the captive
in effect of the Breton duke and latterly a pawn in the hands of the
French court. It had been a narrow and restricted life for him, with
little in it to instruct and inspire a future monarch, offering for many
years only the most dubious prospects. He had perforce to rely mainly
upon his own inner resources with which to focus, preserve, and enhance

[1] *Materials*, I, 4–6; and generally, Anglo, *Guildhall Miscellanea*, II (1960), 3–11.

[2] Edward IV had similarly deposited his banners after Barnet in 1471. *Great
chronicle*, 217, cited Anglo, loc. cit. 4.

[3] Sir Reginald Bray spent £336 18s 4d on clothing materials which were delivered
to the king, partly for Henry himself and partly for servants, as early as 30 August.
John English, king's servant, spent a further £21 3s 7d for clothing for other servants,
including himself, *Materials*, I, 78–183.

his potentiality. He had to make the most of the experience and knowledge of his companions in exile, and his uncle Jasper and the other
substantial men who sooner or later joined him. That he showed signs
of promise as a future leader may be inferred from the fact that a number
of such men did rally to him abroad after the *débâcle* of the duke of
Buckingham's rebellion. Schooled in adversity and disappointment as
he had been, Henry had learnt to bide his time, to calculate his chances,
to be cautious and suspicious, and yet to attract and bind to himself the
support of diverse men whose aid might some day be invaluable. But in
exile he had no means of binding them except by ties of mutual esteem
and hope of future interest; he had no gifts or favours to offer as yet. Up
to the victory at Bosworth his prospects remained so doubtful that only a
high degree of personal magnetism, ability to inspire confidence, and a
growing reputation for shrewd decisiveness could, in all the circumstances, have brought him to that victory and the ensuing acclamation.
Having won that improbable victory, he must needs, if he were to
survive, show to the people that they had acquired a new king who
understood his business. He must without delay set on foot preparations
for his coronation, for a parliament, for the fulfilment of his promise to
marry Elizabeth of York; and must also reward his supporters and
followers, without whose services he could not have succeeded and upon
the continued services of many of whom he must be able to rely; and
above all he must as soon as possible appoint suitable persons to the
principal ministerial and administrative posts to ensure that government could be carried on in his name.

It is not possible to determine precisely in what order Henry tackled
all these and other tasks. No doubt many of them were coped with
simultaneously, but as some of the important appointments appear to
have been made by word of mouth, no exact date can be affixed to
them. At any rate on 15 September writs were issued for a parliament
to meet at Westminster on 7 November,[1] and at some stage the decision
was taken to hold the coronation on Sunday, 30 October. Before these
events occurred or soon after them, much had been done to reward his
supporters, partly by way of honours, grants, or appointments to
offices, so that to some extent the need to reward and the need to
provide for administration were met at the same time. A striking feature
of Henry's efforts in this sphere is the extent to which he rewarded not
only his more eminent kinsmen and supporters, but also numerous
humble folk who had served him in Brittany or France, before Bosworth had been reached. Upon the distinguished among his companions

[1] ibid. I, 6.

in exile Henry would continue to rely in most cases, for the rest of
their lives, but many a grant was made simply 'for service as well
within the realm as in foreign parts' or 'in consideration of true and
faithful service done as well beyond the sea as on this side of our
victorious journey'.[1]

The first three or four months of the reign saw a large number of
rewards for the more important of Henry's supporters. Although not
chronologically the first, the greatest rewards, as was only fitting,
went to the faithful uncle, Jasper, without whose devotion and services
all would have been lost. On 27 October, just before the coronation,
Jasper was created duke of Bedford.[2] By then Jasper was a man of
fifty-five years of age, and had never married, but before 7 November
he was to marry Catherine Woodville, the widow of Henry Stafford,
duke of Buckingham, and a sister of Queen Elizabeth Woodville.[3]
Jasper was to be appointed chief justice of South Wales,[4] steward of all
courts and constable of several castles of many lands pertaining to the
duchy of Lancaster in the Marches of Wales,[5] was granted all the
castles and manors of Glamorgan, Abergavenny, and Haverfordwest,[6]
and was given exemption for life from payment of any fees of the seal
upon any letters patent, charters, or original and judicial writs.[7] The
earldom of Pembroke was restored to him in the parliament of 1485,[8]
and in October 1486 he was appointed lieutenant of Ireland.[9]

John de Vere, earl of Oxford, the chief of Henry's military captains,
was naturally restored to the honours and estates he had lost under the
Yorkists,[10] and as early as 21 and 22 September was appointed admiral

---

[1] The names of some forty persons, mostly of yeoman status, who received grants or
favours of one kind or another on these grounds, starting from as early as 18 September 1485, can be listed from *Materials*, I, *passim*, 8–357. Additional names can be obtained from *C.P.R., Henry VII*, I. The villages of Widerley, Aterton, Feny Drayton,
Manseter, and Atherstone, which had suffered losses of corn and grain at the hands of
Henry's followers before Bosworth, received £72 2s 4d compensation (25 November
1485), *Materials*, 188.

[2] ibid. I, 102. The letters patent were couched in particularly warm terms.

[3] G.E.C., sub.-tit. Bedford. Catherine was allowed 1,000 marks per annum out of
the estate of her late husband as recompense for all dower (*Materials*, 117–18). Jasper
had an illegitimate daughter, Helen, who married William Gardiner, citizen of London, who became the parents of Stephen Gardiner, bishop of Winchester.

[4] *Materials*, I, 215.   [5] ibid. I, 220; *Materials*, 394.

[6] ibid. 334.   [7] ibid. 459.   [8] ibid. 121.

[9] For two years, and thereafter at pleasure, in as full manner as the late George,
duke of Clarence held the office. Appointments to archbishoprics and bishoprics, and
to the offices of chancellor, treasurer, and the chief justiceships were reserved to the
Crown, ibid. 384; cf. Roger S. Thomas, op. cit., *passim*.

[10] *R.P.*, VI, 278.

of England, Ireland, and Aquitaine, and soon constable of the Tower of London, keeper of the lions and leopards within the Tower, with all the usual fees;[1] and was granted other profitable favours.[2]

Thomas, Lord Stanley, and his brother Sir William duly reaped the rewards of their desertion from Richard III at the crucial moment, rewards large in the case of Thomas 'the king's righte entierley beloved father',[3] not so large in the case of William. Thomas, now the king's step-father, became earl of Derby on the same day as Jasper became duke,[4] was to become constable of England,[5] chief steward of the duchy of Lancaster,[6] was granted various manors,[7] and of course saw his wife Margaret Beaufort not only restored to all of which she had been deprived by Richard III, but also granted a large number of favours.[8] William, for some ten years, attained to dignities and profitable offices. He became very quickly chamberlain of the Household, a chamberlain of the Exchequer (vice Sir James Tyrell[9]), and later on constable of Caernarvon Castle,[10] and chief justice of North Wales,[11] as well as the recipient of grants in land. Powerfully entrenched as he became in the royal household and in North Wales, his fall, when it came in 1495, was all the more sensational.

The two Courtenays (not relatives) received recognition for their fidelity to Lancaster and to Henry. Peter, bishop of Exeter, became a king's councillor and keeper of the Privy Seal and was granted the temporalities of the see of Salisbury,[12] whilst the earldom of Devonshire was revived in favour of Sir Edward Courtenay.[13]

Those who had rendered substantial military assistance at one time or another in 1483 or 1485, were rewarded. Henry's French protagonist, Philibert de Chandée, as already mentioned, actually received an earldom – of Bath[14] – and some financial favour.[15] Sir Richard Edgecombe became one of the chamberlains of the Exchequer (vice Sir William Catesby[16]), and was given other substantial grants;[17] the Savages, Sir

---

[1] *Materials*, 23, 31, 38.

[2] e.g. ibid. 33, 211, 213. Sir James Blunt, who had come over to Henry with the earl of Oxford, was restored to the lieutenancy of Hammes Castle (ibid. 368), and was granted the stewardship of the honour of Tutbury (ibid. 551).

[3] ibid. 76.   [4] ibid. 241.   [5] ibid. 345.   [6] ibid. 574.

[7] ibid. 76, etc.   [8] *See* below, p. 57.   [9] *Materials*, 41.   [10] ibid. 258.

[11] ibid. 271.   [12] ibid. 9, 81.   [13] ibid. 100.

[14] So created, 6 January 1486 (ibid. I, 246; II, 152), with 100 marks a year; *see* above, p. 40.

[15] *Materials*, I, 227, 494. Early in 1486 he appears to have been reckoned one of the ambassadors from France, whose expenses in England were reimbursed (ibid. II, 103, 104, 105).   [16] ibid. I, 19.

[17] e.g. office of escheator and feodary of the duchy of Cornwall and constable of

John and several brothers, received minor offices of profit.[1] Sir Richard Guildford became master of the Ordinance[2] and a chamberlain of the Exchequer (vice Lord Hastings[3]). Sir John Cheyney obtained some modest favours, but after Stoke became a baron.[4] Sir Giles Daubeney became master of the king's hounds,[5] lieutenant-governor of Calais,[6] and in March 1486, a baron.[7] The equivocation of Henry Percy, earl of Northumberland, received its reward with the office of warden of the East March and Middlemarch[8] towards Scotland, which he doubtless coveted above all others. Sir Rhys ap Thomas, whose attitude in Wales during the 'journey' may not have altogether pleased Henry, does not appear to have received very substantial solace. With the necessity for providing handsomely in Wales for Jasper and Sir William Stanley, it was perhaps hardly practicable to do a great deal for Rhys ap Thomas. However, he was made chamberlain of South Wales in the counties of Carmarthen and Cardigan, steward of the lordship of Builth Wells,[9] and constable and steward of the lordship of Brecnoc.[10]

The men of administrative talents among Henry's companions soon found their offices, in which they were to remain for many years, in most cases for the rest of their lives. John, Lord Dynham, became treasurer of England,[11] Thomas Lovell, chancellor of the Exchequer,[12] Reginald Bray chancellor of the County Palatine and the duchy of Lancaster,[13] Richard Fox, already the king's secretary and 'beloved counsellor', became bishop of Exeter and keeper of the Privy Seal in succession to Peter Courtenay in February 1487.[14] Christopher

---

Launceston Castle (*Materials*, 1, 18, 290); steward of the earldom of March (ibid. 79); comptroller of the king's Household (ibid. 195); *see* also ibid. 448, 451.

[1] ibid. 10.   [2] ibid. 68.

[3] ibid. 40, 66; constable of Southampton Castle, 344.

[4] ibid. II, 194.   [5] ibid. I, 83.   [6] ibid. 361.   [7] ibid. 385.

[8] With the same authority and power as wardens had in the reign of Richard II and the three Lancastrian kings, 3 January 1486 (ibid. 242). On the significance of this passing over of Yorkist practice, *see* below, p. 98.

[9] ibid. 109.

[10] ibid. 105. On the whole subject, *see* J. M. Lloyd, 'The rise and fall of the House of Dinefwr (the Rhys family) 1430–1530', unpublished M.A. thesis (University of Wales, Cardiff, 1963).

[11] His patent was dated 14 July 1486 (*Materials*, I, 499), but he probably acted as such before the parliament of 1485.

[12] ibid. 84; Lovell became speaker in the parliament of 1485; *see* below, p. 111.

[13] ibid. 549. Many offices, especially connected with finance and estate management, were granted in due course to Bray, including that of steward and surveyor of all the possessions of the late Henry, duke of Buckingham, during the minority of his son and heir Edward, so long as in the hands of the Crown (ibid. 212).

[14] ibid. 154.

Urswick, the faithful priest, became king's almoner and the recipient of a number of favours and preferments.[1]

There were two other personages to whom Henry owed more than he could measure, both prime movers in the original plots. One was his mother Margaret Beaufort, and the other John Morton, refugee bishop of Ely. Margaret became in all but name the dowager Queen Mother, well endowed[2] to sustain her many acts of piety and patronage. Morton was to become chancellor of England on 6 March 1486,[3] and archbishop of Canterbury before the end of that year, cardinal in 1493, and so remained until his death in 1500.[4] John Morton, born about 1420, had been educated at Cerne Abbey and Balliol College, Oxford, where he became a doctor of civil law, and afterwards practised in the court of Arches. He attracted the favourable notice of Thomas Bourchier, archbishop of Canterbury, and was appointed chancellor of the duchy of Cornwall and a master in Chancery. He strongly supported Lancaster, and was present at the battle of Towton. Subsequently he was attainted and went into exile with Queen Margaret at St Mihiel, where he had the opportunity to discuss affairs with Sir John Fortescue and others of

[1] ibid. 275; 3 September 1485, Urswick was granted in augmentation of the king's alms, all the goods and chattels of felons and all deodands falling to the Crown. He was appointed master of King's Hall, Cambridge (ibid. 71, 184), to various preferments (*C.P.R.*, I, 154, 170, 339, 472), and became, before December 1485, dean of York (*Materials*, II, 377).

[2] Among numerous grants and favours shown to Margaret Beaufort, now countess of Derby as well as of Richmond, the most notable were the grant to her of the marriage and wardship of Edward, son and heir of Henry Stafford, duke of Buckingham, and his brother Henry (*R.P.*, VI, 285–6; and *C.P.R.*, I, 113); and the grant for life of a very large number of manors and lordships (ibid. 154). She was allowed to sign herself as Margaret R. (Pollard, *Henry VII*, I, 218.)

[3] On Monday, 6 March 1486 the king, in the presence of Peter, bishop of Exeter, Jasper, duke of Bedford, Christopher Urswick, and others, delivered the Great Seal to John Morton, bishop of Ely, and appointed him chancellor (*C.P.R.*, I, 360). The assignment of this transaction to the year 1487 in some reference books is an unfortunate error. The *congé d'élire* to the prior and chapter of Canterbury was dated 8 June 1486 and Morton was translated to Canterbury on 6 October 1486.

[4] Nor did Henry ignore what were soon to be his Woodville relatives, Edward Woodville, and Thomas Grey, marquis of Dorset, who along with the fellow pledge, John Bourchier, left behind in France, were shown some favour. One would like to know what lay behind Henry's grant dated 26 February 1486 of special protection and safeguard to Ann Devereux, countess of Pembroke, the widow of his former guardian William Herbert, who at the command of the king and for no other reason, came out of Wales to London (*Materials*, I, 320). The grant of the earldom of Huntingdon to her son William, made in exchange for the earldom of Pembroke by Edward IV in 1479, was confirmed on 17 May 1488 (*C.P.R.*, I, 137). The earldom of Pembroke was to be restored to Ann's grandson in 1551.

the party. He was concerned in the negotiations which led to the Readeption of Henry VI, but after the battles of Barnet and Tewkesbury he came to terms with Edward IV, and his attainder was reversed. In March 1473 he was appointed master of the Rolls, and became a councillor and bishop of Ely on 31 January 1479. He remained a valuable servant to Edward IV, but attracted the hostility of Richard, duke of Gloucester, who on 13 June 1483 caused him to be ousted with other councillors, was sent to the Tower, but was shortly committed into the custody of the duke of Buckingham, with results that have already been noticed. After fleeing from Buckingham's custody, he had sought refuge in Flanders. Many other companions in exile, as well as other persons who participated in the risings of 1483 received grants and favours. Some were knighted shortly before or after Bosworth. Some such as Fox and Bray, and others such as Thomas Lovell, were designated councillors from an early date, and a number of others were so designated.

Preparations for the coronation proceeded apace. No expense was going to be spared to make the occasion an impressive and glittering display, and every effort was to be made to ensure the maintenance of the traditional ceremonies and rituals. By 19 October, a commission was issued to Peter, bishop of Exeter; Jasper, the king's uncle; John, earl of Oxford; John, earl of Nottingham; Thomas, Lord Stanley; John, Lord Fitzwalter, steward of the Household; Robert Morton (John Morton's brother), keeper of the Rolls; Sir Thomas Brian, chief justice of the King's Bench; Sir Humphrey Starkey, chief baron of the Exchequer, and Sir Richard Croft, treasurer of the Household, to do all pertaining to the office of steward of England at the coronation.[1]

The joint steward of the Household, Sir Robert Willoughby de Broke, must long before this date have put in hand the ordering of vast purchases of sumptuous cloth and clothing of every hue; silks and satins, furs, skins, leather, trappings, ribbons, shoes and boots, spurs, harness and banners; and had hired tailors and workmen, and the total bill for his efforts alone was to come to £1,506 18s 10¾d.[2] Additional large sums were spent by the keeper of the Great Wardrobe on the clothing and equipment of the household, partly before and partly after the

[1] *Materials*, I, 92; *C.P.R.*, I, 46.
[2] The very detailed and illuminating account surviving fills twenty-eight pages in *Materials*, II, 2–29. It is not possible to state the modern value of the money of Henry VII's time. A basis for comparison can be obtained by noting the prices paid in this and other accounts. Thus, for example, Willoughby paid 13s 4d for the king's gilt spurs; 8s for a sword with a point; 6d for 1,000 small nails. The wages for the tailors employed in the Great Wardrobe were 6d per day.

coronation.[1] Henry VII was, of course, obliged to provide a new royal household from scratch.

With all the officials and workmen concerned doubtless working overtime, as the day approached, Henry began to take up positions appropriate to the occasion.[2] On 27 October he dined at Lambeth Palace, with the archbishop of Canterbury, that veteran member of the progeny of Edward III, Thomas Bourchier, who had been archbishop for thirty years and had officiated at the coronations of Edward IV and Richard III, and now was to participate in the third and last coronation of his life. Then came the procession to the Tower of London, the traditional apartments for the sovereign prior to his coronation. Unlike those unhappy princes, soon to be his deceased brothers-in-law, Henry had no difficulty in re-emerging from the Tower at the appropriate moments. Next day came the bestowal of the dukedom upon Jasper, and earldoms on Thomas Stanley and Edward Courtenay, who afterwards dined together at one table in the king's great chamber. Seven new knights of the Bath were thereafter appointed, including Reginald Bray,[3] and the traditional ceremonies for their installation followed. On the Saturday morning Henry created a new pursuivant, Rouge Dragon. In the afternoon the great procession from the Tower to Westminster Hall filled the streets with pageantry. The heralds and serjeants-at-arms, the esquire of the body, the king's secretary (Richard Fox) and almoner (Christopher Urswick), the mayor of London and Garter king of Arms, and the earls of Derby and Nottingham, of Oxford and Lincoln, preceded the King's Grace, who was bare-headed, clad in a long gown of purple velvet edged with ermine and a rich baldric, under a royal canopy supported by four knights on foot. The only two dukes, Bedford and Suffolk, followed, with six henchmen,

---

[1] The account of Alvered Corneburgh, keeper of the Great Wardrobe, for the period 22 August 1485 to 2 February 1486, is printed, ibid. 163–80. The items include provision for the queen, and the sums involved were of the order of £1,300.

[2] The fullest account of the coronation proceedings is to be found in S. Anglo, 'The foundation of the Tudor dynasty; the coronation and marriage of Henry VII', *Guildhall Miscellanea*, II (1960), 3–11. A late sixteenth-century MS., now B.M. Egerton 985, fo. 41b–48, provides a narrative of Henry VII's procession and coronation proceedings (ibid. 3–6); the coronation order is available in several MS. versions, cited ibid. 5, and is commented on in L. G. Wickham-Legg, *English coronation records* (1901), 220–39; cf. P. E. Schramm, *A history of the English coronation* (1937). On Archbishop Bourchier, *see Registrum Thome Bourgchier*, ed. F. R. H. Du Boulay, Cant. and York Soc., LIV (1957); cf. S. Anglo, *Spectacle, pageantry and early Tudor policy* (1969).

[3] The others were Edward Stafford, John Fitzwalter, Thomas Cokesge, Roger Lewkenor, Henry Haydon, and John Verney.

trapped with 'divers arms and badges'. Sir John Cheyney, knight now of the king's body, led the courser of state trapped in a cloth of gold and arms.

On Sunday, 30 October Henry was anointed and crowned king. The text of the service was the same as that used for Richard III, hastily amended to omit references to a queen. Archbishop Bourchier, too infirm to perform the whole rite, performed only the anointing and crowning; the officiating bishops, John Shirwood of Durham, and Robert Stillington of Bath and Wells, were supported by Peter Courtenay of Exeter, and John Morton of Ely. The new duke of Bedford had the honour of bearing the crown, and the new earl of Derby the sword of state; Oxford bore the king's train. To Bishop Peter Courtenay fell the agreeable task of asking the will of the people, and Thomas Kempe, bishop of London, said mass.

The consecration and crowning, the taking of the oath,[1] and the acclamation over, Henry, now king *dei gracia*, accompanied and supported by all his *entourage*, could emerge from the abbey and show himself to the populace *en route* again to the Tower for the banquet. At this Jasper was steward, and rode up and down on horseback, trapped with ermined cloth of gold. Sir Robert Dymoke, the hereditary king's champion, could appear on horseback trapped this time with the arms of Cadwallader, and challenge all-comers, just as he had for Richard III two years before, and as he was going to do for Henry VIII twenty-four years later. The extreme irony of the present challenge must have struck all beholders as rich indeed. The banquet ended, proceedings lapsed, as the coronation tournament[2] originally fixed for the following Sunday had been postponed until 13 November, for on Monday, 7 November the first parliament was to assemble.

The legal problems confronting the new regime were formidable, and some of these at least had to be resolved before the parliament met. No time was lost in appointing justices and legal officers; many such appointments were made during September and October,[3] and by the time Michaelmas term opened (usually 6 October), the king was in a position to consult the justices on several difficult questions. The most awkward of them was the fact that Henry himself was an attainted

[1] The text of Richard III's coronation oath, presumably the same as that taken by Henry VII, is printed in S. B. Chrimes and A. L. Brown (eds), *Select documents of English constitutional history 1307–1485* (1961), 354–5.

[2] An order was made on 23 October for the payment of 100 marks to Sir Richard Guildford, who had been deputed to prepare the jousts, *Materials*, II, 97–8.

[3] *See* below, p. 156 ff.

person, disabled in the law. The justices of the Exchequer chamber discussed this problem and decided, apparently without difficulty, that he was discharged of his attainder *ipso facto* on taking upon himself to reign and to be king. This evasion of the problem had at any rate the advantage of simplicity and enabled Henry to appear as a lawful person and to hold his parliament in the normal way. No other solution indeed was practicable, for it would not have been possible to annul the act of attainder in a parliament without a lawful king.[1]

On Monday, 7 November, with the king seated on the throne, John Alcock, bishop of Worcester, chancellor of England since 7 October, opened the parliament with the usual *pronunciatio,* in the room called the Cross in the palace of Westminster.[2] He gave a solemn discourse on the text *Intende, prospere, procede, et regna,* exhorted members to pursue not private convenience, but the public and common good, with edifying examples culled from Roman history and supported with a variety of the commonly used anthropomorphic concepts. The commons were instructed to assemble *in domo sua communi* to choose a speaker, and receivers and triers of petition were appointed. On the next day the commons chose a speaker but were inhibited from mentioning his name, presumably because he was a man who had been attainted by Richard III's parliament, as one of the rebels in 1483, and one who, though he had not been in a position to put off his attainder, had already been appointed to several important offices. None the less the commons were ordered to present him next day, 9 November, which they did, *coram domino rege in pleno parliamento* (before the lord king in full parliament). The decision taken must have been simply to ignore the attainder, for no difficulty was raised to the appointment of the man of their choice, to wit, Thomas Lovell.[3]

The primary business of the first parliament, so far as the king was concerned, was to declare his title, to reverse certain attainders and enact some new ones, to obtain financial grants and authorize certain financial arrangements, and to try to ensure observance of the laws for the better preservation of public peace and order.

Declaration of the king's title was made in the form of a bill put forward (nominally at least) by the commons, assented to by the lords spiritual and temporal, and by the king. The bill thus became an act of parliament, though it was not at the time enrolled as a statute. Whoever

---

[1] *Y.B. 1 Henry VII, Mich.*, pl. 5; *see* Chrimes, op. cit. 51, 378.

[2] *R.P.*, VI, 267–384. Extracts from the rolls are given in *Materials*, I, 110–37.

[3] On Thomas Lovell, *see* J. S. Roskell, *The commons and their speakers in English parliaments, 1376–1523* (1965), 298–9, 358–9.

drafted the bill produced a masterpiece of terse assertion which, as a statement of the *fait accompli*, could scarcely have been bettered.

> To the pleasure of All mighty God, the Wealth, Prosperite, and Suretie of this Roialme of England, to the singular comfort of all the Kings Subjects of the same, and in avoiding of all Ambiguities and Questions, be it ordained, stablished, and enacted, by the auctorite thys present Parliament, that the Inheritance of the Crownes of the Roialmes of England and of Fraunce, with all the preheminence and dignitie Royall to the same pertaineing, and all other Seignories to the king belonging beyond the see, with th'appurtenaunces thereto in any wise due or perteineing, be, rest, remaine and abide in the most Royall persone of our now Soveraigne Lord King Harry the VIIth, and in the heirs of hys body lawfully comen, perpetually with the grace of God so to indure, and in non other.[1]

The king himself addressed the commons, showing how he had come to the right and Crown of England, by just hereditary title as well as by *verum Dei judicium* revealed in his victory over his enemy in the field, and declared that all subjects should have and hold all their properties, except those who offend his royal majesty.

Henry had put off this attainder by becoming king, but a number of persons needed an act of parliament to be freed from the legal dangers and disablements. Some of the stalwarts who had been attainted under Richard III 'late in dede and not in right king' or under Edward IV, whether those who had rebelled and fled to the continent in 1483 or later, or whether persons who had incurred penalties for their faithful service to Henry VI, now received their alleviation. Not only the still living but some of the dead got restitution, for what it was worth – Henry VI himself, Queen Margaret of Anjou, Prince Edward, and Henry Beaufort, duke of Somerset. Margaret Beaufort had all her possessions restored, and so did Edward Stafford, heir to the dukedom of Buckingham, as well as Sir Richard and Robert Wells. The Queen Dowager, Elizabeth Woodville, was also restored to her properties. A number of lesser persons, or their heirs, received similar relief.[2]

---

[1] *R.P.*, VI, 268–70; and cf. notes on texts in *S.R.*, II, 499.

[2] *R.P.*, VI, 273–5, 278–86, 288, 290–1, 298, 305. No one to have any action in respect of the lands concerned until after the end of the parliament, ibid. 275. As regards Henry VI, he had been convicted and attainted of high treason and had forfeited the duchy of Lancaster, ibid. V, 478. It is not easy to reconcile this act, and the present repeal thereof, with the opinion expressed by all the justices (except Townsend) to the effect that he had not been attainted, but only disabled of his crown, kingdom, dignity, lands, and tenements, and that when he recovered the crown, all that disablement was *ipso facto* void. *Y.B. 1 Henry VII, Mich.*, pl. 5, cited above.

Now it was the turn of the sovereign whom the last parliament had declared to be the lawful king, to suffer the penalties of failure, along with the more important of those who fought for him. Richard, 'late duke of Gloucester', calling and naming himself by usurpation King Richard III, and twenty-eight other persons, having assembled a great host at Leicester on 21 August the first year of the now sovereign lord, traitorously intending, imagining and compassing the destruction of the king's royal person, our sovereign liege lord, levied war against him, now stood convicted and attainted of high treason, and were disabled in the law and subjected to forfeiture.[1] The arbitrariness of this action was not lost on the members of the parliament, and privately, it would seem, fears were expressed for its effect on supporters of future kings on the day of battle.[2]

The financial provisions made in the parliament were, on the face of it, straightforward. A subsidy of tunnage and poundage was granted for the king's life.[3] An act of resumption of all lands, etc., held by Henry VI on 2 October in the thirty-fourth year of his reign (1455) in England, Wales, Ireland, Calais, or the Marches, was passed, subject to substantial provisos.[4] The duchies of Lancaster and Cornwall were annexed to the Crown, with provisos in favour of Cecily, the dowager duchess of York.[5] Specific provision was made for the assignment by the treasurer of

---

[1] *R.P.*, VI, 275–8. 'Wherefore oure Soveraigne Lord, calleinge unto hys blessed remembraunce thys high and grete charge adjoyned to hys Royall Majestie and Estate, not oblivious nor puttinge out of hys godly mind the unnaturall, mischevious and grete Perjuries, Treasons, Homicides and Murdres, in shedding of Infants blood, with manie other Wronges, odious offences and abominacions ayenst God and Man, and in especiall oure Said Soveraigne Lord, committed and doone by Richard, late Duke of Gloucester. . . .' Among the twenty-eight others attainted were five peers: John Howard, duke of Norfolk; his son Thomas, earl of Surrey; Francis, Viscount Lovel; Walter Devereux, Lord Ferrers; and John, Lord Zouche; and eight knights, including Ratcliffe and Brackenbury; and among the other fifteen persons were William Catesby and John Kendal, who had been Richard III's secretary.

[2] *Cont. Croyland* (ed. Riley), 511. On the whole subject of attainder and forfeiture, see J. R. Lander, 'Attainder and forfeiture, 1453–1509', *Hist. Journal*, IV (1961), 119–151, particularly 144–8. The actual effect of forfeitures on families varied considerably, as broadly speaking a wife's property was exempt. Attainders could be reversed or ultimately reversed in favour of heirs. The total number of attainders during Henry VII's reign was large, 138 altogether, of which fifty-two were eventually reversed. These figures compare unfavourably with the precedents of the three previous reigns: Henry VI, twenty-one attainders, all subsequently reversed; Edward IV, 140 attainders, eighty-six reversed; Richard III, 100, all except one reversed (ibid. 149–51). Henry VII, moreover, showed a marked tendency to be less willing to allow complete restitution of property even when he agreed to reverse attainders (ibid. 145).

[3] *R.P.*, VI, 268–70. [4] ibid. 336. [5] ibid. 270–2.

England to the treasurer of the Household for the expenses thereof of an annual sum amounting to just under £14,000, from eighty-five different stated sources.[1] Similarly, rather more than £2,000 from eighteen sources was to be assigned to the keeper of the Wardrobe for its expenses.[2] The intention to clarify the king's domestic finances was doubtless good; how far the effort was successful is another matter.

The maintenance of the public peace and the enforcement of law and order were inevitably matters of great concern to the poachers now turned gamekeepers, and a special effort was made in the parliament to remind all concerned of their duties in this matter. All the justices assembled at the Blackfriars to consider the king's business against the opening of parliament, could think of many statutes profitable to the realm, if they could be enforced. But the question was, how were they to be enforced?[3] In the parliament, the only method that could be thought of was to exact an oath couched in very detailed terms from the knights and squires of the royal household, the men *de Domo Communitatis* (of the House of the Community), and all the lords spiritual and temporal.

> Ye shall swere that yee from henceforth shall not receive, aid ne comforte, any persoune openlie cursed Murderer, Felon, or outlawed Man of felony, by you knowen so to be, or any such persoune lett to be attached or taken therefore by the order of Law, nor reteine anie Man by Indenture or othe, nor give Livere, Signe, or token, contraire to the law, nor any Maintenance, Imbracerie, Riotts or unlawfull Assemblie make, cause to be made, or assent thereto, nor lett nor cause to be letted the execucion of any of the King's writts or precepts, directed to such lawfull Ministres and Officers, as ought to have execucion of the same, nor lett any Man to Baile or Mainprise, knowing and deeming him to be a Felon, upon Your Honour and Worship. So God you helpe and hys Seints.[4]

This done, and re-enforced at the end of the session by an exhortation by the chancellor to the lords and commons, especially to those who

---

[1] *R.P.*, VI, 299–303. The largest sources were to be the duchy of Cornwall, at £2,700; the subsidy from London, £2,400; and the duchy of Lancaster, at £2,330. The grand total came to £13,475 12s 4d. The lowest assignment was £7.

[2] ibid. 303. The total was £2,105 19s 11d.

[3] *Y.B. 1 Henry VII, Mich.*, pl. 3; cf. Chrimes, op. cit. 255–378.

[4] *R.P.*, VI, 287–8. The list of peers taking the oath is valuable evidence of who responded to the personal writs of summons. It was taken by thirteen bishops (out of eighteen summoned), seventeen abbots or priors (out of twenty-seven summoned), the two dukes, eight earls (out of eleven summoned), one viscount, and seven barons (out of twenty-two summoned). On the question of attendance of peers, *see* J. S. Roskell, 'The problem of the attendance of the lords in mediaeval parliaments', *B.I.H.R.*, XXIX (1956), 153–204, esp. 197.

were justices of the peace,[1] little remained before prorogation on 10 December but for the commons, through the speaker, to beseech the king to marry Elizabeth, daughter of Edward IV, a request which, supported by lords spiritual and temporal standing in their places, the king in person expressed himself happy to accede to.[2] Before the prorogation was over on 23 January 1486, Henry would, in fact, have carried his intention into effect.

Historians have often sought to make much of the fact that the marriage of Henry and Elizabeth of York, which he had solemnly promised to perform at the meeting in Rennes Cathedral on Christmas day, 1483, did not occur until some four months after Bosworth. Much play has been made of the idea that there was some profound political motive for getting himself crowned and his title declared in parliament before he entered into a matrimonial union with the Yorkist house. But it is difficult to see how he could possibly have proceeded in any other way. He was necessarily obliged to ascend the throne on the merits of his own claims, to which marriage with Elizabeth could add nothing. It was only their heirs who could obtain a strengthening of their title from adding the Yorkist to the Lancastrian strain of descent. Henry must become king and attend to the urgent business of the new regime before he could possibly spare time and energy for marriage. Besides, there were other considerations, some of them awkward ones, to be dealt with, before the point of actual marriage could be reached. For one thing, it is a tolerable certainty that at 22 August 1485 he had never set eyes on his intended bride, certainly not for fourteen years, even if he had caught a glimpse of her during the Readeption of 1470–1, which is hardly likely since Elizabeth, at that time four or five years of age, was in sanctuary in Westminster Abbey with her mother. Even Henry could hardly have plunged into matrimony with a total stranger. He must have time for making the lady's acquaintance, and opportunity for a little wooing. Unfortunately there is no evidence of this process, but it must surely have occurred. In any event, there were two serious obstacles to the wedding, which had to be got over before it could be celebrated. At the time of Henry's arrival in England, Elizabeth was, by the law of the land, stigmatized as a bastard, and it would not have done for Henry to marry a person of that status. Furthermore, the parties were related in the fourth degree of kinship and perhaps in the fourth degree of affinity, and could not be married without dispensation. To overcome these obstacles took time, and, on

[1] *R.P.*, VI, 278.　　　　　　　　　　　　　　　　　　[2] ibid.

the whole, things moved fast to enable the marriage to take place on 18 January 1486.

The first of these difficulties was a very delicate matter indeed, for the subject-matter of the act of Richard III's parliament had now become so scandalous to think of that all the justices in the Exchequer chamber advised that it would be best to avoid rehearsing the actual words in the act of Henry's parliament designed to nullify it.[1] Nullified, however, it was,[2] without being too specific about its contents, and until this was done, the legitimacy of Elizabeth remained questionable.

It still remained to go through the elaborate procedure to obtain dispensation for the marriage to be unequivocably canonical. To wait for the papal court itself to make the decree would have been to delay the wedding unduly, and even as it was the services of the apostolic delegate to England and Scotland, James, bishop of Imola, in the matter did not produce a faculty of dispensation in proper form, after due consideration of the testimony of eight witnesses, until 16 January.[3] Two days later the wedding took place, but the papal confirmation of the decree was dated 2 March. When confirmation did come, however, it was worth having, for it not only ratified all that had been done in the matter, but also threatened excommunication to all who should rebel against Henry VII and his heirs.[4]

Little is known of the marriage itself, except that Archbishop Thomas Bourchier is said to have performed the ceremony,[5] which was certainly made an occasion for celebration by the panegyrists and chroniclers, contemporary and later,[6] as well it might, for at last the union of the two houses of Lancaster and York had occurred, even though, as time showed, not all parties and persons were disposed to acquiesce in the turn of events.

There remained to stage a coronation for the new queen. But that was not to be until after the birth of a son and heir, nor until after the first major trial of strength with the Yorkist malcontents. Prince Arthur

---

[1] *Y.B. 1 Henry VII, Hil.*, pl. 1; *see* Chrimes, op. cit. 266, fn. 4, 379.

[2] *R.P.*, VI, 288–9, printed in full in *Materials*, I, 122–3. The justices (*see* fn. 1 above) considered the act so scandalous that they were unwilling to rehearse it, and advised against its recital in the repeal, in order to avoid the perpetuation of its terms. But they considered that the record could not be deleted without the authority of parliament. Every person having a copy of Richard III's act was ordered to hand it in to the chancellor before Easter, on pain of imprisonment and making fine at the king's will. Nothing in the act was to be deemed prejudicial to the act of establishment of the crown on the king and his heirs.

[3] *Cal. Papal Reg.*, XIV (1960), 1–2, 14–28; *see* below, Appendix D.

[4] loc. cit. 2, and Appendix D, below.   [5] *Croyland chron.*

[6] cf. Anglo, op. cit. 18–21; P.V. (ed. Hay), 5; Hall, 424–5; André, *Vita*, 38–40.

was born on 19 September 1486, and the battle of Stoke was fought on 16 June 1487. On 10 November a commission was issued to Jasper, duke of Bedford, John, earl of Oxford, and Thomas, earl of Derby, William, earl of Nottingham, and three others, to discharge the office of steward of England at the coronation of Elizabeth the queen consort,[1] which took place on 25 November.[2] The dynasty was established, but with what measure of security time alone would prove. Many years would pass before even the first Tudor sovereign could feel that the ghost of York was laid, and although his union with Elizabeth was to produce eight offspring, the rate of mortality among them was destined to be very disquieting.[3] Of the three sons (Arthur, Henry, and Edmund) who survived long enough to have any name known to us, only one (Henry) was still alive at the end of April 1502, and only two of the daughters (Margaret and Mary) survived to maturity. For Henry VII, therefore, the problem of security for the dynasty which he had founded remained the fundamental problem which he must solve at all costs. But to obtain security proved far more difficult than could be imagined in 1485.

[1] *Materials*, II, 202, 5 October, a mandate to pay 100 marks to Sir Richard Guildford for expenditure upon jousts to be held in connection with the coronation, ibid. 198.

[2] A full account of the coronation is contained in J. Ives, *Select papers, chiefly related to English antiquities* (1773), 120–56.

[3] Several children, names not known, died in infancy. Arthur died 2 April 1502; the third son surviving, Edmund, born 21/2 February 1499, died 19 June 1500; Henry, born 28 June 1491, lived to be Henry VIII. The eldest daughter, Margaret, born 29 November 1489, married, firstly, James IV of Scotland, lived until 18 October 1541; the second surviving daughter, Mary, born March 1496, married firstly Louis XII of France, and secondly as his third wife, Charles Brandon, duke of Suffolk, grandson of Henry's standard-bearer slain at Bosworth by Richard III, and survived until 24 June 1533. The allegation that has often been made that Sir Roland de Veleville, appointed constable of Beaumaris by Henry VIII, was a bastard son of Henry VII, begotten in Brittany, appears to be untenable. *See W.H.R.*, 3 (1967), 287–9.

Chapter 3

THE PROBLEM OF SECURITY

The problem of security remained a besetting preoccupation of
Henry VII for the whole of his reign, except perhaps for the last two
or three years of it, and even then, though the basic problem had become
largely solved, there were still anxieties which could only be passed on
to Henry VIII, with whom the problem became an obsession. The
dangers confronting Henry VII after his accession were great. He
himself can have known personally very few of the important people
upon whom he would have to rely for support; very few of them could
have known him either. He could not quickly take their measure, nor
they his. It was not surprising therefore that he used at once and brought
into service at high levels the only persons that he did know personally,
the men who had joined him in exile at one time or another. Nor was
it a coincidence that one of the very first things he did was to form a
bodyguard for himself, a most necessary precaution. About two hundred
men, 'the yeomen of the guard', were retained, in imitation, it is said,
of the practice of the French Kings, so that he might be better protected
against treachery.[1] Moreover, he was seeking to establish himself and
his future family, after some twenty-four years of the Yorkist regime.
Not all the influential supporters of that regime perished at Bosworth,
and some of those who survived could be expected to seek to resist the
new government, to embarrass it, and if possible to overthrow it in
favour of one or other of the numerous sprigs of the white rose that were
still unpruned, or even spurious sprigs if genuine ones should prove to
be unavailable. It was not exactly that some of these people were
devoted to the Yorkist house as such – few of them can have inspired
any great enthusiasm, as Edward IV had done in his time; it was
rather that some people had thrived under the Yorkist regime, and
not unjustifiably calculated that they would thrive better under a
restored Yorkist than they would under the unknown Tudor. Nor
could Henry VII, even though claiming to be the heir of Lancaster,
make any great capital out of Lancastrian precedents, which can
hardly have seemed very encouraging in 1485. With what could
Lancastrian tradition be identified? Only with failure in the arts of

[1] P.V. (ed. Hay), 6.

government, and Henry VII could not afford to play too much upon what remains there might be of Lancastrian sentiment. He had to walk alone and to walk warily, and well might he develop a suspicious nature. The plots and conspiracies with which he found himself obliged to grapple were numerous and prolonged. The remarkable circumstance of the Yorkist plots was to be the small amount of support that they gained in England and Wales at any time. Far more menacing was the interest that foreign powers took in some of these enterprises. The weaving of plots against him on an international scale was the most serious threat to his security, and when, as happened at one time or another, Margaret of Burgundy, Maximilian, and France, Brittany, Ireland, and Scotland became involved, inevitably Henry VII's security problems became also problems of foreign policy. At no time, until perhaps the last years of the reign, could Henry VII afford to pursue lines in foreign policy without regard to possible consequences in terms of Yorkist or other plots and the repercussions on internal security. Other powers, for the most part, called the tune, and Henry VII must needs pay the price. In the arena of continental politics, he remained for many years largely an inactive participant, unable to play decisive roles, to a great extent used by the other powers as a make-weight to procure preponderance for one or other of them in the course of their own rivalries. That Henry showed himself an astute diplomat in these exchanges there can be no doubt, but he could hardly aspire to do much more than hold his own and ensure that there would not be another Bosworth staged against himself.

The first armed uprising, that of Viscount Lovel and the Stafford brothers, came early, at Eastertime 1486, and was no more than a flash in the pan. Much more menacing were the circumstances which enabled the first of the Yorkist imposters, Lambert Simnel, to become crowned king of England in Dublin, and, with the heir of York, John, earl of Lincoln, and Burgundian and Irish help, actually to give battle at Stoke in June 1487. Stoke did not turn out to be a Bosworth, and maybe it can be regarded as the last battle of the 'Wars of the Roses', but nobody at the time could be sure of that. Coming as it did at the time when France was in process of invading Brittany, a year before the death of James III of Scotland, and fifteen months before the death of Francis II of Brittany, Henry VII's embarrassments did not end on that field. The acute problem of what part to play in Franco-Breton politics beset Henry in 1488–9. By October 1491, Perkin Warbeck appeared in Cork and began his career as a Yorkist imposter, with its involvements in Ireland, France, Scotland, and Burgundy, which was not to be suspended until his surrender six years later, nor terminated until his execution two years later on. One of Richard III's heirs presumptive, the earl of Lincoln, had lost his life at Stoke, and then, twelve years later, the other one, the earl of Warwick, was also eliminated. But the spectre of York continued to distract Henry VII, now in the shapes of the earl of Suffolk and his numerous brothers. Not until early 1506 did circumstances enable Henry VII to persuade the Archduke Philip to surrender the person of the earl of Suffolk, and even then the circumstances were largely fortuitous. With the earl of Suffolk safely in the Tower of London, Henry VII could at last feel that the house of York could not offer any serious rival to himself. When in 1508 the continental powers negotiated the League of Cambrai, Henry VII could stay out of the league, without calculating the risks for internal security, and could freely maintain amicable relations with the members without apprehensions.

Whether or not James III of Scotland had allowed a Scottish contingent in France to take part in Henry Tudor's expedition and therefore to participate in the battle of Bosworth,[1] he himself viewed the change of dynasty with favour. Although the hostilities between Scotland and Edward IV's regime had given way to uneasy truce under Richard III, there was every expectation that the relations between James III and Henry VII would soon be put on to an altogether more promising footing, and these expectations were, for the short time that remained to James III, to be realized.[2] In the early days of the new reign in England, however, there were fears that the usual Border tensions might erupt into some sort of invasion by Scots, and for this reason, as early as 25 September 1485 Henry VII felt obliged to issue commissions of array to the Border counties to guard against such a contingency.[3] But these hostilities did not materialize, and Henry VII's efforts at raising a loan from the City of London, not enthusiastically responded to,[4] proved to be unnecessary. The reluctance of the city of York to abandon its Yorkist sympathies and to carry out Henry VII's instructions regarding civic elections,[5] although irritating and dis-

---

[1] No English chronicler mentions the presence of Scots in Henry's forces at Bosworth, but the evidence for it adduced by Agnes Conway, *Henry VII's relations with Scotland and Ireland, 1485–98* (1932), 5–9, cannot be lightly dismissed.

[2] *See* below, p. 279.   [3] *C.P.R.*, I, 39–40.

[4] *See* references in Busch, op. cit. 30, fn. 3.

[5] *See* P. M. Kendall, op. cit. 385–9.

quieting to the new monarch, hardly constituted a serious threat to security.

More disturbing was the news that reached Henry in April 1486, then at Lincoln, concerning Francis, Viscount Lovel, and Humphrey and Thomas Stafford. Francis Lovel was son and heir of John, Lord Lovel of Tichmarsh, whom he succeeded at the age of nine in 1463. He had been knighted in 1480 by Richard, duke of Gloucester, for service in Scotland, and was summoned to parliament by writ in 1482. He was created a viscount by Edward IV on 4 January 1482/3, and made Chief Butler. Richard III made him K.G. in 1483, chamberlain of the Household, and constable of Wallingford Castle. Humphrey Stafford, the second but eldest surviving son of Sir Humphrey Stafford of Grafton, was sheriff of Worcestershire, 1470–9 and 1484 to 12 September 1485. In October 1483 he had held the fords of the Severn against his distant kinsman Henry Stafford, duke of Buckingham, and had been attainted in November 1485. Francis, Humphrey and Thomas, who had all been in sanctuary at Colchester since Bosworth, had broken sanctuary and were seeking to raise an insurrection, Lovel heading for Yorkshire and the Staffords for Worcestershire.[1] Henry VII, it is said,[2] could scarcely believe this news, and although the plotters were of no great personal significance, the news was alarming because at that stage Henry could not estimate with any assurance what degree of pro-Yorkist support would be aroused. In fact, the plot was a total failure and very quickly collapsed. Viscount Lovel disappeared for the time being.[3] The Staffords were captured, notwithstanding their recourse again to sanctuary; Humphrey was executed but his young brother Thomas was apparently pardoned. The manner of their arrest in sanctuary gave rise to a *cause célèbre* in King's Bench, in the course of which the judges decided that henceforth sanctuary was not pleadable in treason.[4]

[1] The circumstances of the insurrection were fully discussed by C. H. Williams, 'The rebellion of Humphrey Stafford in 1486', *E.H.R.*, XLIII (1928), 181–9.

[2] *See* Sir Hugh Conway's reminiscences disclosed at a later date, *L. & P.*, I, 234. Conway was told of Lovel's escape and plan by a friend, and decided to pass the news to Sir Reginald Bray, who informed the king.

[3] After the fiasco in 1486, he fled to Sir Thomas Broughton's house in N. Lancashire and thence to Flanders. From there he was sent by Margaret, the dowager duchess, to Ireland to aid Lambert Simnel. *See* below; cf. G.E.C., and *D.N.B.* On Humphrey Stafford, *see R.P.*, V, 276; and J. C. Wedgwood (ed.), *History of parliament, biographies, 1439–1509* (1936), 792–3. For land forfeited by Stafford, *see* numerous references in *C.P.R.*, and *Materials*.

[4] Reported in *Y.B. 1 Henry VII, Trin.*, pl. 1, and *Pas.*, pl. 15. An extract from the latter is in S. B. Chrimes, op. cit. 381 (79). The significance of this case is discussed by

The failure of Lovel and his fellow-plotters had shown that the Yorkists, if they were to challenge Henry, must have a Yorkist prince to set up against him.[1] But there was no male descendant of York who was available and suitable for so formidable an undertaking. Edward IV's sons, Edward V and Richard duke of York, had never left the Tower of London, so far as anyone knew, and although their names and claims would have been an enormous asset to the Yorkist cause, they could not be conjured up in person. George, duke of Clarence's son Edward, earl of Warwick, a weakly boy already in the Tower of London, was clearly neither available nor suitable.

The numerous sons of Edward IV's sister Elizabeth by her marriage to John de la Pole, duke of Suffolk, offered a more promising field for recruitment, but the eldest of them, John, earl of Lincoln, at this time aged about twenty-four, had made his peace with Henry VII and was shown some favour, and his younger brother Edmund had also been received amicably by the new king. These gestures would not prevent them from entering into treasonable activities in due course, but it must be presumed that the earl of Lincoln could not have shown his hand too soon after Henry's accession, and in any event, although he became available, he does not seem to have been regarded as particularly suitable. In the absence of a candidate available and suitable, recourse was had to training two youths who could pretend, in turn, to be one or other of the Yorkist princes of the male lines. The first of them, Lambert Simnel, notwithstanding that everyone of importance knew perfectly well that the son of Clarence was decidedly not available, was passed off as the earl of Warwick. Some four years later, Perkin Warbeck, the son of John Osbeck or Werbeque, controller of Tournai, was to go one better and claim to be Richard, duke of York, mysteriously escaped from the Tower. Henry VII could easily demonstrate that Simnel was not the earl of Warwick by simply parading the latter in the streets of London and making him appear on 19 February before the council and convocation and stand in front of Morton;[2]

Isobel D. Thornley, 'The destruction of sanctuary', *Tudor Studies*, ed. R. W. Seton-Watson (1924), 199 ff. The eagerness of Henry VII to obtain the judicial ruling ultimately given is revealed by the fact that Hussey, chief justice of the King's Bench, was obliged to visit him and ask him not to press for a judicial opinion on the point as the case was to come before the justices in King's Bench. Henry VII agreed to refrain but urged that no time should be lost when the case came on. Later, he ordered the justices to issue writs to proceed with all similar cases which had been surceased by writs of Privy Seal of Edward IV and Richard III. *See* below, p. 161.

[1] R. B. Wernham, *Before the Armada* (1966), 30–1.

[2] C. Jenkins, 'Cardinal Morton's register', *Tudor Studies*, 37.

but he could not prove that either Edward V or Richard, duke of York, was dead. If the princes in the Tower had still been alive after Bosworth – a most unlikely conjecture – they would hardly have survived that event very long. But Henry VII was never able to demonstrate the fact of their death. Hence the imposture by Warbeck retained some aura of plausibility for several years, whilst that by Simnel was implausible from the start, even though supported by the earl of Lincoln for his own purposes. There is indeed no evidence that anyone of significance at any time professed to believe in either imposture except those who had strong political motives for so professing. Of the two impostures, Simnel's, although by far the more far-fetched, yet for a time attained a startling and menacing success, whilst Warbeck's, though much longer protracted and involved in wider international complications, never attained such distinction. The reason for the difference is to be found in Irish politics. To comprehend how it came about that Lambert Simnel, the ten-year-old son of an Oxford joiner, could come to be crowned King Edward VI in Christchurch, Dublin, on 24 May 1487, supported by many Irish lords, including Gerald, eighth earl of Kildare (the 'uncrowned' king of Ireland), and several Irish bishops, is impossible without some excursion into the circumstances of Irish history during the preceding decades at least.

The crucial fact in Anglo-Irish relations in this period was that Richard, duke of York, during his time as king's lieutenant in Ireland in the reign of Henry VI, had not only seen in Ireland 'a jumping off ground for his party', but by the time he finally left Ireland in June 1460, he 'had won almost all Ireland to the cause of the White Rose for some forty years to come'.[1] Richard of York, first appointed lieutenant on 9 December 1447, for ten years, and reappointed on 1 December 1454, was resident in Ireland from 6 July 1449 to September 1450, and again from 25 October 1454 to July 1460. As Miss Conway justly observed,[2] Henry VI would never have sought this way of freeing himself of his most dangerous opponent at home, if he had been able to anticipate that Richard's great popularity would make Ireland a centre of Yorkist sedition for half a century.

When appointed in 1447, York was a man of about thirty-seven years of age. As heir to his uncle, Mortimer, he was earl of March and

---

[1] For much of what follows on Irish affairs, *see* E. Curtis, *A history of mediaeval Ireland* (1923); Agnes Conway, op. cit.; Art Cosgrove, 'The Gaelic resurgence and the Geraldine supremacy', *The course of Irish history*, ed. T. W. Moody and F. X. Marten (Cork, 1967), 158–73; cf. H. G. Richardson and G. O. Sayles, *The Irish parliament in the Middle Ages* (1952), 244–68.   [2] op. cit. 44–5.

Ulster, lord of Trim and Connacht. Even the Celtic Irish saw him as the true heir of Lacey and De Burgo, and could regard him as partly Irish, and the Anglo-Irish were eager to have him as king's lieutenant. When he arrived on 6 July 1449, with the black dragon standard of Ulster carried before him, his personal appeal was widely felt among the Irish lords, many of whom flocked to make submission and pay respects. When on 21 October 1449, York's son George, later duke of Clarence, was born in Dublin Castle, the extraordinary spectacle was seen of both the powerful Anglo-Irish lords, James Fitzgerald, sixth earl of Desmond, and James Butler, fourth earl of Ormond, standing sponsors at the baptism.

But the effect on Irish politics of York's first visit was, in brief, only to promote the aspirations and interests of the 'Home Rule' lords, who aimed at ruling Ireland themselves, with as little interference as possible by the lord of Ireland, viz, the king of England, or his representative. His second visit, after reappointment as lieutenant, carried the process still further, and by this time it may be said that York set himself more specifically to win over to his personal causes the support of the Irish magnates, especially Thomas Fitzgerald, seventh earl of Kildare, who had as deputy lieutenant since 1455 been virtual ruler of Ireland. York was still nominally king's lieutenant when, after the 'rout of Ludlow' on 12 October 1459, he was obliged to flee to Ireland for safety. The Irish lords might welcome their favourite king's lieutenant (even though he would shortly be attainted by the English parliament), but the opportunity which now presented itself for pressing their desires to the full was too good to miss. The parliament at Drogheda called by York early in February 1460 defied his attainder in England by attainting in Ireland his enemies the Butlers and others, confirmed his position as viceroy in Ireland, pronounced it high treason to compass his death or rebel against him, and then declared in forthright terms the legislative and legal independence of Ireland.[1]

This startling triumph of the 'Home Rule' lords of Ireland was perhaps more than York could have viewed with equanimity if he had himself become king of England and lord of Ireland, but when the turn of events in England brought his son to the throne and with him the merging of the whole Mortimer inheritance in Ireland and Wales with the crown, there was little Edward IV could do to undo what had been done. Not even the ruthless intervention of John Tiptoft, earl of

[1] Curtis, op. cit. 380–1.

Worcester, as king's lieutenant in March 1470, could achieve much more than procure the execution of the greatest of the Anglo-Irish exponents of statecraft, Thomas Fitzgerald, earl of Desmond, and to antagonize those Irish lords who did not rejoice at the loss of one of their number.

Dominance in Ireland soon passed for many years to Thomas Fitzgerald, seventh earl of Kildare, and from 1478, with intermissions, to his son and heir Gerald, eighth earl. Gerald became the real king of Ireland, and had behind him almost all the Anglo-Irish, except the Butlers, and wielded a sway over the Celtic-Irish that had been beyond the reach of any of the Anglo-Irish before him. Richard III's short reign could not achieve anything in Ireland, and the Kildares continued to rule as deputies no matter who was king's lieutenant *in absentia*, whether Richard III's baby son, Edward, or John de la Pole, earl of Lincoln, or from 11 March 1486, Jasper Tudor.

The change of dynasty in England after Bosworth brought to Kildare and the 'Home Rule' lords the prospect that they could not indefinitely rule Ireland in the name of the Yorkist regime with the connivance of the new dynasty in England. They must either abandon Yorkist associations and support the Tudor regime, whatever the political consequences might be, or they must at all costs hold on to the Yorkist pretensions and defy the Tudor, if possible to the point of overthrowing him. It was the latter course that they chose, for a time. When, therefore, Lambert Simnel appeared in Dublin, suitably trained beforehand, the Irish lords had no difficulty in deciding that he was the earl of Warwick, the very son of George, duke of Clarence, who had been born in Dublin in 1449, and who, with his alleged son, could be regarded as in some sense an 'Irish' prince. The chance of getting a king of their own was too great for the Irish lords; and in their eagerness they went so far as to allege that the boy in the Tower of London was the real imposter foisted upon the people by Henry VII to deprive the lawful inheritor – the good duke of Clarence – their 'countryman and protector'. Hence Lambert Simnel found himself crowned with a circlet of gold filched from a nearby statue of the Blessed Virgin Mary and proclaimed King Edward VI in Dublin on 24 May 1487.

How long it took for Richard Simons, a priest of twenty-eight years, to train Lambert Simnel sufficiently to make him into a plausible Yorkist imposter is not known.[1] It can hardly be supposed that Simons

[1] The odd remark made by Thomas Betanson in a letter to Sir Robert Plumpton, dated 29 November 1486, to the effect that 'also here is litle spech of the erle of

acted on his own initiative alone, and probably John, earl of Lincoln, had some share in the plot at an early date. It is possible that rumours began to circulate by the end of November 1486, but there is no evidence that Henry VII had any intimation of the nature of the plot until early 1487. By the end of January, steps were taken against a few suspects,[1] but the continued presence of the earl of Lincoln at the council meeting at Sheen on 2 February,[2] at which measures to combat the plot were considered, suggests that even then Henry did not realize that the leading Yorkist himself was implicated. Possibly enough suspicion, however, had fallen upon the queen mother to induce Henry to deprive her of her widow's jointure, which was transferred to Queen Elizabeth, and to remove her to the convent at Bermondsey on an annual pension. But it is very doubtful if the reason for this action was suspicion at all.[3]

The subsequent flight of the earl of Lincoln to Flanders, where he joined Viscount Lovel, must have startled Henry into a fuller realization of the gravity of the conspiracy.[4] The ever-ready sympathy and support of Margaret of Burgundy for such purposes was quickly extended to Lincoln and Lovel, and with her aid and money they were able to land in Ireland on 5 May, backed by some two thousand German mercenaries led by the redoubtable soldier of fortune Martin Schwartz. The arrival of this potentially formidable support contributed to the decision of the Irish lords not only to recognize Lambert Simnel – for reasons indicated above – but also to proceed to a coronation of him as Edward VI on 24 May. Doubtfully reinforced by a number of ill-equipped Irishmen, the conspirators set out to try their luck at another Bosworth, and made a landing at Furness on the Lancashire coast on 4 June.

Warwyk now, but after Christenmas, they say ther wylbe more spech of', is too vague to build any theories upon. (*Plumpton correspondence*, ed. T. Stapleton, Cam. Soc. 4 (1839), 54.)   [1] *C.P.R.*, I, 179.   [2] Leland, *Coll.*, IV, 208.

[3] *Materials*, II, 148, etc. It is by no means certain that the reason for her deprivation had any connection with the plot. The records make no such suggestion. The arrangement may have been voluntary, as R. Pauli, *Geschichte von England* (1858), V, 536, suggested, or may have been induced by family or health reasons. Vergil's explanation (loc. cit. 18), that the reason was her conduct before Bosworth, seems to be rather far-fetched. It is difficult to reconcile with this allegation the words of a writ to the Exchequer dated 10 March 1488, ordering the payment of 200 marks to the 'right dere and right well beloved Quene Elizabeth, late wif unto the noble prince of famous memory King Edward the IVth, and moder unto oure derrest wif the quene' (*Materials*, 273). The king made gifts to her on a number of occasions (ibid. 225, 296, 322, 392, 455, 500). He would hardly have done this if he had felt vindictive towards her.

[4] Numerous commissions of array were issued on 7 April, *C.P.R.*, I, 179.

Henry meantime had taken precautions, caused likely coasts to be guarded, and as information received pointed to the probability of an invasion from Ireland, gradually moved himself westwards and by 8 May fixed his headquarters at Kenilworth. On receipt of news of the landing, he moved towards Newark, and near Stoke encountered the rebels on 16 June.

Little reliable information from contemporary sources exists as to what happened at the battle of Stoke, and we have to rely largely on what Polydore Vergil said some thirty years later.[1] It seems that the fighting was stubborn, and no easy victory was obtained by Henry's forces. The German mercenaries led by Martin Schwartz, experienced and hardy soldiers, fought pertinaciously; the Irish showed spirit and courage, though weakened by lack of body-armour, and suffered heavy losses, but the battle continued without much advantage to either side for some time (the actual time is not stated), and Vergil specifically states that only the 'first line' of the king's forces was committed to the fray and sustained the combat. Why only a part of the royal forces participated is a matter for speculation, but it is hardly justified to suppose that the other parts 'dragged their feet' awaiting a crucial moment to interfere on one side or the other, after the style of the Stanleys at Bosworth. In fact, it seems, the final charge of the first line alone proved decisive and provoked a rout of the rebels. Complete disaster for them was the outcome. John, earl of Lincoln, Martin Schwartz, Thomas Broughton, Thomas Geraldine, the Irish leader, were all slain; Viscount Lovel was either killed or fled and disappeared for ever. Lambert Simnel and his tutor Richard Simons were captured. Simnel was to be found a place in the royal kitchens, and later to be promoted to king's falconer, and was still alive when Vergil wrote.[2] Simons, as a priest, was destined for life imprisonment.

Whether the plot 'came near to shaking Henry's throne' is doubtful.[3] The rebel invaders failed to attract any appreciable recruits even in the Lancashire districts where Thomas Broughton held sway and which had been chosen as a favourable landing place. Without the German and Irish soldiery no battle could have been staged, and the incursion of these in itself was not likely to evoke much enthusiasm even among the pro-Yorkist elements. But the fact that a battle had to be fought within two years of Bosworth must have given Henry VII much food for anxious thought. The risks from his personal participation were

[1] P.V., 12–26, esp. 24. Some antiquarian information and an attempt to reconstruct the battle are given in R. Brooke, *Visits to fields of battle in England in the fifteenth century* (1857).   [2] P.V., 24.   [3] Wernham, op. cit.

too great, for his own death or capture on the field would certainly bring the dynasty to a sudden end. There were to be no more Bosworths or Stokes, in fact, but Henry VII's wary diplomacy would be exerted to the full in the years to come to avoid the chances of any repetition of a similar military threat, whether on behalf of another imposter or any more genuine Yorkist pretender. As has, very rightly, been remarked, 'Henry VII was a man who had learned in years of precarious exile to abhor needless risks'.[1]

Two measures Henry had to take as soon as possible. He must attaint the principal rebels and try to strengthen the executive. He must try, so far as he could, to deal with the chief source of the recent threat – Ireland.

His second parliament met on 9 November, the first with Morton as chancellor, and was dissolved by 18 December.[2] The inevitable act of attainder was passed, and twenty-eight of the rebels were brought within its scope.[3] Some of the king's councillors were given statutory powers to deal with certain kinds of offences especially likely to under-mine law and order – so called, but wrongly, 'Star Chamber' act.[4] A notable additional provision was an act authorizing a jury of the king's Household to enquire whether any member of it below the rank of a peer had conspired to murder the king, or any lord or member of the King's Council, or the steward, treasurer, or controller, and making any such offence a felony. Before the short parliament was over, and with the principal Yorkist claimant killed at Stoke, Henry could proceed to stage the coronation of his queen,[5] who by then had been the mother of his son and heir Arthur, for more than a year.

It was less easy to deal with Ireland. There could be no hope of any major moves as yet to restore the legal position in Anglo-Irish relations that had existed before 1460, but steps had to be taken to recall the Irish lords to their allegiances. As early as 5 July 1487 Henry VII wrote to the pope[6] asking for the excommunication of the Irish bishops who

---

[1] Wernham op. cit.   [2] R.P., VI, 385–402.

[3] ibid. 397–402. Twenty-seven persons were attainted in addition to the earl of Lincoln. According to an act of attainder of 1495 (ibid. 502–7), Francis, Viscount Lovel was ignorantly left out and omitted from the act of 1487, and the error was then rectified. But Lovel had been attainted in 1485 (ibid. 276), and apart from pin-ning down his activities in 1487, the omission was more formal than substantial. Some curious information regarding the more obscure features of the plot is provided by a further act of attainder passed in 1489 (ibid. 436), by which five more persons were convicted.

[4] S.R., II, 509–10; see below, p. 154 ff.   [5] See below (ibid. 520).

[6] L. & P., I, 94–6. In this letter Henry VII refers to rumours that had been spread in England to the effect that he had been routed at Stoke.

had participated in the coronation of Simnel, which request was complied with in a bull of January 1488. The town of Waterford had stood out for Henry VII and had suffered a six weeks' siege by the Desmonds, and in October 1487 was sent a communication from the king commending their loyalty and giving it letters of marque to act against the earl of Kildare and Dublin.[1] But it was not until May 1488 that Sir Richard Edgecombe, a counsellor and comptroller of the Household, was commissioned to go over to Ireland, with power to treat for 'the sound rule of peace, armed with pardons for those who would submit, and to administer oaths of fealty and allegiance, and to imprison rebels and traitors'.[2] Landing at Kinsale on 27 June, Edgecombe with five hundred men proceeded by way of Waterford to Dublin, but it was not until 21 July that the lords assembled took the oath of allegiance, and thereupon received their pardons. The earl of Kildare and some forty others who had supported Simnel now made their peace with the king, enabling Edgecombe to leave Ireland by 30 July. His mission can hardly have made any great impression upon the Irish 'Home Rule' lords of the might of King Henry, but at least they were reminded of the existence of the lord of Ireland and of their legal relationship to him. At the time no doubt it was as much as Henry VII could undertake to do. Six years were to elapse before a more formidable visitation, in the person of Sir Edward Poynings, was to be staged. Before then the second imposter, Perkin Warbeck, was to appear, without however receiving much comfort in Ireland; and international entanglements in Brittany, France, the Netherlands, and Scotland were to preoccupy Henry VII. In the meantime, Gerald, eighth earl of Kildare, remained deputy in Ireland.

In 1491 Perkin Warbeck raised the internal security problem again in a new form. But in the meantime Franco-Breton relations reached a climax, and obliged Henry to take some sort of stand, reluctant though he was to commit himself too far on either side. The embarrassment of the situation, from his point of view, was acute. He owed his early preservation from Yorkist designs to Duke Francis II, and he owed his successful expedition in 1485 and therefore his throne to Anne of Beaujeu's regime on behalf of Charles VIII. It was not to England's interest to acquiesce too readily in the overrunning of Brittany by France and the consequential expansion of the influence of the

---

[1] Printed in Ryland, *History of Waterford* (Dublin, 1824), 26.

[2] *C.P.R.*, I, 225, 227; the wording of the oaths to be taken was very specific and precise, and it is not surprising that the Irish lords were reluctant to take them. *See* below p. 260.

French monarchy to the Breton coast and ports. But he could not dismiss the possibility that France, if provoked, might support a rival claimant to the throne of England, just as it had assisted him to over-throw Richard III. He could not, in any case, aid one side without incurring charges of ingratitude from the other. His military resources were slender; he could not afford a very active intervention, and, although there was some pro-Breton and anti-French feeling among his subjects, some of them did not stop short of a murderous insurrection in order to evade contribution to a tax for war purposes, the collection of which generally fell far below the total sum authorized.[1] The murder of Henry Percy, earl of Northumberland, at Topcliffe in Yorkshire on 28 April 1489, was an ugly incident, induced partly by opposition to his collection of the tax voted in the parliament of January of that year and partly also by his personal unpopularity. The death of the equi-vocal earl who had failed to show his hand at Bosworth may have been viewed with mixed feelings by Henry VII, but the insurrectionary assassination of the warden-general of the East and Middle Marches towards Scotland who was also sheriff of Northumberland called for swift action. One of the leaders of the rising, John à Chambre, was captured and executed, but another, Sir John Egremont, fled to Margaret of Burgundy's court.[2] It is not surprising, therefore, that Henry VII's first considerable involvement in foreign affairs did not bring any manifest lustre to the crown, but the Franco-Breton problem did bring him squarely into the framework of international diplomacy and into foreign commitments, in which he was either deserted or outsmarted by his allies. Notwithstanding his undertaking after the death of Duke Francis on 9 September 1488, to aid Anne, the twelve-year-old heiress of Brittany, at Breton cost by the terms of the Treaty of Redon, February 1489; and notwithstanding his negotiation of a coalition with Maximilian, 'whose will to injure France was as constant as his inability to achieve his purpose',[3] and with Spain (Treaty of Medina del Campo, 27 March 1489), the Breton cause was irretrievably lost well before the time when, on 6 December 1491, Duchess Anne was married to the king of France.[4]

The Treaty of Medina del Campo,[5] the first substantial alliance into which Henry VII entered, apart from its somewhat delusive provisions

---

[1] The total amount voted was £100,000 (*R.P.*, VI, 420–4), but of this only some £27,000 appears to have been raised (F. G. Dietz, *English government finance* (Illinois, 1920), 55).   [2] Busch, op. cit. 47.   [3] Bridge, op. cit., I, 180.

[4] For Henry VII's foreign policies at this time, *see* below, Pt III. On Anglo-Breton relations, *see* B. A. Pocquet du Haut-Juissé, op. cit. 271–99.

[5] *Cal. S.P. Spanish*, I, 21–4.

aimed at France, not only foreshadowed the later marriage between his son and heir and a Spanish princess, but also included a reciprocal undertaking that neither sovereign would harbour or aid any rebels against the other. To Henry this was probably the most important point at the time. For before the year was over, fresh plots against him were being weaved, and in October or November 1491, Perkin Warbeck made his first public appearance at Cork, and soon Henry had to reckon with a Yorkist ghost that could not be easily laid, for now it was that of Richard, duke of York, whose demise in the Tower of London was generally assumed, but could not be proved. From now on, the recognition or otherwise by foreign powers of Warbeck as the son and heir of Edward IV became a major consideration in Henry VII's framing of policy.

The precise origins of the plot that brought Perkin Warbeck into the arena as a Yorkist pretender remain obscure and uncertain.[1] Whatever the earlier stages may have been,[2] it seems clear that his appearance at Cork in the autumn of 1491 and his acceptance as a pretender was no unpremeditated accident but was the first overt action in the unfolding of the plan; it seems equally clear that, whether Margaret of Burgundy had been a party to the plot at this stage, or not,[3] Charles VIII was

[1] Apart from a few points of substance noted below which have been revealed subsequently, there is little on Warbeck's career to be added to the very full and judicious account published by J. Gairdner in the Appendix to his *Richard III* (new ed., 1893). The most important additional point concerns the implication of Sir William Stanley, which was revealed a few months after the publication of Gairdner's work and which has largely escaped notice. *See* below, p. 85, fn. 2. A portrait from a drawing in the town library of Arras is given in Gairdner, op. cit. 282, *see* pl. 11c.

[2] It has been shown that Perkin Warbeck could have learnt a good deal about the court and family of Edward IV from his employer Sir Edward Brampton, a converted Portuguese Jew who had risen high in Yorkist favour, was appointed governor of Guernsey in 1482 and knighted by Richard III, but had fled to the Low Countries after Bosworth. Warbeck accompanied the Bramptons on a voyage from Middelburg to Lisbon in 1487. There is not, however, any evidence that a plot was contemplated by Brampton at this stage. Mr Roth, however, in his valuable article, 'Perkin Warbeck and his Jewish master', *Trans. Jewish Hist. Soc. of England*, IX (1922), 143–62, shows clearly that Warbeck may well have learnt much from Brampton that he put to effective use later on. It remains conjectural why it was that Henry VII granted a general pardon and restitution to Brampton on 21 August 1489. At a later date, however, Brampton may well have been able to tell Henry VII what he knew about Warbeck, and may indeed have been the source of the information which the king disclosed as early as July 1493. *See* below, p. 83, fn. 2.

[3] Although the contrary has been alleged, it seems there is no evidence, and no probability that Margaret of Burgundy could have had any personal acquaintance with Warbeck as a possible Yorkist pretender until he left France in late 1492 or early 1493.

H — D

implicated[1] and intended to use Warbeck as a threat to Henry VII should his participation in Franco-Breton politics become too inconvenient.

At first, it seems, the intention was to pass Warbeck off as another Warwick. Apparently Warbeck himself declined this role, and no doubt it would have been too much for the Irish lords to be expected to swallow another impersonation of the prisoner in the Tower. Nor was there any virtue in the suggestion that he was a bastard son of Richard III. Far better for the newcomer to figure as one of the princes who had disappeared into the Tower and of whose demise no one could offer positive proof. Warbeck was therefore very quickly acclaimed, not indeed as Edward V – he would have been a little too old perhaps, and certainly too embarrassing a personage, as a previously proclaimed king, to impersonate. But his younger brother Richard, duke of York, offered an excellent target for the purpose, and Warbeck henceforth assumed the guise of the younger prince, and could at convenient times by some of the powers involved be designated King Richard IV, even though he was never to obtain a coronation by anyone.

His reception in Ireland in 1491, however, was no more than cool. He did receive some welcome and support from important men of the town of Cork, which was within the domain of the earl of Desmond, who extended him some aid. Probably the earl of Kildare was also implicated, even though two years later he asserted in a letter to the earl of Ormond that he had not countenanced 'the French lad'.[2] Clearly, however, Warbeck was not going to secure the acclaim from the Irish lords that Simnel had received in 1487, and by early 1492 he was making overtures elsewhere. Early that year he wrote, supported by Desmond, to James IV of Scotland seeking aid.[3] More immediate even if short-lived prospects were opened up by Charles VIII, who invited him to France, and received him as a prince with appropriate honours.[4] But Henry VII's military intervention in defence of Anne of Brittany in October rapidly turned itself into a diplomatic negotiation which ended on 3 November in the Treaty of Étaples, and one item

[1] The letter from John Taylor dated 15 September 1491 from Rouen to John Hayes, received 26 November, referred to Charles VIII's and his council's resolve to aid 'Clarence's son'. John Hayes had been in Clarence's service, and John Taylor was an exiled Yorkist active in plot-making. The French King and Council said that they would take nothing in recompense for their aid, but undertook to act because of the 'wrong they had done in making Henry king of England'. Hayes was convicted and attainted of misprision of treason (*R.P.*, VI, 454–5).

[2] *L. &. P.*, II, 55, 9 February 1493.   [3] ibid. 326–7.

[4] Gairdner, op. cit. 274.

included in that agreement was that Charles VIII would not aid any
of Henry VII's rebels.[1] Warbeck's French holiday was therefore
abruptly terminated, and he now turned to Margaret of Burgundy,
who made no difficulty about 'recognizing' him as her nephew, even
though she herself had been out of England for twenty-five years,
except for a short visit in 1480, when her real nephew was aged about
seven years. Now indeed Margaret could train Warbeck and prime
him with recollections of Edward IV's court and Yorkist family
memoirs. Warbeck soon found himself under the protection of the
Archduke Philip and his father Maximilian, who at this time was on
bad terms with Henry VII and eager to patronize Yorkist exiles.

Henry VII, who clearly knew the basic facts of the impersonation
and plot, and had identified Perkin Warbeck's origins by July 1493,[2]
if not earlier, went to considerable lengths to scotch the threat of a
Yorkist incursion based upon the Netherlands. First he sent envoys[3] to
remonstrate with the archduke, whose council eventually evaded the
issue by dissociating the archduke but blandly disclaiming any power
to interfere in Margaret's affairs. Henry's response to this subterfuge
was sharp. He prohibited commercial intercourse with Flanders,
banished Fleming merchants, recalled the Merchant Adventurers
from Antwerp, and moved the Staple to Calais.[4]

At about this time Warbeck sought to extend the threads of his web
by writing to Isabella of Spain to invite her support,[5] and in November
1493 he was taken by Albert, duke of Saxony, to Vienna to attend the
funeral of Emperor Frederick III, and met Maximilian, who received
him as rightful king of England. By the summer of 1494 Maximilian
was back in the Low Countries with Warbeck, who now sported a
white rose and the arms of Richard, prince of Wales.[6] According to
Charles VIII, now eager to depart on his expedition into Italy and
anxious both to oblige and to embarrass Henry VII, Maximilian was
preparing to render material assistance to Warbeck. Henry expressed
his thanks to Charles VIII, professed to treat the matter of '*le
garçon*' lightly, and sought to make diplomatic hay by asserting that

[1] *Foedera*, XII, 710–12; *R.P.*, VI, 507.

[2] This is clearly revealed in a letter from Henry VII at Kenilworth, 20 July, to Sir
Gilbert Talbot, printed by Gairdner, op. cit. 275–6, who shows that the year must be
1493; and Ellis, *Letters*, 1st ser., I, 19.

[3] These were two formidable persons, Sir Edward Poynings and William Warham,
later archbishop of Canterbury. *Foedera*, XII, 544.

[4] Busch, op. cit. 69–70, and refs; and *see* below.

[5] Printed by F. Madden, 'Documents relating to Perkin Warbeck', *Archaeologia*,
XXVII (1838), 199.   [6] Gairdner, op. cit. 280–1.

Maximilian's secret objective was to sow dissension between England and France.[1]

Henry could at least profess in his exchanges with Charles VIII to discount the threat from the Netherlands, for he need not suppose that Maximilian would ever be able to muster sufficient resources to stage any formidable incursion; but he was not treating the plot light-heartedly on the home front. When he heard of Warbeck's appearance at Cork, he had sent in December 1491 a small military force to Ireland,[2]

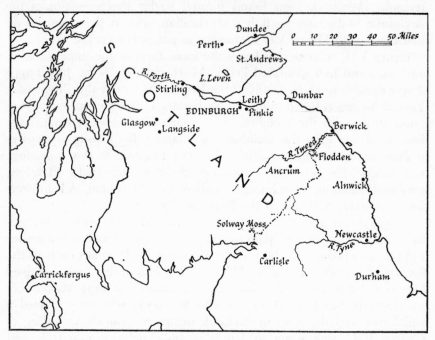

Map 2 Southern Scotland

and had absolved the Irish from obedience to the deputy, the earl of Kildare, who was dismissed on 11 June 1492. The Irish problem continued to occupy him for some time, until eventually the mission of Sir Edward Poynings could be prepared and sent over in October 1494, with large consequences for Anglo-Irish history.[3] In the meantime, in England, he struck at persons whom his agents and spies had informed him were implicated in the Yorkist plots.

The first crop of attainders relating to treasonable acts connected with the Warbeck conspiracy came in the parliament of 1495 (14

[1] *Archaeologia*, loc. cit. 200.   [2] Conway, op. cit. 49.   [3] *See* below, Pt III.

October to 21 December),[1] but a number of the accused had previously been arrested and some executed. By far the most eminent of these was Sir William Stanley, the chamberlain, Henry VII's step-uncle, and the man whose intervention at Bosworth had saved the day, who was tried for treason in Westminster Hall on 30 and 31 January, and beheaded on 16 February 1495. It is quite clear that as early as 14 March 1493 Stanley had entered into an agreement with Sir Robert Clifford to the effect that the latter would go abroad, which he did on 14 June, to communicate with Warbeck at the court of Margaret of Burgundy.[2] At what stage Clifford informed the king of what was afoot is uncertain, but it was on his information that Stanley was arrested and tried. Clifford may have been in Henry VII's service all along, and at any rate received a pardon and rewards for his part in shattering the conspiracy at home.

For there can be little doubt that the effective work of Henry's agents, the sudden arrests of Yorkist malcontents, and their speedy trial and conviction, and the downfall of so powerful a personage and one so near the king as Sir William Stanley broke the plot before it had reached any overt point at home. The result was that when Warbeck made his attempt at landing at Deal on 3 July, it proved to be a fiasco. After entering into grandiose agreement with Margaret of Burgundy and Maximilian,[3] and Margaret had written to the pope for support,[4] Warbeck had at length been equipped with a small expedition, which had appeared off the Kentish coast; some of his forces landed near Deal, but failed to gain any local support, were quickly captured, killed or executed.[5] Warbeck abandoned them to their fate, and set sail for Ireland. Some more names were added to the attainted in the parliament at the end of the year.[6]

In Ireland Warbeck received a welcome from the earl of Desmond,

---

[1] *R.P.*, VI, 503. In addition to Sir William Stanley, three others now attainted had been convicted of high treason by *oyer et terminer*, and sixteen others were now convicted and attainted.

[2] The reports of the trials of Stanley and others are missing from the *Baga de secretis* (*see* below, p. 92, fn. 1), but a sixteenth-century copy was found in Camb. MS. Ee. 3.1, and published by W. A. J. Archbold, *E.H.R.*, XIV (July, 1899), 529–34; too late to be used by Gairdner in the revised edition of his *Richard III*, who, however, added comments to Archbold's note, loc. cit. 529–30. As Gairdner observed, the facts revealed are valuable.

[3] The terms of these fantastic agreements are set out in Gairdner, *Richard III*, 289–91. The documents are still in the archives of Antwerp. See M. Gérard, *Bull. de la commission royal d'histoire* (Brussels), 4th ser., II, 9–22.

[4] *Memorials*, ed. Gairdner, App. A, 393–9.   [5] Gairdner, op. cit. 294–5.

[6] *R.P.*, VI, 503–7. Fourteen persons were included.

and an attack was made on the town of Waterford, which resisted stoutly for eleven days (23 July to 3 August), and was relieved by Sir Edward Poynings from Dublin. Making no progress, and with no visible prospects in Ireland, Warbeck finally decided to retire to Scotland, to seek aid and comfort from James IV,[1] who received him at Stirling on 27 November 1495. Until July 1497 Warbeck found himself befriended by James IV, who not only extended every favour to him, perhaps even believed in him for a time at least, but also was certainly eager to use him as a means of injuring Henry VII, if he could. The explanation of James IV's conduct can be found only in the previous history of Anglo-Scottish relations.

Relations between England and Scotland had taken a turn for the worse some six years before Henry VII came to the throne.[2] A truce which had endured for thirteen years was broken in 1479 largely as a result of Louis XI's intrigues, who sought to embarrass Edward IV by fomenting trouble on the Border. But Scotland itself was to be for many years embroiled by internal factions and bedevilled by the ambitious hostility of Alexander, duke of Albany, towards his brother, James III. Edward IV and Richard III both tried to take advantage of the situation by aiding Albany against the king, and Albany was able to dangle before them the prospect of the return to England of Berwick, which had been ceded to Scotland by Queen Margaret of Anjou as the price for assistance in 1461. James III himself, although a man of many good personal qualities and cultivated tastes, was somewhat ineffectual as a ruler, made many mistakes and was as little able to dominate his turbulent and violent relatives and magnates as Henry VI of England had been. Little impediment therefore confronted Albany and Richard, duke of Gloucester, whom Edward IV sent up to help the faction, and Richard was able to take Berwick, which has remained part of England ever since. Albany was enabled to secure the person of James III, and became the effective governor of Scotland in the king's name.[3] His extremism and obvious ambition, with Edward IV's aid, to obtain the crown for himself, led to a reaction among a number of the malcontent barons, who rallied to James III, forcing Albany to come to terms with his brother, and obliging him to give up his offices. His flight to England in March 1483 brought no comfort, for Edward IV died on 9 April. Richard III could not afford adventures in Scotland, dropped Albany, and sought to improve relations with James III, and entered into negotiations for a truce, which was eventually agreed upon in Septem-

---

[1] Curtis, op. cit. 404; Conway, op. cit. 78–9, 84–6, 175, 233–4.
[2] See Conway, op. cit. 1–41. [3] Foedera, XV, 160.

ber 1484, for three years.[1] But in all the circumstances it is not surprising that James III should have favoured and welcomed Henry Tudor when the time came, and it is possible that a small Scottish contingent from France participated at Bosworth.[2] But although relations between the two kings were cordial, tension between the two countries was not relaxed, for the opponents of the Scots king in Scotland did not scruple to threaten the Border territories,[3] and renewed bitter struggles with James III. In this struggle, Henry VII did not remain neutral, as has sometimes been supposed. He maintained his agents in Scotland, who kept him fully informed of the course of events,[4] entered into negotiations with James III, and made with him in June 1486 a treaty for a three-year truce.[5] James III, it seems, would have liked to make a more permanent peace, but dared not avow his purpose publicly. Further negotiations were arranged, however, early in 1487, and even a three-fold matrimonial alliance considered, whereby James III was to marry Edward IV's widow, and his two sons, two of Queen Elizabeth's sisters. Nothing, however, came of this startling project, partly at least because of the Scots parliament's opposition to a marriage alliance which made no provision for the return of Berwick to Scotland. The most that could be achieved was an extension of the truce until 1 September 1489.[6] But before that date was reached, the struggles between James III and his factious nobles reached a ferocious climax. In February 1485, James III's son and heir was purloined by the opposition and made to serve its ends, and the culmination came with the battle of Sauchieburn, 11 June 1488, ending in James III's defeat and murder.

For Henry VII these events were disastrous to his policy of patiently building up good relations with the Scottish government. He could show sympathy and give aid to some of James III's faithful adherents, and by suitable distribution of pensions could secure the continued service of well-placed agents. He could, very soon, agree to a further truce for three years with James IV,[7] still only fifteen years of age and

---

[1] *L. & P.*, I, 59–67; *Foedera*, XII, 235–47.　　[2] *See* above, p. 70.　　[3] ibid.

[4] Henry Wyatt, later the father of Sir Thomas Wyatt the poet, rose from obscure origins high in the service and favour of Henry VII by performing notable services as an agent in Scotland. Conway, op. cit., John Ramsay, Lord Bothwell, and later James Stewart, first earl of Buchan, were the outstanding Scots magnates who were in Henry VII's pay for many years and supplied him with much information, ibid. 7, 17, 22, 25, 37, 102–3.

[5] *Rot. Scot.*, II, 473–7; Miss Conway, op. cit. 10, 22–3, shows conclusively that these negotiations belonged to 1486, not 1488, as Rymer, *Foedera*, XII, 334, mistakenly supposed. This error was repeated by many historians who consequently attributed the negotiations and treaty to early in the reign of James IV.

[6] *Rot. Scot.*, II, 480–1.　　　　　　　　　　　[7] ibid. 488–90.

badly shocked by the murder of his father and the unwitting part he had played in the plot which had so culminated. But it was not to be thought that the new king of Scots either would or could adopt the attitudes towards the English government which his father had favoured.

It is possible that James IV was apprised of a pro-Yorkist conspiracy, as early as November 1488, when he received a number of English visitors, at the request of Margaret of Burgundy,[1] from whom he received letters in December of that year and in September 1489.[2] In February 1490 he received a herald from Ireland,[3] whom he sent on to Margaret. In the summer of 1491 he renewed a treaty with France, whereby he was to attack England if Henry VII made war on France.[4] The truce he had made with Henry VII expired in October 1491, and its renewal was not ratified.[5]

In November of that year Perkin Warbeck had revealed himself in Ireland and sent his message to James IV in March 1492.[6] But, thereafter Warbeck had repaired to the Court of Charles VIII until the Treaty of Étaples obliged him to travel elsewhere for some three years. In the circumstances James IV eventually succumbed to Henry VII's prolonged blandishments and agreed to a formal truce from 3 November 1492 (the same date as the Treaty of Étaples was sealed) to 30 April 1494,[7] still further extended for seven years, from June 1493.[8] The immense trouble and expense undertaken by Henry VII's envoys in the course of these prolonged negotiations indicates the gravity with which he viewed the possibility of an active alliance between James IV and the Warbeck plotters.

But the threat was not averted. By November 1495 Warbeck was in Scotland, had been acknowledged as Richard, duke of York, and by December had been given to wife James's kinswoman Katherine Gordon, sister of the earl of Huntly – a match which would scarcely have been conceded unless James, for the moment at least, had not genuinely believed Warbeck was what he pretended to be.[9]

Henry VII, although now on the throne for ten years, found himself confronted with a situation of menacing possibilities. The presence of a potential Richard IV across the Border, backed by the unfriendly and

---

[1] Great Seal register, 1424–1513, No. 1798; Conway, op. cit. 31.

[2] Treasurers' Accounts, I, 99, 120. These transactions may have been connected with the conspiracy for the release of the earl of Warwick for which the abbot of Abingdon and John Maine were convicted and hanged in December 1489. R.P., VI, 436–7.

[3] Treasurers' Accounts, I, 130.

[4] Rot. Scot., II, 499; Milanese calendar, Nos 440, 443, 444.

[5] ibid. 503–5.   [6] See above, p. 82.   [7] Foedera, XII, 494–7.

[8] Rot. Scot., II, 508.   [9] See generally, Conway, op. cit. 99–117.

calculating James IV, supported by Margaret of Burgundy and any pro-Yorkist malcontents who might show their hand in England, was not a prospect that he could view with equanimity. It not only endangered his government, but threatened the most cherished objective in his foreign policy – to conclude a marriage alliance between his son and heir and a daughter of Ferdinand and Isabella, who would not conclude any such proposal whilst a pretender could threaten Henry's position and dynastic hopes, and who, moreover, at this time were anxious above all to get Henry into the Holy League as an additional means of tarnishing Charles VIII's triumphs in Italy. Much depended upon the outcome of Henry's handling of the situation, and international interest in the unfolding of the drama was acute. No one could at first predict that the drama would soon turn out to be a farce.

Henry VII lost no time in preparing to resist invasion, but at the same time commissioned his ablest diplomatic negotiator, Richard Fox, strategically located at this time in the episcopal see of Durham, to treat for a marriage alliance between James IV and his daughter Margaret.[1] Other diplomatic commissions were issued and even a scheme to kidnap Warbeck was apparently mooted.[2] In the meantime the possibility of additional complications with Ireland had largely been removed by the earl of Desmond's having been brought to terms,[3] and by other measures.

James IV's attitude soon became somewhat equivocal. He hoped, it seems, to agree satisfactory terms with Richard Fox, but if he did not, he proposed to honour his pledges with Warbeck and to invade by 17 September 1496, on terms with Warbeck which as finally agreed included the return of Berwick and a substantial refund of costs should Warbeck be successful.[4] But he declined Charles VIII's offer to buy Warbeck off him.[5]

The very small reinforcement which Margaret sent to Warbeck at this stage was not encouraging, though the pretender no doubt made much of it and of letters he received from his 'aunt'.[6]

The invasion of England started on 17 September as threatened. But it proved an utter failure. Not even the banner of Richard IV evoked any response south of the Border, and a penetration of four miles and the capture of a couple of watch-towers, with some devastation of the countryside, which, to his credit, shocked the unwarlike Warbeck, ended in retreat back to Scotland. The alarm served Henry VII's turn

[1] *Rot. Scot.*, II, 520.   [2] Conway, op. cit. 103.
[3] ibid. 104 and Apps XXXVIII, XXXIX.   [4] ibid. 105.
[5] ibid.   [6] ibid. 107–8.

by enabling him to raise considerable financial aid in England and to make military preparations which, although not needed to repel the incursion from Scotland, could be adapted next year to suppress the formidable Cornish rebellion at the battle of Blackheath on 17 June.

The Cornish insurrection was ostensibly not against the king but against the counsellors who had advised him to raise the taxation voted in the parliament of January 1497, largely for preparations to resist the threatened invasion by James IV and Warbeck. The most serious feature of the insurrection was the ease with which a large number of rebels were able to march up from Cornwall to near London, with no opposition until they reached Kent, in spite of insignificant leadership. The explanation no doubt lies in the circumstance that Henry VII's preparations at that time were directed towards Scotland, and the Cornish rising was no part of a preconceived plot, or any pro-Yorkist conspiracy, so that no advance warning of it could have been obtained. The quick diversion southwards of forces already engaged under Lord Daubeney ensured a speedy conclusion to the rising, which can scarcely be said 'to have shaken Henry VII's throne'. The battle on Blackheath was decisive; some thousand rebels were killed, and the rest surrendered or fled. Only the three ringleaders, a local lawyer and a blacksmith, and James Touchet, Lord Audley, were executed. The main consequence of the episode was to induce Henry VII to try to come to terms with James IV so as to avoid the costs and preoccupations of a war on the Borders.[1]

But Henry's urgent preoccupation with his truculent Cornishmen was not taken advantage of by James IV, who by then was clearly preparing to drop 'Richard IV'. Whether he had become disillusioned as to Warbeck's pretensions and potentiality, or appreciated that Henry VII would not be easily displaced, or whether he now seriously believed that his best interests would be served by marrying Henry's daughter Margaret, cannot be told. Certainly he counted the cost of pressing Warbeck's pretensions, and decided to cut it. The wily Fox was commissioned with elaborate instructions to negotiate once again,[2] and on 6 July Warbeck departed from Scotland in a Breton vessel hired by James IV for the purpose.[3] With that stumbling-block out of the way, long and tortuous though the negotiations proved to be, at last a seven-year truce was agreed in September 1497, at Ayton, renewed in 1499,

---

[1] Busch, op. cit. 110–12, and refs. therein. For the attainders of Lord Audley and fourteen others, ten of whom were yeomen, see R.P., VI, 544. Twelve more, all except three being yeomen, were attainted in connection with Warbeck's incursion into Cornwall, ibid.   [2] L. & P., I, 104–9.   [3] Gairdner, op. cit. 318.

leading on to the first full peace treaty with Scotland since 1328.[1] By the Treaty of Ayton, January 1502, James IV was to marry Princess Margaret, which he did in August 1503. For Henry VII this triumph of his diplomacy was both rewarding and most opportune. For in April the previous year his son and heir Prince Arthur had died and in so doing had brought to naught the hard-won marriage with Catherine of Aragon, and now only his younger son Henry stood between the queen of Scots and the succession to the throne of England. But a hundred years was to pass before the union of crowns was to occur, and then only because by then all Henry VII's English grandchildren were dead without lineal descendants, a catastrophe which he could have neither predicted nor contemplated without horror. Yet it was his astute diplomacy which in the long run protected England, in 1603, from calamities which would have proved worse than the succession of a king of Scots to its throne.

For Warbeck the departure from Scotland began the last phase of his pretension. He appeared at Cork on 26 July, but finding that Irish support was not forthcoming, he set sail with two small ships and a pinnace, and a hundred or so men to land at Whitesand Bay, near Land's End on 7 September, in the hope that in Cornwall, the only region now in England which might be expected to show hostility to Henry VII, substantial aid might be rendered to 'Richard IV'. But within a fortnight all was over. A few thousand countryfolk joined him. But Exeter drove him and them off, and Taunton did not want him. The rapidly mobilized forces of the king soon terminated any further hopes. Warbeck fled, surrendered; made a full confession as to his real name and origins; soon wrote to his real mother giving an account of his adventures and touted her for money, and was now at the king's mercy.[2] Henry VII could by now afford to be generous to his humiliated and no doubt winsome and charming captive. Besides, Warbeck was not a subject of his, and it might have been difficult at this stage to pin

---

[1] *Rot. Scot.*, II, 526; *Foedera*, XII, 680; Conway, op. cit. 116; Wernham, op. cit. 46–7.

[2] Gairdner, op. cit. 317–33. The confession, which was printed, is analysed, ibid. 265–8; and Warbeck's letter to his mother is printed, ibid. 329–30. There is no reason to doubt the authenticity of either the confession or the letter. Warbeck's wife, Katherine Gordon, was courteously treated by Henry VII, pensioned, and put into the queen's care. She subsequently, in the time of Henry VIII, married three times, (1) James Strangways, a gentleman usher of the chamber; (2) Mathew, later Sir Mathew Cradock, a gentleman of Glamorgan; and (3) Christopher Ashton, another gentleman usher of the chamber. She died in 1537, and was buried in Fyfield Church, Berkshire. *See* Gairdner's note to Busch, op. cit. 440–1.

charges of treason upon him. No restraint was put upon him, and he was treated as a member of the court. But there were to be no more wanderings, and it was folly indeed for Warbeck to try to flee from Henry's silken shackles. On 9 June 1498 Warbeck was arrested at Sheen, brought back to London, made to repeat publicly his confession, to sit in the stocks twice, and to repair to the Tower. What exactly happened in that fortress during the following months, we shall probably never know. Whether he was 'framed', or whether he was given or merely took an opportunity to initiate a hare-brained plot with the earl of Warwick, who was still a prisoner, one cannot tell.[1] In any case, it can hardly be doubted that he abused the leniency shown him, and by 16 November 1499 he was tried on a charge of trying to escape and on 29 November was hanged. Two days previously, the court of the lord high steward (John de Vere, earl of Oxford, for the occasion) in Westminster Hall considered the findings of a grand jury returned against Edward, earl of Warwick, found him guilty of treason, which he admitted. A week later he was beheaded on Tower Hill. The most innocent sprig of the white rose was thus lopped off. Tudor reason of State had claimed the first of its many victims.

But there were still other sprigs that had to be taken into account – numerous sons of Edward IV's sister Elizabeth and John de la Pole, duke of Suffolk. There had been seven of them altogether, and as yet only two were accounted for. The eldest, John, earl of Lincoln had, as we have seen, lost his life at Stoke in 1487; the second son, Edward, died before 1485; the fourth, Humphrey, was a cleric and a country rector, who died c. 1513. Nothing significant is known of the sixth, Geoffrey. But the third son, Edmund, earl of Suffolk, the fifth, William, and Richard the seventh son,[2] could still claim to be the representatives of York, and might at least embarrass the Tudors for years to come.

Edmund, a month or two after the marriage of Arthur and Catherine had been celebrated by proxy in May 1499, resenting judicial process in respect of a private murder which he had committed, although promptly pardoned, took offence and fled to Flanders.[3] He spent some time with Sir James Tyrell, the governor of Guisnes, near Calais. But he

---

[1] That a minor conspiracy, in which the prime movers were a few citizens of London, existed, intended to procure the release of Warwick and Warbeck, seems clear from the indictments in the *Baga de secretis*, *53rd annual report of the deputy keeper of the Public Record* (1892), App. II, 30–6. The suspicious circumstance is that most of the commoners who were found guilty of treason were subsequently pardoned. Busch, op. cit. 118–21, and n. 14, 349.

[2] G.E.C., XII, 2 (1953), App. 1.

[3] On Suffolk's movements, *see* Busch, op. cit. ch. v, and refs.

was persuaded to return and remained along with his brothers in Henry VII's good grace until in July or August 1501, he fled, together with his brother Richard, to the court of Maximilian, whose aid he sought in starting a new conspiracy in his own favour. But Henry did not remain uninformed of the plot's ramifications. Edmund's brother William found himself in the Tower, where he stayed until he died thirty-eight years later. Other persons who were implicated were imprisoned, and in some cases executed. Among the latter was included Sir James Tyrell.

Henry VII could no longer afford to take chances. His own dynastic prospects had recently become more precarious than he could contemplate with any equanimity. In June 1500 his third son Edmund had died. The marriage of Arthur and Catherine of Aragon, for which he had striven for many years, was solemnized on 14 November 1501, but Arthur died on 2 April 1502. His only male heir now was the ten-year-old and as yet not very robust second son, Henry. In these circumstances, it is far from surprising that within five weeks of Arthur's death, Sir James Tyrell, before his execution, should be alleged to have made a confession which was calculated to lay the ghosts of the princes in the Tower for ever. Tyrell was the ideal candidate for such a confession, especially as he would shortly be dead, and it was most important to take the opportunity, such as it was, to make it very difficult for any further imposter to claim to be a son of Edward IV. But the manifest expediency of the allegation does not make it true.[1]

Several years were to elapse before the live Yorkist male heir, Edmund, earl of Suffolk, could be brought into safe custody. Before then, Henry VII's own queen and devoted consort, Elizabeth, the eldest of the heiresses of York, died (11 February 1503); his daughter Margaret had departed to be James IV's queen (August 1503); his daughter Mary was as yet only seven years of age, and Henry VII's efforts at getting Edmund de la Pole out of Flanders were unremitting,

---

[1] There is no reliable evidence that the confession was ever made by Tyrell, or that it was ever published, as it surely would have been if it had been made. The most that can be said is that it appears that Henry VII let it be known that Tyrell had confessed before he was executed, and the reasons for his so doing are obvious enough, as indicated above. The essential incredibility of the whole story as embroidered and enlarged upon by Sir Thomas More in his *Richard III*, and vaguely referred to by Polydore Vergil and the *Great chronicle*, was fully exposed by P. M. Kendall, *Richard the Third* (1955), 398–406. For the attainders of Suffolk and Tyrell, and fifteen others, see *R.P.*, VI, 545. In this parliament of 1504, the king announced that he did not intend to summon another parliament without 'grete necessarye and urgent causes', ibid. 526.

and unavailing, until chance and adverse winds brought the Archduke Philip and his wife Joanna of Castile to England in 1506, when Henry's hospitality proved to be so flattering and so prolonged that before Philip was finally able to leave he not only agreed *inter alia* to surrender Edmund and to cause him to be brought home (with assurances as to his safety), but also to a commercial treaty which was markedly favourable to England.[1] In the Tower of London Edmund was safe until 1513, when his brother Richard, still at large, got himself recognized for a time by Louis XII as another Richard IV,[2] whereupon Henry VIII thought it best to terminate Edmund's custody once and for all. Merely to be a De la Pole was fatal in the reign of Henry VII's heir, as many of the family discovered when the only surviving male Tudor ruthlessly sought to extinguish the White Rose for ever.[3]

Henry VII's problem of security was thus not solved with the death of Warbeck and of Warwick in 1499. Not until 1506 could he feel that so far as Yorkist claimants were concerned he had little to fear. But by then his dynastic hopes had come to rest solely upon his surviving son Henry. His line of succession was very slender, and his continued fears for the future of his house induced his pertinacious efforts in his last years to find a second queen for himself. His endeavours were to be in vain, but the same fears and efforts were to be inherited and enormously magnified by his successor.

[1] Archduke Philip and his wife set sail on 7 January 1506, but their fleet was scattered by a storm and his ship was driven ashore at Melcombe Regis near Weymouth on 16 January. Elaborate arrangements for their hospitality were made as soon as possible. They did not leave England until 23 April. Among the agreements reached was that neither party should harbour any rebels against the other. On 16 March, Suffolk was handed over at Calais and conveyed to England on 24 March. Busch, op. cit. 192. For the treaty with the archduke, *see* below, p. 290.

[2] Richard de la Pole had escaped to Hungary in the summer of 1506, but later took service in France, and survived until 1525, when he was killed fighting for Francis I at Pavia.

[3] For a list of Yorkists and descendants who suffered execution under Henry VIII, and the later Tudors, *see* Chrimes, *Lancastrians, Yorkists, and Henry VII*, 2nd ed. (1966), 163, fn.

PART II

The Personnel and Machinery of Government

Chapter 4

THE KING'S COUNCIL

Though the surviving records are sparse and inadequate, and the problems of detail probably insuperable,[1] the difficulty of envisaging the council under Henry VII has been greatly, though unnecessarily, enhanced by historians' misconceptions and reluctance to accept existing evidence realistically. It does not help our understanding of the council under Henry VII to look at it in the light of developments under Henry VIII. The first Tudor could only build his governmental structures on what existed in 1485, and it is to the then past, not the then unknowable future, that we have to look for the basis of our comprehension.

If we examine the considerable material that has already been published relevant to the council in the time of Henry VII,[2] nothing could be more obvious than the essential unity and flexibility of the council throughout the reign. The King's Council was simply the king's council;[3] there was no court of Star Chamber; there were no commit-

[1] G. R. Elton, 'Why the history of the early Tudor council remains unwritten', *Annali della Fondazione italiana per la storia amministrativa*, I (1964), 268–96.

[2] The indispensable commentary and texts are contained in *Select cases in the council of Henry VII*, ed. C. G. Bayne and W. H. Dunham, S.S. 75 (1958). This valuable volume, however, was largely preoccupied with the judicial activities of the council, and the criticisms of it by G. R. Elton, *E.H.R.*, LXXIV (1959), 686–90, need to be taken into account. Important contributions were made, mostly in relation to a later period, by W. H. Dunham, 'The Ellesmere extracts from the "Acta Consilii" of King Henry VIII', *E.H.R.*, LVIII (1943), 301–18; and 'Members of Henry VIII's whole council 1509–1527', ibid. LIX (1944), 187–210. Professor Elton, *Annali*, loc. cit. 272, has shown that the expression 'whole council' merely meant all the councillors. For other materials on the judicial activities of the council, *see* below, p. 147 ff., fn. The articles by A. F. Pollard, 'Council, Star Chamber and Privy Council under the Tudors', *E.H.R.*, XXXVII (1922), 337–60, 516–39, although superseded in some respects and erroneous in others, contain a number of points that are still valid. The older books and articles relevant to the subject are now mostly superseded. Useful material is contained in I. S. Leadam (ed.), *Select cases before the King's Council in the Star Chamber*, I, *1477–1509*, S.S. XVI (1963), but the editorial comment is almost entirely out of date.

[3] 'Henry's board was the council, and his generation never called it by any other name' . . . 'we do not possess the means of dividing the members of this council into separate bodies according to the nature of their duties.' (Bayne, op. cit. xxii, xli.) Unfortunately Bayne was not wholly consistent in observing these undoubtedly

tees of the council, and no statute created any such committee; there was no 'whole' council, no 'privy' council, no 'inner' council, no 'attendant' council, no offshoots in the North[1] or Wales.[2] The origins of the later Tudor Council of the North are attributed to the private council established by Richard, duke of Gloucester, as the greatest northern landowner. When he became king a council continued to exist as a kind of regional council vested with powers of administration and justice, and he clearly regarded it as a King's Council in the Northern parts. Henry VII, however, does not appear to have followed this precedent, and no comparable institution appeared in his reign. He did not even revive the wardenship of the West March, but quickly restored Henry Percy, earl of Northumberland, to the wardenship of the eastern March until his murder in 1489. Thereafter he appointed Prince Arthur as warden-general and Thomas Howard, earl of Surrey, as his lieutenant. The warden appointed councillors with a president, but this was not the king's council nor an offshoot thereof.

The King's Council, in the sense of 'all the councillors', never met at any time. All that was ever done by the council was done by groups of councillors, the composition of which varied greatly from time to time and according to the nature of the business and to whether the business was such that it recurred frequently. These groups were not committees of the council in any modern sense of the term. There is no evidence that the council, or anyone else, at this time, delegated or relegated any business to a committee of itself, and indeed it is very doubtful whether the conception of such a procedure existed. The King's Council consisted of the king's councillors, and any number of them might be used for the king's purposes without in any way changing

---

correct statements. He thought, for example, that the Statute of Retainers (or Liveries) of 1504 (19 Henry VII, c. 14) allows us to regard the 'council in attendance as a recognized body' (ibid. xxiv), but the reference in the statute is simply to 'the King and his Council attending upon his most royal person wheresoever he be' (*S.R.* II, 658; extract in J. R. Tanner, *Tudor constitutional documents* (1930), 10). This can only mean to refer to those councillors who happened to perambulate with the king and does not identify a 'body' in any institutional sense. Kings had always had councillors 'in attendance'. G. R. Elton, *Annali*, loc. cit. 290.

[1] See the memorandum printed in *L. & P.*, I, 56–9, and in Chrimes and Brown, *Select documents*, 357–8; discussed in R. R. Reid, *The King's Council in the North* (1926). See also R. L. Storey, *Henry VII*, 147–9: and 'The wardens of the Marches of England towards Scotland 1377–1489', *E.H.R.*, LXXII (1957), 593–615; R. R. Reid, op. cit.; F. W. Brooks, *The Council of the North* (Hist. Association, 1953, rev. ed. 1966); G. R. Elton, *The Tudor constitution*, 196–7.

[2] See below, p. 245 ff.

their status as members of the King's Council. The fact that some might habitually attend to judicial business in the room commonly called (because of its ceiling *décor*) 'Star Chamber' did not create a 'court of Star Chamber' – the term except in a locative sense was almost never used in the reign of Henry VII.[1] Star Chamber at this time was merely the convenient location for groups of king's councillors to conduct their business, whether it was judicial or other kinds of business. Most judicial business, however, by its nature, needed a more or less fixed location if it was to be conducted in an orderly and practicable manner, but it could be conducted wherever the king or a suitable group of councillors might be. Usage and convenience might encourage the idea that judicial business would normally be conducted by some of the councillors sitting in Star Chamber, and seekers after justice often came to look for what they wanted there, but the truth remained exactly as the anonymous law book called Fleta had observed a hundred years and more earlier – *rex habet curiam suam in concilio suo* (the king has his court in his council).[2] The fact that a particular group of councillors, considered to be especially well qualified for the tasks set them, and including among their number a high proportion of persons 'learned in the law', attracted to themselves the occasional label of 'Council Learned' did not make them a committee of the council; they were a part of the King's Council who habitually gave their attention to particular tasks.[3]

[1] Bayne, op. cit. lxxv–lxxvi.

[2] Aptly cited by A. F. Pollard, loc. cit. 340. The original sentence in Fleta continues with the words '*in parliamento suo*'.

[3] R. Somerville, 'Henry VII's "Council Learned in the Law"', *E.H.R.*, LIV (1939), 427–42. Sir Robert Somerville clearly showed that the members of the Council Learned exercised their jurisdiction as members of the King's Council, and that the records refer indifferently to proceedings before the Council Learned and the King's Council (op. cit. 439). There is, therefore, no validity in describing the Council Learned as 'a committee of the council' (ibid.), any more than there is in similarly describing the council in Star Chamber as a committee of the council. Both are merely groups of councillors for some purposes. They do not derive their functions by delegation from the council: they *are* the council for their occasions. The references to the dispute between the Corporation of York and the abbey of St Mary contained in *York Civic Records*, II (1941), ed. Angelo Raine (Yorks. Arch. Soc., Record Ser., CIII, 169), cited by Bayne, op. cit. xxvii, as evidence that the matter was heard and examined by the King's Learned Council, and then 'referred back to the council proper for final decision' do not appear to support Bayne's interpretation, if it was meant to imply that the Council Learned referred back to the council as a whole in the sense that a modern committee refers back to its appointing body. There are no such words as 'referring back' in the record, or any suggestion that the King's Learned Council was thought of as a committee of the council. In any event the decision of the King's Council was that the matter should either abide the rule of the bishop of Winchester,

The most unfortunate labelling at a later date of the act of 1487 with the totally inappropriate words '*Pro camera stellata*' bedevilled the historiography of the Tudor council for generations. No one now supposes that the act had anything to do with either the council or the court of Star Chamber,[1] but the point also has to be made clear that it did not in any sense establish a committee of the council. What it did do was to establish a tribunal consisting of the three principal officers or two of them, who were required to call to their assistance a bishop and a temporal lord from among the king's councillors, for the judicial purposes specified. The act of 1487, therefore, not only had nothing to do with Star Chamber, but also nothing to do with the King's Council as such. Its only point was to establish a tribunal distinct from the council.[2]

It is also an unfortunate circumstance that the evidence surviving for the judicial activities of council, although not very extensive, is much greater than that for the far more important and basic work of the king's councillors, i.e., the work of giving the king counsel on any and all the multifarious affairs of state. This circumstance has resulted in a distortion of our picture of the council under Henry VII. For the king himself the essential importance of his councillors was not to be found in the efforts of some of them to supplement the jurisdictional labours of the common law courts, but in the efforts of all or any of them to aid him in reaching decisions in the pressing problems of government. It is a commonplace that no king could govern without the advice and counsel of councillors of some kind, and it seems a safe generalization to assert that Henry VII, coming to the throne in the way he did in 1485, stood in greater immediate need of counsel in affairs of state than any of his predecessors. For he came to it devoid of any personal experience of government of any kind. It is, therefore, to the King's Council as an organ and instrument of government that we need to direct our attention first, whilst leaving its judicial activities for consideration where it properly belongs – under the heading of judicature.[3]

The nucleus of what was to become Henry VII's council was formed from the time when in Brittany he first began to assume overt preten-

---

two of the King's Council and two judges, or else be dealt with under the common law (ibid. 172).

[1] The fullest discussion is in Bayne and Dunham, op. cit. xlix–lxiv. For a brief summary and references, *see* G. R. Elton, *The Tudor constitution* (1960). It is unfortunate that Professor Elton, although well aware that the controversy is dead, should have perpetuated the old untenable label by printing the words 'Star Chamber' both in his list of statutes and in his imaginary title to the act, op. cit. xi and 163. For a facsimile of the act, *see B.I.H.R.*, III (1925–6), 114.

[2] *See* below, p. 154 ff.   [3] *See* below, p. 147 ff.

4 6 7 9 1

sions to royal dignity, and this appears to have occurred early in 1484. A number of his close associates at that time[1] remained his most confidential advisers for the rest of their lives, were after Bosworth appointed to offices, and figure among his councillors during his reign. It is not possible to say when exactly his formal council was established, if indeed there was at any time any specific establishment. Most likely the personnel were picked upon and added to the nucleus from time to time according to circumstances, and gradually as Henry made the acquaintance of likely persons or felt able to accept recommendations. Polydore Vergil's notion[2] that a council was constituted after the dissolution of the first parliament on 4 March 1486 cannot be accepted at its face value, although it may well be that after the parliament some opportunity may have been taken to publicize the names of some at least of the councillors. Henry clearly could not have done without councillors from the moment he took over the government, and in any case there is record evidence that a council was functioning formally in the first month of the reign.[3]

Nor is there now any great difficulty in determining where Henry VII looked to obtain recruits to add to the nucleus of a council which he brought with him from Brittany and France. He looked and found a substantial number of them from the ranks of those who had had experience as councillors to either Edward IV or Richard III, or to both. No less than twenty-nine of his councillors had been councillors to one or other of the Yorkist kings, thirteen of them to both, nineteen of them to Richard III. Fifteen of his councillors were near relatives of Edward IV's councillors, and others had prominent administrative careers under the Yorkist regime.[4] Evidently Henry VII was fully prepared to employ as councillors men of experience regardless of their Yorkist associations. 'Loyalty and ability were the only criteria of service – mighty lord, bishop, doctor of canon or civil law, or official, all were there, but only at the king's will.'[5]

With so substantial an overlap in personnel between the Yorkist and the first Tudor council, it would be a natural supposition to make that Henry VII's model for his council, in so far as he had a model, was the Yorkist precedent.[6] Enough is now known about both councils, even

---

[1] See above, p. 56.   [2] P.V. (ed. Hay), 5–6.   [3] Bayne, op. cit. xviii.

[4] J. R. Lander, 'Council, administration, and councillors, 1461–85', B.I.H.R., XXXII (1959), 138–80. The names of the overlapping councillors are listed, 179–80.

[5] ibid. 165.

[6] J. R. Lander, 'The Yorkist council and administration, 1461–85', E.H.R., LXXII (1958), 27–46. The wide scope of the administrative activities of the Yorkist council is amply illustrated in both of Professor Lander's valuable articles.

though there remain many gaps in our knowledge, to show that this supposition is correct. Until comparatively recently not enough information was available about either council, but it has always been difficult to perceive what Henry VII in the circumstances of his accession could have done, at least for some years, but follow Yorkist patterns.

How large Henry VII's council was at any given time cannot be ascertained, but the total number of councillors identified for the whole reign is 227; of these 183 are known to have attended one or more of 135 meetings of the council in one form or another spaced over twenty-one of the twenty-five years of the reign.[1] Of the total number a rough division into classes has been made as follows: peers 43, courtiers 45, churchmen 61, lawyers 27, officials 49.[2] This division cannot be taken as exact, since serious overlapping of classes is unavoidable, but it does give an indication of the diversity of the personnel of the council over the reign, and invalidates any idea that Henry VII drew his councillors mainly from any particular class. It is, for example, calculated that about two-thirds of the peerage were present at one or more meetings of the council over the reign,[3] and it cannot be said therefore that Henry VII neglected the lay peers in composing his council, even though only a few of them appear to have been used frequently. The spiritual lords were likewise heavily drawn upon, as many as seventy-three, if those who were also officials are included; of these thirty were bishops, and most meetings were attended by several bishops, even though again only those who were also officials attended frequently and attained to importance as councillors.[4]

Among the common lawyers, the chief justice and chief baron, and the law officers figure most prominently, but their activities were not confined to judicial business; any business might be dealt with at meetings at which some of them were present.[5] Of the officials, the chancellor, treasurer, and keeper of the Privy Seal may be described as *ex officio* councillors, and were the most regular attenders, although it cannot be shown that any one of them was always present at a meeting. Probably the chancellor was normally present and presided unless the king were present, which he frequently was,[6] or until the time came (probably in 1495) when the preoccupations of the chancellor induced the appointment of a president of the council for at least some occasions.[7] Specific

---

[1] Bayne, op. cit. xix–xxii.   [2] ibid. xxix.   [3] ibid.
[4] ibid. xxxi.   [5] ibid. xxxii.   [6] ibid. xxxiii.
[7] ibid. xxxvii–xl. Three presidents can be identified for the reign: 1497–1502 Thomas Savage, bishop of Rochester 1493–6, of London 1496–1501, archbishop of

references to 'the president of the council' occur from March 1497, and by October to such a president by name. The probability is that the appointment for such an officer arose from the need to have someone to preside over meetings of the council when the chancellor was not available, and since Morton was by then approaching eighty years of age and was to die on 15 September 1500, the need must have become apparent. During the ensuing years – and no chancellor was to be appointed until 21 January 1504 – further appointments of presidents were made, but references to the presidents remain singularly few, and only slight inferences can be drawn therefrom. Certainly it seems clear that the presidents among other activities acted judicially in Star Chamber and were especially associated with, and even regarded as the presiding officer at jurisdiction over 'requests'. Several other officials frequently attended, but not so much because of their offices as because of their personal standing with the king.[1]

There is no evidence that anything like a meeting of all the council ever took place or that such an unlikely event was ever envisaged. The limited evidence we have suggests that at most perhaps two dozen councillors were summoned to and attended habitually and composed what was normally regarded as a meeting of the council.[2] It is a misnomer to call these an 'inner council'; it *was* the council in so far as the council was manifested in general meetings. Most of the councillors attending these meetings were there frequently because they were regarded by the king as his most confidential and reliable councillors, but it was the king's will in the prevailing circumstances of the moment that decided just which councillors should be summoned to attend. Any councillor could be required to take the councillor's oath, but it is unlikely that all the persons designated councillors were expected to do so.[3] Designation as a king's councillor undoubtedly gave a man a status that was honorific in itself and also served to associate him with the regime. A wide range of actual or potential services could be readily brought within the compass of the king's call by such designation. Persons whose services in diplomatic missions were desired; lawyers whose special talents were wanted for some particular tasks; magnates

York 1501–7; 1502–6 Richard Fitzjames, bishop of Rochester 1497–1503, of Chichester 1503–6, of London 1506–22; 1506–9 Edmund Dudley. The evidence cited by Bayne, op. cit. xxxix, from the *Plumpton correspondence* (Cam. Soc. 4, 114), is too slight to justify the suggestion that the president (who appears to be called Lord President only when he was also a bishop) controlled the Signet Office.

[1] Bayne, op. cit. xxxv–xxxvi.
[2] ibid.   [3] ibid. xlix.

whose support for the government it was desirable to recognize; other persons for other purposes; all could be brought within the ranks of the councillors. But only a few could be entrusted with the secrets and tasks of government at its highest level; only those to whom by reason of office or trust the king was prepared to open his mind, upon whom he relied for advice and the formulation of policy and decision in any matter of state that might arise. It is upon these men and the nature of their business that attention needs to be focused if Henry VII's government at its apex is to be depicted. Although the surviving evidence of conciliar activity remains comparatively scanty, both as regards advisory and judicial functions, enough is now available to provide a general picture. Contrary to formerly common belief, it is certain that a register of council business was kept both for executive and judicial business, at this time. All the volumes for Henry VII's reign remained in the custody of the later clerk of the Star Chamber, until the eighteenth century, when they disappeared. We are consequently dependent for our knowledge of their contents upon a number of extracts made from them in the sixteenth and seventeenth centuries.[1]

The outstanding feature as regards the three principal offices, the chancellorship, treasurership, and the keepership of the Privy Seal, was the long tenure of office enjoyed by those whom Henry VII appointed. Only four chancellors were appointed throughout the reign; two of these held the office for nearly twenty years between them, whilst two keepers of the Great Seal held posts for periods of under two years each. Two treasurers held office, between them, for very nearly the whole reign, and only two keepers of the Privy Seal were appointed throughout the reign. It is clear that Henry VII knew how to select his chief administrative officers and principal councillors, retained his confidence in them, and continued to rely upon them in most cases for the duration of their or his life.

The first two chancellors appointed were both men who had had experience of the office under the Yorkists and were clearly stop-gap appointments, no doubt pending the return to England of John Morton. Thomas Rotheram (1423–1500), archbishop of York since 1480, had had extensive administrative and legal experience under Edward IV, and had been chancellor from 1474 (with a short interval in 1475) when he attained a reputation as an 'equity' judge until he was dismissed by Richard, duke of Gloucester, then protector, in April 1483. Henry VII made use of him as an interim chancellor from 18 September to

[1] These are printed in Bayne, op. cit. 1–59; and the problem of sources discussed, ibid. xi–xviii; cf. Elton, loc. cit. 285–90.

7 October 1485.[1] The second stop-gap was the man who had been chancellor in England whilst Rotheram accompanied Edward IV to France in 1475, John Alcock (1430–1500), bishop of Worcester since 1476, who had once been tutor to Edward V, was destined to succeed to the bishopric of Ely when Morton became archbishop, and who retained the chancellorship until 6 March 1486.[2] From that date John Morton, bishop of Ely since 1479, held the office until his death on 15 September 1500.

Although there can be little doubt that Morton was the key figure in Henry VII's government for many years, nothing approaching an adequate study of his life and role has yet been published, and here we can only sketch his career and recall estimates of his qualities that have been made at different times.[3] That he was an astute politician and a sagacious lawyer and administrator cannot be doubted. It was not only his longevity that enabled him to serve in turn Lancastrian, Yorkist, and Tudor kings. He was well able to trim his sails according to prevailing winds, but it could only have been great abilities that enabled him to anticipate Thomas Wolsey by becoming at the same time chancellor, archbishop, and cardinal. A doctor of laws of Oxford, he began his career as a practising lawyer in the court of Arches, managed to attract the patronage of Thomas Bourchier, archbishop of Canterbury from 1454, and soon himself became an outstanding pluralist. He did not, however, climb very high on the ladder of officialdom under Henry VI, but became chancellor of the duchy of Cornwall and a master in Chancery, and he was sufficiently attached to the Lancastrians to throw in his lot with them when disasters overtook them, was present and captured at the battle of Towton, escaped and eventually joined Queen Margaret in exile at St Mihiel. He acted as keeper of the Privy Seal to Henry VI and he was concerned in the negotiations that led to the Readeption of Henry VI in 1470. After Tewkesbury, he made his peace with Edward IV, and then in time had a chance to use his talents in the service of the new regime. His attainder was reversed; he became master of the Rolls and a king's councillor in 1473, was employed on several diplomatic missions, and assisted in the negotiations leading to Edward IV's Treaty of Picquigny with Louis XI in 1475; by then he was deemed to be of sufficient importance and influence to be made the recipient of a pension of six hundred crowns from Louis XI. In 1479 he

[1] See D.N.B.   [2] ibid.
[3] See D.N.B. A. B. Emden, *Biographical register of the University of Oxford* (1958), has a full sketch, pp. 1318–20; the list of benefices to which Morton was appointed fills a whole column in this volume; More's *Richard III*, ed. Sylvester, 211–12, etc.

became bishop of Ely. His hopes of further service and promotion, however, appeared to be terminated by Richard III's usurpation. For whatever precise reason, Richard ordered his arrest along with Stanley and Hastings and others, in June 1483. As we have seen, Morton came into the custody of the duke of Buckingham at Brecon, and there took a major share in the concoction of the conspiracy to overthrow Richard III and to promote the cause of Henry of Richmond.[1] The total failure of Buckingham's rebellion did not prevent Morton from fleeing to Ely, thence to Flanders, and thence to Rome.[2] He was back in England, apparently, by mid-October 1485. On 6 March 1486 he became chancellor of England, and archbishop of Canterbury on 6 December of that year.[3] His cardinalate came in 1493.

Not for nothing did Dominic Mancini in 1483 describe Morton as being 'of great resource and daring, for he had been trained in party intrigue since King Henry's time', and a man who 'enjoyed great influence'.[4] Sir Thomas More, who as a boy had cause to know Morton well, had some revealing remarks to make. Morton, he wrote, was 'a man of great natural wit, very well learned, and honourable in behaviour, lacking no wise ways to win favour', a man who 'had got by great experience the very mother and mistress of wisdom, a deep insight in politic worldly drifts'.[5] Elsewhere More wrote of him, 'the Kynge put muche truste in his counsel, the weale publique also in a maner leaned unto hym'. Even an anonymous and not specially friendly London chronicler could say of him that he was 'a man worthy of memory for his many great acts and especially for his great wisdom . . . in our time there was no man like to be compared with him in all things'.[6] It may be that when the council dealt with affairs of state the lord chancellor was merely one among other members,[7] but in fact Morton was present at almost all meetings of the council of which we have a record, and there can be no doubt that he was preeminent among the councillors and Henry VII's most trusted adviser. It may well

[1] See above, p. 20.

[2] More's assertion that Morton went to Rome (*Richard III*, ed. Sylvester, 91, 269) has hitherto been deemed to be the only evidence for the visit. That Morton did in fact visit Rome and signed on at the Fraternity of the Holy Spirit and St Mary on 31 January 1485 is proved by the evidence printed in Pietro Egidi, *Fonti per la Storia d'Italia* (Institutia Storia Italiana, 45 (1914), 309). His nephew Robert Morton, and Oliver King, the future secretary to Henry VII, and others were also there at much the same time, I am indebted to my former pupil, Mr M. Pronay, now of the University of Leeds, for this reference.   [3] See above.

[4] *Usurpation of Richard III*, ed. C. A. G. Armstrong, 102.

[5] *Richard III*, ed. Sylvester, 90.   [6] *Utopia*, ed. Reed, 12.

[7] Bayne, op. cit. xxxvi.

be that Morton began as a careerist and opportunist, but having weathered such vicissitudes of fortune and gained such knowledge of affairs, he survived to provide Henry VII with what he most lacked – indispensable experience of statecraft in all its diverse forms.

On Morton's death, the gap was filled temporarily from 13 October 1500 by the appointment as keeper of Henry Deane, bishop of Salisbury since earlier in the year, formerly since 1494 bishop of Bangor, who had been chancellor, deputy, and justiciar in Ireland in 1496. He was destined to succeed Morton as archbishop of Canterbury from 26 May 1501, but he died in 1503.[1] Another future archbishop, more renowned, William Warham (1450–1532), a former practitioner in the court of Arches and distinguished diplomat extensively employed by Henry VII, about to become bishop of London, was appointed keeper on 11 August 1502. After succeeding to the archbishopric in 1503, he was promoted to be chancellor on 21 January 1504, and retained the office not only until the end of the reign but until the end of 1515, when he was displaced by Wolsey.[2]

How far the functions of the treasurer were mainly honorific at this time remains a matter of some doubt, but it is clear that the holder of the office was regarded as one of the three principal officers, and was usually present at council meetings. The patent appointing John, Lord Dinham (d. 1501) to the office is dated 14 July 1486,[3] and there is evidence that Archbishop Rotheram in fact was retained as treasurer after his displacement as chancellor, doubtless to preserve a further degree of continuity in administrative experience.[4] But it is also clear that Dinham was appointed in February 1486 by the king's express command by the advice of his council, so that Rotheram's retention was by way of filling the gap temporarily. Lord Dinham was another outstanding instance of a man whose early career and advancement had been wholly at the favour of Edward IV and Richard III. He had materially assisted Edward to escape to Calais after the rout at Ludford in 1459, and had led the attack on Sandwich which resulted in the capture and humiliation of Lord Rivers and others. On return he became sheriff of Devon in 1460–1, a king's councillor, and was summoned to parliament in 1466 and held to be a baron thenceforth; he received a

[1] See D.N.B.

[2] C.P.R., Henry VII, I, 118; Materials, I, 495. See W. C. Richardson, Tudor chamber administration, 1485–1547 (1952), 100, fn. 45.

[3] Materials, I, 226. Extracts from payments, etc., Michaelmas Term, 1485. 'To Thomas, archbishop of York, treasurer of England, for his fee and diet, £133 6s 8d', cited by R. L. Storey, The reign of Henry VII (1968), 223.

[4] See D.N.B.; G.E.C.; L. & P., I, 14, etc.

number of grants, was appointed commander of the forces at sea in 1475, and from that year was numbered among the king's councillors. By February 1483 he had become chief steward of the duchy of Cornwall, but before the year was over he had been appointed Richard III's lieutenant of Calais, where presumably he remained until he had made his peace with Henry VII. His value to the new king must have been considerable; from him he received various grants, was appointed to many commissions, was very active as councillor, and remained in office as treasurer until his death in January 1501.[1]

Henry VII's choice of a successor to Dinham was even more remarkable, being none other than Thomas Howard, earl of Surrey (1443–1524), the only son of Richard III's stalwart supporter, John Howard, who had been created by him the first duke of Norfolk (of the Howard line) and had fought and was killed at Bosworth. Thomas Howard had followed his father in a Yorkist career, had fought for Edward IV at Barnet, been created earl of Surrey when his father was made a duke, became steward of the Household, 1483–4, and also fought for Richard III at Bosworth, when he was wounded and at first reported dead, but was captured alive, attainted, and imprisoned in the Tower. By some means, however, he placated Henry VII, who pardoned him, restored his earldom in 1489, appointed him lieutenant-warden-general of the Scottish Marches on the death of the earl of Northumberland, and advanced him in his service. His military achievements in the Yorkshire rising and against the Scots in 1497 secured him in favour. He was to hold the treasurership from 1501 to 1522, to be the victor at Flodden in 1513, and to have the dukedom of Norfolk restored to him in 1514. That he was a man of distinguished abilities and large political ambitions cannot be doubted, and Henry VII seldom showed his talent for selecting valuable servants to better advantage than when he decided to forget antecedents and win over Thomas Howard, who was doubtless eager enough to be won over. He could not anticipate that the Howard family might not always enjoy the goodwill of the Tudor dynasty.[2]

Henry VII was fortunate also in having to find only two keepers of the Privy Seal. Both for differing periods had been his companions in exile. Peter Courtenay (d. 1592), the third son of Sir Philip Courtenay of Powderham (not the same family as the Courtenays who became earls of Devon), began his career as a civil lawyer, a doctor of Oxford and perhaps Padua, had made his way and obtained preferments under Henry VI, became dean of Windsor in 1477 and bishop of Exeter in 1478. His advancement under Edward IV, however, did not induce

[1] *See D.N.B.*; G.E.C.; Richardson, op. cit. 134.   [2] *See D.N.B.*

him to support Richard III, and he joined the duke of Buckingham's plots in 1483, was attainted but fled to Brittany. He was appointed keeper of the Privy Seal as early as 8 September 1485, and was translated to the bishopric of Winchester in 1487, when he gave up the Privy Seal.[1]

His successor, Richard Fox (1448–1528), also a lawyer of Oxford, had been accepted into Henry's service straight from the University of Paris, and very soon acted as the king's secretary, probably informally in France, formally from at least November 1485. In 1487 he succeeded Courtenay both as keeper of the Privy Seal and as bishop of Exeter. He was to remain keeper until 1516, and was promoted to a bishopric from 1492. As keeper he was frequently in attendance at the council, but was extensively employed on diplomatic missions, and became Henry VII's ace negotiator.[2]

The five councillors who appear to have attended meetings most frequently without holding one of the three principal offices, and who were clearly high in the king's confidence and upon whom he relied for intimate service over many years, were very diverse types, and each appears to have brought special talents to bear upon the work of government. All five in one way or another aligned themselves with Henry before Bosworth. These were Reginald Bray, who in the earliest days of the Buckingham conspiracy enlisted at least two of the others – Giles Daubeney and Richard Guildford; the other two, Thomas Lovell and John Riseley, also joined Henry in exile. All five as councillors or holders of various offices retained great importance in Henry VII's regime and great personal influence with the king himself, in most cases for the rest of their lives. The testimony of foreign ambassadors, even though ambassadors were often wrongly informed in such matters, is of value in this connection. In 1497 the Milanese ambassador described Daubeney, Bray, and Lovell as the leading men of the realm.[3] In the same year Venice was informed that Morton and Fox, Bray, and Lovell were the king's principal ministers.[4] The following year the Spanish envoy reported that these four men, together with Daubeney, Thomas Savage, and Margaret Beaufort were the most influential persons in England.[5] It is remarkable that as late as 1507 Catherine of

---

[1] Emden, op. cit.; *D.N.B.*   [2] *Milan Cal.*, I, 335; Bayne, op. cit. xl.

[3] *Venetian Cal.*, I, 256; Bayne, ibid.

[4] *Spanish Cal.*, I, 163; Bayne, ibid. For Thomas Savage, *see* above, p. 102, fn. 7.

[5] *Spanish Cal. Supplement*, 131; Bayne, ibid. xli. It is noticeable that according to Bacon's version of the proclamation made by Warbeck in 1496 (the original of which he said was among the Cottonian MSS), Warbeck included Fox, Bray, Lovell, and Riseley, as well as Oliver King, and Empson, among the fifteen persons of whom he

Aragon could write to her father King Ferdinand and say that Daubeney was the man who could do most in private with Henry.[1]

These five councillors merit a far more detailed study than has yet been accorded to them. Here we can only sketch their careers, and much must be left to surmise. Bray and Lovell were the most important in the work of government, and both were preeminent in the sphere of finance; Daubeney's *métier* was military command, but he was clearly a great deal more than a soldier. Richard Guildford had a speciality which marks him out among the others. He was expert in military and naval engineering. John Riseley remains the least known of the five, but performed important diplomatic services, including that of acting as interpreter in 1492, and presumably therefore was more than usually expert in at least the French language; but he attended council meetings with remarkable frequency and was presumably well within the more intimate circle of councillors. All five, except Daubeney, who was in the Lords, were frequently elected members of parliament during the reign; all except Riseley became knights of the Garter.

Bray (d. 1503) had been used as the go-between by Buckingham and Morton and Margaret Beaufort in 1483.[2] Of an old Norman family, he had begun his administrative career as receiver-general to Sir Henry Stafford, Margaret Beaufort's second husband, and remained in her service, after her remarriage, and had become a member of parliament in 1478. He rendered invaluable services in the early stages of the plot. Whether he actually went into exile is not clear, but at Bosworth he became a knight banneret and a knight of the Bath at the coronation, as well as a knight of the Garter later on. He was almost at once singled out as a principal financial administrator and property manager, made chancellor of the duchy, appointed to numerous offices, mostly with financial bearings; served on about a hundred commissions of various kinds, and was a member of parliament many times. In the process he acquired a great reputation as financier and administrator, as well as large property for himself. Constantly in demand as a trustee, he seems to have escaped adverse criticism from his contemporaries.[3]

---

said Henry VII had 'none in favour and trust about his person except these, and such other caitiffs and villains of low birth' (*Henry VII*, ed. Lumby, 142). In Speed's edition of the work, Guildford is also included in the list, with two more names (ibid. 281).

[1] *See* below, p. 139.

[2] W. C. Richardson, op. cit., App., 451–8, has the fullest account; cf. R. Somerville, *Duchy of Lancaster*; *D.N.B.*; Wedgwood, *Hist. Parl.: Biographies*.

[3] W. C. Richardson, op. cit. 67 ff.; J. S. Roskell, *The Commons and their speakers*, esp. 298–9, 358–9; Wedgwood, *Hist. Parl.: Biographies*.

Thomas Lovell (1453–1524) acquired substantial financial interests and could be described by the Venetian ambassador in 1499 as the king's 'chief financial officer'. But of the five councillors he was probably preeminent in the general political sense. So far as the evidence goes, he attended more council meetings than any other man except John Morton. As the fifth son of Ralph Lovell of Barton-Bendish, Norfolk, he doubtless had to make his own way in the world, which he did by entering Lincoln's Inn and successfully following a common law career for some twenty years before he threw up the likelihood of further advancement in his profession by joining the uncertain prospects of Buckingham's rebellion in 1483. Exile and attainder followed. The impression he made upon Henry in exile must have been considerable, for after Bosworth he was very quickly appointed chancellor of the Exchequer, treasurer of the Household, an esquire of the body (i.e. a squire in attendance on the king's person) and a councillor, and was chosen to be the speaker in Henry's first parliament. He was a member of probably all the parliaments of the reign, but not again speaker. He was knighted after Stoke in 1487, appointed to numerous offices and given many rewards, including the Garter in 1503, was retained in many of his offices by Henry VIII, who gave him others as well, and he remained associated with the government until his death in 1524.[1]

Giles Daubeney (1451–1508), son and heir of William Daubeney, began his military career in the service of Edward IV. He accompanied him to France in 1475, became an esquire of the body in 1477, was knighted in 1478, and was sheriff of Somerset and Dorset in 1480–1. But he joined Buckingham's revolt in 1483, was attainted and fled into exile with Henry. He was at Bosworth, after which his attainder was reversed and he was rapidly advanced. Appointed master of the Mint and lieutenant of Calais in March 1486, he was made a baron, largely, it would seem, on the grounds of his descent from an ancestor who had been a baron by writ in the fourteenth century. He went on to the embassy in Burgundy in the same year. He was made a chamberlain of the Exchequer from December 1487; he participated in minor military successes in Flanders during the half-hearted English intervention in the Breton interest in 1489; he came closer to the king's person as chamberlain of the Household in 1495, and from then on he was a frequent attender at council meetings. He was in command of forces that had been intended to march against the Scots in 1497, and his rapid change of objective and direction enabled him, with some difficulties, to suppress the Cornish rising at Blackheath in 1497.[2] His services were

[1] See D.N.B.; G.E.C.   [2] Annali, 60, 116–19.

considerable, but it is not easy to see from his career why Catherine of Aragon should have described him in the terms that she did. Bernard André, Henry VII's poet laureate, thought fit to extol Daubeney very highly, to give him a lengthy obituary notice, and to provide him with an epitaph, whereas he scarcely mentions any of the other councillors. Daubeney, he says, was a sound, most prudent and faithful man, *'vir bonus, prudens, justus, probus, et omnibus dilectus'* (a good man, prudent, just, honest, and loved by all).[1]

Richard Guildford (1450–1506) was probably a more sophisticated man than Daubeney. He had participated with his father Sir John Guildford of Rowerden, Kent, in Buckingham's rebellion, was attainted, and fled to Brittany. He was knighted on the landing in Milford Haven, and made a chamberlain at the Exchequer, and appointed master of the Ordinance in 1485. This was a post for which he was especially fitted, as he apparently had a flair for 'engineering', and busied himself with the building of forts, artillery, and shipbuilding, and played a notable role in building up the new regime in this field. He became controller of the Household in 1492 and was frequently at council meetings. In 1499 he was commissioned with another to seek Edmund de la Pole in Flanders and try to persuade him to return.[2] A surprising change of outlook came when he decided in 1505 to set out on a pilgrimage to Jerusalem, where he died in September 1506.[3]

John Riseley's (1450–1512) place in the regime is less easy to assess. He was the son of John Riseley of Chetwode, Bucks, became an esquire of the body and accompanied Edward IV to France in 1475, and received financial favours before 1484. He did not, it seems, serve Richard III, but apparently took no part in Buckingham's insurrection. He fled to join Henry abroad, as he, like Richard Guildford, was knighted at the landing in Milford Haven. He received a number of rather minor grants and offices after the accession, and became a councillor before 1490. In that year he acted as interpreter at the reception of the French ambassador and was employed in diplomatic service of one kind or another on several occasions. He appears never to have held any important office.[4] Perhaps he should not be reckoned one of the closest advisers of the king, but he attended the council nearly as many times as Lovell, and he would not have been so fre-

---

[1] See *D.N.B.*; Wedgwood, *Hist. Parl.: Biographies*.

[2] A journal of the visit was kept by his anonymous chaplain, printed by Pynson and edited by Sir H. Ellis, (Cam. Soc., LI, 1857).

[3] See *D.N.B.*; Wedgwood, *Hist. Parl.: Biographies*.

[4] Bayne, op. cit. xliii–xlviii.

5. Henry VII as a young man, by Jacques Le Boucq, mid-sixteenth century.
Source unknown (*Library of Arras, MS. 266*)

6a. Sir Reginald Bray, *c.* 1499–1502
(*Great Malvern Priory Church, transept window*)

6b. Richard Fox, bishop of Winchester,
Johannes Corvus, *c.* 1528
(*Corpus Christi College, Oxford*)

6c. Sir Thomas Lovell, bronze relief attributed to Pietro Torrigiano. (Originally on
the gatehouse of Lovell's house at East Harling, Norfolk. *Westminster Abbey* since 1910)

quently summoned without reasons that seemed sufficient to the king himself.

The number of councillors attending a meeting of the council varied greatly. As few as four and as many as forty are recorded, and the commonest number was seven. There is no means of ascertaining what determined the summons of few or many. All depended on the circumstances of the occasion, who was available, and the nature of the business to be considered. No doubt the king's wish was the dominant factor, but the king himself would hardly decide on every occasion on each individual summons, and normally the chancellor would see to it that a suitable group of councillors was got together; and the personnel varied a good deal according to whether the business was primarily political or judicial in character. Although the council was always the King's Council whatever its business, some of the judicial work clearly called for a considerable degree of specialization, whether it was jurisdiction before the king, or exercised in Star Chamber, or of the 'requests' variety, or conducted by the 'Council Learned', or however conducted. Conciliar jurisdiction in its various forms is best considered as part of the judicial structure.

But the business of the council in Henry VII's time made no distinction between judicial and administrative work.

> So far as the evidence that we possess shows, it turned, without change of personnel or place of sitting, from dealing with foreign relations or internal administration to hear a charge of riot or decide a disputed title to land. Foreign affairs, the government of Ireland, trade and commerce, privacy, coinage, the maintenance of internal order, the government of London, city guilds, criminal trials and civil litigation, all these subjects engaged its attention at one time and another.[1]

It is not indeed possible to catalogue or specify all the subjects of conciliar concern. It is evident that any topic that might concern the king's government might engage the council's attention. Proclamations remained a royal prerogative, and most of Henry VII's were issued without mentioning the council, but nonetheless the council's agreement to some of them was obtained beforehand.

The council existed to advise the king on all or any matters as he thought fit. He himself was often but not always present, especially if the business was of a routine judicial character. Deliberation might be formal or informal, meetings large or small. That he personally intervened in deliberations, even sometimes in judicial matters, and specifically sought councillors' opinions, particularly in matters of foreign

[1] Bayne, op. cit. xlii.

E — E

policy, is clear. It is equally clear that it was advice that he sought, and that the ultimate decision in matters about which he wished to decide for himself remained with him. There is no hint that the council or any of the councillors would, or could overbear him. 'Henry was master in his own house.'[1]

<hr />

[1] Bayne, op. cit. xlv.

Chapter 5

THE SEALS AND SECRETARIATS

The elaborate secretarial organizations that had come into existence over the preceding centuries underwent little change in the reign of Henry VII, so far as we know. The Great Seal in the custody of the chancellor, the Privy Seal in that of the keeper, and the Signet Seal in that of the king's secretary, continued to be used at this time in much the same way, and for much the same purposes as they had been before. Certainly no marked change in secretarial routine is discernible. It was still normal for a petition to be approved by the sign manual and for this signed bill to constitute a warrant to the Signet office to draw up a warrant to the Privy Seal office, which repeated the process to authorize the Chancery to issue the grant under the Great Seal.[1] No attempt appears to have been made under Henry VII to curtail this long-winded and repetitive process. Whether it did not occur to anyone to try to simplify the elaborate procedure, which had grown up for historical reasons that had become largely otiose with the lapse of time, or whether the jealousies and vested interests of the offices concerned were too strong and entrenched to enable any reforming efforts to be made at this time, it is hard to say. That the vested interests were tough, and the sacrosanctity of routine hard-bound, we can well assume; but there is no evidence that any one sought to overcome either at this time. Such developments as occurred in the secretarial arrangements were therefore slight, and the result of changing circumstances rather than of any deliberate plan. The secretarial activities of the Chancery remained formal, and although legally indispensable for many purposes had little or no independent status in general administration. The Privy Seal continued to occupy a central position, as the seal for conciliar business and as easily movable for administrative purposes either by the king directly or through the Signet. The secretary and Signet remained close to the king, but as yet showed little sign of the great magnification of the practical importance they were to develop at a later period.

[1] G. R. Elton, *The Tudor revolution*, 30–1; *England under the Tudors*, 11–13; 'The problems and significance of administrative history in the Tudor period', *Journal of British Studies*, IV (1965), 18–28; and *The Tudor constitution*, 116–19; cf. S. B. Chrimes, *An introduction to the administrative history of mediaeval England*, 3rd ed. (1966), Epilogue, 241–70.

There is nothing to suggest that either Morton or Warham,[1] however important they were in other spheres, made any special mark upon the purely secretarial side of Chancery's work. Their importance as councillors has been touched upon, and their significance as judges in the court of Chancery must be considered later. For secretarial functions, the masters and clerks in Chancery proceeded in the time-honoured routine to deal with the work that required the Great Seal, moved by authority from elsewhere, the making of grants, the issuing of original writs and other sorts of writs, and serving the needs of judicial administration, and authenticating instruments of state. 'There is no sign,' we are told, 'that the routine of Chancery and the Great Seal was in any way affected in these years.'[2]

Only two keepers of the Privy Seal had to be found during the whole reign, Peter Courtenay and Fox. Peter Courtenay, bishop of Exeter from 1478, a doctor of canon laws of Padua and later of Oxford, had acted as secretary to Henry VI during the Readeption, but this did not prevent Edward IV from using him in the same capacity in 1472–4. But he had thrown in his lot with the rebellion of 1484, been attainted by Richard III, fled to Brittany, and received his reward by being appointed keeper, 8 September 1485; he retained his office until 24 February 1487, when he was further promoted to the rich see of Winchester.[3] His successor, one of the outstanding personages of the reign, was Richard Fox, whose services Henry had acquired whilst in France. Fox retained the keepership until 1516, and was promoted successively to be bishop of Bath and Wells (1492), of Durham (1494), and of Winchester (1501). He became one of the most influential of Henry VII's officers and councillors, employed especially on major diplomatic missions. He was to be the chief negotiator in the Treaty of Étaples and the 'Magnus Intercursus', the marriages of Princess Margaret with James IV and of Prince Arthur with Catherine of Aragon, and the alliance with Archduke Charles in 1508. His retention of office and influence for the first seven years of Henry VIII's reign testifies to his outstanding abilities and resource, and marks him out as one of the principal builders of the early Tudor regime. The fact that he could perform his distinguished services whilst remaining the whole time keeper of the Privy Seal made him the greatest minister to hold that

---

[1] *See above, p. 106.*

[2] G. R. Elton, *The Tudor revolution*, 30.

[3] *See D.N.B.*; Emden, *Biog. Reg. Oxf.*, sub nom.; J. Otway-Ruthven, *The King's Secretary and the Signet office in the fifteenth century* (1939), 155, 177–8; cf. above, p. 109.

office up to that date, and rounded off the long slow climb of the keeper to preeminent ministerial rank.[1]

The promotion of Fox left a vacancy in the secretaryship and Signet office[2] which Henry decided to fill by calling on the services of a former Yorkist official, Oliver King, who had been a clerk of the Signet in 1473, French secretary, 1476–80,[3] and king's secretary to Edward IV and Edward V, 1480–3. His close associations in these years did not commend themselves to Richard III, who replaced him. Henry VII, however, in 1487 thought well enough of him to appoint him in Fox's place and retained him in office apparently until November 1495, notwithstanding that he became bishop of Exeter in 1492.[4] On his translation to the see of Bath and Wells in 1495, however, he was replaced before July 1496 as secretary by Robert Sherborne,[5] an Oxford graduate who had been Morton's secretary, and was to be used as envoy at the papal court in 1496, 1502 and 1504, and to Scotland in 1503.

Sherborne became dean of St Paul's in 1499, but was replaced as king's secretary, probably to be ambassador at Rome, before he became bishop of St David's in 1505; he was translated to Chichester in 1508.[6] He was succeeded as secretary by Thomas Ruthall, a doctor of canon laws of Oxford, and an ambassador to France, in March 1500,[7] who was not only able to retain the office until 1516, when he succeeded

---

[1] For references, *see* above, p. 109. He was also the founder of Corpus Christi College, Oxford, to which he bequeathed a very large number of books and MSS. He was interested in humanism and corresponded with Erasmus; cf. Emden, *Biog. Reg. Oxf.*, *sub nom.*

[2] For the office in the period before 1485, *see* J. Otway-Ruthven, *The King's Secretary and the Signet office in the fifteenth century* (1939); and F. M. G. Evans, *The Principal Secretary of State* (1932), ch. I.

[3] He was succeeded as French Secretary by Stephen Fryon until 1490, when Francis Dupon, a former secretary to the duke of Brittany, was appointed, with John Meautis as an assistant, who from 1491 took the office and retained it until 1522. *See* J. Otway-Ruthven, op. cit. 104. A Latin secretary was appointed from 1495, with Peter Carmeliano as the first appointee; ibid. 190–1, and below, p. 307.

[4] *See* Otway-Ruthven, op. cit. 102–4, 155, 156, 159, 178–9; *D.N.B.*; and Emden, *Biog. Reg. Camb.*, *sub nom.*

[5] *Cal. Venetian P.*, I, 691, 712, 722.

[6] Emden, *Biog. Reg. Oxf.*, *sub nom*; cf. *D.N.B.*, *sub nom.* That Henry VII thought well of him is suggested by the fact that he supported him in the unsavoury episode in which Sherborne was alleged to have forged the papal bull providing him to the see of St David's; cf. G. Williams, *The Welsh church from the Conquest to the Reformation* (1962), 298, 306; Emden, *Biog. Reg. Oxf.*, III, 1686; *L. & P.*, I, 246; II, 169. He was not only extensively employed by Henry VII on foreign missions, but was used for the more undiplomatic task of extracting ruthless pecuniary penalties from Warbeck's adherents (P.V., 108).

[7] *L. & P.*, I, 132, 405, etc.; *Cal. Venetian Papers*, 795, 799.

Fox as keeper of the Privy Seal, but also to hold it with the bishopric of Durham from June 1509.[1] The fact that Ruthall retained the secretary-ship for some years after he had become a bishop is not so significant a fact as has been argued, for the precedent had apparently already been set by Oliver King. But it seems clear that Ruthall's appointment to the great see of Durham whilst continuing to be the king's secretary to Henry VIII and Wolsey's *alter ego* in foreign affairs did mark a stage in the growth of the importance of the office. But in the long run it was to prove a matter of more importance for the subsequent development of the secretaryship whether the holder was prominent in the king's council than whether he was a bishop. From William Hatcliffe's tenure of the office in the time of Edward IV, *c.* 1464, the secretary is generally found to be among the king's councillors.[2] Whilst still in the office of secretary, Fox[3] and King[4] were so to be found; so was Sherborne, and later as bishop he was a member of the Council Learned.[5] Ruthall was a member and could be required by the council 'to conceive a minute for a reasonable answer' to the archduke's letter regarding Calais,[6] and by 1504 it was thought most expedient that 'Mr Secretary' should be associated with my lord Chancellor and my lord Privy Seal to deal with diplomatic business.[7] By that time it would seem, the king's secretary was well advanced on the path to ministerial rank.

[1] Emden, *Biog. Reg. Oxf., sub nom.*; *D.N.B.*

[2] J. F. Baldwin, *The King's Council*, 424, where the name given is erroneously Hatfield; F. M. G. Evans, op. cit. 17. From the time of Thomas Cromwell, secretary from 1533, all the king's secretaries were to be laymen.

[3] Bayne, op. cit. 1, 8, 14, etc.

[4] ibid. 18.   [5] ibid. 32, xxv.   [6] ibid. 32.   [7] ibid. 38.

Chapter 6

FINANCIAL ADMINISTRATION

No man succeeded to the throne of England with such a total lack of financial experience and resources as did Henry VII. Unlike any of his predecessors, Henry VII succeeded to the crown without any personal experience of estate management, or any knowledge of financial administration. All he had had personally was dependence upon his guardian's provisions as a boy, and thereafter penury and dependence upon the charity of the duke of Brittany and of the government of France during his years of exile. The impecuniosity of his early years doubtless to some extent explains his assiduous attention to his financial interests for the rest of his life, the meticulous fostering of his revenues, and the prominence of his trusted financial agents during his reign. He could not do other than rely greatly upon those who had had experience of financial management in the past, necessarily for the most part under the Yorkist regime, and although time was needed for the due consideration of the problems and possibilities, it was not long before the usefulness of Yorkist methods of improving the royal finances was appreciated, and these methods adopted, adapted, and carried to a much higher degree of efficiency. There was to be little that was entirely novel in Henry VII's financial administration.[1] Nearly all of its methods were derived from Yorkist or even Lancastrian precedents; many of the new king's financial officers and agents, whether they had joined Henry in exile or not, had been trained and acquired their expertise in previous reigns. What was to be new was the degree of the king's sustained personal supervision and stimulus in financial matters, and the measure of success attained in rehabilitating the royal revenues. The time came when annually the rate of expenditure was substantially less than the annual income, and the Crown obtained an unwonted spell of solvency. Henry VII undoubtedly enjoyed his personal affluence. It was not just

---

[1] F. C. Dietz, *English government finance, 1485–1558* (1921, repr. 1964), was insufficiently aware of the Yorkist precedents and consequently exaggerated the novelty of Henry VII's Chamber organization. The indispensable background and correctives are provided by B. P. Wolffe, 'The management of English royal estates under the Yorkist kings', *E.H.R.*, LXXI (1956), 1–27; and 'Henry VII's land revenues and Chamber finance', ibid. LXXIX (1964), 225–54; and now more fully in his *The royal demesne in English history* (1971).

that he could and did maintain his court in magnificence and thereby impressed his subjects and foreign powers; he could and did display liberality in pecuniary gifts (all meticulously recorded by his clerks) to a great variety of those who pleased him in important or in trivial matters, or who sought his charity.[1] Much more than a question of personal affluence was involved; it was a question of adequately financing the king's government in nearly all its aspects. Whether or not Henry VII had ever imbibed Fortescue's wise views on 'the harme that comyth off a kynges poverte', passed on perhaps by Jasper Tudor and John Morton, he certainly acted in the spirit of the Lancastrian chief justice's conclusion that 'we most holde it for undoubted that ther mey no reaume prospere, or be worshipfull, under a poure kynge'.[2]

Inevitably in the circumstances of his accession, it took time for Henry VII to obtain knowledge of the financial procedures that were open to him, and to consider and devise the arrangements that were to prove to be the most advantageous and eventually to be characteristic of his reign. Necessarily at first he could not do other than rely mainly upon the Exchequer for the administration of his revenues. The Household of Richard III ceased to exist with the death of the king, and with it the financial organization of the chamber upon which the Yorkist kings had pivoted their financial innovations. It was not possible at first to exempt from Exchequer audit and divert from Exchequer coffers the large land revenues that for many years had been collected by special receivers and paid direct into the chamber. The pressing necessity was to get in the proceeds of the parliamentary grants of 1485 and 1486 of such landed revenues as existed, augmented by the fruits of the acts of resumption of 1485–7, as quickly as possible, and to provide for the immediate needs of the government. It was the Exchequer,[3] therefore, that received a sudden and substantial increase of income from the endowed revenues soon after the accession of Henry VII, and for some four years the Exchequer was not only by far the most important

[1] See extracts from the account books of the chamber, as printed by S. Bentley, Excerpta historica (1831), 85–133; passim; and below, Appendix E. On these accounts, most of which are still unpublished, see W. C. Richardson, Tudor Chamber administration, 1485–1547 (Louisiana, 1952), App. III, 463–6. Professor Richardson's monograph is invaluable for the whole subject, even though over-weighted with detail and somewhat repetitive in arrangement. A. P. Newton's pioneer essay, 'The King's Chamber under the early Tudors', E.H.R., XXXII (1917), 348–72, is still a valuable short survey.

[2] Sir John Fortescue, The governance of England, ed. C. Plummer (1885), 119–20.

[3] B. P. Wolffe, 'Henry VII's land revenues', loc. cit. 239. A useful short account of Exchequer methods is contained in G. R. Elton, The Tudor revolution in government 1955), 20–30.

financial agency but seemed to be well on its way to recovering the accounting supremacy it had enjoyed before the Yorkist magnification of the chamber. For the first ten years of the reign the land receipts in the chamber remained small and less than the total attained under the Yorkist kings. But in the course of the second ten years the total greatly increased and almost the entire revenues were handled by the chamber. But the process of reviving Yorkist policy and carrying it out further in practice took time; suitable financial officers had to be found; the advantages of diverting accounts and cash away from the Exchequer to a chamber organization close to the king himself had to be appraised. But the time came when the fullest effect was given to that policy, and the supervision of the bulk of the revenues was brought to the king himself or his immediate nominees.[1]

We have seen the remarkable continuity in the tenure of the office of treasurer of England, with Lord Dinham and Thomas Howard, earl of Surrey, as the only holders of the office for the whole reign, after the first few months.[2] The same observation has to be made regarding the office of under-treasurer. Two holders of that office, of more practical importance than the treasurership in Exchequer business, spanned almost the entire reign. Two holders certainly, but perhaps one should add a third, and that one no less a person than Reginald Bray, who as early as 16 October 1485 was being described as 'under-treasurer of England', as well as chancellor of the duchy of Lancaster.[3] He continued to be so described from time to time, but no formal appointment has ever been found. If Alfred Cornburgh, who was Richard III's under-treasurer, remained in office after Bosworth, the probability is that Bray was appointed informally to keep an eye on him and the Exchequer, and to keep a grip on that side of the financial administration, for a period. But what exactly that period was remains unknown at present. Alfred Cornburgh had been a servant of the Crown from 1455, as a yeoman of the chamber and controller of mines, as a sheriff, and as a soldier by land and sea. He served Edward IV well and became under-treasurer by April 1485 and remained in that office until his death in 1487, and was keeper of the Great Wardrobe as well during his last year. He was a member of parliament at least five times, but was essentially the permanent official, whose career survived and bridged all the political vicissitudes from 1455.[4]

His successor in the office, Robert Lytton, knighted in 1494, was

[1] Wolffe, loc. cit. *passim.*   [2] *See* above, p. 107.
[3] Richardson, op. cit. 67, 100.
[4] ibid. 44n, 86, 100n, 107; and Wedgwood, *Hist. Parl.: Biographies.*

another survivor of the Yorkist regime, who had been a clerk of the Exchequer from 1470, clerk of the Issues, 1478, promoted to be under-treasurer and councillor from 1487, apparently until his death in 1505, keeper of the Great Wardrobe from 1492, and treasurer at war 1501–2.[1] As for the chancellorship of the Exchequer, this office was held for the whole reign by Sir Thomas Lovell and he combined it with the treasurership of the Household for very nearly the whole reign. Only five persons appear to have been appointed chamberlains of the Exchequer during the reign. These were such prominent figures as Sir William Stanley, Sir Richard Edgecombe, Sir Richard Guildford, Giles, Lord Daubeney, who replaced Guildford at the end of 1487, and Sir Sampson Norton, who had been master of the Ordinance and a soldier, who replaced Sir William Stanley after his dismissal and execution in 1495.

These then were the high officials in the Exchequer of Henry VII, and if, as we are given to understand, it was the under-treasurer of England who was the effectual head in practice, then there can be no doubt that Sir Robert Lytton was the key man, but of him little is at present known. But it is evident that Henry VII could have experienced little difficulty in imposing on the Exchequer whatever policies and procedures he wished to adopt, even though there might be friction between the barons of the Exchequer over the question of 'foreign accounts', and equally clear that the time came when he decided to reverse the process whereby the Exchequer in the early years of his reign had regained its financial preeminence, and to revive the dominance of the chamber.

Whether or not Henry VII carried out completely the plans for the reform of financial administration envisaged by Richard III,[2] there can be no doubt that the Yorkist policy of making special arrangements for the management and accounting of revenue from crown lands had produced results sufficiently promising to induce Henry VII, when he had had time to appreciate the advantages, to emulate these arrangements and to carry them further with a drive and vigour exceeding anything that the Yorkists were able to use. The need to tackle the problem was all the greater because the circumstances of the reign

[1] Wedgwood, *Hist. Parl.: Biographies.*

[2] The text is printed in Chrimes and Brown, *Select documents*, No. 304, pp. 358–60, from *L. & P.*, ed. J. Gairdner, I, 81–5. The document is discussed by B. P. Wolffe, 'The management of royal estates', loc. cit. The memorandum is perhaps too terse to be fully intelligible. Mr T. Brynmor Pugh has made the suggestion that the memorandum may in fact have been composed in the early years of Henry VII's reign, on the grounds that the implication in the text may be that the duchy of Norfolk was forfeit at the time. But this is hardly a conclusive argument, even if the implication can be sustained.

magnified the extent of the territories in the Crown's hands. Further acts of resumption, forfeitures following upon numerous convictions for treason, and determined exploitation of feudal rights, all combined to make the Crown lands a potential source of large revenues. It was not a question of desiring to undermine the Exchequer system as such; it is misleading to speak of 'a breakdown of the Exchequer system'.[1] The fact was, as the Yorkists had realized, that the Exchequer had at no time been competent to organize the effective administration of Crown lands, to enhance their profitability, or to cope with the immensely detailed work of estate management, most of which necessarily had to be done locally. The Exchequer could, in its laborious and slow ways, audit the accounts of receivers and such agents, if routine so required, but mere audit was not enough. The responsibility for management, collection of revenues and accounting must be pinned down upon care-fully selected agents and the results of their labours supervised by persons close to the king, or even by the king himself, if the king were to be satisfied that he was actually receiving all that could be obtained from these sources. Once the advantages of side-tracking the Exchequer in these processes had been grasped, it doubtless followed inevitably that the actual cash accruing should also be diverted away from the Exchequer of Receipt and paid into 'a counting house' very close to the king himself, and all the precedents for this purpose pointed to the chamber of the Household. It was not difficult to provide for the resump-tion of a normal flow of cash from the Exchequer to the Household departments, including the chamber, for current expenses, as well as for the payment of the wages of the king's officials in general, and this was done under letters of Privy Seal as early as 24 December 1485.[2] But it took longer to attempt the task of appointing *ad hoc* receivers of Crown lands. The preamble to the act of resumption of 1487 admitted the fact. Henry, it was stated, had been so busy for the defence of the Church of England, his own royal person and his realm since the beginning of his reign that he and his council had so far not found time to 'set, make nor ordain Receivers, Auditors . . . and other officers accountants, such as should be to his profit and avail, nor providently make leases, grants . . . by occasion whereof, his honours, manors, lands, tenements, possessions and inheritances be greatly fallen in decay, and further in decay shall daily fall: if remedy in this behalf be not provided . . .'.[3]

The crisis ending with the battle of Stoke was now passed; the act of resumption itself brought much business in land into the Crown's

[1] As W. C. Richardson, op. cit. 41–57.   [2] *Materials*, I, 217–19.
[3] *R.P.*, VI, 403, cited by B. P. Wolffe, 'Henry VII's land revenues', loc. cit. 233.

purview, and the forfeitures after the battle added to the accumulation. Soon steps were taken to remedy the deficiencies in administrative mechanism in these connections. The same act annulled all grants of office of receivers and auditors, etc. and revoked all leases on the royal manors and lordships to enable new leases to be made for the king's 'most profit and approvement of his revenues'. In 1495 similar action was taken as regards leases in the principality of Wales.[1] This action was doubtless the result of Reginald Bray's advice, for as early as 28 February 1486 he had been given a commission to look into the whole problem of the landed revenues in the duchy of Lancaster. The king, it was said, had been given to understand that he and his progenitors had suffered great loss in the duchy by negligent feodaries, receivers, and bailiffs. Bray, therefore, was instructed to discharge, with the advice of the council of the duchy, all officers who should fail to act diligently and profitably and to appoint others in their place.[2] The experience gained by Bray as chancellor of the duchy presumably stood him in good stead as one of the chief financial advisers of the king, and he was in a very strong position to guide the royal policy in the right directions. Once again, as in the past, the experience acquired in the estate management of the duchy could be turned to royal advantage.

By 17 May 1488 the point was reached of appointing a commission under the terms of the act of resumption of 1487 with authority to nominate auditors and receivers, farmers, customers, ulnagers, and other accounting officers in England, and to let to farm all castles, honours, and lordships to sufficient persons according to the value thereof. The commissioners, who were thus given large power to overhaul the management of Crown lands, were Richard Fox, bishop of Exeter, the keeper of the Privy Seal, Dinham, the treasurer, Robert Lytton, the under-treasurer, Sir William Hody, the chief baron of the Exchequer, Sir Reginald Bray, and Thomas Savage, clerk.[3] No list of all the officers appointed or reappointed by these commissions has so far been compiled, but enough names have become known to make it clear that some of the most experienced Yorkist appointees were among them.[4] Many of these men had in previous years been accustomed not to have to account at the Exchequer, but to conciliar or *ad hoc* auditors, and to see the revenues they collected paid direct into the chamber. The advantages of such methods could hardly remain concealed from the king's

---

[1] *R.P.*, VI, 405.

[2] *Materials*, I, 324. Dietz, op. cit. 26, failed to note that Bray's commission related only to the duchy of Lancaster.

[3] *C.P.R.*, I, 230.   [4] B. P. Wolffe, loc. cit. 224-5.

chief financial advisers, nor therefore from the king himself, and before very long, even though gradually, these well-tried methods were being revived. By 2 March 1493, for example, Bray himself, with two others, receivers of the Warwick, Salisbury, and Spencer lands, and of lands lately belonging to William, marquis of Berkeley, Lord Morley, and Earl Rivers, were instructed by the king, on the advice of his council, to pay their issues into the king's own hands and nowhere else, and submit their accounts to be 'overseen and examined' by the king and his council. As from Michaelmas 1491, the barons of the Exchequer were commanded to cease all process against these receivers and were restricted merely to requiring delivery of accounts for custody into the Exchequer from the 'foreign auditors' only after they had been determined by the king and council.[1]

No general rule exempting receivers of Crown lands from Exchequer process seems ever to have been made. Each case appears to have been considered on merits, and receivers had to earn Henry's approbation by reputation and efficiency before such exemptions were made, and then granted only to the individuals concerned. Numerous examples of such exonerations exist, but little specific information is available as to who the auditors were – 'the king and some councillors' is as precise a description as can be given. But a number of the resulting 'declarations of account' survive, and 'there can be no doubt whatsoever that the work of all these receivers, foreign auditors and conciliar surveyors was under the closest personal supervision of the king'.[2] All the relevant documents reveal the immense personal labour in which the development of his chamber of Receipt, fed by these officials, relentlessly involved Henry.

The effect on the amount of receipts in the chamber of the diversion to it of general income and land revenue can be shown from the chamber books that survive. These run from 4 July 1487 to 4 July 1489; from 30 September 1489 to 1 October 1495; and from 1 October 1502 to 1 October 1505. The first book shows that Thomas Lovell, the treasurer of the chamber, had no balance in hand on 4 July 1487 (he must however have had some receipts during the preceding period and a reference is made in this book to an earlier book), but received £10,491 during the next twelve months. The yearly average receipts for the period covered by these three books were: total £17,000, land revenues £3,000; total £27,000, land revenues £11,000; total £105,000, land revenues £40,000. These figures were still smaller than in the late Yorkist period,

[1] ibid. 241.   [2] ibid. 240-4.

but they were to increase substantially over the remaining years of the reign and it has been calculated that some four-fifths of the total average annual revenue of about £113,000 (c. £42,000 from land revenues) found its way into the chamber.[1]

The immense increase in the receipts and responsibilities of the chamber could not be handled without a development in the personnel and organization of the chamber itself. Once policy determined that the chamber should be not only revived but elevated into the chief financial office it was necessary to find the right men to head it, and to take such steps as might be necessary to free it from Household entanglements and complications. Henry, almost always felicitous in his choice of officers, had to find only two treasurers of the chamber for the whole reign. Richard III had formally appointed Edward Chaderton to the office in April 1484 in succession to the unfortunate Sir Thomas Vaughan whom he, as duke of Gloucester, had found it expedient to eliminate along with Anthony Woodville, Earl Rivers, on 23 June 1483. Chaderton continued in Henry VII's service in various capacities, but was displaced as treasurer of the chamber by the redoubtable Thomas Lovell in the autumn of 1485.[2] We may well believe that Lovell, with the financially ubiquitous Reginald Bray in the very near background, was the architect of the revived chamber system, and that these two between them prepared the ground so thoroughly that it was possible by 1492 for Lovell's assistant accountant in the chamber, John Heron, to succeed him as treasurer and to retain the office for little less than thirty years, far into the reign of Henry VIII. Sir John Heron, as he became before April 1515,[3] was destined to fulfil the role of a key figure in early Tudor financial administration; an accountant rather than a minister, but a civil servant, or at least a court official *par excellence*, without whose meticulously kept account books, scrutinized and initialled by Henry VII himself very frequently, we should be greatly impoverished (as indeed the king himself would have been).

The gradual elevation of the chamber into the major financial

---

[1] B. P. Wolffe, loc. cit. 237–8.   [2] W. C. Richardson, op. cit. 93, 111–12.

[3] ibid. 114–16. The difficulties of ascertaining the date when Heron actually became treasurer of the chamber are however brought out by J. R. Hooker in his valuable article, 'Some cautionary notes on Henry VII's Household and chamber system', *Speculum*, XXXIII (1958), 69, 75. Lovell was still being referred to in some records as the chamber treasurer as late as 1505–6, notwithstanding his appointment to be treasurer of the Exchequer in 1492. The evidence suggests that Lovell remained the chamber treasurer, whilst Heron, whose salary continued to be paid as a 'servant' from the chamber until 1506, and kept the accounts all the time, acted as Lovell's deputy in the chamber from 1492 until he was appointed treasurer of the chamber in 1506.

bureau, with its treasurer becoming the principal financial officer and after 1492 the effective head receiver-general of all the newer Crown revenues, was facilitated by some reorganization within the Household and the chamber itself.[1] The Wardrobe continued to be the nucleus of the Household, but its keeper became merely a court official, whilst a number of separate Household 'chambers' dealt with the financial arrangements for various branches of the Household. It was the king's 'privy chamber' that was built up to cope with its enlarged business. It was staffed with a number of gentlemen, serjeants, yeomen, grooms, servers, messengers, ushers, and pages, resident at court and in close attendance in varying ways according to their status and capabilities. Some of them could be used to serve on general commissions, special missions, confidential enquiries, and administrative tasks. It was from this larger class of Household officials that the lesser Tudor ministers were drawn. Practically all the newer civil servants who attained the important stewardships, masterships, receiverships, and surveyorships prior to 1547 had risen from their ranks.

The financial business of the chamber, however, was carried on by a comparatively small group of clerks and accountants under the treasurer. Before long the king's Jewel House, the depository for cash and jewels associated with the chamber, grew so much in importance as its deposits multiplied that its keepership was separated from the treasurership. To the keepership Sir William Tyler was appointed, though the real work was done by the clerk, Sir Henry Wyatt,[2] whose effective management and devotion to the king's service in a variety of ways both enhanced the importance of the Jewel House as a sort of 'private bank' for the king, and advanced Wyatt's own position. He succeeded to the office of keeper, probably in 1486, and retained the office for the rest of the reign, was continued in it by Henry VIII, who showed him much favour, and promoted him to the treasurership of the chamber in 1524.

The process of development whereby the treasurer of the chamber became in effect the receiver-general of Crown revenues was a slow one. No doubt John Heron performed his functions for some years under the supervision of the two prominent financial administrators, Bray and Lovell, and remained overshadowed by these powerful personages. But the time came, by about 1500, when Heron was clearly the chief of the Receipt division of the chamber, the general receiver of all revenues of Crown lands and all forms of revenues not processed in the Exchequer,

[1] ibid. 58–78, 84–109.   [2] ibid. 99.

the controller of disbursements and the keeper of the accounts. He received the payments and accounts of the particular receivers of the estates of Lancaster, Cheshire, and other units of Crown lands, of Calais, Berwick, and the merchants of the Staple, of the chamberlains of Wales, the customers, the agents for the sale of offices, wardships and marriages, and the collection of fines for favours or grace, and of the agents who collected the profits from prerogative rights. In 'Heron's house within the sanctuary of Westminster', i.e. the chamber office, were deposited all manner of financial documents, indentures, lists of debts, recognizances and obligations, tallies for uncollected sums, and the like. The profits of the Hanaper were paid in to him, and the proceeds of transactions with Italian and other financiers. Many of the sums paid into his hands were small, but some were large, and by 1505-9 the annual receipts were totally more than £100,000 a year.[1] Periodically he submitted his accounts to the king himself, who personally scrutinized them. By 1506 it was possible to describe Heron as the 'general receiver to our sovereign lord'.

The monies paid into the chamber were mainly intended for immediate or speedy use. Sometimes advances were made to the Exchequer or Household departments; it constantly financed the private expenses of the king. It paid the salaries and wages of officials, disbursed alms, and rewards; paid the costs of espionage, defrayed the costs of regalia and clothing of the king's navy and soldiers. The excess of income over expenditure was seldom great in any one year, but such surpluses were frequently invested in jewels and plate or used to float loans of one kind or another.

John Heron's handling of these large responsibilities was such as to earn him golden opinions for his efficiency and honesty. When the time came for Henry VIII to consider his position with regard to the chamber and its treasurer, he could hardly have paid a greater compliment to both than the one he adopted. He himself was not going to take the close personal interest in the accounts and business of the chamber that his father had done. But he in effect departmentalized the chamber and by a statutory declaration confirmed all the acts of 'his trusty servant John Heron his general receiver'.[2] Henceforth the treasurers of

---

[1] W. C. Richardson, op. cit. 114-16, 161-6, 217-19.
[2] St. 1 Henry VIII, c. 3; S.R., III, 2. 'Wher as the Kyng oure Souveraign Lorde entendythe that divers Revenues and Duetys dewe and to be dewe to hys Highness shalbe payde to his trusty servant John Heyron his general Receyvor and to other Persones by his Highness hereafter in lyke office to be deputed and assigned as in the tyme of the late Kyng of famus memory Henry the VIIth hath been used. . . .'

the chamber were officially also the king's receivers-general, and the Exchequer officials could no longer attempt to contest the validity of chamber audits of accounts, as they had occasionally done in Henry VII's reign. But the time would arrive later on when the Exchequer would come into its own again and the chamber and its system would sink back into a minor role.[1]

Two of the interests and substantial sources of revenue falling within the scope of chamber finance were sufficiently specialized and coherent to inspire further departmentalism in Henry VII's time. The proper exploitation of the profits of wardship could be lucrative. In the earlier years of the reign, up to as late as 1503, the disposal of wardships and marriages was handled in a haphazard fashion mainly either by Bray or the king himself, who disposed of many of them either by favour or by sale. For some years the proceeds remained small, only £350 in 1487, rising to £1,588 in 1494, but reaching £6,000 by 1506–7. Before then, in 1503, a special officer was appointed to supervise the management of the business, the master or surveyor of the King's Wards, with Sir John Hursey as the first appointee, to be succeeded in 1513 by Sir Thomas Lovell.[2] The foundations were now laid for the future statutory court of Wards set up in 1540.[3]

The king himself retained a close interest in the evaluation and final dispersal of his rights in wardships and marriages, and he himself would often assess the relevant obligations and fines. But wardships and marriages were only one strand in the tangled skeins of the king's prerogative rights, most of which sprang from the king's ancient rights as feudal overlord. The deliberate intent to ferret out and exploit to the full the financial rights of the king arising from tenurial obligations was unquestionably a major feature of Henry VII's financial policy,[4] and must be considered later. Here we are concerned only to note that the legal problems and administrative complexities of the policy were great, especially after decades of comparative neglect consequential upon the civil wars and local disturbances. No doubt for these reasons in the early years of the reign no better device for reviving and exploiting the rights was resorted to than the appointment of numerous *ad hoc* commissions to enquire into concealed lands (i.e. lands legally held in chief of the king but concealed from the officials who should enforce the king's financial interests therein), into escheats, reliefs, wardships, licences for the marriage of the king's wards and widows, and the like. But though the growing revenues from the prerogative sources mostly found their

[1] W. C. Richardson, op. cit. 414–41.   [2] ibid. 166–75.
[3] St. 32 Henry VIII, c. 46; *S.R.*, III, 802–7.   [4] *See* below, p. 209 ff.

way into the chamber, for many years no consolidated centralized machinery for the management of the business was devised until the last year of the reign. A precedent for the establishment of an officer specifically charged with these duties had been set in October 1499, when William Sever (or Senhouse), bishop of Carlisle, had been appointed receiver and surveyor of the king's prerogative rights in the northern parts, i.e. Cumberland, Westmorland, and Yorkshire.[1] Not until August 1508 was 'a surveyor of the king's prerogative' set up, with an office organization and wide powers.[2] Edward Belknap, an esquire of the body, who was to figure prominently in the financial administration of Henry VIII's reign, was the first surveyor appointed. But although Belknap was not formally relieved of his office until 1513, it seems that the function of his post effectively ceased with the death of Henry VII. Whatever the reasons for this suspension of the short-lived activities of this particular organization may have been, the activities themselves were carried on in different ways.[3] Henry VIII was not going to forgo the financial profits of his prerogative rights, even though he found it expedient at his accession to make modifications and provide scapegoats as concessions, more apparent than real, to the popular reaction against his father's methods. The office of Wards remained to administer not only wardships, but the other prerogative rights, whilst after 1509 the general surveyors of Crown lands took over the supervision of all the chamber estates, including lands acquired by forfeiture and prerogative rights incidental to feudal tenure. Among the general surveyors appointed early in the new reign figure Sir Robert Southwell, Bartholomew Westby, and Belknap himself,[4] all three of whom had been prominent in one capacity or another in Henry VII's administration.

Southwell and Westby had both emerged into some eminence in Henry's VII's financial affairs as auditors in the chamber system. *Ad hoc* audits of particular accounts, of units of Crown lands, of specific sources of revenues, were one thing; but it was quite another thing to

---

[1] W. C. Richardson, op. cit. 136-9. He was translated to Durham in 1502, and was succeeded by Roger Leybourne at Carlisle.

[2] *C.P.R.*, II, 591.

[3] ibid. 192-214; and 'The surveyor of the King's Prerogative', *E.H.R.*, LVI (1941), 52-75. Professor Richardson's valuable account of this office is somewhat coloured by his mistaken conception that 'the prerogative rights' in question had some equivalence to later ideas of 'sovereignty'. The prerogative rights however meant at this time little more than either the king's financial interests in the criminal law or in the incidents of feudal tenure.

[4] On Southwell, *see* W. C. Richardson, *Tudor chamber administration*, App. II, 455-462, 177-9; on Westby, ibid. 251-3; on Belknap, ibid. 201-5.

provide for the audit of the accounts of the chamber itself. It seems clear that the ultimate auditor of these accounts was the king himself; this is the conclusion to be drawn from the frequent initialling of pages of chamber accounts with the royal sign manual. 'Both Lovell and Heron as Treasurers of the Chamber presented their Chamber account "to the king's highness", who regularly examined them, weekly, monthly, or quarterly. When the accounts were thus accepted and signed by the king, the accountants were discharged without any other accompt or reckoning.' But necessarily much preparatory work in auditing chamber accounts and in preparing 'declarations' of account needed to be done, and was done, by officers charged with the task. There is no evidence that such an office of Audit was part of the chamber itself, nor that the officers concerned were regarded as a 'committee of the council', though they might be deemed councillors or members of the Council Learned. Reginald Bray might perform the essential function himself in the early years of the reign, but the time came when the task was being undertaken regularly by the two officials, Bray's former assistant Sir Roger Southwell, and Roger Leybourne, bishop of Carlisle (who was succeeded by Bartholomew Westby, a baron of the Exchequer, in 1509), and their activities were sufficiently regular and judicial in character as to become recognized as 'a court of audit meeting habitually in the Prince's Chamber at Westminster'. By February 1505 it was possible even for an indenture to be entered into between Southwell and Carlisle as the king's principal auditors and the barons of the Exchequer to clarify the relative claims of the two parties to be the final auditors of certain accounts.

The general accounts or declarations, three of which survive, were drawn up annually by Southwell and submitted to the king for final scrutiny. The under-treasurer at the Exchequer was also required to submit an annual summary or 'declaration of the state of the treasury', so that Henry VII was in a position to obtain knowledge of the state of his finances, at least in the later years of his reign.[1]

In these tentative and somewhat informal ways, the problem of audit was solved in Henry VII's time. That it worked reasonably satisfactorily seems assured by the fact that the court of Auditors continued to function until it was merged into the statutory court of General Surveyors of Henry VIII.[2]

That Henry VII's government succeeded in developing a chamber organization efficient in receiving and accounting for the great bulk of

[1] *See* generally, ibid. 176–91.
[2] ibid. 257 ff; St. 27 Henry VIII, c. 62; *S.R.*, III, 631–2.

the royal revenue, and in making disbursements according to the king's will, and the needs of the moment, whether for large expenses of State or for trivial purposes, can hardly be doubted. It is perhaps odd that it was thought proper for the treasurer of the chamber to record precisely every item of insignificant expenditure down to the last shilling or penny, little sums for the king's losses at gaming, for small gifts and rewards, all lumped together with expenditure sometimes of thousands of pounds for the army and navy or foreign loans and payments. It is surprising that no attempt at analysing and classifying expenditure seems to have been made, and that Henry VII, so closely and intimately concerned with his accounts as he was, should not, apparently, have interested himself in what proportions of his income were being disbursed on what sort of expenses. A certain naivety and lack of sophistication seem to have been characteristic of his handling of financial affairs. It remains something of a mystery why it took so many years to establish the chamber system – if 'system' is the right word.[1] It is not obvious why years passed before the arrangements became fully effective. It is not clear to us why the flow of revenues into the chamber could not have been increased much more rapidly and earlier in the reign than it was. The Yorkist precedents were there, and many of the officials employed by Henry VII must have been well aware of the advantages accruing to the Crown from the exploitation of these methods. But doubtless there were many obstacles to be overcome, difficulties to be ironed out, and time was required before Henry could know which officials and agents were trustworthy and reliable and what methods were practicable in the changed political circumstances. The reign of Edward IV and its useful examples was in any event separated in time by the interlude of Richard III's usurpation, and although Richard's financial administration had not differed materially from his brother's, it must have been politically and psychologically difficult for Henry to follow

---

[1] Some of the difficulties in regarding Henry VII's chamber organization as a clearcut system are rightly emphasized by J. R. Hooker, loc. cit. Mr Hooker calls attention to Professor G. R. Elton's well-justified observation (*Tudor revolution in government* (1957), 9) that Professor W. C. Richardson's term 'chamber system' covers too much when he uses it to describe all the administrative changes of the first two Tudors and that he speaks too definitely of 'offices' (Audit office, office of Wards) where it may be preferable to speak of individuals working in a somewhat unorganized and haphazard manner. Mr Hooker appears to be right when he says (loc. cit. 75), 'One should hesitate to conclude that men administered because they occupied certain posts. In fact they administered because Henry authorized them to do so and not by virtue of powers inherent in specific offices. So much depended upon personality and proximity to the throne, that it is impossible to separate performers from performance.'

too quickly and too closely the methods of the usurper. Caution and some degree of experimentation were no doubt imperative, apart from preoccupations with more pressingly urgent affairs for several years at least. In any event the sources of royal revenues were so diverse and miscellaneous in character, each encased in its own traditional usages and complications, that the problems of administration would have baffled a far more experienced financier than Henry VII. The chamber and its satellites were too close to and too dependent upon the king himself to survive the succession of a differently-minded king, and did not in fact survive more than a few decades. Moreover, although the chamber of Henry VII could cope with receiving, disbursing, and accounting, it was inadequate to deal with all the problems connected with the applications of financial policy[1] and the exaction of debts to the king. It could not take punitive action; it could not haggle; it had not the legal expertise and authority to act in any sort of judicial or quasi-judicial capacity. For these sorts of activity Henry VII resorted to his Council Learned from 1500 at latest. The Council Learned acted not only as a court of law for the adjudication of cases, based partly on private suits, but mostly on government prosecutions. It was also a Royal debt-collecting agency. It could and did call upon Crown debtors to pay their debts or to appear and show cause why they should not. It used the weapon of the Privy Seal and applied the screw.[2] Its two members most prominent in these connections, Richard Empson and Edmund Dudley, could be later called *judices fiscales*.[3] It, or its members, could extract payments-down from debtors and impose bonds and recognizances for the later payment of balances. The debts it sought to collect were doubtless for the most part lawfully incurred, but its methods of collection were not known to the common law and were very open to abuse; its debasement of the dignity and authority of the King's Council to such purposes was not likely to endear it to the public nor to enhance the prestige of the king's highness. It did not survive the king himself, and the time would come when the old Exchequer, with its established judicial and accounting methods, supplemented by those

---

[1] For financial policy generally, *see* below, ch. 11.

[2] Many Privy Seal writs exist ordering the payment of monies to John Heron, treasurer of the chamber, often of unspecified amount but all described as a debt due to the king, or else to appear before the Council Learned on a certain day (Somerville, loc. cit. 435). Dudley's account book of sums received by him, presumably mainly as a member of the Council Learned, for the use of the king, from 9 September 1504 to 28 May 1508, survives in B.M. Lansdowne MS. 127. The entries for each day are initialled by Henry VII himself; cf. Dietz, op. cit. 38.

[3] P.V. (ed. Hay), 133 fn.

parts of Henry VII's 'chamber system' that could earn a statutory recognition, would revive.[1]

[1] Henry VII himself took steps to improve the machinery of the Receipt of the Exchequer at least by 1504–5, if not earlier. The under-treasurer and teller took over custody of money from the Treasury chamberlains, who became more specifically honorific in character. The multiplicity of rolls kept was reduced. The Issue rolls were abolished and two of the Receipt rolls; transactions were recorded in the tellers' rolls only and these were the basis for the compilation of the annual Declaration of the state of the Treasury from at least 1504–5. cf. G. R. Elton, op. cit. 24, citing an early seventeenth-century description in B.M. Lansdowne MS. 151, fos 104–6.

Chapter 7

PARLIAMENTS
AND GREAT COUNCILS

Little or nothing of much significance occurred in the history of parliament in the reign of Henry VII; or, in other words, parliament as an institution was not in any way notably different at the dissolution in 1504 of Henry's seventh parliament from what it had been at the meeting of his first parliament in 1485. The precedents already set over the previous century or so were followed; there were no significant innovations in procedure, so far as we know; no change in composition or electoral arrangements; few legislative measures enacted were of any great importance. No change in the relations between the king's government and any part of parliament occurred. The summonses of parliament were infrequent, only seven in the whole reign, and in the assembly of 1504, the king expressly stated that he was not minded for the ease of his subjects to summon another for a long time without 'grete and necessarye and urgent causes'.[1] Throughout the twenty-three years and eight months of the reign, parliaments sat for about seventy-two weeks in all.[2] But Great Councils, lords without the commons, were summoned five or six times, and the continued existence of these assemblies has to be borne in mind if the consultative activities of Henry's government are to be assessed.[3]

For certain purposes, however, Henry VII, like his predecessors for more than a hundred and fifty years, could not do without the representative parliament. First and foremost, he could not do without financial grants in parliamentary form, and each of his seven parliaments made some kind of fiscal contribution.[4] He must also have parliamentary assent to numerous acts of attainder[5] and of restitution for those previously attainted; and for the substantial acts of resumption

---

[1] *R.P.*, VI, 526.

[2] G. R. Elton, *The Tudor constitution* (1960), 228, unaccountably says, 'perhaps twenty-five weeks'; R. L. Storey, *Reign of Henry VII* (1968), 118, says, 'fifty-nine weeks'.   [3] *See* below, p. 141.   [4] *See* below, p. 195 ff.

[5] The judges held that an attainder without the assent of the commons was invalid. *See Y.B. 4 Henry VII, Mich.*, pl. 11, reprinted in Chrimes, op. cit. 382; and Pollard, *Henry VII*, II, 19.

that it was his policy to obtain. Inevitably the measures of importance to the government were initiated by the government, and the attempts that have been made to distinguish between official bills and commons bids as the sources of statutes, in so far as the attempts are not illusory, have not resulted in any very significant conclusions.[1] Few of the statutes that emerged from Henry VII's parliaments can be regarded as of major importance; many are little more than administrative improvements; some are trivial or transitory; few amended the common law.[2] Undoubtedly the commons could have initiated bills that might have become important statutes, but in fact they did not do so. At best the government procured some measures which seemed to it sufficiently worthwhile to procure parliamentary sanction for them. But it is difficult to believe that the reign of Henry VII was particularly notable for its legislative activity.[3]

As yet no one spoke of the 'Houses of Parliament', though references to 'Parliament House', and 'Common House' are quite frequent, and the latter expression had already some years earlier come to bear a certain institutional as distinct from a merely locative sense.[4] The 'Common House' was sometimes called the 'lower house', an expression which would imply the existence of an 'upper house'. The phrase 'Higher House before the Lords' did appear as early as 1454, but remained rare. There was as yet no such term as the lords' house or House of Lords.[5] There was no need for such a term, for the lords' house *was* the Parliament House. A contemporary document expresses the realities neatly

[1] H. L. Gray, *The influence of the commons on early legislation* (1932), 141–56, was justified in stressing the importance of government bills in this reign, and emphasizing that many of the acts which became statutes originated similarly; but much of his elaborate argument was based on the fallacious belief that the heading 'communes petitions' in the rolls of parliament meant bills originating among the commons themselves, and must therefore be treated with great caution. See K. Pickthorn, *Early Tudor government*, I, *Henry VII* (1934), 127; S. B. Chrimes, *English constitutional ideas in the fifteenth century* (1936), ch. III, 236–49; Excursus III, 'Critical memorandum on H. L. Gray's *The influence of the commons on early legislation*'.

[2] *See* below, p. 177.

[3] The not uncommon laudation of Henry VII's legislative activity springs from F. Bacon's *History of King Henry VII* (1622). Bacon, as a lawyer, was naturally interested in this aspect of Henry VII's government, and was right to stress the importance of taking into account the legislative performances of any government in making historical assessments (ibid., ed. Lumby (1885), 75), and was right to describe a number of the statutes of the reign as 'good', but he does not convince us that the reign was especially remarkable for its legislation.

[4] *See* Chrimes, op. cit. 126–30.

[5] It is said that the term has not been traced earlier than 1544 (Elton, op. cit. 241, fn. 1, citing A. F. Pollard, *Henry VII*, I, xxxiii).

when it uses the expression 'in the comen Howse besyde the parlement house of the kynges grace and the lordes'.[1] Such terminology is in no way surprising, for as yet there was no such thing as a 'House of Lords' in any sense of the term. The Commons House came into existence, in a locative and an institutional sense, long before the House of Lords could do so, because the commons met outside the Parliament House, and had a fixed electoral composition, whereas to the Parliament House came, except on the formal occasions, only such persons, councillors, prelates, lords, lawyers, and others, as the king thought fit to summon individually and personally. 'A plague on both your houses' is a poetic malediction that might well be adapted and applied to historians of the early English parliaments, for to see two houses of parliament where none or only one existed is merely to make confusion worse confounded.

The injury to a realistic history of the Commons caused by anachronistic thinking is by now generally understood and guarded against. But the damage done to the history of the Lords by the effects of the doctrines of modern peerage law still vitiates many attempts at sketching that history. It is perfectly plain, as J. C. Wedgwood pointed out more than thirty years ago, that a personal summons to parliament did not necessarily create a prescriptive right even by 1509, and that some persons attended for whom no writs of summons were endorsed on the Close rolls, and for whom no writ appears ever to have existed. Some who might be said to possess an hereditary peerage were not summoned to some parliaments, even though the persons were available; it was common practice not to summon those who were known to be unavailable, by reason of absence on service at home or abroad, infirmity, or even poverty. It is more than likely that some were summoned by word of mouth, but certain that no one would come and be admitted unless the king was willing. It has been pointed out that Henry VII's first parliament was 'perhaps the first occasion on which names had been omitted from the list of summons on grounds of partisanship'.[2] Nor can it be denied that Henry VII showed himself to be extremely reluctant to create dignities that can rightly be called 'new peerages'. He has often been credited with having made seven, or even nine of these

---

[1] 'List of members of the fourth parliament of Henry VII, 1491–2', ed. Winifred Jay, *B.I.H.R.*, III (1925–6), 175. The list is printed from B.M. Harl. MS. 2252, and is said to be in an early sixteenth-century hand. But there is no reason to suppose that the document is not a contemporary one.

[2] J. Enoch Powell and Keith Wallis, *The House of Lords in the Middle Ages* (1965), 529; cf. Wedgwood, *History of parliament, register* (1938), lxi–lxviii.

new creations, but the number really dwindles to one or two, and if he imagined that in other cases he was creating new hereditary peerages, he was singularly unlucky; nor, in most of the instances, was he creating a new 'baron' – he was issuing a personal summons to particular parliaments.

But an hereditary presumptive right to a summons, did, indeed, exist in the case of many of the 'peerage' families, and Henry VII was prepared to recognize this, unless there were reasons to the contrary, and to recognize the principle to the extent of summoning a descendant or relative of a person who might be said to have had some sort of claim; and this kind of summons accounts for at least six of the so-called nine new creations.[1] Thus John Ratcliffe de Fitzwalter was summoned in September 1485, in the 'right' of his mother, but he was destined to be attainted and subject to forfeiture in 1495. A viscounty was created in 1485 for John Welles, the king's half-uncle, but he was an heir to a 'barony', and the viscounty became extinct in 1498.[2] Robert Willoughby de Broke received a writ of summons in November 1488, but he was descended from an old established barony, and he died in 1503, was succeeded by his son and heir in 1511, who died in 1522 without male heir, and the barony remained in abeyance until 1696. The position of Thomas Ormond de Rochford was peculiar; he was already eighth earl of Carrick and seventh earl of Ormond when he was summoned as Thomas Ormond de Rochford, *chevaler*, in November 1488. It was not the practice to summon the Irish earls to the English parliament, but for personal reasons Henry VII decided to summon him. Ormond died without male heir in 1515 and the 'barony' supposedly created in 1488 remained in abeyance. The case of Charles Somerset also had its unique features. He was knighted at Milford Haven in 1485 and presumably therefore had joined Henry in exile, which is not surprising, for he was a natural son of Henry Beaufort II, duke of Somerset, and therefore Margaret Beaufort's cousin and Henry VII's second cousin. He married Elizabeth, the only daughter and heiress of William Herbert, earl of Huntingdon (by his first wife, Mary Woodville, the Dowager Queen's sister), the son and heir of William Herbert, earl of Pembroke, who had been Henry VII's guardian. The creation of Charles Somerset by

---

[1] For the cases that follow, *see* G.E.C.; *D.N.B.*; and *The historic peerage*, ed. Sir H. Nicolas and W. Courthope. For valuable details regarding each of these cases, *see* J. Enoch Powell and Keith Wallis, op. cit. 481, 524 ff. For Sir Charles Somerset, *see* also Rhys Robinson, 'Early Tudor policy towards Wales; the acquisition of lands and offices in Wales by Charles Somerset, earl of Worcester', *Bull. Bd of Celtic Studies*, XX (1964), 421–38.   [2] *See* above, p. 35, fn. 2.

patent as Baron Herbert of Ragland, Chepstow, and Gower in November 1506, and the continuance of his summons in 1509 and 1511 as Charles Herbert, *chevaler*, can hardly be regarded as the creation of a 'new peerage'. The fact that he was created earl of Worcester in 1514 does not, of course, affect the position under Henry VII. Thomas Darcy de Darcy was certainly summoned to Henry VII's first parliament, and may have been summoned in 1509, but he was the great-grandson of the fifth baron Darcy of Knaith, and was destined to be attainted, beheaded, and forfeited in 1538, although his son was restored ten years later.

We are left then, with Thomas Burgh, Giles Daubeney, and John Cheyney. There is evidence of an intention to create a barony for Thomas Burgh, who was descended through a junior line from Hubert de Burgh, earl of Kent, but there is no evidence that he received more than a writ of summons in September 1487, or that he ever attended; his eldest son and heir, however, was of unsound mind and was never summoned, but his brother and his heirs were summoned from 1529 until 1597, after which the heir died in infancy and the barony went into abeyance.

John Cheyney was summoned by writ in September 1487, but died without heirs in 1499. Of all these nine persons, only Giles Daubeney was given a barony by charter, to him and his heirs male, in March 1486 (and even he could be deemed to be the heir of the Ralph Daubeney who had been summoned in 1342, but neither he nor his intervening heirs had been thereafter so summoned). But this new barony became extinct in 1548. The redoubtable Giles Daubeney had, however, been clearly singled out for a mark of special honour, granted to him in most laudatory terms.

Henry VII was therefore extremely restrained in adding to the personnel of the secular lords. He did give some recognition to presumptive hereditary claims to a summons, but at the same time he kept as free a hand as possible in committing himself to the implications. It is open to doubt whether he thought in terms of creating additions to an hereditary peerage by issuing a few personal summonses, except in the case of Daubeney. The circumstance, remarkable at first sight, is that he did not think in terms of rewarding his most distinguished and faithful servants with 'peerages', as would have been the case in a later generation. But in reality many of his intimate associates, as councillors, or as elected members of parliament, or as both, were necessarily present at parliaments, to do the king service; their rewards were in the tangible form of grants of office and lands and profits, and when it came to dignities, it seems clear that the Garter rather than anything that could be called 'a peerage' was the ultimate mark of honour favoured by Henry VII, and for men of comparatively modest birth and beginnings who had climbed solely by service to the king, the honour was great. He created no fewer than thirty-seven knights of the Garter, of whom more than half were men who were among his closest associates in government or in war.[1]

The number of persons known to have been summoned to Henry VII's seven parliaments remained remarkably constant.[2] The normal number of archbishops and bishops was twenty-one, but this figure varied from seventeen to twenty-one according to circumstances; the number of abbots and priors was a constant twenty-seven; the total number of lords temporal varied only slightly, from thirty-four in the first parliament to forty-three at most, made up of two dukes, or one prince and one duke; one marquis from the third parliament (when the marquis of Dorset had again secured a writ), from nine to twelve earls; two or three viscounts, and from twenty to twenty-seven 'barons'. The men of law summoned varied from nine to twelve. At its smallest (in the first parliament) the total number of persons summoned was eighty-eight, and at its largest, 101. The variations in the totals are accounted for by prevailing circumstances and material causes, including the king's pleasure, but even allowing for the probability that a few persons may have been summoned verbally or without surviving evidence, it is clear that Henry VII's attitude in the matter was extremely conservative, and apparently devoid of any particular policy beyond the continuance of existing practice and avoiding more than minimal additions to the personnel either of his parliaments or of the 'hereditary' peerage. It is as well to recall Professor Roskell's cautious but carefully chosen phrases when he wrote: 'it would perhaps not be going too far to say that, in practice, parliaments were called in order to get together a full meeting

---

[1] G.E.C., II, App. B, 565–7. Of these thirty-seven creations (or re-creations) eight were in favour of home or foreign royal personages; of the remaining twenty-nine more than half were in favour of persons who were the king's close associates in the government or court, and among these were included John de Vere, earl of Oxford, John Cheyney, John, Lord Dinham, Giles Daubeney, Sir William Stanley, Sir Edward Woodville, Viscount Welles, John Savage, Robert Willoughby, Edward Courtenay, earl of Devon, Edward Poynings, Gilbert Talbot, Henry Percy, earl of Northumberland, Charles Somerset, Thomas Lovell, Richard Guildford, Reginald Bray, Thomas Grey, marquis of Dorset, and Thomas Brandon. Only one lady was awarded Garter robes by Henry VII, viz, his mother, Margaret Beaufort. (His mother-in-law, wife and two sisters-in-law had been granted them by Edward IV.)

[2] See analysis and tables in Wedgwood, op. cit. liii–lxxviii, 404–612.

of the ordinary council, afforced by as large a number of other lords as possible, and so that they should meet the elected commons'.[1]

But Professor Roskell has taught us[2] also to remember that the number of persons summoned to mediaeval parliaments was different from that which actually attended, which was smaller, and often very much smaller. It is clear that the number of lords who attended those mediaeval parliaments about which we have enough information to be able to calculate varied a great deal, and was never equal to the number summoned. This fundamental fact inevitably modifies the traditional views of the 'upper house'. Unfortunately the attendances at Henry VII's parliaments are not known,[3] and no conclusions can be drawn. But it can hardly be insignificant that the oaths to preserve law and order, etc., supposed to have been administered to all the lords in the first parliament, were taken by only thirteen out of seventeen prelates summoned; seventeen out of twenty-seven abbots and priors summoned; and by eighteen temporal lords out of thirty-four summoned, and of these, two were dukes and eight earls, so that only eight out of the other twenty-four lay lords took it.[4] The circumstances were, of course, exceptional, yet we cannot suppose that the attendance of lords was necessarily at all full in Henry VII's parliaments, and apparently it is not until the later years of Henry VIII that a rate of attendance much higher than the usual mediaeval average becomes evident.

Notwithstanding the extraordinary neglect with which the Great Council of mediaeval and early Tudor periods has been treated by historians, it must be remembered that the lords spiritual and temporal might receive writs of personal summons to assemblies other than parliaments; that at these assemblies major questions of policy, of peace and war, might be considered, questions of State which might transcend in importance most of the matters, largely routine and legalistic in character, which came before the lords and commons in the parliaments.

That these meetings could be important is not open to doubt, but available information on the subject remains as slight now as it did sixty years ago. An assembly of the new King's Council and other persons in London in September 1485, at which Henry VII renewed his promise to marry Elizabeth, and which accepted him as successor to Edward IV, not Henry VI, seems to have been a Great Council. A meeting at Charterhouse, Sheen, in February 1487, which decided to

---

[1] 'The problem of attendance of the lords in mediaeval parliaments', *B.I.H.R.*, XXIX (1956), 199.

[2] ibid. 153–204.   [3] ibid. 197.   [4] ibid.

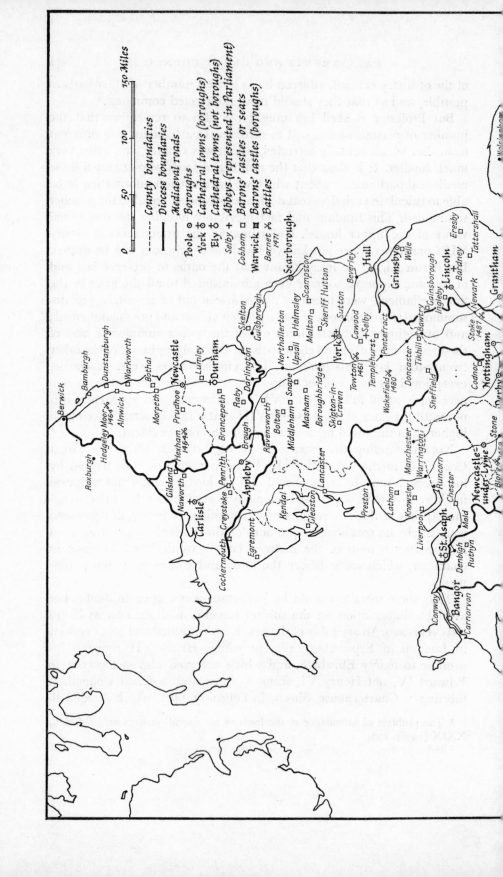

Poole ○ Boroughs
York ✠ Cathedral towns (boroughs)
Ely ✟ Cathedral towns (not boroughs)
Selby + Abbeys (represented in Parliament)
Cobham □ Barons' castles or seats
Warwick ⊠ Barons' castles (boroughs)
Barnet ✕ Battles
1471

- - - - - County boundaries
———— Diocese boundaries
———— Mediaeval roads

0   50   100   150 Miles

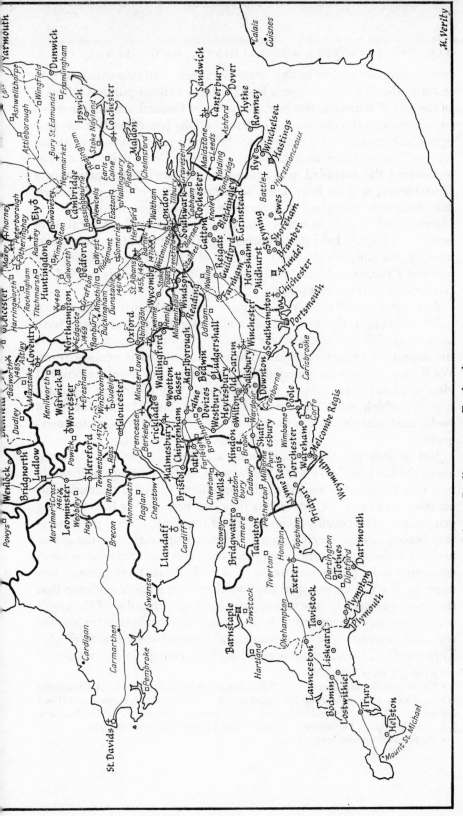

Map 3 Parliamentary England 1439 to 1509

offer a general pardon to any would-be rebels who submitted, to take in hand the Queen Dowager's lands, and to make a public exhibition of the earl of Warwick, was probably a Great Council. Another meeting in November 1488 discussed the state of affairs regarding Brittany and apparently authorized the levy of a subsidy of a tenth which was ratified by parliament three months later. A Great Council in June 1491 authorized the intended war against France and the exaction of a benevolence, said to have been *ad instancium et specialem requisicionem tam dominorum spiritalium et temporalium quam aliorum nobilium* (at the instance and request as well of the lords spiritual and temporal as of other notables).[1] In 1496, between 24 October and 6 November, another assembly considered the threat of invasion by Scotland, and granted £120,000, at least as a loan, a grant subsequently ratified by parliament in January 1497.[2]

Five meetings of the Great Council are thus known to have been held; all except the first, which was inaugural to the reign, were concerned with the threats of war or rebellion; three of them authorized the imposition of financial aid in advance of any parliamentary grant. We do not know who attended these meetings, but from the point of view of Henry VII's urgent political needs, they clearly performed a function which must have seemed indispensable. The machinery of parliament was clearly too slow and cumbersome to respond to emergencies.

Just as little or nothing of an innovatory nature can be discovered about the lords in Henry VII's parliaments, so also nothing significantly new can be found in regard to the commons. Electoral arrangements continued, so far as we can tell, as they had been during the preceding generation.[3] The constituencies remained the same; no new parliamentary boroughs were created, so that seventy-four knights for the shires, and 222 citizens and burgesses for the boroughs, 296 members in total, continued to be summoned; there is no evidence that any attempt was made by the Crown to 'pack' the commons, nor is there evidence that there was any need for the government to do so. A number of the king's councillors were frequently elected, and the speakers were clearly regarded as primarily king's servants, and received rewards accordingly. They made the usual protestations, and no change in the matter of

[1] Rymer, *Foedera*, XII, 466.

[2] For details, the only account is still that furnished by R. Steele (ed.), *A bibliography of royal proclamations of the Tudor and Stuart sovereigns, 1485–1714*, I, *England and Wales* (1910), lxxvi–lxxvii. The valuable *Tudor royal proclamations*, ed. P. L. Hughes and J. F. Larkin (1964), has nothing material to add to this particular subject.

[3] Wedgwood, op. cit. lxxix–cxxvii.

7. Wax impressions of the seals of Henry VII
a. Great Seal (*B.M. Seal XLV, 13*)
b. Privy Seal (*P.R.O., appended to Henry VII's Will, E 23/3*)
c. Signet Seal (*ibid*)

8. Extract from Book of Chamber Receipts kept by Sir Thomas Lovell, treasurer of the chamber, 27 August to 6 September 1492. Each entry is initialled by the king, who changed the style of his royal sign manual after 27 August (*P.R.O., E 101, 413/2/2, fo. 36*)

privilege occurred. Each of Henry VII's seven parliaments had a different speaker; they were Thomas Lovell, John Mordaunt, Thomas Fitzwilliam, Richard Empson, Robert Drury, Thomas Englefield, and Edmund Dudley. All of them were lawyers by profession, all (except Dudley) received knighthoods, and most of them were otherwise prominent in the king's service.[1] There is no evidence of anything that could be called serious friction between the king and the commons, although it is not to be supposed that all the king's measures put to parliaments were equally popular, and some might arouse criticism and perhaps opposition.[2] But nothing approaching a crisis, or even strained relations, occurred. The king's pleasure prevailed whenever pressed, and further steps in constitutional history do not materialize out of mere agreement and acquiescence.

For only one of the seven parliaments have we a full record of the names of the elected representatives; apart from this, and the parliament of 1491–2,[3] for which we have 294 names out of 296, and for that of 1495, for which we have 114, we know only about seventy for each of the other parliaments and it is not possible therefore to obtain any complete picture of the personnel. But from the materials available, no significant conclusions emerge. The kinds of people elected were much the same as had been elected in previous decades. A modest proportion of members had served in previous parliaments, and some were re-elected during the reign; some knights of the shire class got elected in boroughs, but there was nothing new in this phenomenon; various kinds of men sought and obtained seats: 'King's servants, nobles' servants and relations, local administrators, lawyers within and without the bar, knights and squires, farmers both of land and revenue, traders and tradesmen' all can be found in the existing records.[4] Two hundred and ninety-six of them were elected, but since we have no means of knowing the names of most of them, we cannot know how many of them actually attended, all the more so because many exceptions to the traditional payment to them of wages by their constituencies had occurred for one reason or another.[5] There is, however, no reason to

[1] Roskell, *The commons and their speakers in English parliaments, 1376–1523* (1965), 298–308, and App.; cf. Wedgwood, op. cit., *Biographies*.

[2] The remark by Thomas Betanson in his letter to Sir Robert Plumpton, dated 13 December 1485, referring to the bill of attainder in the first parliament, is revealing, but it would be unwise to build too much upon it. 'How beit,' he says, 'ther was many gentlemen agaynst it, but it wold not be, for yt was the King's pleasure.' *Plumpton correspondence*, ed. T. Stapleton (Cam. Soc. (1839), 49).

[3] *See* above, p. 137, fn. 1.   [4] Wedgwood, op. cit., *Register*, lxxxvii.

[5] ibid. cxxiii–cxxvi.

suppose that attendance was not the normal practice, and there is evidence that some people eagerly sought election. Private careers, regional and sectional interests could be advanced during the comparatively brief sessions; public concerns and a share in implementing the king's will were attractive occupations for many who might not otherwise come to Westminster and reside for a few weeks on the fringes of the court. All of Henry VII's parliaments were summoned to Westminster, as the practice had been since 1470, and was to be the subsequent practice with rare exceptions. Few who had the opportunity would fail to rise to the occasion.[1]

[1] If we had more evidence such as that contained in a brief report made by Colchester M.Ps in 1485–6 (contained in the *Red Paper Book of Colchester*, ed. W. Gurney Benham (1902), 60–4; extracts in Wedgwood, op. cit. App. XIV, 752–4), we should know more about what interested at any rate burgesses and their constituencies.

Chapter 8

JUDICATURE

To survey the whole field of royal jurisdiction in the reign of Henry VII would be a task impossible to attempt in a work of the present sort, and would in any event be impracticable until such time as far more detailed investigations into the legal history of the period have been undertaken than is at present the case. In some fields much has been done, in others nothing at all. For our present purposes, however, some features of the administration of royal justice need to be taken into account, especially conciliar jurisdiction and the activities of certain special tribunals, the activities of the justices in the Exchequer chamber and the courts of common law, the equitable jurisdiction of the chancellor, and the functions of the justices of the peace, who, however, would perhaps better be considered as among the local agents of the royal government.

The King's Council was not only an advisory and executive body, it was also a court of law.[1] It exercised the residuary jurisdiction vested from time immemorial in the sovereign lord king. As a court it held sittings either in the Star Chamber at Westminster or anywhere in the realm whither councillors might accompany the king. But it was not yet the court of Star Chamber. Star Chamber was still a place, not a tribunal.[2] No instance has been found of the address of a plaintiff's bill or petition to a court of Star Chamber in this period. The bulk of known bills were addressed to the king; some others to the king and council, or to the chancellor, or to the council.[3] The functions of the council as an executive body are barely distinguishable from its functions as a court. Its jurisdiction was not primarily criminal and did not extend to treason or felony; it dealt at least as much with civil disputes. There is no known instance of litigation before the council being initiated by the government; all such litigation began with the presentation of a bill or petition, submitted either by the plaintiff in person to the council in

---

[1] For references, *see* above, p. 97.

[2] Bayne, op. cit. lxxv. In ninety-three references to Star Chamber in the period, all except three are references to a location not to a tribunal. Some useful points are made by S. E. Lehmbergin, 'Star Chamber, 1485–1509', *Huntingdon Library Quarterly*, XXIV (1960–1), 189–214.   [3] Bayne, op. cit. xxx.

session, or to individual councillors, or to the king himself, or to the clerk of the council.[1]

The purpose of such bills was to seek redress from the supreme authority for wrongs that could not obtain remedy elsewhere, either because of the applicant's poverty, or the deficiencies of the common law, or of the local power and influence of the other party, or because of a combination of these reasons. Once the council was satisfied as to the *bona fides* of the supplicant's bill, it could proceed by methods not available to the courts of common law. It could summon the defendant by a writ under the Privy Seal requiring him to appear before the king and his council. But the council employed no staff of process-servers and in the great majority of cases the plaintiff or his agent were obliged to serve the writ – a circumstance that must have considerably impeded the securing of remedy. If a second Privy Seal failed to procure the attendance of the defendant, a writ of attachment addressed to the sheriff would follow – and if all else failed a commission requiring the magnates of the county to seize the culprit might be resorted to.

Once the parties had been got to attend, procedure continued by way of answer and demurrer, defendant's oath and examination. No juries were used, but no attempt was made to oblige a defendant to incriminate himself. Replication and rejoinder, and examination of witnesses might follow, and if the whole matter were not referred to special commissioners for decision, a public hearing was arranged for formalities and for the delivery of judgment by decree. Notwithstanding the possibilities of long delays in some instances, the evidence suggests that justice was administered with reasonable promptitude.[2]

Fifty-nine per cent of the cases known to have been adjudicated by the council in Star Chamber at this period were private suits in which rioting, of trivial or large dimensions, was alleged as the origin of the complaint.[3] Various offences against public justice were alleged in a few cases, and some criminal acts in others. Most of the offences were of a commonplace kind, and miscellaneous civil suits and municipal and trade disputes brought up the total so far as is known. The six offences specified in the act of 1487 hardly figure at all in the known cases. The offence of maintenance was normally dealt with in the common law courts and was not regarded as Star Chamber business; the taking of bribes by juries, a common offence, produced no case in

---

[1] *See* Bayne, op. cit. lxxiii–clxxiv, and texts 1–170. [2] ibid. cx.

[3] ibid. lxxiv, cxxix–cxxx. It has to be remembered, however, that the total number of extant cases before the council in Star Chamber for the period is not more than 194. Of these 115 were cases of rioting initiated by private suitors.

Star Chamber; embracery figures only once; there is no evidence that Star Chamber tried a single offender against the laws in restraint of retaining; complaints were made about offences by sheriffs, but were not initiated by the government, which left such cases to the common law courts. Rioting, the sixth offence mentioned in the act of 1487, accounted for more than half the extant cases, most of them initiated by private parties, but in one instance by the attorney-general. The punishment of rioting was a major concern of Henry VII's government and must be considered later; several statutes were made to cope with the problem and one of these provided that where the riot was committed by forty or more persons or was 'heinous' for some other reason, the record was to be sent up to the council, presumably in Star Chamber, so that adequate punishment could be inflicted. Generally, the council left the trial and punishment of rioters to the common law courts.[1]

Such evidence as exists[2] suggests that such punishments as were inflicted by the council at this time were moderate, in the form of fines which were seldom heavy, or imprisonment, usually until the fine had been paid or security for it given. There is no evidence of ruthlessness or extortion in the council penalizations. Star Chamber at this time has been described as a 'very gentle instrument of coercion'. But there were other ways of coercion, other means of ruthless extortion that might be resorted to, if it so pleased the king – by his own executive command, outside the sphere of conciliar jurisdiction altogether. Indeed, the council in Star Chamber was scarcely regarded by the government at all as an instrument of coercion for its own purposes. Its procedures were primarily for the benefit of the aggrieved suitor, not of the government. When the king wanted to coerce or seize opportunities for pecuniary advantage under the guise of legal justification, there were other channels open for the exertion of his will.[3] One of these was the group of councillors, some of whom might indeed sit with others in Star Chamber, but who as a group attained an identity of its own, and whose activities, unlike those of the council in Star Chamber, were largely focused on the king's interest, namely, the Council Learned.

'The king's Council Learned in the law' remains a somewhat obscure body,[4] of which almost nothing would be known except for the fortuitous survival of some of its records among the archives of the duchy of Lancaster, of which Sir Reginald Bray, a leading member of

---

[1] ibid. cxi–cxliv.   [2] ibid. clxv–clxxii.   [3] ibid. clxxiii–clxxiv.
[4] R. Somerville, 'Henry VII's "Council Learned in the law" ', *E.H.R.*, LIV (1939), 427–42; Bayne, op. cit. xxv–xxviii.

the Council Learned, was chancellor. Nothing is known of its activities before 1500, and it disappeared in 1509. It is, however, clear that it performed two functions; it acted as a tribunal or court (though never so called) and it acted as a royal debt-collecting agency. It is misleading indeed to describe it as a 'committee of the council'[1]; rather it was a group of councillors exercising the discretion of the King's Council for certain purposes. Its activities as a debt-collecting agency must be considered later; here its judicial activities need attention.

The names of at most only twelve members of the group are recorded at any time during the nine years of its known existence, but not all of these were members at any one time. Two bishops were among them: Roger Leybourne, bishop of Carlisle from 1504, and Robert Sherborne, who had been the king's secretary, bishop of St David's from 1505.[2] Sir Reginald Bray, and his successor but one as chancellor of the duchy, Richard Empson, were prominent members, so prominent that a closer connection between the Council Learned and the duchy than the merely personal may be conjectured. The other known members at one time or another were Edmund Dudley, Sir James Hobart, the king's attorney, Thomas Lucas, the king's solicitor, and William Mordaunt,[3] clerk of the Common Pleas and duchy attorney there. All these eight are known to have been at one time or another king's councillors. Four other persons are known to have been associated with some of these in judicial activities, and may have been reckoned to be of the Council Learned, though not specifically so called in the surviving records. Three of these were common lawyers: Robert Brudenall, a serjeant-at-law in 1504, king's serjeant in 1505, and a justice of King's Bench in 1507; Humphrey Coningsby, serjeant in 1494, a justice of the King's Bench, but only from 21 May 1509;[4] and Richard Hesketh, a rising apprentice-at-law who was not destined to become a justice, but was twice a commissioner of gaol delivery and once a commissioner to enquire into the king's prerogative rights in Henry VII's time, and was in 1515 to deliver a reading in Gray's Inn on a subject profitable for aspiring lawyers to lecture upon at these times – the *Praerogativa regis.*[5]

---

[1] *See* above, p. 99.   [2] *See* above, p. 117.

[3] Bayne was mistaken in supposing that this was the Sir John Mordaunt who succeeded Bray as chancellor of the duchy from June to his death in September 1504. *See* Somerville, loc. cit. 428, fn. 7.

[4] Foss, *Judges of England, Tabulae Curiales, sub nom.*

[5] *C.P.R.,* II, 546, 560, 627; S. E. Thorne, *Praerogativa regis* (1949), xxviii, fn. 108; and *Readings and moots at the inns of court in the fifteenth century,* S.S., 71 (1954), xiii. *See* also below, p. 210. Somerville, loc. cit. 429, fnn 3, 4, 6, was mistaken in describing all these three men as justices under Henry VII.

The fourth, William Smith, cannot be identified with any assurance.[1]

The feature common to this personnel was legal training. Except for one of the two bishops[2] and Bray, who does not appear to have had a legal training,[3] all the members were lawyers (unless William Smith was an exception), and not for nothing therefore were they known as *consilium domini regis in lege eruditum* or *jurisperitum*.

The cases that came before this tribunal were of two kinds, either private suits, mostly about land, or government prosecutions. It is far from clear why some private suits were heard by this body instead of the council in Star Chamber, though there are some instances of the plaintiff's bill being addressed to the Council Learned. In these private suits there is no apparent difference between the Council Learned's jurisdiction and that of the council in Star Chamber, unless perhaps for some reason the more concentrated legal expertise of the former was thought to be more appropriate. In all such cases the jurisdiction, even if not exactly 'equitable' jurisdiction, was to provide remedies by conciliar discretion.

But the bulk of the cases heard were initiated by the government, and there can be no doubt that the *raison d'être* of the Council Learned was to try certain Crown prosecutions and to collect Crown debts. The connecting link between these two superficially distinct functions was the king's financial interest, and the reason for circumventing the normal recourse to the common law courts in either function can only be surmised as 'reason of State'. It is not surprising that the odium that the tightening of the financial screws by this body produced was sufficient to result after Henry VII's death in its disappearance as such.

The litigation initiated by the Crown was miscellaneous. Offences

---

[1] As Bayne pointed out, op. cit. xxv, it is very doubtful whether he can have been, as Somerville queried, loc. cit. 422, fn. 5, the well-known William Smith who was a king's councillor and later bishop of Lincoln. This William Smith had become bishop of Coventry and Lichfield as early as 1493, but he is not, in accordance with normal practice, designated a bishop in the record. Bayne suggested, ibid., with plausibility, that he might have been the William Smith who was arrested as an accomplice of Empson and Dudley and imprisoned on Henry VIII's accession. But although this Smith received grants under Henry VII, he seems never to have been more than a groom of the Robes, an office hardly compatible with the status of a member of the Council Learned. But it has to be remembered that it cannot be asserted categorically that either Smith, Brudenall, Coningsby, or Hesketh was so reckoned, *see* Somerville, loc. cit. 429.

[2] Roger Leybourne, a fellow of Pembroke Hall, Cambridge, *c.* 1490, had sufficient legal training to be admitted a notary public by 1496, and vicar-general of Durham from 1500; Emden, *Biog. Reg. Camb., sub nom.*

[3] *See* above, p. 110.

against various kinds of statutes, including trade regulations, the mis-demeanours of sheriffs and jurors, escapes of prisoners, false returns, riots, livery, retaining and maintenance; offences against proclamations, failure to take up knighthood; the king's feudal and seignorial rights – ward of heirs, assignment of dower, entry without livery, all figured in the list. One case of treason and several of murder figure in the records, but why these should have come before the Council Learned is a mystery. However, the bulk of prosecutions ended, so far as is known, with the imposition of a fine, and many Privy Seals are known to have been issued requiring the payment of money to John Heron in the chamber or else ordering appearance before the Council Learned. But these latter demands were often for unspecified amounts and reasons – they ranked as 'debts due to the king', and in this regard the functions of the council as a debt-collecting agency came into the picture.[1] What jurisdictional purpose the Council Learned really served, it is hard to see. Most of the matters considered could have been referred to the common law courts, some indeed were so referred by it. But the processes of the ordinary courts were slow, and the threatening weapon of the Privy Seal was not available therein; nor could the accruing fines be readily diverted to the chamber. If the chief purpose of the Council Learned was to operate to the king's financial advantage then doubtless it was an efficient instrument well designed for the purpose. But it could hardly have expected to become a permanent feature in the administration of justice.

Just as some of the council sitting in Star Chamber performed judi-cial functions, without its being called the court of Star Chamber in Henry VII's time, so some of the council could adjudicate upon what were originally intended to be 'poor men's causes', without as yet being called 'the court of Requests', a term that did not come into use until twenty years after Henry VII's death.[2] It is doubtful whether the councillors who were concerned with this type of business can be called 'a standing committee of the council'. They were a group of councillors, and for many years suitors were obliged to follow the king in his pro-gresses and the councillors who happened to be attendant upon him were the ones who dealt with this species of judicial activity. From 1483 a clerk had been appointed specifically as the clerk of the council of

---

[1] *See* below, p. 209.
[2] I. S. Leadam (ed.), *Select cases in the court of Requests, 1497–1569*, S.S. 12 (1898). Many points in the editor's introduction are superseded; cf. Bayne, op. cit. xix–xx, xxv–xxviii, xxxii, xxxvii–xl, lxxvii, lxxix, lxxxv; J. F. Baldwin, *The King's Council*, 442–6

Requests, in recognition of his good work in the custody, registration and expedition of bills, requests and supplications of poor persons,[1] but the earliest recorded proceeding comes from 1493; from 1497 the council of Requests began to observe the same terms as the common law courts and the council in Star Chamber. Not until 1516 did Wolsey establish a location for it, in the White Hall in Westminster, where it usually though not always met thenceforth. But the location gave it for some time the name of court of White Hall, and although the term 'court of Requests' began to be used from 1529, even then it was still sometimes referred to as the council.[2]

The personnel of the council of Requests under Henry VII seems to have been simply a group of councillors for the time being, some of whom, however, probably never acted as councillors for any other purpose.[3] There do not appear as yet to have been any formal appointments of masters of Requests. The keeper of the Privy Seal frequently functioned as the chairman of the group, but then so also did a president of the council, who is first mentioned in 1497, when he took the place of the Privy Seal in proceedings on Requests; and a president is on a number of occasions mentioned as similarly occupied.[4] What the significance of this alteration may be can at present only be conjectured, but the office of president of the council can hardly have been set up primarily for such a purpose. There is no evidence that the personnel was necessarily constant; there were considerable variations, as one would expect, but there were apparently always present several ecclesiastics qualified in canon and civil law, as well as normally some common lawyers, and these provided the expertise needed for the adjudication of the legal problems involved.

What exactly differentiated the jurisdiction of the council of Requests from that of the council in ¦Star Chamber is difficult to determine. It will not do to say that the former dealt with civil disputes and the latter with criminal causes,[5] for the council in Star Chamber clearly handled both, even though Requests appears to have confined itself to civil causes. The original idea that the requests to be adjudged were only those of poor men unable to obtain remedy by the ordinary courses had already become a fiction, for some of the plaintiffs of whom we have knowlege were certainly not in that category, and there is little to distinguish the petitions considered by the council of Requests from those

[1] *C.P.R.*, *1476–1485*, 413, 496, 535.   [2] Leadam, op. cit. x–xi.
[3] For lists of names of the councillors in the ninth to fourteenth years of Henry VII, *see* ibid. cii–ciii; Bayne, op. cit. xix–xx.
[4] ibid. xxxvii–xl.   [5] Leadam, op. cit. x–xi, following Lambarde.

considered by the council in Star Chamber at this time.[1] What the plaintiffs wanted were remedies for one reason or another unobtainable or difficult to obtain in the common law courts; and the summary procedures by written pleadings and depositions on interrogatories, likely to be cheaper and more expeditious than processes elsewhere, were desirable enough. But there is no evidence that the plaintiffs themselves asked for their petition to go to the council of Requests. They sought remedy from the king their sovereign lord, and it was the officials who decided which petition should go where. On what basis the distribution was made there are no means of determining.

The jurisdiction exercised by the council, whether as a whole, or in Star Chamber, or in the Council Learned, or in the council of Requests, was conciliar jurisdiction exercised by virtue of the residuary discretion of the king himself. Jurisdiction exercised by virtue of royal commissions or by statutes was a quite different matter. The bulk of Henry VII's judicial commissions were of the normal common law variety (commissions of *oyer et terminer*, gaol delivery, of assize, and the like) and do not call for special comment. The occurrence of the rather numerous conspiracies, plots, and rebellions and insurrections during the reign induced the king from time to time to appoint special commissioners[2] to pacify the region or regions concerned, and pacification in this sense involved judicial or quasi-judicial activities with strong emphasis upon the summary extraction of financial penalties rather than strict course of the common law.

Of the statutory tribunals set up the one which has attracted the most attention is that established by the act of 1487, the entirely erroneously-called '*pro camera stellata*' act. The tribunal set up by this act had in fact nothing whatever to do with the council in Star Chamber or with the council in any form.[3] The essential purpose of the act was

---

[1] Bayne, op. cit. lxxxv, mentions instances of the transfer of cases from Requests to Star Chamber. Only five cases from Henry VII's reign are printed by Leadam, op. cit. 1–14.

[2] Numerous commissions of this sort are to be found in *C.P.R.*, *passim*. A good example is the commission to Robert Sherborne, dean of St Paul's (*see* above, p. 117) and Amias Poulet, knight of the body, to cite before them and examine the adherents in Somerset, Dorset, Wilts, and Hants, of Michael Joseph and Peter Warbeck, to pardon those who surrendered and fine or imprison others (*C.P.R.*, II, 203). The ruthlessness of these commissioners is commented on at length by Polydore Vergil (ed. Hay), 108.

[3] For references, *see* above, pp. 99–100. The indispensable discussion now is in Bayne, op. cit. l–lxxii. Bayne made it quite clear that the tribunal was nothing to do with the council in Star Chamber, but was not equally emphatic that it had nothing to do with the council either.

to create a tribunal quite distinct from the council, which, as the King's Council, could and did exercise all the jurisdiction envisaged without any statutory provision. The whole point was that in 1487 it was thought necessary to establish a tribunal which was not the council or a common law court, to deal with certain classes of offences against the public peace, the very offences the committal of which tended to vitiate the slow traditional process of the common law itself. The aim was to confer summary jurisdiction in these matters upon the principal officers of state. The chancellor, the treasurer, and the keeper of the Privy Seal, or any two of them, were empowered to call to their assistance a bishop and a temporal lord of the king's most honourable council, and the two chief justices or two other justices in their absence. The tribunal so established was authorized to proceed upon any bill or information put to the chancellor for the king or otherwise against any person 'for any misbehaving' (of the kind specified), with authority to summon by writ or Privy Seal, by examination at discretion, and to punish them according to their demerits and in accordance with statutes already made with regard to the specified offences, as they should be punished if they were convicted after the due course of law.[1]

The six offences specified were: maintenance, retaining by indentures, by promises, or oaths, and by giving liveries, signs and tokens, embracery, corrupt conduct of sheriffs in returning juries, bribe-taking by juries, and riots. These were the particular offences against public order and the proper operation of the common law which were giving the government special concern. All of them had been the subject of statutory provision over the past century,[2] most of them had been condemned by the oath administered to the commons and lords in the parliament of 1485.[3] The object of the establishment of what can best be described as this ministerial tribunal was to enforce the provisions of statute law expeditiously and summarily, primarily so as to free the common law procedures from the abuses and corruptions that were impeding the course of justice.

It is clear from the evidence, scanty though it is, that the tribunal

---

[1] St. 3 Henry VII, c. 1; S.R., II, 509–10. The terms of the act are perfectly clear and self-explanatory. Printed by Bayne from the MS., op. cit. 60; and in modernized spelling by J. R. Tanner, Tudor constitutional documents (1930), 258–9; and G. R. Elton, The Tudor constitution, 163–4.

[2] For references to relevant acts, see C. Plummer (ed.), Fortescue's Governance of England (1885), 27–30; W. Stubbs, Constitutional history, III (5th ed., 1903), 278–80; Bayne, op. cit. lii–liii; the fullest discussion of statutes against livery and maintenance is in W. H. Dunham, Lord Hastings's indentured retainers (1955).

[3] See above, p. 64.

did operate in Henry VII's reign. Most of the few cases for which record is extant were initiated by the government; there is no evidence that the offenders prosecuted were particularly outstanding or highly placed, but it is possible that the discovery of new material might put a different light upon the matter. It is certain that the tribunal was operating in 1493, when the common law justices in the Exchequer chamber ruled that the chancellor, treasurer, and Privy Seal, or two of them, were the only judges under the act of 1487, and the other persons only assistants, although they must be associated with the judges to give validity to the judgments of the tribunal.[1]

In the absence of more than the ten cases the records of which have become available,[2] any wide generalizations about the effectiveness of the act of 1487 are hazardous. How far the tribunal it set up was successful in suppressing the offences it dealt with, we do not know. It may well be that it made no mark on the history of the time and that it was superfluous[3] because the council in Star Chamber could and did deal with the same kinds of offences, but the framers of the act must have been well aware of such an alternative, but still have had good reason to enact the measure. Only time showed in the long run that the council in Star Chamber would make the tribunal redundant. But that time did not arrive for many years, otherwise there would have been no point in re-enacting the whole measure in 1529 and adding the president of the King's Council to the ministers, two of whom were to be the judges.[4] There was probably a good deal more to the history of the tribunal set up by the act of 1487 than has yet been revealed.[5]

All the justices of the common law courts appointed soon after his accession by Henry VII had been previously appointed by Richard III, or in the time of Edward IV.

Sir William Huse was appointed to be chief justice of the King's Bench, Sir Thomas Brian to be chief justice of Common Pleas, and Sir

---

[1] Printed by Bayne, op. cit. 60–1.

[2] ibid. liv–lix, and 60–70.   [3] ibid. lxxii.

[4] 21 Henry VIII, c. 20; *S.R.*, III, 304; printed in J. R. Tanner, *Tudor constitutional documents* (1930), 259–60. Tanner pointed out that in this act the authority to call persons before the tribunal was to be by writ of Privy Seal, whereas in 1487 it was by writ *or* Privy Seal. The change of word, whether deliberate or inadvertent, had the effect of excluding the use of letters of Privy Seal, which do not appear to have been used in this connection up to 1529.

[5] It is questionable whether the provisions of the act of 1487 should be regarded as an experiment (Bayne, op. cit. lxi), even though another act of the same year set up a court to deal with offenders in the Household (3 Henry VII, c. 14), and an act of 1495 set up a special court to deal with corrupt jurors (11 Henry VII, c. 25).

Humphrey Starkey to be chief baron of the Exchequer; all by signed bills with date 20 September 1485.[1]

Huse (or Husey), of Gray's Inn, had become the king's attorney-general in 1471, a serjeant-at-law in 1481, and been appointed chief justice of the King's Bench in 1481, and continued in office by Richard III. Brian, also of Gray's Inn, became a serjeant as early as 1463, and was appointed chief justice of Common Pleas soon after Edward IV's restoration in 1471, and continued under Richard III. Starkey, of the Inner Temple, became a serjeant in 1478 and was appointed chief baron ten days before the dethronement of Edward V, received a new patent from Richard III, and was soon appointed a justice of Common Pleas by him and by Henry VII.

Only one other chief justice of the King's Bench had to be found by Henry VII, and his choice was to promote John Fineux in November 1495, who less than two years earlier had been appointed a justice of Common Pleas, despite Morton's opposition to the elevation of a lawyer (a serjeant, of unknown inn, before 1485), who had expressed criticism of the government's fiscal policy. Fineux, a man outstanding in his profession, remained chief justice until his death in 1525.

A more rapid turnover occurred in the chief justiceship of Common Pleas. Brian died in October 1500, and was succeeded by Thomas Wood, who had been included among Henry VII's first call of serjeants in 1485, appointed king's serjeant in 1488, and a justice of Common Pleas in November 1495. But he died in 1502, and was followed by Sir Thomas Frowyk, of the Inner Temple, a serjeant since 1494, of such eminence that he was promoted direct to the chief justiceship. But he held the office for four years only and on his death in 1506 was succeeded by Sir Robert Read, who had been a justice of King's Bench from 1495, after having been of Lincoln's Inn, reader there, and serjeant from November 1485. He continued in the office until his death in 1519.

When Starkey died in October 1486, his successor as chief baron was William Hody, whose father John had been chief justice of the King's Bench in 1440–1, immediately before Sir John Fortescue. Hody retained the office for the whole of the rest of the reign and for the first eight years of Henry VIII's reign. He had been made attorney-general and a serjeant by Henry VII as recently as 1485.

---

[1] *Materials*, I, 13. But *Y.B. 1 Henry VII*, Mich., pl. 4, implies that all the justices' patents were made on 26 August. For the justices generally, *see* E. Foss, *Tabulae Curiales* (1865), 44–5; *Judges of England* (1870), *sub nom.* For the serjeants, *see* A. Pulling, *The order of the Coif* (1884).

Apart from those who were sooner or later promoted to be chief justices, fourteen further judges of the benches were appointed during the reign, and ten barons of the Exchequer. In the King's Bench these were Guy Fairfax and John Sulyard from September 1485 (both previously Yorkist appointees), Thomas Tremayle from 1488, and Robert Brudenall. One chief justice and two puisine judges at a time sufficed for the King's Bench, but double that number of puisne judges were appointed to Common Pleas. All four justices appointed in 1485 – Richard Neele, John Catesbey, Humphrey Starkey, chief baron, and Roger Townsend – had previously been appointed by Richard III. William Calowe and John Haugh followed in 1487, William Danvers in 1488, John Vavasour in 1490, Fineux and Thomas Wood, later chief justices, in 1494 and 1495, John Fisher in 1501, John Kingsmill in 1503, and John Boteler in 1508.

Similarly, Henry VII's first three barons of the Exchequer had served under Richard III, Bryan Roucliffe (or Radcliffe), Edward Goldsborough, and John Holgrave. Nicholas Lathell and Thomas Roche followed in 1487 and 1488; Thomas Barnewell in 1494, Andrew Dymock in 1496, Bartholomew Westby and William Bolling in 1501, and John Alleyn in 1504.

All the justices of both benches, and the two chief barons of the Exchequer had, in accordance with custom, been called to the degree of serjeant-at-law, before being appointed justices; none of the barons of the Exchequer, however, had been, and so far as is known, only three of them were members of an inn of court; the normal course of promotion to the bench in the Exchequer was service as an official therein. The outstanding feature of all these judicial careers was continuity of tenure despite the political vicissitudes of the times. All justices held office at the king's pleasure, but none was dismissed for political reasons, or indeed for any reason in the Yorkist and early Tudor periods, except after the Readeption of Henry VI in 1471. Sir John Fortescue had been replaced by John Markham as chief justice of the King's Bench in 1461, but Fortescue, who was perhaps the only politically minded justice of the whole period, had removed himself by fleeing with Henry VI. In any event, the number of serjeants available for promotion to the bench was quite small at any given time.[1] The common lawyer's profession, with its own system of training, its own hierarchy of apprentices, benchers, readers, its order of the Coif, could maintain its

[1] *See* E. W. Ives, 'Promotion in the legal profession of Yorkist and early Tudor England', *L.Q.R.*, 75 (1959), 348–63. The number apparently never exceeded fourteen at any one time in this period, and might fall much lower.

standards, pursue its rewards, often large, and serve the king and the law whoever happened to occupy the throne at any given time. Entry into the order of the Coif was by royal command to take up the status and degree of serjeant-at-law, admission to which was designed to furnish recruits to the judicial benches, and in any event normally entailed inclusion in judicial commissions of Assize, gaol delivery, etc. Not only was this – the first and most lucrative of the laymen's professions – a way for able men to climb to wealth and influence in the State, but it also contributed a salutary element of stability, continuity, and professional standards to a society which had need of these qualities, even though not all lawyers enjoyed public approbation.[1]

The king's justices had not only their own courts of King's Bench or Common Pleas, or Exchequer to attend to; they served regularly as itinerant justices on commissions of Assize, of *oyer et terminer*, gaol delivery and others, as well as sometimes on special commissions, and were also sworn of the commissions of justice of the peace for counties with which they might be connected. Some might perform other services on behalf of the government. All were liable to be summoned from time to time to an assembly of all the justices of England for matters of law, meeting usually but not always in the Exchequer chamber. This assembly for deciding difficult points of law was very much a fifteenth-century creation: the first reported assembly was in the reign of Henry IV. Reference to it was extensive from Henry VI's time, when its authoritative position became fully recognized. Some two hundred cases are reported in the Year Books from 9 Henry IV to 19 Henry VIII.[2] The function of this assembly, at which many of the serjeants and some apprentices assisted by argument, was to advise on points of law, which might be raised by the chancellor on a point of equity or common law, by parliament, by council, by any court of importance, or by the king himself. It was not a court of first instance; no individual litigant would get advice from it. Legal difficulties were referred to it, whether arising from complexities, the absence of precedents, equal division of opinion in the courts, or from reasons of policy. All kinds of law were its concern, whether common law, canon law, the law of the constable's and marshal's courts, law merchant, or palatinate custom. The opinions of the

---

[1] *See* E. W. Ives, 'The reputation of the common lawyer in English society, 1450–1550', *B.H.J.*, VII (1959–60), 130–61.

[2] *See* M. Hemmant (ed.), *Select cases in the Exchequer chamber before all the justices of England*, I, *1377–1461*, (S.S. 51, 1933); II, *1461–1509* (S.S. 64, 1943). There are instances of such meetings in the Parliament chamber, in the Inner Star Chamber, at the Blackfriars, and in the Whitefriars.

assembly, even of a majority thereof, were accepted without question, and no more authoritative pronouncement on legal problems could be got.[1]

The use made of the assembly by the king and others in the early years of Henry VII, especially on some difficult constitutional problems, is very relevant to our purpose. Indeed, the key to some of Henry VII's actions at the time of his accession and in ensuing years is to be found in the opinion of all the justices in Exchequer chamber.

Before the opening of Henry VII's first parliament, all the justices, it is reported,[2] met at the Blackfriars to consider '*les matters le Roy encontre le Parliament*'. There were, it was asserted, plenty of good statutes very profitable for the realm, if they could be executed. But how were they to be executed? That was the question. That indeed was the question which beset Henry's government, and it was often difficult to find satisfactory answers to it.

Two fundamental difficulties confronted Henry at the start. He was an attainted person, and his prospective wife and her sisters had been stigmatized as bastards by act of parliament. Both points were resolved by the justices in Exchequer chamber. As to the first, it was decided that no act reversing the attainder was necessary in the case of Henry, for it was held that on taking upon himself to be king, his attainder was *ipso facto* discharged.[3] The second point was more difficult. The problem was how to procure the reversal of the act which had bastardized Edward IV's children. Its contents were now deemed to be so scandalous that rehearsal of it in the parliament would be undesirable and recital of it in a repealing act should be avoided so as not to perpetuate its terms. But it could not be taken out of the record without an act of parliament to protect those who had custody of the records.[4] In the upshot the offending act was nullified without recital.

Also in the Exchequer chamber all the justices except two held that assignments against collectors of tenths made under Richard III were still valid even though Richard III had died before the collection had been completed.[5] All agreed, at the Whitefriars, that in the matter of the payment of the arrears of their own fees due from the customers and collectors of London, an act of Henry VI providing for this payment as a first charge on the customs must be followed notwithstanding an

[1] Hemmant, op. cit. I, xix, xxv.

[2] *Y.B. 1 Henry VII, Mich.*, pl. 3; extract in Chrimes, *English constitutional ideas in the fifteenth century*, 378, No. 72.

[3] *Y.B. 1 Henry VII, Mich.*, pl. 5; Chrimes, op. cit. 378, No. 74; cf. above, p. 60.

[4] *Y.B. 1 Henry VII, Hil.*, pl. 1; Chrimes, op. cit. 379, No. 75; cf. also above, p. 66.

[5] *Y.B. 1 Henry VII, Hil.*, pl. 5; Chrimes, op. cit. 379, No. 76.

Exchequer difficulty arising from the dates of patents appointing them as justices. The law was that they were to have their rate for each day of service, without regard to the date (26 August) of the patents made by the new king for the justices and the customers in relation to the Michaelmas or Easter days at which Exchequer practice normally made the payments.[1]

The chancellor put a 'great question' to all the justices about the legal effect of a bill sent from the 'Common hous' to the lords for their assent. Would the bill declaring that the inheritance of the crown of England and of France, with all the preeminences and prerogatives, had passed to our sovereign lord the king Henry VII and the lawful heirs of his body have the effect of a resumption of the franchises and liberties of all manner of persons, or not? The reply of the justice was 'not'.[2]

On other occasions the justices held that the statute of England bound the king's subjects in Ireland, and the king could not by licence give exemption from a statutory felony;[3] that letters patent ratified by parliament would be void if they did not adhere to the terms of the parliamentary confirmation;[4] and that the assent of the commons was necessary to give validity to an act of attainder.[5]

It may sometimes have been the case that acceptable advice was given by the justices to the king rather than that the advice given was accepted,[6] but this was rare, and in one outstanding case the king received a rebuff when he sought their opinion on a case of great importance to him, but which was *sub judice*. The king sought the opinion of all the justices on the legality of Humphrey Stafford's claim, in advance of the trial, that sanctuary rights made illegal his arrest on charge of high treason. But the justices would not do this. 'It is not good order to argue the matter and give our opinions before it has come before us judicially.'[7] Chief Justice Huse went to the king and besought him to excuse them, which with some reluctance he agreed to do. In due course, all the justices of both benches sitting in King's Bench decided that the claim to give sanctuary for treason could not be upheld when based on presumptive right alone, and all concurred in sentencing Stafford to death.[8]

---

[1] *Y.B. 1 Henry VII, Mich.*, pl. 5; Chrimes, op. cit. 378, No. 73.
[2] *Y.B. 1 Henry VII, Hil.*, pl. 2; Chrimes, op. cit. 381, No. 78.
[3] *Y.B. 1 Henry VII, Mich.*, pl. 2; Chrimes, op. cit. 377–8, No. 71.
[4] *Y.B. 10 Henry VII, Mich.*, pl. 20; Chrimes, op. cit. 386, No. 93.
[5] *Y.B. 4 Henry VII, Mich.*, pl. 11; Chrimes, op. cit. 382, No. 81.
[6] Hemmant, op. cit. I, xxxvi.
[7] ibid. lxvii.
[8] ibid. II, 115–24; *Y.B. 1 Henry VII, Trin.*, pl. 1.

It still remains impracticable to survey the functioning of the courts of King's Bench, Common Pleas, Exchequer, or Chancery in the reign of Henry VII. This is not because there is a lack of unprinted source material for these subjects; on the contrary the bulk of it is immense[1] and this circumstance is doubtless one reason why very few research workers have so far been attracted to the formidable task of coping with it on a scale sufficient to enable conclusions to be drawn. We cannot here attempt to summarize the legal history of the reign, nor would it be within our scope to try to do more than estimate the effect of Henry VII's government on the functioning of these courts.

It seems that the reign of Henry VII made little or no difference to the workings of the common law courts. There is not much evidence that Henry VII's government interfered with or modified the functionings of the common law courts in any marked degree, except that in matters especially touching the king's financial advantage greater reliance was put upon the conciliar machinery than upon the common law courts, which however continued to be the principal resource for maintaining law and order. It would be a delusion to suppose that Henry VII's government in any way undermined or distorted the work of the common law courts. The basic difficulties of these courts arose from the inherent weaknesses of common law procedure, not from interference by the Crown; indeed these weaknesses persisted, perhaps because of the Crown's inability or unwillingness to intervene by legislation to improve procedure. The introduction of the 'Bill of Middlesex' device helped to curtail procedure in some cases, but this had occurred in the mid-fifteenth century, and was in no respect novel in Henry VII's reign. In the only serious study of the work of King's Bench in the reign, still unpublished,[2] we are told that, although the court's intentions were good, it was often very busy doing nothing, busy recording failure rather than success. Its most serious defect was not slowness or expense, but the futility of its frequent recourse to outlawing as an expedient in judicial procedure. In the course of Michaelmas term 1488, when some two-thirds of the 958 cases were civil suits, outlawing, which was seldom reversed, was resorted to in the bulk of the cases, and few final judgments were recorded. Even in Crown Pleas, only about a fifth reached judgment. Outlawing as a means of getting

---

[1] cf. G. R. Elton, *The sources of history, England 1200–1640* (1969), 54–7.
[2] Marjorie Blatcher, 'The working of the court of King's Bench in the fifteenth century', unpublished Ph.D. dissertation (University of London, 1936). A summary of this was published in *B.I.H.R.*, XIV (1937), 196–9. The dissertation was based upon a meticulous investigation of the sources for Michaelmas term, 1488.

defendants into court was singularly ineffectual, but its financial possibilities did not pass unnoticed by the Crown. The time came when royal administrative action was taken to profit from outlawries and inlawries.[1] The Crown benefited therefrom, but the ineffectiveness of outlawing as a weapon in judicial procedure remained. But there was nothing new to Henry VII's reign in this, except perhaps the will to extract financial profit from it, and although national crises might still further slow down the machinery of King's Bench, it did not break down.

If what we know of the working of King's Bench in the reign is limited, at least we know something, which is more than we can say of Common Pleas. There has been no continuation of Professor Margaret Hastings's work,[2] and we must assume that that court continued in much the same way under Henry VII as it had during the Lancastrian and Yorkist periods with which her work was mainly concerned. Her conclusion as regards the working of Common Pleas was much the same as Dr Blatcher's for King's Bench – slow and ineffectual functioning bogged down in mesne process, but no breakdown. She was doubtless right in thinking that 'reforms were necessary when Henry Tudor seized the throne'.[3] Yet, as she herself recognized, the enactments of Henry VII's reign were, for the most part, not new in principle. She might, perhaps have gone further, and observed that the 'enactments' of Henry VII as regards the court of Common Pleas were negligible or non-existent.

As regards the court of Exchequer, we know nothing of its working for this period, except its efforts in enforcing penal statutes.[4] When we come to the question of the equitable jurisdiction of Chancery, we are confronted with grave difficulties. On the one hand we have almost no facts for the period; on the other hand we have a good deal of historian's generalities almost wholly derived from theorizings about earlier or later

---

[1] Dr Blatcher, 356–7, in the dissertation above mentioned, drew attention to Belknap's power as surveyor of the King's Prerogative (*see* above, p. 130) to enquire into lands of all persons convicted of felony and of outlaws, and to seize them for the Crown. He was to be remunerated with a ninth of lands so seized, and his deputies were to receive a tenth of the residue (citing P.R.O. Exchequer, Misc. Acts, E 101/ 517/14–15). The result of this pressure was to enable inlawries to be made expensive. Holinshed, *Chron.*, III, 553, says that Empson persuaded the king that it was lawful for pardons for outlaws not to be issued by Chancery until half the issues of all their lands had been paid into the king's use for two years. Dr Blatcher suggests that this profit may have been equivalent to the forfeiture of goods and chattels if the outlaws had been convicted of felony (op. cit. 357). But of course they had not been actually convicted.

[2] *The court of Common Pleas in fifteenth-century England* (New York, 1947).

[3] ibid. 239.   [4] *See* below, p. 191 ff.

periods, none of which can safely be applied to Henry VII's reign. Legal historians' inferences drawn almost wholly from studies of Christopher St Germain's treatise, *Doctor and student*, published in 1523 at the earliest,[1] cannot be taken as evidence of what the Chancery was doing under Henry VII, if indeed that treatise can be taken as evidence of actualities at any time. The concrete study of the equitable jurisdiction of Chancery in the later fifteenth century is only just beginning, and has not reached the reign of Henry VII.[2] But the results so far obtained are disturbing to received dogma on this subject.

Miss Avery may be right in asserting that 'the most striking institutional development of the Lancastrian period was the growth of the equitable jurisdiction of the court of Chancery',[3] but there are formidable difficulties in demonstrating with precision what this development amounted to. In the first half of the period the material consists of little more than petitions presented; only after 1440 do answers, replications, and examinations become at all common, and recorded judgments remained extremely rare. The petitions themselves can seldom be dated with accuracy, and it is only from the long chancellorship of John Stafford, from 1432 to 1450, that materials survive in substantial numbers, but the number of cases tended to increase during the period as a whole. Certain conclusions can be drawn.[4] The chancellors in this period were not administering a self-sufficient body of law; they were supplementing the common law. In the 'equitable' as distinct from the common law cases coming before the chancellors, the petitioners complained that no remedy was available at common law; in common law cases they complained that although a remedy at common law was available, it could not be obtained because of obstacles such as poverty or maintenance. In the absence of more than a few recorded judgments

---

[1] *See* P. H. Winfield, *The chief sources of English legal history* (1925), 321–4; cf. S. E. Thorne, preface to D. E. C. Yale (ed.), Hake's *Epieikia* (1953), vi, 'only after the appearance of the very influential *Doctor and student* . . . did English lawyers generally begin to differentiate between law and equity'.

[2] Margaret E. Avery's article, 'The history of the equitable jurisdiction of Chancery before 1460', *B.I.H.R.*, XLII (1969), 129–44, is indispensable. W. D. Baildon, *Select cases in Chancery*, S.S., X (1896), is inadequate and useless for the late fifteenth century. The generalities in W. S. Holdsworth, *History of English law*, V (1924), 215–18, are of no precise value for the reign of Henry VII. The latest legal history exposition, S. F. C. Milsom, *Historical foundations of the common law* (1969), 74–85, carries us no further on this subject. W. J. Jones, *The Elizabethan court of Chancery* (1967), is valuable for the later Tudor period. Stuart E. Prall, 'The development of equity in Tudor England', *American Journal of Legal History*, 8 (1964), is a useful generalized article, but has nothing to contribute on the subject before *Doctor and student*.

[3] Avery, loc. cit. 129.

[4] ibid. *passim*.

it is not possible to generalize about the remedies provided, but some cases show that the rules of common law were closely followed, and it can be assumed that these rules would be followed where appropriate. But the growth of equitable jurisdiction proper depended upon cases where the common law courts had no remedy to offer, and these cases were almost wholly concerned with contract and uses. The advantages to the petitioners in cases of contract arose from the fact that the common law courts largely restricted themselves to remedy in cases where written and sealed documents of contract could be cited. Chancery could offer equitable remedies where such documents could not be produced, or where strict performance could be deemed inequitable, or where protection was needed for victims of agreements made by force or fraud; or where specific performance or recovery of goods rather than damages[1] were sought.

But the great expansion of the chancellor's jurisdiction, Miss Avery concludes, in the fifteenth century, resulted from his defence of the interests of the *cestui que use* (the person for whose profit the land is held by someone else), and this became in the reign of Henry VI the main *raison d'être* of the court, 'and was due to the inability of the Crown to halt a process which was so damaging to its real interests'.[2] Henry VII's attempts to deal with the problem of uses by legislation is a matter to be considered below, under law-making,[3] but here, whilst bearing in mind the limited success which Henry VII met with in these attempts, the point to note is that 'the great development of the court was the result of pressure from the propertied classes', who sought to get the court to protect their recourse to the creation of uses in various forms. 'The equitable jurisdiction developed in spite of, or even because of, the weakness of the king' in this sphere. Chancery was not primarily a court for the poor and needy, nor a royal court for the suppression of disorder and the control of the overmighty subject. It was rather a tribunal for landowners who wished to escape the restrictions imposed by common law upon their freedom to deal with their lands as they wished.[4]

Whether or not Miss Avery's conclusions regarding the development of the equitable jurisdiction of Chancery before 1460 will be sustained for the period 1485–1509 must depend on detailed research upon the material for the period. But it seems highly likely that these conclusions will be upheld when that work comes to be undertaken, and some sense

---

[1] *See* W. T. Barbour, *The history of contract in early English equity* (1914), a valuable monograph which does not go beyond Richard III's reign.

[2] Avery, loc. cit. 135, 143.

[3] *See* below, p. 181.   [4] Avery, loc. cit. 143.

and substance is at last introduced into the theme. It still remains to be revealed just what part John Morton, chancellor for the fourteen years 1486–1500, played in the exercise of equitable jurisdiction. It would be interesting to ascertain how far his declaration that 'no one who came to Chancery should leave the court without a remedy' accorded with practice.[1] But until this revelation is made, conclusions concerning the court of Chancery under Henry VII are impossible.

However little Henry VII's government may have interfered with the common law courts, and whatever the development of the equitable jurisdiction of Chancery may have been, there is no doubt that his government concerned itself actively with the work of the justices of the peace. By 1485, we are told, 'the work of defeudalizing local government had been to a great extent accomplished, and the justices of the peace were undertaking the administrative work as well as the judicial duties of the counties, not only superseding the feudal lord but encroaching very considerably on the sphere of the sheriff'.[2] We are not here concerned directly with the administrative work of the justices, but it is worth bearing in mind that the importance of the sheriffs tended to decline in this period, that their reliability diminished, and that their malpractices attracted the vigorous intervention of Henry VII's government.[3] There were to be no lords lieutenant of counties before 1549,[4] and the concern with which Henry VII's government viewed the importance and potentialities of the justices of the peace is reflected in the fact that every parliament of the reign passed one or more statutory provisions relevant to the work of the justices. As many as twenty-one out of the total one hundred and ninety-two statutes of Henry VII's reign[5] had something to say about the justices, and one of these[6] represented a major attempt to oblige the justices to perform their duties properly.

By 1485, the justices had in theory all the powers as criminal judges that they had had by 1380, with some notable additions, but in practice the justices of Assize were encroaching upon some of their highest judicial powers. But in local government as Crown-appointed and Crown-controlled officials and administrators of a great body of legislation, much of it economic, they were superseding the old institutions, both criminal and feudal. By then the justices of the peace, although still

---

[1] Barbour, op. cit. 152, citing *Y.B. 4 Henry VII*, 4.8.

[2] Gladys Scott Thomson, *Lords lieutenant in the sixteenth century* (1923), 3. The present writer provided in Holdsworth, *History of English law*, I, 7th ed. (1956), a summary of recent work on the justices, 24*–29*, supplementing 285–95.

[3] *See* below, p. 187.

[4] Gladys Scott Thomson, loc. cit. 24.

[5] *See* below, p. 168.

[6] 4 Henry VII, c. 12; *see* below, p. 187.

acting in some degree in competition with other judicial commissions and controlled by writs from King's Bench, or more rarely from Chancery, or the council, had made good their position. The commons had been successful in pressing for the extension of the judicial powers of the justices, but had failed in trying to get them elected in the county courts. The development of quarter sessions helped to undermine the criminal jurisdiction of the county courts and the sheriff's tourn and courts of private jurisdiction, even though it was the judges of *trailbaston*, whose descendants were the justices of *oyer et terminer* of the fifteenth century, who 'stole the thunder' of the justices in eyre.[1]

It was doubtless no accident that the first printed treatise on the justices of the peace, and the first reading in the inns of court on their position date from Henry VII's reign. The anonymous *Boke of Iustyces of peas*, first printed in 1506, ran through thirty-two printings before 1599. This treatise concerned itself mainly with summaries of statutes up to 11 Henry IV relevant to the justices, with precedents, forms of writs and indictments, and charges to jurors. The most notable of the few expressions of the author's opinions is to the effect that 'A justice of the peace is a statute creature, and ought to act no further than the statutes empower him'. The work is mainly backward-looking, and is not reliable for a picture of the practice of the early sixteenth century. It no doubt served as a manual for the justices, and the frequency of its reprinting shows that it was popular for the purpose. Fitzherbert's better known *L'office et auctoryte des Iustyces de peas* did not appear until 1538, in French, but then in English in eleven subsequent editions; Lambard's oft-quoted *Eirenarcha* not until 1581.[2]

Three years before the anonymous *Boke* appeared, Thomas Marowe gave his reading on '*De pace terre*', which, however significant in itself, received no mention in the *Boke*, nor in Fitzherbert's treatise, and indeed no mention at all for half a century, though it came into its own in Lambard. A reading in the inns of court was not suitable as a manual of practice, and although Marowe's exists in eleven manuscript copies, it was destined not to be printed until Professor Putnam produced her edition in 1924.[3]

Marowe's reading, though providing a substantial analysis of the history of the office, a descriptive account of the difference between the

---

[1] Holdsworth, op. cit. 28*. The most important study of the early history of the justices of the peace is B. H. Putnam, *Proceedings before the justices of the peace in the fourteenth and fifteenth centuries, Edward III to Richard III* (1938).

[2] *See* B. H. Putnam, *Early treatises on the practice of the justices of the peace in the fifteenth and sixteenth centuries* (1924), 6–42.   [3] ibid. 145–222.

work of the conservators and the justices of the peace, and of the authority of the justices, is remarkable for its omissions. It quotes no writs or
indictments, no list of statutory offences falling into the justices' scope,
no account of their administrative duties, no adequate account of their
powers outside sessions. At best it can be described as a legal treatise for
such justices as might be learned in the law. But of course its primary
purpose was to provide an erudite reading in the Inner Temple, and
we may doubt whether Marowe had any other purpose in mind.

Marowe himself died on 5 April 1505, and his early death may account for the obscurity which befell his work. But there may have been
other reasons for its neglect. Marowe had succeeded Frowike as common
pleader of London in 1491, but became under-sheriff of London, for
some years jointly with Edmund Dudley, and both of them were appointed to the degree of serjeant-at-law in Michaelmas term, 1503.[1]
Marowe's friendship with Frowike, the future eminent chief justice,
may not have saved him from the odium later to be visited upon his
closer associate, Dudley. There is no evidence of any unpopularity of
either of them in London during their terms of office, and both were
rewarded with pensions by the City council, but in view of the later
turn of events it is perhaps unnecessary to seek further for the reasons
why Marowe's reading remained in manuscript.[2]

But our primary concern here is to examine the extent to which
Henry VII's parliaments made statutory provision for justices of the
peace. The twenty-one relevant enactments, taken as a whole, reveal
the extent to which the government relied upon the justices to perform
numerous duties, some old and some new, including the matter of dealing with riots, unlawful assemblies, retainers, and the extortions of
sheriffs; but also reveal the anxiety and doubts of the government as
to whether the justices actually performed these duties properly.

Among the comparatively minor duties reiterated or imposed may
be reckoned the task of examining the accused on information laid of
persons hunting in forests in disguise;[3] of taking inquests to enquire
into concealments by other inquests assessing amercements;[4] of taking
recognizances for the keeping of the peace and of certifying the same
into Chancery or King's Bench or Exchequer;[5] of allowing bail for

[1] *See* B. H. Putnam, 134–5.
[2] cf. generally, D. M. Brodie, 'Edmund Dudley, minister of Henry VII', *T.R.H.S.*,
4th ser., XV (1932), 133–62.
[3] 1 Henry VII, c. 7 (1485–6); *S.R.*, II, 505–6.
[4] 3 Henry VII, c. 1 (1487); *S.R.*, II, 509–10.
[5] 3 Henry VII, c 2; *S.R.*, II, 512.

persons arrested on suspicion of felony only under certain conditions;[1] of enquiring into 'damnable bargains grounded in usury, coloured by the name of new chevisaunce contrary to the law of natural justice';[2] of hearing and determining defaults in weights and measures;[3] of hearing complaints against collectors of fifteenths and tenths;[4] of punishing keepers of houses for dicing and other unlawful games and regulating ale houses;[5] of reviewing panels of inquests returned by the sheriff for the king;[6] and of panels of inquests set up to enforce the laws against perjury;[7] of assessing subsidies and of being associated with the commissioners;[8] of compelling officers to accept certain coins as legal tender;[9] of assigning persons as searchers of pewter and brass;[10] of enquiry into destruction of deer and herons and of committing offenders to prison pending surety for payment of consequential forfeitures.[11]

Five acts referred to the duties of the justices in regard to riots, unlawful retainers, and the extortions of sheriffs. Statute 11 Henry VII, c. 3[12] alleged that certain offences, such as riots, unlawful assemblies, maintenance, embracery, retainers, giving and use of liveries and tokens, not to mention the taking of wages in excess of lawful standards, the playing of unlawful games, or the wearing of inordinate apparel, went unpresented and unpunished because of the bribery and corruption of juries; it empowered the justices to proceed against committers of such offences upon information, whether they were indicted or not, except in treason, murder, or other felonies, provided the offences were committed in their respective counties. In the same parliament the commons prayed that procedure in cases of riots, routs, and unlawful assemblies should be improved, and it was enacted that the justices, whether on complaint or indictment, should make proclamation of the leaders in such activities in the next general sessions to appear, or, failing their appearance, should commit them to custody. If the offenders could not be seized, then they should stand convicted and be bound over

---

[1] 3 Henry VII, c. 3; S.R., II, 512–13.
[2] 3 Henry VII, c. 5; S.R., II, 514.
[3] 7 Henry VII, c. 3 (1491–2); and 11 Henry VII, c. 4 (1495); S.R., II, 551–2, and 570.
[4] 7 Henry VII, c. 11; S.R., II, 551–2.
[5] 11 Henry VII, c. 2; S.R., II, 569.
[6] 11 Henry VII, c. 24; S.R., II, 598.
[7] 11 Henry VII, c. 25; S.R., II, 589.
[8] 12 Henry VII, c. 13; S.R., II, 644.
[9] 19 Henry VII, c. 5; S.R., II, 650.
[10] 19 Henry VII, c. 6; S.R., II, 652.
[11] 19 Henry VII, c. 13; S.R., II, 655.
[12] ibid. 570.

to keep the peace. If the riots were heinous, the offenders were to be kept in prison until surety on their behalf had been forwarded to king and council. The record in such cases was to be certified under the seal of the *custos rotulorum* and be likewise sent to king and council. 19 Henry VII, c. 13,[1] took the point further by insisting that the justices should specify the names of such offenders under penalty of £20 for each omission, and that such specification should be equivalent to the verdict of a jury. 19 Henry VII, c. 14,[2] sought to enforce acts against unlawful retainers. The justices were at each general sessions to be held four times a year to send warrant to the sheriff to return a panel of twenty-four jurors having lands of the annual value of £5 or 40s at the least, to enquire into all unlawful retainers, to enquire into such offenders and certify the cases to the King's Bench under penalty of £100 for each omission. Such offenders might be proceeded against before the council in Star Chamber, King's Bench, or the king and his council. Any informer might lay information of such cases before the chancellor, the King's Council in Star Chamber, King's Bench, or the king and his councillors attendant upon him, provided that three councillors, including two lords spiritual and temporal, were present. Informers were to get costs and reward. Extortions by sheriffs, undersheriffs, and sheriffs' clerks were dealt with by 11 Henry VII, c. 11.[3] The justices were to receive complaints of this kind of abuse and were given power to examine the offenders, or to forfeit 40s for each default or failure to certify into the Exchequer.

Notwithstanding these numerous statutory intentions to rely upon the justices of the peace in such a variety of ways, early in the reign another statute then enacted could hardly be construed as a token of the government's confidence in their reliability. 3 Henry VII, c. 12,[4] expressed the king's great displeasure at the negligence, misdemeaning, and favour shown by the justices, whereby the laws and ordinances made for the 'politique wele peace, and gode rule and for the profit, surety and restful living of his subjects' are not duly executed. For to him 'nothing is more joyous than to know his subjects live peaceably under his laws and increase in wealth and prosperity'. Therefore it was enacted by authority of parliament that every justice of peace should cause to be proclaimed four times a year in general sessions, under penalty of 40s for each and every omission, a proclamation in the king's name, to the effect that the king (considering daily how his coinage

[1] *S.R.*, II, 657. [2] ibid. 658. [3] ibid. 579.
[4] ibid. 536–7. These statutes were surveyed by K. Pickthorn. *Early Tudor government, Henry VII* (1934), 63–6.

was counterfeited, murders, robberies, felonies occur, how unlawful retainers, idleness, unlawful games, extortions, misdemeaning by sheriffs, escheators, and others were common, all because the said laws are not put in execution as they ought to be by the justices) charged all justices of the peace to execute their commissions, under threat of being dismissed. All persons aggrieved by the mischiefs of the justices might complain to some other justice, or if not able to obtain redress, to any justice of Assize, or to the king, or to the chancellor. The king would make enquiry into such allegations, and put offending justices out of the commission and impose further punishments.

That this statute was drastic in intention cannot be doubted, and its candid exposure of the shortcomings of some at least of the justices was unflattering to their reputation. But how far it was justified by the facts, and how far it was effective in gaining its objectives cannot be estimated until much further research into the activities of the justices of the peace for the reign has been undertaken. The unusual phrasing of its preamble, however, suggests strongly that although the king's government was largely dependent upon the justices of the peace for the implementation in the shires of many parts of the law, it felt no great assurance that its principal instruments for the enforcement of law and order in the localities could be relied upon. If this is a fair inference, it follows that Henry VII's government did not notably succeed in solving the perennial problem that had beset his predecessors – how to enforce the laws of the realm.

PART III

Statecraft

Chapter 9

LAW-MAKING

(A) By Proclamation

The deliberate making of new law by the constituted authority of the realm was a phenomenon less conspicuous in the England of late mediaeval times than in that of the more modern period. But it had, of course, occurred often before 1485, and had been specifically recognized for what it was during the fifteenth century. By 1454, for example, Chief Justice Sir John Fortescue enunciated that parliament was so high and mighty in its nature that it might make law and unmake that which was law.[1] To make a change or addition to the existing law of the land, which was mostly the common law derived from custom and judicial decisions, was necessarily a solemn act of government, often with far-reaching consequences upon the life and activities of some or all of the people. To give authority to such legislation was always a significant and basic exercise of statecraft. Law-making, therefore, must be our first theme under that general heading.

Any consideration of law-making in the reign of Henry VII must take account of the possibility of legislation by royal proclamation. The emphasis placed by historians upon statutory law made by king in parliament has tended to obscure the historical importance of the Tudor monarch as the source of law. Royal enactment of statutes is certainly the best known form of legislation at this period, but the other, until recently less well known form, was by proclamation issued by the king with at most the consent of the council.[2] A proclamation has been defined 'as a public ordinance issued by the king, in virtue of his royal prerogative, with the advice of his council, under the Great Seal, and by royal writ'.[3] A proclamation conveys an express royal command; it is validated by the royal sign manual or signature; it is promulgated

---

[1] On the subject generally, see Chrimes, *English constitutional ideas in the fifteenth century*, 192–203, 249–53. For Fortescue's assertion, see *R.P.*, V, 239.

[2] R. Steele (ed.) *A bibliography of royal proclamations of the Tudor and Stuart sovereigns 1485–1714* (Bib. Lindesiana, V), I, *England and Wales* (1910), provided a general commentary and list of fifty-two proclamations by Henry VII. P. L. Hughes and J. F. Larkin printed the text of fifty-eight such proclamations, *Tudor royal proclamations*, I, *1485–1553* (Yale, 1694), and four more in the Appendix to vol. III (1969). Some comments on this valuable work are provided by G. R. Elton in his review of it in *Hist. Journal*, VIII (1965), 266–71.   [3] Hughes and Larkin, op. cit. xxiii.

by the terms of a royal writ, and the penalties to be imposed for viola-
tions of the command expressed are at the king's discretion. Few of the
extant proclamations by Henry VII specifically refer to the council's
consent, but there is evidence that the council was sometimes consulted
before promulgation or was involved in follow-up action, though since a
proclamation was essentially an exercise of royal prerogative, council
consent to it can hardly have been a necessity for its validity.

A royal proclamation was a legislative act and would have the force
of law,[1] and during the course of the Tudor period the importance of
proclamations greatly increased,[2] and even early Tudor examples show
'an uncanny skill in presentment',[3] but any appraisal of the significance
of such promulgations in the reign of Henry VII must be based upon
an analysis of the sixty-two proclamations issued by him and known
to us.

By far the largest category into which Henry VII's proclamations fell
was that of general administrative arrangements. Twenty-five fell into
that category, dealing with such matters as the mustering and victualling
of troops,[4] the surrender of rebels,[5] distraint of knighthood,[6] the maintenance of public order and prohibition of the spread of false news,[7] and
other miscellaneous matters.[8] Two more,[9] making announcements
about the payment of certain classes of the king's debts, are hardly in
any other category. No fewer than ten others[10] refer to monetary and
coinage matters, and though the royal concern for this question is
vividly revealed, administration is still the primary theme, and the
same can be said for six more devoted to the regulation of trade.[11]
Eleven proclamations[12] are given over to announcing truces, treaties,
peace, war, and courtesies to foreign potentates. Two[13] exercise the
prerogative of pardon; three seek to enforce statutes.[14] Two might be

[1] Hughes and Larkin, op. cit. xxvi–xxx.
[2] As under Henry VIII, see the standard histories, and the statistical tables in
G. R. Elton, loc. cit. 268–9.
[3] Hughes and Larkin, op. cit. xxvi, citing John Craig, The Mint (1933), 106.
[4] ibid. Nos 4, 6, 12, 20, 27, 36, 37.
[5] ibid. Nos 8, 15, 41.   [6] ibid. Nos 9, 48, 49, 53.
[7] ibid. Nos 11, 13, 14, 16, 19, 22, 24, 46, 47.   [8] ibid. Nos 32, 58.
[9] ibid. No. 55; and III, 20.5.
[10] ibid. Nos 10, 25, 38, 42, 43, 44, 54, 57; and III, 20.6, 20.7.
[11] ibid. Nos 18, 26, 27, 31, 45, 56.
[12] ibid. Nos 3, 7, 21, 23, 29, 33, 34, 40, 51, 52; and III, 23.5.
[13] ibid. Nos 2, 35.
[14] ibid. Nos 17, 30, 50. The first of these refers to 4 Henry VII, c. 12, regarding the
duties of justices of the peace; the second to 3 Henry VII, c. 2, and earlier acts
regarding felonies and other offences; the third to acts of earlier reigns prohibiting
retainers.

described as of constitutional significance and are of substantial interest;[1] one of these announces the death of Richard III and seeks to impose a pacification immediately after the battle of Bosworth; the other summarizes the papal bull recognizing the king's title.

There may, of course, have been other proclamations made that have not survived or are not known, but it is unlikely that any such were of greater importance than these. It seems evident therefore that Henry VII did not resort to his prerogative power to issue proclamations in order to add significantly to the law, and it is to the statute law of his reign that we must turn if we are to assess the legislative activity of his reign.

(B) By Statute

Francis Bacon was of the opinion[2] that the laws (i.e. the statutes) made in the reign of Henry VII were his 'preeminent virtue and merit', and it is upon this judgment that Henry VII's reputation as a legislator has mainly been grounded. So far as quantity is concerned, the 192 statutes enacted in his seven parliaments,[3] an average of slightly above twenty-seven per parliament, testify to considerable legislative activity. But only an analysis can reveal the importance of these numerous enactments. The largest category, with thirty-five items, are acts of attainder or restitution. Next, with thirty-one items, come trade, prices and wages regulations. Twenty-eight are so miscellaneous in content that they can scarcely be otherwise categorized. Twenty-two fall into a group of major concern to the lawyers, in as much as they in some degree modified the common law. Nineteen are of a personal character, affecting only the individuals specified. Fourteen come under the heading of law enforcement. Thirteen confer privileges or pardons, but of these no fewer than ten relate to the king's own rights. Twelve make fiscal provisions. Seven are largely concerned with the justices of the peace. Six refer to the merchants' position, especially alien merchants. The remaining five relate to church matters and include a further restriction on the privilege of 'benefit of clergy' in criminal trials.

Of these eleven main categories, a number – the acts of attainder and restitution, and the miscellaneous acts, the personal provisions, privileges and pardons – throw little light on Henry VII's reputation

---

[1] ibid. Nos 1, 5. [2] *Henry VII*, ed. Lumby, 74.
[3] Ten in 1 Henry VII (1485); sixteen in 3 Henry VII (1487); twenty-four in 4 Henry VII (1488–9); twenty-four in 7 Henry VII (1491); sixty-five in 11 Henry VII (1495); thirteen in 12 Henry VII (1496–7); forty in 19 Henry VII (1504); *see S.R.*, II, 499–694.

as a legislator. The acts largely concerned with the justices of the peace, along with others relating to them, have already been considered.[1] Those concerned with trade and mercantile regulations,[2] with law enforcement,[3] fiscal provisions,[4] and the Church[5] will receive attention below. Here our main consideration must be those twenty-two acts of significance in the juristic sphere.

Of those twenty-two statutes, two are of a general or even constitutional import; four touch upon criminal law; nine relate to procedural law; and seven modify land law in some respects.

The first two are the only ones that have attracted general attention; both have suffered the disadvantage of misnomer and misinterpretation springing ultimately from Bacon's eloquent misunderstanding of them. The first of these is the so-called but wrongly called 'Star Chamber' act of 1487, which has already been discussed.[6] The second of them is the so-called but wrongly called 'De facto' act of 1495.[7]

In spite of the fact that A. F. Pollard (more than forty years ago)[8] demonstrated beyond any doubt the significance of this act, misunderstanding of its manifest nature is still hard to eradicate, so long-lived are Baconian ideas buttressed by Coke's phrases.[9] There is nothing whatever in the act about kings '*de facto*' or '*de jure*'; nothing whatever about a distinction between a king's person and the king's office. The only king envisaged in it was the king for the time being. The main provision of the act was henceforth to protect faithful service and allegiance to the king for the time being from charges of treason, but excepting from this provision any one who should fail in his allegiance in future, i.e. in his allegiance for the king that then was, Henry VII. The purpose of the act was to reassure Yorkists (or other rebels) who had so far escaped attainder or forfeiture that no proceedings would be taken on the grounds of what they had done before Henry VII became 'the king for the time being'. It suspended the principle of '*nullum tempus occurit regi*' (time does not run against the king) for the benefit of those persons who remained faithful in their allegiance to Henry VII. It assumed, as Pollard also observed,[10] that the question of the succession to the throne

---

[1] *See* above, p. 164.   [2] *See* below, p. 220 ff.   [3] *See* below, p. 186 ff.
[4] *See* below, p. 195 ff.   [5] *See* below, p. 243 ff.
[6] *See* above, p. 100.   [7] 11 Henry VII, c. 1.

[8] 'The de facto act of Henry VII', *B.I.H.R.*, VII (1929), 1–12. The correct interpretation and the text of the statute were given by G. R. Elton, *The Tudor constitution* (1966), 2, and No. 2.

[9] *Henry VII*, ed. Lumby, 133. The terms '*de facto*' and '*de jure*' appear to have been introduced into the discussion by Sir Edward Coke, *Third Institute* (ed. 1809), 6 ff.

[10] Pollard, loc. cit. 12.

was closed. The only then conceivable sovereign, after ten years of possession, was Henry VII himself. It was a 'measure of temporary expediency of very limited scope'.

The attempt in the act to prohibit any future change is hardly a serious assertion of the principle of the inability of a future parliament to make a change in the law by statute. The conception of repeal of an act by parliament was perfectly well understood and practised before this time.[1] The Baconian phrase on this part of the act may well be allowed to stand, for it can scarcely be bettered. 'Things that do not bind may satisfy for the time.'

The act of 1495, therefore, along with that of 1487, must be interpreted realistically. The latter created a ministerial tribunal which had nothing to do with the court of Star Chamber and made little mark upon the jurisdictional activity of the time; the former retrospectively justified allegiance to Richard III whilst he had been 'king for the time being', even though it had been treated as treason from 1485 to 1495.[2] It would indeed be difficult to regard such a manifest expedient as the enunciation of a great constitutional principle. It was no more than a prudent attempt at a pacification, dictated (albeit belatedly) by 'reason and good conscience', as the preamble to the act suggested.

Of the four statutes that dealt with matters within the sphere of criminal law, the first alleged that murders daily increased, and sought to oblige coroners to exercise their office according to law and made some improvements in the procedure of dealing with persons accused of murder.[3] The second statute[4] declared the abduction of women, whether maids, widows, or wives, and marrying them against their will or defiling them, or procuring or abetting such an offence, to be felony[5] unless the woman was in ward or a bondwoman. Another statute pronounced penalty of forfeiture of goods and imprisonment upon captains retained to serve the king overseas if they failed to produce the proper

---

[1] See Chrimes, *English constitutional ideas*, 265–6.

[2] It is notable that from 1495 onwards the description of Richard III as 'king indede but not in right', until then common in acts of parliament and elsewhere, appears to have been dropped, and thenceforth he figures as 'Richard, late duke of Gloucester, otherwise called King Richard III', or as 'the said King Richard'. Pollard, loc. cit. 2.

[3] 3 Henry VII, c. 2. Under other terms of this act murderers might be arraigned within a year and a day without waiting for an appeal to be initiated; if acquitted an accused person was to be imprisoned pending a possible appeal until a year and a day had elapsed. Townships were to be amerced for escapes of prisoners by day, and the coroners were to enquire into, and justices of the peace were to certify, such incidents.

[4] 3 Henry VII, c. 3.　　　　　　　　　　　　　　　　[5] 7 Henry VII, c. 1.

number of soldiers and failed to pay them their full wages, and declared desertion by the soldiers to be felony without benefit of clergy. The same benefit was taken away from any lay persons found guilty of petty treason by the murder of their masters, by the fourth statute in this group.

Eight statutes may be said to have related to procedural matters. But two of these were confined to arrangements in one locality only;[1] one other was passed and repealed in the same parliament; another passed in the last parliament complained[2] that an act in the second parliament was not being enforced, confirmed it and ordered it to be put in execution. We are left therefore with only four acts to be examined. The first of these was aimed at penalizing the suing out of writs of error only to delay judgments.[3] The second sought to restrict forfeit of lands and goods by persons outlawed in the county of Lancaster to that shire only, but this was repealed in the same parliament.[4] The third provided that poor persons should at the discretion of the chancellor have original writs and *writs of subpoena* free, and that the justices should appoint counsel for them likewise free of charge.[5] The fourth decreed that, because of delays in actions on the case, like process should be had in such actions as in trespass or debt.[6]

Of the seven statutes relating to land law five were concerned with feoffments to use (i.e. grants of land to be held to the use or profit of some other person), and this is clearly the question of major importance in the legislation of the reign, and requires consideration. Of the other three acts, one merely decreed that freehold in Calais chargeable for guarding Calais should be forfeit to the king on neglect of duty for a year and a day,[7] and hardly comes into the land law category at all. St. 4 Henry VII, c. 24, re-enacted and improved 1 Richard III, c. 7, in the matter of procedure on fines. Fines were to be proclaimed (in accordance with 27 Edward I, St. 1, c 1) in the court of Common Pleas during the term when they were levied and the three succeeding

---

[1] 12 Henry VII, c. 7. A further statute, 4 Henry VII, c. 13, concerned with other restrictions of benefit of clergy, must be borne in mind, but is better dealt with under another heading. *See* below, p. 243. It is, however, considered to be of some importance in the history of the legal concept of murder. *See* J. M. Kaye, 'The early history of murder and manslaughter', *L.Q.R.*, 83 (1967), 569.

[2] 19 Henry VII, c. 16, fixed the qualifications for jurors in the sheriff's tourn in Southampton, Surrey, and Sussex. 19 Henry VII, c. 24, decreed that the shire courts of Sussex should be held alternately at Chichester and Lewes.

[3] 3 Henry VII, c. 11, confirmed by 19 Henry VII, c. 20.

[4] 7 Henry VII, c. 10, repealed by c. 20.   [5] 11 Henry VII, c. 12.

[6] 19 Henry VII, c. 9.   [7] 11 Henry VII, c. 16.

terms, and then to be final, saving the rights and interests of others (if under certain disabilities at the time) and reversionary and future actions and rights, for five years. Henceforth fines could be levied either at common law or under the act.[1] St. 11 Henry VII, c. 20, was of some but limited importance in the history of the doctrine of seisin and of conveyancing.[2] This act was doubtless interesting to the conveyancers, but the other statutes concerning feoffments to uses,[3] although also somewhat technical, were of much wider significance. But to put these in some perspective, it is necessary to review the background to Henry's legislation in this field.[4]

For more than a hundred years before this period feoffments to uses had been accepted as the most convenient and advantageous way for a landholder to make settlements of his land, and provided a lord did not deprive the king of all his rights, the royal escheators usually did not interfere in such arrangements. In any event without specific legislation the powers of escheators and other officials were insufficient to prevent losses of incidents due to the Crown by the evasive possibilities of the practice. Little, however, was done to limit the erosion of royal revenues from this source by this practice until the reign of Edward IV.[5] The first Yorkist king addressed his attention to the problem, particularly in the duchy of Lancaster, by setting up commissions of enquiry to investigate evasion of royal rights, and is reported to have imposed heavy fines on those who entered on inheritances without licence. By the time of his last parliament, Edward IV[6] was attempting to legislate on the problem by act of parliament, but only in relation to the duchy of Lancaster. The act as passed, however, was weaker than the bill upon

---

[1] cf. Holdsworth, *History of English law*, III, 120, 244; IV, 483. A fine in this context meant a legal agreement between parties, especially to convey land.

[2] ibid. IV, 484.

[3] Three of these may be dealt with summarily. 3 Henry VII, c. 5, related to uses but not to land and strictly speaking does not fall in the present group. By it deeds of gift of goods and chattels made in trust for the use of the donors (to defraud creditors) were to be void. Two other statutes dealt with minor points and can best be mentioned here. 1 Henry VII, c. 1, allowed demandants informed on to proceed against the pernor of profits, i.e. the *cestui que use*, and were not to be obliged to sue the feoffee. By 3 Henry VII, c. 16 (apparently only until the next parliament), a person having action or such 'hanging to the use of other persons', was not to be excluded from proceeding, notwithstanding outlawry, attainder, or conviction; cf. Holdsworth, op. cit. IV, 443, 444, 428.

[4] It would scarcely be practicable to do this but for the valuable work of J. M. W. Bean, *The decline of English feudalism, 1215-1540* (1968), on which the passages that follow are largely based: cf. Holdsworth, op. cit. IV, 407-49, generally. Some useful information is contained in J. L. Barton, 'The mediaeval use', *L.Q.R.*, 81 (1965), 562-77.   [5] Bean, op. cit. 235-40.   [6] *R.P.*, VI, 207.

which it was based, and it would appear therefore that he was obliged to accept amendments made to it in the course of its passage through parliament. Even so, this act of 1483 was repealed by Richard III's parliament of 1484,[1] presumably in the hope of getting the political support of the tenants of the duchy. Edward IV's attempt, however, was remarkable as the first legislative effort to prohibit the evasion of feudal incidents – the essential *raison d'être* of feoffments to uses. The very legislation itself was based on the assumption that the *cestui que use* was the real occupier of the land. Uses had become an inherent part of the structure of land ownership, and neither the Yorkists nor Henry VII could alter the fact. Henry VII sought to put some limit on Crown losses of feudal incidents, but was unable to do more than a very little. St. 4 Henry VII, c. 17 (1490), was the first attempt to legislate on uses on a national scale, and was followed fifteen years later by St. 19 Henry VII, c. 15, which if anything revealed how little he could do in the matter.

That Henry VII made the collection of the feudal incidents which were his due a major feature of his financial policy is not open to doubt,[2] but here our concern is with his legislation on the point, and it is the modest nature of his achievement in a sphere so close to his financial interests that is the outstanding feature, pointing as it does at once to his consciousness of the importance of the problem and the weakness of his political position vis-à-vis the vested interests of the landed classes.

The statute 4 Henry VII, c. 17, was passed in the third session of the parliament of 1489–90, and its passage then was inspired by apprehension of the situation which would arise in the lands of Henry Percy, fourth earl of Northumberland, who had been murdered on 28 April 1489, leaving an heir of eleven years of age and roughly three-quarters of his landed revenues in the hands of feoffees to his use.[3] The act of 1490 was a legislative recognition on a national scale of the state of affairs in which tenants-in-chief, by employing feoffments to use, were manipulating after their death revenues which belonged to the Crown. The act[4] provided that if a *cestui que use* died without making a will of his lands, the lord should secure the incidents of tenure which would have been due to him if his tenant had died seised. This provision applied to all sub-tenants, and although the writ of ward procedure specified for enforcing the lord's rights could not apply to the king there is no doubt

---

[1] *R.P.*, VI, 261–2; H. G. Hanbury, 'The legislation of Richard III', *American Journal of Legal History*, 6 (1962), 95–113, has little historical value, and p. 99 misses the essential point of this act.

[2] *See* below, p. 209.   [3] Bean, op. cit. 242–5.   [4] *S.R.*, II, 540.

that the act, which the Crown had initiated, gave to it the advantage of its provisions. Even so, the act was in no sense a radical one; it could operate only where the *cestui que use* had not made a will at the time of his death.

If St. 4 Henry VII, c. 17, is no great tribute to Henry VII's power as a legislator, St. 19 Henry VII, c. 15[1] is almost a monument to his humiliation in tackling the problem. It reveals the extent to which he was obliged to continue to accept loss of incidents by the practice of uses. The act, apart from useful but minor provisions,[2] laid down that the *cestui que use* shall have all the advantages in law as if he were sole seised, but if he were a bondman, his lord might enter on land held to his bondman's use, as if the land was held in fee or otherwise. 'No doubt the Crown, as the lord of the largest number of bondmen in the kingdom, gained most from this statute. But only in the case of unfree manorial tenants did it succeed in securing legislation which in effect enabled it to oust their feoffees.'[3]

The conclusion to be drawn is that Henry VII, even towards the end of his reign, was not strong enough to prevent the loss of feudal revenues because of uses; he could neither abolish uses completely nor adequately safeguard loss of incidents consequential from uses. He could not deprive landowners of the great advantages accruing from uses. He could but tacitly accept the practice, whilst striving to obtain increased revenue from feudal incidents by methods which, according to Professor Bean, verged on, or approximated to, blackmail.[4]

So far it seems that there is little to support Bacon's encomium to the effect that Henry VII 'may justly be celebrated for the best law-giver to this nation, after King Edward the first'.[5] We cannot, of course, here examine the legislative achievements of all the sovereigns between Edward I and Henry VII in order to comment more fully on Bacon's claim, still less those of Henry VII's successors to James I, but useful as many items in the legislation of the reign may have been, they are hardly of sufficient novelty or substance to confer upon Henry VII any great reputation as a legislator.

Nor can we accept the assertion that 'to the parliaments of Henry VII there was to be presented a greater number of official bills than of commons' bills or that the government was largely to replace the commons as the initiator of statutory legislation'. These assertions were

---

[1] ibid. 660.

[2] The other main points were to make the lands of the *cestui que use* liable for execution of judgments of debts, and to secure to lords the relief and heriots of the *cestui que use* of lands in socage, cf. Holdsworth, op. cit. IV, 428, 443, 449.

[3] Bean, op. cit. 255. [4] ibid. 256. [5] *Henry VII*, ed. Lumby, 69.

originally made[1] on the assumption that there was such a thing as an 'official bill' (i.e. a bill initiated by the government subjected to procedure different from that accorded to other bills). But this assumption was not proved at the time it was made.[2] There has in fact never been such a thing as an 'official bill', but naturally the government could and did initiate bills which became statutes in the time of Henry VII, as it has always been able to do. But there is no simple means of identifying for certain in what way many of the statutes of Henry VII originated, unless the content reveals it. A substantial number of these statutes specifically refer to the prayer of the commons or to the petition to the commons by some other body. Such instances as these can be taken as not having been initiated by the government. Others make no such reference, and the inference in these cases must be that the government had taken the initiative, an inference which is certain when, as occasionally happened, the king's will was explicitly mentioned. We may doubt very much whether such instances account for the majority of the statutes enacted and there can be no supposition of the 'dominance' of official bills over commons' bills in the parliaments as a whole, though this may have occurred in some parliaments, provided we mean by 'dominance' merely 'arithmetical majority'. Naturally the content of these bills was more significant than that of other bills, for the government would not bother to initiate legislation that was not of substantial government interest, except when it was moved to support some private or individual interest. In any event, there was not any doubt that the commons, the lords, and the government had the right to initiate, and who did originate and what the fate was of any bill depended upon the play of political forces at the moment.

[1] H. L. Gray, *The influence of the commons on early legislation* (1932), 141–61.
[2] S. B. Chrimes, *English constitutional ideas in the fifteenth century* (1936), 236–49. K. Pickthorn, *Early Tudor government*, I, *Henry VI* (1934), appreciated that the caption *communes petitiones* did not necessarily mean 'commons petitions' (p. 127), but failed to discount the notion of 'official bills' (p. 128). G. R. Elton was very right to question the assumption that much of the legislation of the reign necessarily represents the king's policy, except in the sense of mere acceptance, 'State planning in early Tudor England', *E.H.R.*, 2nd ser., XIII (1961), 433–9. *See* below, p. 219 ff.

Chapter 10

LAW ENFORCEMENT

At present it is difficult to find much evidence that Henry VII's government attained any marked success in tackling the perennial problems of law-enforcement. There is indeed little evidence that any very striking attempts were made to enforce it, except where such attempts redounded to the financial advantage of the Crown. At least fourteen statutes were enacted that can be considered to fall within the sphere of enforcement, and the preambles to some of these manifest acute awareness of the unsatisfactory observance of the law, but with a few exceptions, the substance of the enactments did little but reiterate what had previously been enacted or provide some further measures that reveal how little the law was in reality being enforced. Clearly the will to enforce the extant laws was often lacking in those whose position, powers, and influence should have provided the impetus without which the government could only partially function. Chief Justice Huse put his finger on the essential point at that meeting of all the justices at Blackfriars early in the first year of the reign. 'The law,' he said, 'will never be well executed until all the lords spiritual and temporal are of one accord, for the love and dread they have for God or for the king, or both, to execute them effectually, and when *the king on his part* and the lords on their part both want to do this – and do it.'[1]

The basic problem was of course a moral one, as it always is. If the great and powerful (including the king himself) did not exert themselves to enforce the law and to refrain from abusing legal process, inevitably the standard of observance would not be high. Whilst we may well believe that Henry VII desired to secure the maintenance and enforcement of the laws, and sought by statutory and other means to improve the prospects, it is not easy to find much concrete evidence of his government's action to enforce the laws, except in spheres of financial interest.

As we have seen, surprisingly little initiative was taken by the

[1] *Y.B. Henry VII, Mich.*, pl. 3, cited above, p. 64. Otherwise, he went on to say, all would take them lightly, and if they were chastised or punished others would be ready to stand surety for them. I have ventured to italicize very significant words in this quotation.

government, so far as we know, in prosecuting offenders before the
council in Star Chamber or elsewhere, or before the ministerial tribunal
set up by the statute of 1487. That more was done in King's Bench is
possible, but the only study of its workings so far available is not very
encouraging to the idea.[1] We do know, however, that a good many
prosecutions were initiated in the court of Exchequer.[2] In any event,
whatever the government may have desired, it was to a very large
extent dependent upon instruments which were often decidedly unreliable. The statutes of the reign in themselves reveal the shortcomings of
justices of the peace, the corruptions of sheriffs and sheriff's officers, and
of jurors. The weakness of the common law courts in the face of the old
practices of maintenance, champerty, embracery, the giving of liveries,
and of retainers by indenture or otherwise – the very offences which the
tribunal of 1487 had been set up to deal with – is obvious. But these
offences continued to be legislated against until the last parliament of
the reign, and we can therefore hardly suppose that the tribunal or the
other courts met with any marked success in suppressing these notorious
evils during the first nineteen years of the reign.

The parliament of 1487 (assembled, it will be remembered, some
five months after the battle of Stoke), which saw the enactment of the
ministerial-tribunal statute, also saw the enactment of a very remarkable measure, testifying at once to the dangerous weakness of Henry
VII's position even at that date and to the difficulty he evidently
experienced in using the normal procedures for coping with treason.
St. 3 Henry VII, c. 14, alluded to the fact that in the absence of actual
deeds, there was no remedy for treasonable intentions against the king,
the king's councillors, great officers of the Household, or any lord, but
the envy and malice of the king's Household servants had of late been
such as likely to lead to the compassing of the death of the king himself.
For this reason, the steward, treasurer, and controller of the Household,
or any one of them, was to have power to enquire by twelve 'sad and
discrete' persons of the Check Roll of the Household, whether any
servant sworn and named on that roll, under the rank of a lord, had
taken part in any confederacy, compassings, conspiracies, or imaginings
to destroy or murder the king or any such aforesaid persons. If enquiries
suggested that any such servants had so participated, any two of the
great officers were empowered to put them on trial by a jury of twelve
other members of the Household, and if found guilty, the offenders were
to stand convicted of felony and attainted at common law.[3]

[1] See above, p. 162; and below, p. 191.
[2] See below, pp. 191-2.   [3] S.R., II, 521.

If in 1487 Henry VII was driven to such a measure as this by suspicions as to the intentions of some of his own Household servants, it is
not surprising that local officers and agents were exposed to statutory
censure and threatened with penalization for defaults in most of his
parliaments. The justices of the peace were frequently reminded of their
duties, especially in the act 4 Henry VII, c. 2, which very stridently
invoked them to perform their lawful tasks.[1] The sheriffs were likewise
censured and penalized under the terms of St. 11 Henry VII, c. 15.[2]
This act referred to the great extortions brought about by the subtle and
untrue demeanour of sheriffs, undersheriffs, and shire clerks and sought
to provide remedies. St. 11 Henry VII, c. 26,[3] reminded sheriffs of
the qualifications for jurors in sheriffs' tourns that had been laid down
by 1 Richard III, c. 4, but allowed relaxation if sufficient persons
with the requisite qualifications were not available. By another statute,[4]
the sheriffs were made responsible for the keeping of all the king's
gaols (except those held in fee), and were to be fined for all negligent
escapes.

Jurors were similarly visited with statutory correction. London jurors
were to be highly qualified with the possession of 40 marks in land or
chattels and subjected to forfeiture for non-appearance; their false
verdicts were to be liable to attaint by bill in the court of Hastings, and
their corruptions subject to enquiry even if their verdicts complained
of were found to be true.[5] The false verdicts of any jurors were to be
remedied by writ of attaint obtainable by the aggrieved party against
the jurors and the party benefited; jurors in attaint actions were to
possess 20 marks of freehold in ancient demesne, and the penalty for
jurors attainted was to be £20 each, half to go to the king and half to
the aggrieved party.[6] But this provision was to continue only until the
next parliament. Then the duration of the validity of this and other acts
was extended until the next parliament, 'because they had not been put
into execution for shortness of time'.[7] Why it was deemed appropriate
to enact important measures of this kind temporarily only, is a mystery,
but it hardly testifies to the firm intentions of the government. Still, this
act was continued again in the next parliament,[8] which proved to be
the last of the reign.

Four statutes of the reign sought to deal with the old problem of
livery and retaining and the abuses resulting. Of these, none except

[1] See above, p. 166.
[2] S.R., II, 522.
[3] ibid.
[4] 19 Henry VII, c. 10; S.R., II, 654.
[5] 11 Henry VII, c. 21; S.R., 584.
[6] 11 Henry VII, c. 24; S.R., II, 588.
[7] 12 Henry VII, c. 2; S.R., II, 636.
[8] 19 Henry VII, c. 3; S.R., II, 649.

perhaps the last (19 Henry VII, c. 14) was particularly original. Edward IV, in his substantial act of 1468, had sought to define what was lawful retaining, but the vagueness of the terms of that act had left uncertainty behind it. There was undoubtedly in 1485 such a thing as lawful retaining, and this continued to be the case throughout Henry VII's reign. The problem was to define exactly what species of retaining was unlawful and to prescribe penalties for such unlawful practices. Henry VII made some progress with this definition and prescription; but it still remained open to the Crown itself to prosecute or not to prosecute for infringements of the law, and in this respect it is difficult to see that the government pursued any very consistent policy. It can hardly be said that Henry VII sought to abolish the practice of retaining. On the contrary he clearly wished to preserve it, but so far as possible only so that he himself got the benefit of it for his own purposes. He sought to repress it in so far as its practice by his subjects redounded to the public disadvantage and the corruption of public order, but to ensure its continuance so far as his own interest was engaged. It was not possible to connive and even encourage retaining for the king's service without also risking the abuses inherent in the practice. In fact the practice and its risks continued long after Henry VII's death.[1]

In his first parliament[2] Henry VII had shown himself well aware of the dangers of the practice, by persuading the commons and the lords to take an impressive oath not to retain or be retained unlawfully, and a similar oath was in January 1486 to be taken locally by other persons in the presence of royal commissioners. But the futility of mere oath-taking was expressed by Chief Justice Huse on the same occasion as he made other forthright pronouncements.[3] In any event, the ambiguity of the act of 1468 remained and it was hard for even judicial opinion to decide whether the retaining of persons other than household servants was necessarily unlawful.[4] Henry VII's first relevant statute, 3 Henry VII, c. 15,[5] did not take the point any further, but did seek to oust from office any of the king's local officers if they allowed themselves to retain or be retained unlawfully or participate in any field, assembly, or rout

---

[1] The fullest discussion of these matters is to be found in W. H. Dunham, *Lord Hastings's indentured retainers 1401–83* (New Haven, 1955), esp. 90–116.

[2] *See* above, p. 64.

[3] *See* above, p. 64. He remarked that as king's attorney in Edward IV's time he had seen the lords swear to keep the laws and an hour later in Star Chamber break their oaths by other oaths completely contrary to the first: *Y.B. 1 Henry VII, Mich.*, pl. 3. As Dunham, op. cit. 92, observes, the oath here referred to was not the same as Henry VII promoted in 1485.

[4] ibid. 91–2. [5] *S.R.*, II, 522.

without the king's command, and to forfeit the grants and leases of any of the king's farmers or tenants, should they similarly offend.

The next relevant statute rather tamely referred to 'the many good statutes' that existed against unlawful assemblies, riots, livery, maintenance, embracery, as well as such different practices as the taking of excessive wages and the playing of unlawful games, and passed some of the responsibility for enforcing the law to the justices of the peace.[1]

The same parliament, however, in another act complained that notwithstanding the good statutes, the king's officers were failing to refrain from retaining and being retained, and tightened the powers of the justices of the peace to correct them.[2]

Certainly Henry VII on several occasions tried to bring home to various classes of his subjects the overriding obligation to observe their allegiance to him, and consequently to refrain from entering into retainer relationships that might conflict with that obligation.[3] But all retaining always had been explicitly or implicitly saving allegiance to the king, and Henry VII's desire to emphasize the fact was not in itself a limitation or further definition of lawful retaining. The best that Henry VII could do was set forth in the statute of the 19th year, c. 14.[4] But in substance this act was little more than a repetition of 8 Edward IV, c. 2,[5] which, along with all other relevant statutes, it ordered to be observed and executed. Both acts forbade any person to give any livery or sign or to retain any persons other than his menial servants, officers or men of law, by any writing, oaths, promise, livery, sign, badge, token, or in any other wise *unlawfully* retain. It is true that Edward IV's act in another passage appears to include among permitted classes of retainers, in addition to menial servants, officers, and men of law, persons 'for loyal service done or to be done', but it is far from clear whether this omission in phraseology was deliberate or significant. It still remained

[1] 11 Henry VII, c. 9; *S.R.*, II, 57.
[2] 11 Henry VII, c. 7; *S.R.*, II, 573.
[3] 11 Henry VII, c. 18; *S.R.*, II, 582; declared the duty of all the king's subjects to serve him in war if required, except the master of the Rolls, other Chancery clerks, officials of the courts and Exchequer, the king's attorney and solicitor, and the serjeants-at-law; St. 19 Henry VII, c. 1, insisted that grantees of land from the king must attend him in war if needed, on pain of forfeiture. cf. Dunham, op. cit. 92–4, where however the connection between such measures as these and the problem of retaining is perhaps over-emphasized.
[4] *S.R.*, II, 658. Proclamation to enforce the statutes against retaining had been made, 10 March 1502. *See* Hughes and Larkin, op. cit. I, No. 50; cf. *C.P.R., 1494–1509*, 286–7. Extracts from the statute are printed in Elton, *The Tudor constitution*, No. 18.
[5] *S.R.*, II, 426–9. Extracts printed in Chrimes and Brown, op. cit. No. 280.

true that what was forbidden was unlawful retaining, but there was no novelty in that. The penalties prescribed for infringements were the same as in 1468. The giver of every livery or badge was to forfeit 100s, and every person who should unlawfully retain or be retained was to forfeit 100s, in each case per month. The act of 1468 defined the courts and the procedure to be used for cases of infringement, and the act of 1504 specified that any person could sue or complain before the chancellor or the keeper of the Great Seal, in the Star Chamber, or before the King's Bench, or before the king and his council attending upon him, and the usual conciliar procedure was to follow, with 'reasonable reward' for the plaintiff or informer. The act of 1504 was more forthright and stringent in the procedures it envisaged than that of 1468, and both acts contained provisos which made exceptions from the act in favour of the use of liveries at certain ceremonies and the practice of retaining in defence of the realm. Henry VII's act was very specific in excepting from its provisions persons who, by virtue of the king's placard or writing signed with his own hand and sealed with the Signet or Privy Seal, should enter into retaining to do the king service. The king might therefore issue licence for retaining, and so long as he used this power there would be no abolition of the practice. But the astonishing feature of the act was the temporary and uncertain duration of its validity. It was to apply from the feast of Pentecost next ensuing for the term of the king's life and no longer. Naturally no one then knew that by Pentecost five years later the king would be dead, but the reason for such a limitation is an inexplicable mystery.

Evidence for prosecutions under the act is not abundant. Very few such cases appear to have come before the council, none in Star Chamber, some but not many of much importance in King's Bench.[1] The only peer known to have been prosecuted for retaining in Henry VII's reign was George Neville, Lord Burgavenny.[2] He was certainly a very major offender against the act, but he can scarcely have been the only one. He had however been implicated in the Cornish rebellion in 1497, and no doubt this was one of the circumstances which induced Henry VII to extract very large financial penalties from him in 1507 on charges of retaining contrary to the act. Other entries in Dudley's Account Book suggest that compounding for retaining offences may

[1] Dunham, op. cit. 100–5, gives references.

[2] ibid. 103–5. There is still no documentary support for Bacon's story about Henry VII's dealings with John de Vere, earl of Oxford, in the matter of his retainers. But the story itself makes no reference to litigation, it merely alleges that the earl compounded for the offence. Bacon, *Henry VII*, ed. Lumby, 192–3.

have staved off other prosecutions and given a fillip to Henry VII's financial advantage, if not indeed a suggestive of the motive for the act.

It was after the turn of the century that Henry VII's government took steps to tighten up the law in these matters. That more effort was taken to enforce the law, at any rate in certain spheres of particular interest to the king, in the later years of the reign, is one of the conclusions to be drawn from the only substantial work so far done in the field of law enforcement.[1] So far as prosecutions for offences in the sphere of retainer, livery, maintenance, and so forth are concerned, Dr Guth's researches amply confirm the impressions indicated above, and reveal facts that must be taken into account in any assessment of Henry VII's policy, or at any rate, activity. There was a striking lack of prosecution for these offences. Retainer, Dr Guth reminds us, was only a social evil when it conflicted with the king's interests. Little rigorous repression was undertaken, either in the Exchequer or elsewhere. An investigation of the plea rolls of King's Bench shows that after 1490 about two actions of this kind occurred per term, revealing moderate activity by the Assize justices and justices of the peace. But the bulk of these cases in King's Bench ended in pardon or dismissal. In the Exchequer only nine prosecutions for retainer occurred, all after 1501. Most of these actions were against the retainor, and the average number of men alleged to be retained was four. The attorney-general did not initiate any of these actions, two of which remained unresolved; two were dismissed, and five ended in acquittal by a jury. None of them ended favourably to the king. Only one action against maintenance occurred and that ended in a pardon.[2]

Taking into account *all* the cases of penal law enforcement in the Exchequer for the whole reign, Dr Guth comes to the conclusion that 'the picture remains relatively unimpressive'. 'There is,' he writes, 'very little evidence on the Exchequer record that the Crown was seriously interested in the general enforcement of parliamentary statute.'[3] Some significant expansion in law enforcement did occur after 1500, particularly on the initiative of Crown officers, but this initiative was largely restricted to matters of foreign trade. Infringement of the law relating to customs duties was the sphere which attracted most prosecutions and

---

[1] I am indebted to Professor de Lloyd John Guth, now of Michigan University, for allowing me to use his valuable unpublished Pittsburgh Ph.D. dissertation, 'Exchequer penal law enforcement, 1485–1509', and to Professor G. R. Elton for his kindness in lending me his copy of this work, the publication of which is greatly to be desired.

[2] Guth, op. cit. 271–4.   [3] ibid. 275.

the most profit to the king. Crown officials of one kind or another
initiated the bulk of these actions; some but few private informers took
any part in them, and 'the notion of an army of private informers is
pure myth, at least for Henry VII's Exchequer'.[1]

On the whole, the Exchequer was efficient and effective in enforcing
the penal law, once actions were initiated, but for the most part it
functioned only in those areas which directly pertained to the king.
Outside those areas enforcement remained haphazard, tied to the
vagaries of the private informer system – a system which did not receive
much encouragement from the Crown except when the informers happened to be also Crown officers or servants.[2]

Henry VII's government therefore did not greatly exert itself to
enforce penal statute law, with the exception perhaps of those laws,
such as customs regulations, in which the Crown had a direct financial
interest and in relation to which the machinery for enforcement existed
and was comparatively easy to operate. It is indeed doubtful how far
any mediaeval king expected to be able to enforce penal statutes at all
fully. It is probable that machinery adequate for the purpose had not
come into existence. The Crown could do little but rely upon its not
always reliable local agents, whether justices of the peace, sheriffs,
customers, escheators, or bailiffs, and other officers.[3] The potential utility

[1] Guth, op. cit. 277.

[2] ibid. 278; out of the 1,804 prosecutions in the Exchequer for the whole reign,
1,140 were for customs violation, i.e. smuggling. 990 informers can be identified, but
in 891 cases out of the total of 1,804 the informers were Crown officers, and in
addition 322 informations were laid by the attorney-general. Some two-thirds of the
total cases were thus initiated by Crown activity in one form or another; 84 per cent
of the cases were for offences committed within a year, and there was no question of 'reviving' old statutes for prosecution purposes. In 1,359 cases a formal conclusion was reached, but of these 40 per cent ended in dismissal. In 682 cases
judgment for the king was reached. The total monetary award to the king was
£7,965 5s 5½d, and informers' moieties amounted to £3,062 0s 4d, see Guth, op. cit.
167–75. As Dr Guth observes, 'the entire system of Exchequer penal enforcement wa'
therefore limited in effectiveness, very narrow in application, and hardly harsh when
successful'.

[3] Prosecutions in the Exchequer against local officers for failure to observe statutory
regulations were remarkably few, and these all belonged to the 1490s and later. Only
two prosecutions of justices of the peace occurred, and both were dismissed. Far
more attention was given to escheators, with twenty-eight prosecutions in all. Of these
twenty-three were initiated by the attorney-general, on two occasions only in 1493 and
1499. Eight cases ended in pardons and thirteen were unresolved. Five charges were
entered against one sheriff, all unresolved, and twelve other sheriffs were prosecuted
(nine of them after 1505); of these five were dismissed, five unresolved, and two acquitted by jury. Some other sheriffs were prosecuted, on the initiation of private informers, under St. 23 Henry VI, c. 9.

of private informers who were not also Crown officials was necessarily limited and probably inadequately motivated. In this whole sphere, there is no reason to suppose that Henry VII's government was any more or any less efficient than previous governments. It cannot be accused of any particular ruthlessness or harsh administration, or of any special innovatory ingenuity. That Henry VII was markedly anxious to increase his revenue is not open to doubt. This increase was to come most of all, however, not from the laborious and slow processes of litigation on the penal statutes, but rather from the more expeditious, more profitable, more ruthless and more certain exploitation of the potentiality of the royal prerogative rights. In this sphere the king might be able to secure substantial revenue with the minimum recourse to litigation in the courts.

Chapter 11

FISCAL AND FINANCIAL POLICY

The division of royal revenues into 'ordinary' and 'extraordinary' is a distinction drawn by historians rather than fifteenth-century commentators.[1] Fortescue used this distinction with reference to expenses, not revenues. The important difference then was not between 'ordinary' and 'extraordinary' revenues, but between certain and casual. Another distinction which can usefully be drawn is between the revenues, whether certain or casual, which the sovereign received as king, or as landowner, or as feudal overlord, and this kind of classification so far as practicable is the one attempted here.

As king, Henry VII from time to time obtained taxation, indirect or direct, by parliamentary grant or grant of the convocation of the Church; he could obtain loans and benevolences, and payments from a foreign potentate; he got the profits of justice, whether in fines or fees, and financial advantages from purveyance and similar royal rights. As a landowner he got land revenues similar in kind to those that any large landowner got, but as king he could enlarge these by acts of attainder and forfeitures for treason or felony, and as overlord by the falling in of escheats. As overlord he could exploit his prerogative rights and secure the feudal incidents due from tenants in chief – reliefs, wardships, marriages, aids, escheats – and could find here a sphere in which careful and thorough exploitation could greatly improve his income. In the manipulation of bonds, whether obligations or recognizances, he could obtain further financial advantages both as king and overlord. A survey of these various categories will enable us to form a picture of his finances and some conclusions as to his financial position. This was a subject which, next to his life, throne, and dynasty, lay nearest to Henry VII's heart. Whatever modern research may have done to modify or destroy Baconian phrases, there is no reason to revise the one which asserts 'of nature assuredly he coveted to accumulate treasure'.[2]

Each of Henry VII's parliaments made a contribution to his revenues in one form or another, even though the fifth parliament (1495) had

---

[1] B. P. Wolffe, *The Crown lands, 1461–1536* (1970), 16–17; and now more fully in the same author's *The royal demesne in English history* (1971).
[2] *Henry VII*, ed. Lumby, 213.

little to offer beyond giving statutory authority to tighten up the collection of the arrears of the benevolence previously sanctioned.[1] Most of the parliamentary grants of taxation were paralleled by the usual corresponding grants by the convocation of the Church. The parliamentary grants of fifteenths and tenths (a tax on movables in the shires and boroughs, respectively) were conventional in character and followed well established form and procedure, but in 1488 the grant of an aid to be assessed on individuals followed a precedent set in Edward IV's time, and although a failure at the time nevertheless it formed a link in the chain of experiments that was to lead on later in the Tudor period to the all important development of the subsidy as distinct from the old fifteenths and tenths. The form of the grant in 1504 of a lump sum in lieu of the levy of two of the ancient customary feudal aids may have shown novel features, but the basic principle behind it was not new.

Henry VII's first parliament (1485) only followed the precedent set by Richard III's first and only parliament in the previous year when it granted for the king's life *both* the subsidy on wool, etc., *and* the subsidy of tunnage and poundage.[2] Both subsidies had been granted for the remainder of the lives of Henry V in 1415, of Henry VI in 1454, and to Edward IV in 1465, but not, of course, in the first parliament of their reigns, whilst Richard II had obtained in 1398 for the short remainder of his reign only the subsidy on wool.[3] Having obtained this life grant of customs duties, in effect on almost all the commodities of import and export from the start of his reign,[4] there was little he could do to improve the yield except to encourage the necessary commerce as far as possible, to improve the book of rates for London,[5] to increase in certain respects the rates payable by alien merchants,[6] and to show a

---

[1] *See* below, p. 204.   [2] *R.P.*, VI, 268–70.

[3] N. S. B. Gras, *The early English customs system* (1918), 84, and refs. therein.

[4] The 'custom and subsidy' as it was sometimes called, consolidated the ancient custom of 1275, part of the new custom of 1303 and the later parliamentary subsidy, on wool, woolfells, and hides. The 'petty custom and subsidy of tunnage and poundage' covered duties in wine, cloth, corn, wax, spices, and most commodities of import or export (ibid. 85–6).

[5] A book of rates was promulgated, 15 July 1507, for the port of London, mostly on imports, by the King's Council by the advice of the surveyors and collectors and the Merchant Adventurers of London, said to be the earliest known, and is printed in Gras, op. cit. App. C, 694–706.

[6] e.g. the parliament of 1485 included in its grant a provision that alien merchants becoming denizens should continue to pay the duties at the higher rates applicable to aliens. *S.R.*, II, 501–2.

greater activity in enforcing the law in this sphere than in any other statutory field.[1] Even so, if the calculations that have been made are valid, the increase in receipts from the customs during the reign, though useful, was not very striking. The average annual receipts for the first ten years of the reign are put at about £33,000, and for the remainder at about £40,000.[2] The proceeds apparently could vary greatly from as little as £11,500 (1491–2) to as much as £27,500 (1503–4) from the port of London alone, and from as little as £25,000 (1491–2) to as much as £48,200 (1508–9) overall, according to fluctuating circumstances that would be hard to identify. During the reign as a whole rather less than £900,000 was derived from this source, half of which came from London.[3]

The grants of fifteenths and tenths by the second, fourth, and sixth parliaments were levied in the form that had been standard for a hundred and fifty years and which was to be resorted to again many times up to 1623, even after the newer 'directly-assessed' subsidy had come into more frequent usage.[4] A grant of a fifteenth and tenth was the grant of a specified sum of money fixed in 1334, little altered since, from every vill and urban ward, levied first on the communities, each of which then decided how the tax was to be assessed on individuals. Four of Henry VII's parliaments (1487, 1490, 1491, and 1497) granted respectively two, one, three (the third was never levied), and two, fifteenths and tenths. The levy when made was still based on the movable goods and chattels of all persons, secular and clerical, and remained traditional, except that it was apparently a Tudor innovation to allow the nomination of the collectors by the commons themselves.[5] But the total sum levied remained stereotyped and the yields, gross or net, stayed remarkably constant throughout the reign. The gross yield of each fifteenth and tenth was just over £31,000; net approximately

[1] *See* above, p. 191 ff.

[2] Dietz, op. cit. 25; G. Schanz, *Englische Handelspolitik gegen ende des mittelalters*, 2 vols (Leipzig, 1881). It should be remembered that these figures are by no means necessarily valid. Schanz's methods of calculation are open to considerable objections, such as those set out in *Studies in English trade in the fifteenth century*, ed. E. Power and M. M. Postan (1933); but these studies did not reach the reign of Henry VII.

[3] Schanz, op. cit. II, tables, 37–47.

[4] For what follows I am greatly indebted to Dr R. S. Schofield of Clare College, Cambridge, for his kind generosity in lending me a copy of his valuable unpublished Cambridge Ph.D. dissertation (1964), 'Parliamentary lay taxation 1485–1547'; and to Professor G. R. Elton for his good offices in this connection. Dr Schofield's thorough and meticulous research on all the available record material puts the whole subject on a footing of lucidity and accuracy far exceeding any published account.

[5] Schofield, op. cit. 65.

£29,000; the actual sums known to have been received never fell short of the net yield by more than a few hundred pounds, about one per cent on average.[1] Henry VII was evidently very successful in obtaining, usually with expedition and efficiency, the most that could be got out of the traditional subsidy of fifteenths and tenths. No opposition in parliament to these grants is apparent.

The grant of two fifteenths and tenths in 1487 was said to have been partly in lieu of the uncollected balance of a fifteenth and tenth granted to Richard III in 1484.[2] The grant of two fifteenths and tenths in 1491–2 was in aid of the war impending with France, and was payable in two instalments; if the army remained abroad for more than eight months, a further fifteenth and tenth was granted,[3] but this was never levied. Two more fifteenths and tenths were granted in 1497,[4] specifically to finance the war impending with Scotland, and was to be void if peace were made. In the event this grant proved to be insufficient and recourse was had to a different form of subsidy, to amount, however, to the equivalent of another two fifteenths and tenths.[5]

There were, therefore, grants of seven fifteenths and tenths between 1487 and 1497, the total gross and net yields of which may be put at about £217,000 and £203,000 respectively. The collection of these stereotyped sums by the traditional methods carried out smoothly and with little apparent difficulty or friction clearly offered advantages to both Crown and taxpayers, but being for fixed sums, the Crown did not obtain revenue that would reflect that growth in local wealth which it had some justification in looking for, nor could it by these means attempt to procure a more equitable distribution of tax among the different classes of the population. It was moved, therefore, to seek other fiscal policies.[6]

[1] ibid. 413–24; and table 40, p. 416. The gross yield never rose above £31,171, and only once (the second grant leviable in 1492) fell below £31,000 (to £28,964). The net yield at its highest was £29,874 and only once fell below £29,000 (to £27,735, corresponding to the lowest gross yield). The difference between the gross and net figures is accounted for by collectors' remuneration, permitted exemptions and deductions, and bad debts. The actual sums known to have been received were less than the net yield in every case, but never by more than a few hundred pounds. The difference between gross and net yields was generally about 2½ per cent, but 99 per cent of the net yield was actually received.

[2] *R.P.*, VI, 400–1.   [3] ibid. 442–4.
[4] ibid. 513–19.   [5] *See* below, p. 200.

[6] A subsidy which the commons were willing enough to grant without reservations was a poll tax on aliens. Five of these had been granted before 1485; in 1439, 1442, 1449, 1453, and 1482. In 1487 such a subsidy was granted along with the grant of two fifteenths and tenths. The rate varied according to occupation and residential status, from 2s for the alien artificers who were not householders, to 40s for

The history of parliamentary taxation from 1485 to 1547 is, Dr Schofield says, the history of a successful attempt to replace the fifteenth and tenth as the main form by the directly assessed subsidy.[1] In this history, Henry VII's reign made a small, but very significant contribution. This took the form of a grant of a tax fixed at varying rates levied on each individual according to prescribed criteria, with the yield unfixed, open, and according to rates and results. Such subsidies had been granted seven times before 1485;[2] of these, two were failures and withdrawn, and the others were not very successful. The proposals were viewed with suspicion and hostility in parliament. The commons not unnaturally did not like fiscal proposals which would raise an unfixed total yield, and likely to exceed the product of a fifteenth and tenth. They were prone to impose conditions of one kind or another, including its insistence that no precedents were to be set and no returns were to be made to any court of record.

When in 1489 the government proposed such a subsidy to help finance the military expedition pending to aid Brittany, it is clear that the model in mind was that of 1472, and the reactions of the commons (and of the taxpayers) were very similar to those manifested then.[3] The Crown's proposal in 1489 was for £100,000 to defray the costs of 10,000 archers for one year. After a good deal of controversy, the commons eventually agreed to raise £75,000, and the convocation of Canterbury agreed to raise the remaining £25,000. As in 1472, the parliament insisted on the appropriation of the proceeds to the specific military operation, and if the military need were reduced, the grant was to be reduced in proportion; but if the forces remained abroad for longer, and the expenses rose above £100,000, then the tax was to be renewed up to another two years, provided not more than £25,000 was raised in any one year. The details of private wealth that would be assessed were never to come into the possession of the Crown, and no records of assessment were to be returned to the Exchequer or any other court of record. The total amount from any area was not to be certified to the Exchequer but to parliament. The very cash raised was not to be paid into the Exchequer or any other central treasury but was

---

merchants, factors, and attornies who were householders or resided for three months. Denizens, aliens engaged in husbandry or born in Ireland, Wales, Berwick, Calais, Gascony, Guyenne, Normandy, or the islands, were exempt. *R.P.*, VI, 401–2. No enrolled accounts of this tax exist, and the gross yield can only be roughly guessed, at about £774. Schofield, op. cit. 165.   [1] ibid. 4.

[2] In 1404, 1411, 1427–8, 1431 (withdrawn), 1435, 1450, and 1472 (withdrawn).

[3] *R.P.*, VI, 4–60.

to be deposited in designated repositories until the king should send for it.[1] The grant was never to be a precedent.

As in 1472, the subsidy was in the form of two separate grants, by the commons and the lords respectively. The commons granted the tenth of annual income from all honours, castles, lordships, manors, lands, tenements, rents, fees, annuities, corrodies, and other pensions, fee farms and the temporal lands of the clergy, and 1s 8d for every 10 marks worth of goods and chattels. The lords confined their grant to a tenth of the income of lands and offices (including persons enjoying the use even though not seised thereof). Commissioners were to be appointed under letters patent to discover the value of net incomes and the capital value of goods, after their discretions. Some administrative rules were laid down, and the actual collectors were to draw up indentures of payment for all payers.[2]

But despite the elaborate and cautious procedure, the grant was a failure. The eventual yield was estimated by parliament itself to be no more than £27,000, and even this may have been an exaggeration.[3] The reluctance of parliament to make the grant was matched, it seems, by the reluctance of the people to pay,[4] and probably neither commissioners nor collectors over-exerted themselves. The same parliament in January 1490[5] persuaded the king to accept in lieu of the balance the grant of one fifteenth and tenth as had been done in 1431 and 1472.[6]

Failure of the attempt in 1489 to raise an open-ended subsidy was so great that the experiment was not repeated in the same form for twenty-five years. But by 1497, with the war against Scotland impending, the need for substantial taxation was again pressed upon parliament. In addition to the two fifteenths and tenths which parliament granted in the usual way,[7] it was asked to ratify a grant of £120,000 which a Great Council had previously sanctioned.[8]

Ratification took the novel form of the grant of an aid or subsidy equal in total amount to that of two fifteenths and tenths, but the usual division

---

[1] Actually some 70 per cent was paid into the Exchequer. Schofield, op. cit. 176.

[2] *R.P.*, VI, 420–4. The queen, the counties of Cumberland, Westmorland, Northumberland, and merchants of Castile, Venice, Genoa, Florence, Lucca, and the Hanse were exempt.

[3] ibid. 437. The yield so far as can be ascertained was £20,736, but the actual total may have been more. Schofield, op. cit. 178.

[4] It was in an affray arising from opposition at Topcliffe, Yorkshire, to this subsidy that the earl of Northumberland lost his life.

[5] *R.P.*, VI, 437.

[6] ibid. IV, 409; VI, 149–53.

[7] *See* above, p. 197.

[8] *See* above, p. 144.

of the county total among the vills was abandoned in favour of the assessment of individual contributions by specially appointed commissioners.[1] This aid was thus based upon a compromise between the traditional fifteenth and tenth with its assured total yield and the subsidy with its direct assessment on individuals. At the same time the tax within each county was spread more proportionately to the wealth distributed within the county even though the total for each county remained the same, and the commissioners undertook their duties without prejudice to the total yield that the Crown would get. The advantages to both Crown and taxpayers were manifest, and the device of 1497 set an important precedent for the future. The levy of the second half of the aid, equal to one fifteenth and tenth, was made conditional upon the prosecution of the military campaign against Scotland, but as this condition was not fulfilled,[2] it was not in fact levied. The gross net yields were slightly higher than the usual fifteenth and tenth and the sum actually received by the Crown was as high as £30,088.[3]

The grant of 1497 provoked the Cornish rebellion, not, apparently because of any novelties in the tax, but because of the unwillingness of the Cornishmen to contribute to the cost of a campaign in Scotland, for which they thought a scutage or land tax on knight's fees, especially in the northern counties, was more appropriate.[4]

It may well have been the unhappy repercussions in Cornwall of the 1497 aid that induced Henry VII to come to terms quickly when confronted with parliament's opposition to his proposal in 1504 for the grant of the customary feudal aids for the knighting of his eldest son Arthur and the marriage of his daughter Princess Margaret. Although in principle the request was in accordance with ancient custom the occasion was not auspicious. Arthur had first been knighted in 1489 and had been dead for nearly two years, and Margaret had married James IV in the previous year. It may well be therefore that Henry's motive was not primarily to raise money which he did not specially need at that time, but to set on foot a far-reaching enquiry into tenures *in capite* as part of his policy of exploiting his prerogative rights. He may have

[1] *R.P.*, VI, 513–19.

[2] The expedition to Scotland was recalled to combat the Cornish rebellion, and the renewed invasion two months later was abandoned on account of adverse climatic conditions.

[3] Schofield, op. cit. 416, table 40. The procedures were similar to those of 1489 but the rules for assessments differed in a number of respects; ibid. 188–9.

[4] At any rate this was the Baconian version of the Cornish objections to the tax. *Henry VII*, ed. Lumby, 148–9; P.V. (ed. Hay), 90 ff.

envisaged a sort of Tudor Domesday Book. The commons declined the proposal on the ground of the uncertainty of tenures, and did not welcome the prospect of a far-reaching investigation. After prolonged discussion and the emergence of an opposition such as Henry VII had not before experienced, the commons offered an aid of £40,000, of which the king discreetly agreed to accept £30,000 only, roughly the equivalent of one fifteenth and tenth.[1] The procedure and assessment decided upon were nearly the same as for the subsidy of 1497 and the yield received slightly higher at £30,873.[2] The total received by the four subsidies of the reign was about £80,000.

The subsidies of 1497 and 1504 were thus essentially similar. Both had fixed yields but the taxes were assessed and levied by statutory commissioners. Both were successful, and the precedents thereby set led on to the development of the directly assessed, open-yield subsidies aimed at from 1513 onwards.[3]

To the total figures received by the Crown from parliamentary grants must be added the sums received from the clerical grants of the tenths by the convocations, which paralleled some of these grants. But the value of these grants is not known for this period. An estimate recently made suggests that the average yield per annum from this source during the years 1486 to 1534 may have been about £9,000.[4] How far this figure can be used for 1486 to 1504 does not appear, and at present it seems that the value of the clerical contribution must remain speculative.

In view of the comparatively moderate receipts from parliamentary and clerical grants, it is not surprising that Henry VII and his advisers turned their attention to other possible sources of income which offered better prospects of financial advantage.

The advantages from borrowing were mostly of the short-term kind,

---

[1] R.P., VI, 532–42; 19 Henry VII, c. 32; S.R., II, 674; Schofield, op. cit. 192–8. It has been suggested (ibid. 193, fn. 94) that Thomas More's opposition in the commons to the proposal by the Crown may have been prompted by his common-lawyer dislike for an investigation into tenures, and if this were so it might help to explain Henry VII's vindictive action against his father, John More, who had become a serjeant-at-law in 1503. Roper, Life of More, 7–8; Busch, op. cit. 285; D.N.B.

[2] Schofield, op. cit. 416, table 40.   [3] ibid. 198 ff.

[4] J. J. Scarisbrick, 'Clerical taxation in England, 1485–1547', J. Eccles. Hist., II (1960), 50. For this period, the actual (gross) value of the clerical grant is known only for the southern convocation for 1501. The sums accruing to the Crown for the restitution of temporalities and fines, estimated to amount to perhaps £3,500 per annum over the period 1486 to 1533, are, of course, in a different category, and in any event cannot be estimated with any accuracy, as Professor Scarisbrick shows, ibid. 49.

since at least a considerable proportion had to be repaid, with or without interest, but a benevolence, if it could be extracted, was in a different category since it was in effect a tax not subject to repayment in any form.

The fiscal machinery in any event worked slowly, and Henry VII's financial needs were inevitably most pressing from the moment the battle of Bosworth was won. Recourse was had at once to short-term loans. He could not avoid incurring some debts from the start. Hostages were left in Paris as pledges for money borrowed before the expedition was launched; the duke of Brittany had been given promises for the repayment of 10,000 crowns as soon as the kingdom had been won. Richard III had pawned the royal jewels and these had to be redeemed, and some of his debts had to be met. Within his first year Henry VII borrowed from individuals, from Italian merchants, the merchants of the Staple at Calais, and the City of London, sums amounting to rather more than £10,000, mostly for short periods, all of which were repaid.[1]

But there were to be other loans of a less voluntary nature. These were, if not exactly 'forced', extracted from individuals under the pressure of Signet letters, which might be repaid, and did not require parliamentary or other sanction. Better still a benevolence or 'benevolent loan', although it did require some sanction and the excuse of some dire military need, spread the net much more widely and involved no question of repayment.

It is very doubtful whether the loans invited by Signet letters can justly be called 'forced' in the modern sense of the term. For an individual to refuse a request under Signet was doubtless difficult, if not virtually impossible.[2] But none the less these obligatory loans were in

---

[1] Dietz, op. cit. 51–2.

[2] G. L. Harriss, 'Aids, loans and benevolences', *H.J.*, VI (1963), 1–19, discusses the whole problem. A specimen of such a Signet letter is printed in A. F. Pollard, *The reign of Henry VII*, II (1914), from the Rutland papers (Hist. MSS Comm., i.13), 44–5. The effective words in this letter, addressed to Sir Henry Vernon, dated 26 April 1492(?), were 'wherfor we holding for undoubted that ye bere a singular tendreness to suche Thinges as concerne the suretie and universal weale and tranquillite of our saide reame and subgiettes desire and hertily praye you that ye will lene unto us the somme of C li . . . wherunto ye maye verraily truste, wherein shal not only doo unto us thing of [grete?] and singulier pleaser, but also, cause us to have you therfor moore specially recommended in the honor of oure grace in such thinges as ye shal have to poursue unto us heraftre'. The further specimen of a request for loan, printed by Pollard, ibid. 45–7, from *Christchurch letters* (Cam. Soc. n.s. xix), 62, was issued 1 December 1496/7, after a Great Council had sanctioned the raising of a loan for the Scottish war, and is couched in less conciliatory terms.

form made 'by agreement',[1] the sums assessed could not be seized, they had to be asked for, with a reminder to the lender of his obligation to assist the sovereign, and there was plenty of precedent for requiring the subjects to aid the king financially in lieu of personal service. There is little or no evidence that these requests were resisted or aroused any particular resentment. The sums asked for were generally rather small, generally from people rich enough to pay without demur, and were usually repaid. But the costs of the efforts of the commissioners sent round in 1486 and 1489 were high and the net proceeds comparatively low.[2] Far more substantial sums continued to be lent by individuals and the City of London, apparently without the persuasion of Signet letters.[3]

Even so, the king's intention to invade France in person provided an opportunity to extract a 'benevolence' in July 1491, just as similar circumstances had provided the same opportunity for Edward IV in 1473, with the slight difference that in 1491 the individuals were asked for aid in person or by money gifts. This levy was sanctioned by a Great Council,[4] and the commissioners set about extracting a benevolent 'loan' or rather gift from a substantial number of persons, notwithstanding the terms of Richard III's statute purporting to abolish 'the charge or imposition called "benevolence" and any similar charge'.[5] Whether it was Morton's or Fox's 'fork' (which asserted that those who spent little must have saved and those that spent much must have means) that came in useful in this connection is not very significant, for this was but an echo of an analogous 'fork' invented in 1473–5.[6] But whatever the legal position of the 1491 levy may have been,[7] it certainly

---

[1] cf. *Materials*, II, 95, extract from Treasurers' Receipt Rolls, 2 Henry VII; Cambridgeshire and Huntingdonshire. 'From William Creton, Clerk, Thomas Burton, and other commissioners of the king in the said counties of money received under the name of "agreement" from divers persons in the same counties, in respect of letters specially addressed under the king's signet to the said persons £206 9s.' Other examples, ibid. 91–2, 95–7, 105–6.

[2] Dietz, op. cit. 52, n. 11.   [3] ibid. 52.   [4] *See* above, p. 144.

[5] 1 Richard III, c. 2; extract in Chrimes and Brown, *Select documents*, 355–6.

[6] The attribution of the 'fork' to Morton rests on Bacon's assertion only (op. cit. 93). According to Erasmus, who had the story from Thomas More, Fox was its author, and he merely turned the argument of some of the tax-paying clergy against themselves. Busch, op. cit. 421–2. According to Battesta Oldovini, writing 17 March 1475, Edward IV himself invented a dilemma in a rather different form. 'If the king thought otherwise, he said: "such a man, who is poorer than you, has paid so much: you who are richer can easily pay more",' *Cal. S.P. Milan*, I, 193–4; extract in *E.H.D.*, IV, ed. A. R. Myers (1969), 527–8.

[7] There appears to be no evidence that Henry VII 'had conveniently deemed all Richard III's statutes to be void', as alleged (R. L. Storey, *The reign of Henry VII*

received retrospective parliamentary sanction in 1495, though in the context of statutory authority for the collection of arrears from both individuals and collectors, under heavy penalties.[1] So that it cannot be doubted that the levy of the benevolence of 1491 was not as successful or as satisfactory as had been hoped and expected, and this may account for the apparent absence of any further attempt at this mode of raising money during Henry VII's reign. By the time the next serious military need arose, against the Scots in 1496, another Great Council, reinforced by the presence of some merchants and burgesses, authorized the raising of a loan, but this was by way of anticipating a promised parliamentary grant.[2]

In the meantime, Henry VII's finances had received a bonus from the results of his invasion of France in 1492, in the form of a handsome payment of debts acknowledged by the king of France. The Treaty of Étaples of 1492 provided that France would reimburse the costs of the war, the debts incurred by Anne of Brittany, the expenses of ambassadors, the arrears of the pension promised by Louis XI to Edward IV, amounting in all to the sum of about £159,000, which was regularly paid by Charles VIII and continued by Louis XII.[3]

To estimate the financial advantages of the loans and benevolence to Henry VII seems to be an impossible task, at least at present. Most of the short-term loans appear to have been repaid, and these therefore

---

(1968), 108). What precisely Richard III's statute abolished could be open to doubt, and possibly no statute could be deemed to have abolished the king's right, especially when supported by a Great Council, to act as his did in issuing commissions in the terms, 'whereas Charles of France not only unjustly occupies the king's realm of France and his duchies of Normandy, Anjou, Touraine, and Aquitaine, but threatens the destruction of this his realm of England, on which account the king intends to defend her English subjects, and to enter France with his power and vindicate his right, but the king has not sufficient funds for the expedition' (and therefore the commissioners are) 'to go to the counties . . . and require the assistance of the king's subjects there in this arduous affair, each one according to his means, and to certify the king and council what they do'. C.P.R., I, 353; Foedera, XII, 435. In any case no one, of course, would in 1491 have cited Richard III's statute against the king's commissioners.

[1] 11 Henry VII, c. 10; S.R., II, 576–7. The act asserted that many subjects had granted money, 'of their free will and benevolence, and had many payments full lovingly'. Others had not, and part of their contributions were still in the hands of the grantors or collectors. Proclamation was to be made for the payment of all arrears within three months, with power of recovery in default or death. Commissioners were to render account under penalty of imprisonment, with due allowance for the costs and rewards.

[2] Mackie, The early Tudors (1952), 140; Storey, op. cit. 122; and above, p. 144.

[3] Dietz, op. cit. 57. For the treaty, Foedera, XII, 506, 684.

did not constitute any addition to his long-term revenue. Short-term lending in any case is alleged to have largely ceased by 1490, and if this was so, it can be assumed that he was by then or thereabouts able to meet normal expenditure from other sources. The benevolence of 1491 is said to have raised rather more than £48,000, but the cost of the invasion of France in 1492 is believed very nearly to have reached that figure, so that the surplus from this particular source can only have been very small.[1]

It is also useless to attempt to put any figure on the total or annual average of income from the profits of justice, fines and fees, and from the large number of miscellaneous rights which the king enjoyed as king. It is more profitable for us (as it was for Henry VII) to turn our attention to his profits from land and his prerogative rights as feudal overlord.

Whilst in theory it is possible to distinguish between the king's income from lands of his own, and income from prerogative rights as overlord, in practice the distinction was a good deal blurred, especially in the reckoning of accounts; all in any event were profits from land, except that to some extent it became possible to extend the notion of the financial obligations of tenants-in-chief to tenants who held directly of the king rights other than rights in land. All were equally part of his 'patrimony, his hereditaments, the issues of his kingdom', or simply 'his own'.[2]

If, however, for the sake of convenience we may first examine the position as regards revenues from lands in the king's hands, whether permanently or temporarily, by inheritance or purchase or gift, or in consequence of forfeitures or escheats, we must consider by what means Henry VII could expect to improve upon the profits of such lands as he possessed on his accession. At that date he acquired whatever land estates were left behind by Richard III as king, as heir of York, of Lancaster, and duke of Gloucester and widower of Ann Neville, less such charges on the profits as he might think fit to maintain. Once these 'Crown lands' had been acquired it was open to him to improve the proceeds greatly by several different means. By acts of resumption he could extend their range; by acts of attainder he could make further extensions, not necessarily permanently; and by improved methods of

---

[1] Dietz, op. cit. 57, and nn 45, 46.

[2] B. P. Wolffe, *The Crown lands, 1461–1536* (1970), 30. This work, with the documents provided therein, is indispensable for the subject, together with the same writer's 'Henry VII's land revenues and Chamber finance', *E.H.R.*, LXXIX (1964), 225–54; and 'The management of English royal estates under the Yorkist kings', ibid. LXXI (1956), 1–27.

management and accounting he could enhance the net proceeds from the whole.

His first parliament passed two acts of resumption which together regularized the basis of the Crown lands. The act of the first session roundly declared him to be the heir of Henry VI and of his own father Edmund Tudor.[1] The act of the second session invited him to resume into his own hands all the lands and possessions legally vested in Henry VI on 2 October 1455 or at any time since. All grants of lands, offices, annuities, pensions, etc., made between that date and 20 January 1486, were declared invalid.[2] The actual effect of this act, however, was not so substantial as has often been supposed. Henry VII indeed felt obliged to append no less than 461 clauses of exemption, a far greater number of exemptions appended than to any previous act of resumption, and the great bulk of these exemptions did not represent new grants by the king himself, but rather confirmations of grants by the Yorkist kings.[3] Two further acts of 1495 were not so much acts of resumption as acts clarifying the king's title to the lands which Richard III had held as duke of Gloucester, and to all the lands which the house of York had held by virtue of grants by Edward III and Richard II to Edmund of Langley.[4]

Naturally Henry VII could not retain for himself all the net proceeds of these territories, apart from the specific exemptions. Provision out of the York lands had to be made for the dowager duchess Cecily, and for Edward IV's widow Elizabeth Woodville (subsequently diverted to Henry's queen). Provision for members of the royal family had always been regarded as a proper charge on Crown lands and indeed a justifiable reason for alienation. Substantial grants were made to the king's mother Margaret Beaufort and to his trusty veteran uncle Jasper Tudor, as well as to Sir William Stanley, who might be said to have saved the day at Bosworth. One reason, however, why Henry VII was able to obtain a heavy increase in his net profits from land in the later years of his reign was that the provision he was obliged to make for his family was small and diminished markedly.[5] True, his mother outlived him by a short term, but Jasper died in 1495; the dowager duchess Cecily also died in 1503. The provisions made in Wales, Chester, Cornwall, and the North for Prince Arthur lapsed on his death in 1502, and for a time brought over £6,000 a year into the king's hands, and when Prince Henry became Prince of Wales

---

[1] *R.P.*, VI, 270–3.   [2] ibid. 376–84.
[3] Wolffe, *E.H.R.*, LXXIX, 232–3.   [4] *R.P.*, VI, 459–61.
[5] Wolffe, *The Crown lands*, 68.

in 1504 the duchy of York that had been conferred upon him in 1494 reverted to the Crown.[1] So far as William Stanley was concerned, his attainder in 1495 brought most of his grants back to the Crown.

Acts of attainder did not necessarily result in the forfeiture of all of the attainted person's lands, and such penalties were not uniformly enforced. Some attainders were repealed subsequently, although not necessarily with full restoration of lands. The substantial number of attainders of men of large property during Henry's reign did however redound greatly to the advantage of the king's landed revenues, and Henry VII went far to exploit these possibilities.[2] Though comparatively lenient in his attitude towards the Yorkists defeated in 1485, he resorted to attainders very frequently. Only one parliament of the reign (1497) omitted to pass an act of attainder. The reign saw 138 persons attainted; eight-six of these attainders remained unreversed; only forty-six were reversed by Henry VII or ultimately reversed by Henry VIII in favour of the heirs. His attitude towards the bargains which he allowed to be made with some of those attainted was 'distinctly cynical'. In the case of noblemen he rarely allowed a complete restitution of their property. Parts thereof were often withheld for many years as an incentive to loyalty and good service, no doubt, but the king derived continued profit from those retained parts, and lesser men fared little if any better. The conditions under which restitutions were agreed were more severe than those imposed by Edward IV in like cases. Although it is not possible at present to put any figure on the total financial advantages accruing from the forfeitures following upon attainders, it is clear that these advantages were very considerable even though not necessarily permanent.[3] Rewards for faithful service could be, of course, and often were, made by grants out of lands so forfeited.

The accumulation of lands in the king's hands, by inheritance, purchase, gift, resumption, forfeiture, or otherwise would doubtless have augmented the royal income from this source merely by itself. The gap

---

[1] *R.P.*, VI, 522. The net profits of York lands was £928 in 1503–4. Wolffe, op. cit. 143.

[2] J. R. Lander, 'Attainder and forfeiture, 1453–1509', *H.J.*, IV (1961), 144–8; and tables, 149–51.

[3] Some of the profits from the attainders from 1495 to 1504 are known, including those of the earl of Warwick, the earl of Suffolk, Lord Fitzwalter, Lord Audley, Sir William de la Pole, and Sir James Tyrell. The net proceeds from these forfeitures alone amounted to over £6,400. Wolffe, op. cit. 142–6, doc. No. 16, General Surveyors' accounts, 1503–4. In addition, it is known that from Sir William Stanley's possessions over £9,000 in cash and jewels had been obtained. W. R. Richardson, *Tudor chamber administration*, 12.

between the gross and the net proceeds and the assurance that the net proceeds would expeditiously and effectively find their way into the king's coffers depended upon efficient management, collection, accountancy, and auditing. We have already seen in general terms the ways in which Henry VII sought to improve financial administration,[1] and we need not repeat those generalizations here. A few points of special relevance to the management of landed revenues may, however, be emphasized.

It is quite clear that after a year or two of revival of the Lancastrian traditional methods of reliance upon Exchequer procedures in these matters, Henry VII deliberately decided to revert to the Yorkist system of appointing *ad hoc* receivers of groups of lands, who accounted in the chamber, and were exempted from Exchequer control, with audit of accounts either by specially assigned councillors or by the king. Books of summaries of accounts of some forty receivers appearing before the king and his group of councillors survive for some years of the reign, and these councillors or 'general surveyors' also heard a number of other accounts, and acted as the supreme board of management for almost all the landed revenues of the king. The board became the court of General Surveyors of Land Revenues, and was both very active and efficient. Herein 'lies a major part of the explanation for the augmentation of such revenues for which the opening years of the sixteenth century were remarkable'.[2]

In all this, as in so much else, Henry VII showed that he knew how to take advantage of procedures that were essentially Yorkist in origin and initiation. The heir of Lancaster became the heir of York in more senses than one.

Before we try to see how great was the financial advantage to Henry VII of the exploitation of land revenues, we must turn to the field of prerogative feudal rights, for the ultimate proceeds of both were often lumped together and it is hard to be sure of the size of the profits from these two main sources. In this field of prerogative rights, Henry VII found a source of financial profit which offered large returns if the possibilities were more systematically and more ruthlessly exploited than had been the case in the past, even under the Yorkists. In this field, more than any other, it is possible to see Henry VII applying his

---

[1] *See* above, ch. 6.

[2] Wolffe, *The Crown lands*, 74–5, and see ibid. docs 16 and 17. The court of General Surveyors, however, never became a court of record and following council advice to Henry VIII to abolish such 'by-courts' (ibid. doc. 18) its work was absorbed into the Exchequer by 1510 (ibid. doc. 20).

9. Extract from the Foundation Indentures for Henry VII's Chapel in Westminster Abbey, 16 July 1504. The king is shown presenting a book of ordinances to William Warham, archbishop of Canterbury, Richard Fox, bishop of Winchester, John Islip, abbot of Westminster, and others: the king's arms with supporters are depicted on top; the Beaufort badge of a portcullis surrounds the folio (*P.R.O., E 33.2, fo. 1*)

a b c

d e

10. Some of Henry VII's new coins (*British Museum*)
a. Sovereign (gold), b. Ryal (gold), c. Angel (gold),
d. Testoon (silver), e. Groat (silver)

legal rights for financial gain with a zeal and relentless application which earned him and his agents an unpopularity and a measure of odium which became marked towards the end of the reign and which might well have produced serious consequences for the regime if it had lasted longer. Here in this sphere, if in any, Henry VII might conceivably be described as 'rapacious', but whether or not he felt 'remorse' is a matter not germane to the present discussion.[1]

'Henry's determination to ascertain and enforce his traditional rights as feudal overlord, and particularly to collect his revenues thereto attached, was made clear early in his reign,'[2] and commissions of enquiry of which there were to be many, were set on foot in his first year.[3] Infractions of royal rights in the past decades, coupled with the determination to extract the profits of the rights to the full, led, as we have seen, in due course to the establishment of the office of the surveyor of the King's Prerogative, and later in the next reign to the setting up of the statutory court of Wards.[4] The whole system of enforcing the king's lawful rights came to be put on a fresh footing. New methods of investigation were devised which by-passed the traditional services of the local escheators and the antiquated procedures of the Exchequer. The hearing of cases and the collection of debts from this source passed largely to what was in effect though not in name a conciliar court – the Council Learned in the law.[5]

The policy in this field was essentially to ascertain what the law was in regard to the highly complex mass of rights that sprang from the accumulation of feudal custom determining the financial obligations of tenants-in-chief towards their overlord the king. The more precise the definition of these rights, the greater was the inducement to increase the number of tenants-in-chief, and the more this could be done, the more worthwhile it became to enforce the collection of debts legally due, even if the methods adopted should prove to be unconventional and novel. The job was essentially one for lawyers and officials, and the work they achieved went far beyond the scope and vision of the old escheators, and beyond the strict text of the only extant legal statement of the overlord's rights contained in the thirteenth-century text known as

---

[1] See G. R. Elton, 'Henry VII: rapacity and remorse', *H.J.*, I (1958), 21–39; J. P. Cooper, 'Henry VII's last years reconsidered', ibid. II (1959), 103 ff; and G. R. Elton, 'Henry VII: a restatement', ibid. IV (1961), 1–29. On the general question of Henry VII's character, *see* also below, p. 298.

[2] *Prerogativa regis*, ed. S. E. Thorne (Yale, 1949), v. This work is indispensable for the subject.

[3] *See* refs in ibid. fn. 1, and x–xi.

[4] *See* above, p. 129.   [5] *See* above, p. 113.

the *Statuta de praerogativa regis*. Much of this text, which was not a statute but rather a declaration of common law,[1] had become obsolete and misunderstood by the fifteenth century, but it provided a solid text which could be reinterpreted, glossed, and made to cover possibilities that were not orginally envisaged in the different economic and social circumstances of the thirteenth century. The vigorous new determination of Henry VII's government to exploit the financial potentials of his feudal prerogative inevitably encouraged the lawyers to apply their wits and erudition to the task of elucidating and adapting the strict words of the *Praerogativa regis*, and it is no accident that whilst no readings on that text in the inns of court are known to antedate his reign, the first known is believed to be dated within the first three years of it, and that by 1495 two very full readings were given. The first of these[2] was given in Lincoln's Inn by Robert Constable in the autumn term of 1495, and the second in the Inner Temple by Thomas Frowyk in the same term and year. Evidently by then it was a promising theme for ambitious serjeants-at-law-elect to choose for their lectures, and their example was frequently followed throughout the Tudor period.[3] If by any chance their learned arguments could still further extend the scope and therefore the proceeds of the sovereign's prerogative rights, what more effective step towards favour and advancement could a reader take?

It was common doctrine that land held by tenants-in-chief directly of the king by military service owed him the customary feudal incidents. Thus, to mention the chief incidents, if the holder *in capite* died without heirs then the land escheated (or reverted) into the king's hands permanently, unless regranted to someone else. If the heir was a minor, the wardship of the heir and the land came into the king's hands, with its profits less the costs of maintaining the heir; if the heir was a woman then the rights to her marriage were disposable by the king; any succession to the land involved liability to the payment of a relief or fine. All tenants-in-chief were by custom liable to contribute to an aid to the king on the occasion of the knighting of his eldest son, the marriage once of his eldest daughter, and for the ransoming of the king's body if captured. Henry was never held to ransom, but as we have seen, in 1504 he got what he could out of the other two pretexts. The number of tenants-in-chief never remained static. There were numerous ways in which by the nature of things sub-tenants might find

---

[1] cf. Chrimes, *English constitutional ideas in the fifteenth century* (1936), 44–5.
[2] ed. S. E. Thorne, op. cit.   [3] ibid.

themselves elevated into the position of tenants-in-chief, and find themselves owing the full array of incidents.[1] There was never any legal doubt about these obligations in regard to holdings of land. But the *Praerogativa* did not place any limitation upon the phrase '*qui de ipso tenent in capite per servicium militare*'. It was open therefore to Henry VII's lawyers and officials to bring incorporeal things into the picture. Tenants-in-chief could be extended to include not only those that held land but also those who held any incorporeal thing,[2] and it could be presumed that such things were held by military service if there were no specific indications to the contrary. The possibilities of expanding the sources of profit from prerogative rights were thus very great, and there is no doubt that every effort was made by Henry VII's officials to exploit them to the full. The legal technicalities of the matter are too complex for us to attempt to unravel here, but we may perhaps agree with Professor Thorne that 'though they (the commissioners of enquiry into the king's prerogative rights) perhaps were prepared to resolve all doubts in the king's favour, it is difficult to find evidence . . . that they . . . were engaged in extra-legal exploitation'. No doubt the 'harsh, strict, and uncompromising actions' of Empson and Dudley and other commissioners were responsible for the attack made upon them in Henry VIII's first parliament, but the charges of extortion (made against Dudley in particular), had to be dropped, presumably for lack of evidence. The commissioners' actions were not always upheld, and redress for exactions that could not be legally upheld could be obtained. Harsh and ruthless though the policy doubtless was, it was not pursued outside the framework of the law.[3]

But whether it was a wise policy to pursue is another question. It was, at bottom, a policy that set itself to meet the expanding financial requirements of the state 'by means of a set of rules framed for his tenants-in-chief by a feudal suzerain'.[4] It may well be that it was followed because it was easy to follow; it rested upon the king's will alone and involved no other sanction or consent. It was easier to get financial profit by these means than it was to get adequate supplies from parliamentary grants. What the political possibilities really were is a matter that was doubtless more manifest to Henry VII than it can be to us, but we need to remember that the effects on English law of this artificially prolonged emphasis upon the feudal incidents were profound.[5] In any

[1] Examples are listed in Thorne, op. cit. xii.
[2] Such as advowsons, rents, annuities, stewardships, wardenships, warren, wreck, markets, fairs, and other franchises. *See* ibid. xiii.
[3] ibid. x–xi.   [4] ibid. ix.   [5] ibid.

event, what Henry VII found acceptable in this policy found favour also with his successors.[1]

That the land revenue policies of Henry VII found favour is not surprising when the spectacular increase in the sums from these sources reaching the chamber is considered. If under this heading the proceeds from estate receivers, fee-farmers, and sheriffs, fee farms of towns, bailiffs of liberties, wardships, marriages, vacant temporalities, fines for alienations and other feudal incidents are totalled – it is not possible to differentiate the various items – the figures are, in terms of annual average for 1487-9, £3,000 out of £17,000 reaching the chamber; for 1492-5, £11,000 out of £27,000; for 1502-5, £40,000 out of £105,000.[2] From these sources alone, therefore, Henry VII acquired annually in his later years sums equivalent to more than he would have got from an annual parliamentary grant of one and a third tenths and fifteenths.

Before we can view the state of Henry VII's finances as a whole, we need to consider the matter of bonds, whether in the form of obligations or of recognizances, which not only brought further supplies of cash into the chamber, but constituted something like an instrument of State policy, as well as being matters very closely under the king's personal control.

Both obligations and recognizances were bonds binding a person to a liability of one kind or another, but although the precise nature of the liability is not always made clear in the accounts, there was a distinct difference between the two. Obligations were bonds with specific conditions for the payment of money, the fulfilment of an undertaking, or the performance of a specific duty. Recognizances were obligations which recognized or acknowledged a previously established debt or agreement, often made contingent on future conduct. If the recognizer did not fulfil the terms of his bond, he was liable to forfeit the sum specified in the bond. The full penalty, however, might be compounded for a fine. Most, but by no means all these bonds, were for payment, usually by instalments, of legally justified debts to the king.[3]

The reasons for the giving and taking of bonds were extremely varied and are not susceptible of any logical classification.[4] The clue to the whole device is to be found, if anywhere, in the fact that all the

---

[1] For the later history, see J. B. Hurstfield, 'The revival of feudalism in early Tudor England', History, XXXVII (1952), 131–45.

[2] Wolffe, E.H.R., LXXIX (1969), 252, n. 1, and 237; Crown lands, 48–69.

[3] W. C. Richardson, Tudor chamber administration, 143–4.

[4] See generally, ibid. 141–58; Dietz, op. cit. 33–49.

bonds were given by the king's favour, and all were the result of a bargain entered into with the king's agents or directly with the king himself. All such bargains were closely scrutinized by him and there could be no finality about any of them without his personal sanction.[1]

Many of the bonds entered into represented no more than routine or even commercial transactions. Payments for the restitution of episcopal temporalities, for loans by the king to Italian and English merchants, for arrears of accounts in the hands of the king's receivers, for the purchase of the king's wards, for licences to export wool and import wines, for the deferred payment of customs duties, and for hire of the king's ships; all these were no more than routine obligations. But other bonds fell into a different and more doubtful category. Recognizances for fines imposed in the courts for various offences might be a legitimate means of getting the lawful penalties into the king's hands, but a large element of arbitrariness and undue favour entered into the bonds made for the release of culprits from prison, for the pardon of murderers and other felons, and for the pardon of rebels, especially after the Cornish rebellion.[2]

The financial screws were undoubtedly tightened to supplement the machinery of the law courts. Much could be done by the king's agents to oblige wealthy law-breakers to come to terms and enter into a bond for the king's pardon, conditional perhaps upon future good behaviour, without waiting for the slow machinery of the common law to operate, or even without reference to that machinery at all.[3] Something could be done in this way to uphold the laws against retaining, to enforce respect for the king's prerogative rights. Not only was such procedure expeditious, and comparatively secret, it was also highly lucrative. Even though some of the very large sums assessed were never collected in full, substantial fines could be extracted and the spectre of the whole liability could be threatened in a bond inveighing good behaviour in future.

In this sphere then Henry VII found not only a rich source of income, but also an instrument for enforcing the law which supplemented the creaking machinery of the common law courts, and possibly diverting business from the council and the statutory ministerial council set

---

[1] 'The essential factor common to them all is that they represent personal arrangements reached with the king himself', Wolffe, *E.H.R.*, loc. cit. 246. In one of the chamber books at the bottom of a page of recognizances Heron entered a revealing reminder 'aboute certain persons which are not yet through with the king's grace. And his said grace hath a list of their names'. Cited, ibid.

[2] Dietz, op. cit. 33–4; Richardson, op. cit. 144.

[3] Dietz, op. cit. 44.

up in 1487. A far more detailed study of the evidence known to exist for these transactions is needed before their full import and impact can be adequately assessed. Such a study would be worth making, for in this sphere is to be found the clearest manifestations of Henry VII's personal interventions in finance and in law enforcement. Here Henry could at once gratify his desire to increase his revenues effectively and in terms of hard cash, whilst at the same time browbeat some of his recalcitrant and defaulting subjects into subjection and obedience. No doubt the bulk of the transactions made were grounded in the law; no doubt Empson and Dudley, again very prominent for their activities in this sphere, are not to be regarded as mere extortioners, but the arbitrary and secret character of the 'bargains' struck was bound to incur odium and produce a vigorous reaction in the end. A number of kings before Henry had used similar methods, but few if any of his predecessors had taken such a close personal part in wielding the whips and scorpions of financial pressures to attain their ends. The sovereign lord the king could not play the part of Shylock without incurring loss of prestige.[1]

The extraordinary scope and frequency of Henry VII's exaction of recognizances became more apparent with the publication of the *Calendar of Close Rolls* for 1500–9 in 1963. The number of recognizances on the rolls for these years, as the late Mr K. B. McFarlane observed, was the most remarkable new feature of these enrolments. After examining these entries McFarlane felt obliged to assert that 'the point had almost been reached when it could be said that Henry VII governed by recognizance. In this he was neither mediaeval nor modern, but *sui generis*'.[2]

Over one third of the entries on these rolls after 1500 consist of recognizances in favour of the king, and over fifty of them bear the condition that those so bound should keep their allegiance to Henry VII and his heirs, and probably most of the others had the same intent. Examination has shown that many original recognizances survive in unsorted Chancery files and that the great majority were not enrolled,[3] and the scope of their exaction was much greater than has been supposed.

[1] Heron's chamber accounts were audited only by the king. He himself personally handled many transactions and received cash. The account book for 1502–5 is prefaced with four folio sides of memoranda written by Henry himself. His signature or sign manual appears on every page, sometimes five or six times. Wolffe, loc. cit. 244, fn. 6, and 245–6.

[2] *E.H.R.*, LXXX (1963), 153–4.   [3] *C.C.R.*, II, viii–ix.

Professor J. R. Lander's recent study[1] has focused attention on what Henry VII's policy in this sphere meant to the nobility. Between 1485 and the end of 1499, eleven peers gave bonds and recognizances in amounts varying from £100 to £10,000. After 1502 the number rose sharply to thirty-six.[2]

> Out of sixty-two peerage families in existence between 1485 and 1509, a total of forty-six or forty-seven were for some part of Henry's reign at the king's mercy. Seven were under attainder, thirty-six, of whom five were also heavily fined, gave bonds and recognizances, another also was probably fined, and three more were at some time under subpoenas which carried financial penalties. Only sixteen (possibly only fifteen) remained free of these financial threats. Furthermore, not only did the number of peers concerned increase sharply, but also the number of them who were obliged to give more than one bond; twenty-three gave more than one; five gave five or more, two gave twelve or one (Lord Mountjoy) twenty-three. A situation arose in which a majority of the peerage were legally and financially in the king's power and at his mercy . . . so that in effect people were set under heavy penalties to guarantee the honesty and loyalty of their fellows. The system was so extensive that it must have created an atmosphere of chronic watchfulness, suspicion, and fear.

Polydore Vergil reported that in 1502 the king began to treat his people with more harshness and severity than had been his custom before in order to make them more thoroughly obedient to him. But the people generally attributed his motives to greed.[3] It may be that 'this policy of financial terror was eminently successful', and that the amount of cash actually received by the king was comparatively moderate, nevertheless there were some remarkably arbitrary conditions attached to some of the bonds,[4] and the exaction of these was by no means confined to the peerage.

[1] 'Bonds, coercion, and fear; Henry VII and the peerage', in *Florelegium historiale: essays presented to Wallace K. Ferguson* (Univ. of Toronto Press, 1971), 328–67.

[2] ibid. 339.   [3] ibid. 347–8; P.V., 126–31.

[4] e.g. the humiliating treatment of Henry Percy, earl of Northumberland; the very severe conditions imposed on Thomas Grey, marquis of Dorset; the enormous financial penalties accorded to George Neville, Lord Burgavenny, were doubtless whittled down to comparatively modest actual payments, but it seems to be going rather far to have added another bond for £5,000 to the £100,000 for retaining and for allegiance already imposed as a penalty should he enter Kent, Sussex, Surrey, or Hampshire without the king's licence at any time for the rest of his life. Richard Grey of Ruthven, earl of Kent, was doubtless a spendthrift, but a bond for £10,000 to make no sale or lease or grant of any land or offices or annuities without the king's consent, to attend daily upon the king so as to be seen once daily in the king's house, with no departure therefrom without licence except for eight days each quarter, seems to be remarkably arbitrary.

It could be argued that there was a good deal of 'policy' behind the binding of most of the peers to their allegiance and good conduct especially after the death of Arthur in 1502. But what might be high policy in this sphere could easily turn to greed if the same methods were turned against lesser or even quite humble people who could be harshly treated by such exactions without adequate reason. We know that Edmund Dudley was very well aware that such things did in fact occur, that he confessed as much, and provided a list of such cases whilst he was a prisoner in the Tower under sentence of death. In this place, however, we are concerned with policy. Greed is a theme we must postpone until later.[1]

Just how much cash actually found its way into the royal coffers as a result of payments derived from obligations and recognizances during the reign cannot even be guessed at. But from such figures as are ascertainable for a few years it is clear that the potential profit was very large. One says 'potential' advisedly, for the totals that can be calculated relate to liabilities incurred, not to actual cash received, and since many of the payments made were by instalments and often spread over many years, the actual proceeds in any one year cannot be stated. But for what the figures are worth, the extant accounts show that Dudley alone brought in bonds and cash (to the nearest hundred pounds) to the tune of £44,900 in 1504–5; £60,700 for 1505–6; £65,400 for 1506–7; and £48,400 for 1507–8. Of this impressive total of nearly £219,400, however, only just over £30,000 was in cash. Many bonds were cancelled by the king; others were suspended during pleasure, so that the eventual cash accruing was certainly a good deal less than the face value. But what that cash actually amounted to can only be left to surmise.

Finally, it is equally difficult to know what the total revenues or expenditure of Henry VII were on the average or during the reign as a whole. No one at the time attempted to draw up a statement of total income or total expenditure. Attempts have been made by historians to supply the deficiency for at least some years. Fairly reliable figures are obtainable for the actual amounts of cash reaching the chamber during the years for which the treasurer of the chamber's accounts survive, which were checked and initialled by Henry VII himself – these were the figures which interested him most – the figures of ready cash. But these figures by no means corresponded to all the revenues from all sources, nor was all expenditure recorded in the chamber. All attempts at estimates of total income and expenditure are hazardous. Those made

[1] *See* below, p. 313.

by Dietz have been shown to be erroneous in some respects,[1] and no reliable estimates of a comprehensive nature can be made. An indication can perhaps be got from the latest calculation, which asserts that the total revenues during the last five years of the reign probably averaged £113,000 a year, excluding however the proceeds of lay and clerical subsidies but including some items which were no more than temporary or casual windfalls.[2]

More pertinent, and more feasible perhaps, is to consider how far Henry VII succeeded in obtaining revenue in excess of expenditure. There is enough evidence, mainly from the chamber accounts surviving – and these accounts, after all, came to include the great bulk of revenue and expenditure – to show that Henry VII did become solvent quite early in the reign, and was able to secure some considerable surplus annually during his later years. The cessation of short-term loans by 1490 suggests that the government no longer had need of hand-to-mouth methods. The chamber accounts at the end of September 1489 appear to show a surplus of £5,000. From 1492 at least Henry found himself able to put by substantial sums in the purchase of jewellery, plate, cloth of gold and the like, and to spend money on building. From 1497 onwards, but not before, foreign ambassadors began to allude to his apparent wealth. Between 1491 and 1509 he appears to have spent between £200,000 and £300,000 on jewels and plate – clearly his favourite form of 'investment', even though some of these purchases were doubtless intended to be gifts or for normal use and personal display.[3] But at the end, he was left with little but what he had so 'invested'. At the end of the reign the chamber cash balance was exhausted, and the issues of the new reign had to be used to pay the debts of the old. Whether he expected to get any return from another quarter of a million pounds he had invested in loans to the imperial family is not knowable, but in fact he got nothing but some political advantage. More probably he did expect to get return from the £87,000-odd that he loaned to English and Italian merchants, but information is lacking.[4]

Henry VII did, then, no doubt enjoy 'the felicity of full coffers' for the last few years of his reign[5] but the other Baconian tradition that he left behind him a surplus of some two million pounds[6] cannot be maintained. At most, it seems, his legacy to his son and heir amounted

[1] Dietz, op. cit. 39; Richardson, op. cit. 158.
[2] Wolffe, *E.H.R.*, loc. cit. 249–50.
[3] ibid. 521.   [4] ibid. 253; Dietz, op. cit. 78–87.
[5] Wolffe, loc. cit. 253–4.   [6] Bacon, op. cit. 210.

perhaps in jewels and plate to something like the value of two years' gross yield of his permanent revenues.[1] No mean achievement, but it was accomplished at great cost in terms of personal application, of the distortion of administrative machinery, and the straining of the royal repute. It was an achievement that would never be repeated in anything like the same form.

[1] Wolffe, loc. cit. 254.

Chapter 12

ECONOMIC AND SOCIAL POLICY

No doubt Professor Elton was justified in his exhortation to historians to 'get away from impressionism too common in these matters',[1] but as he well realized, lack of much pertinent evidence or investigation in the matter of Henry VII's economic and social policies makes it difficult if not impossible to avoid some degree of impressionism. The impression one gets from the scattered and not at all comprehensive work done so far is that Henry VII, although clearly interested in some economic and social matters, had no consistent policies and took few measures in these fields that were not conventional or repetitive of actions taken by previous governments. He was interested in bringing commercial interests into his diplomatic relations with other countries; he was interested in reforming the coinage and in encouraging shipping, exports, and maritime exploration. He took some initiative in these matters; he gave his assent to a variety of measures for the regulation of merchant companies, trade, wages and prices, weights and measures, for the restraint of enclosures, and the treatment of vagabonds and beggars. Some of these measures were precedents for more far-reaching governmental action in later decades, but many though not all of these appear to have been initiated by others than the government in Henry VII's time, and how far the mere giving of assent to proposals for minor regulations amounted to acceptance as serious government policy is a matter for speculation rather than dogma. We can scarcely accuse Henry VII of adopting 'paternalistic' attitudes. Whatever else Henry VII was, he was essentially an opportunist and sought to achieve few broad or far-reaching aims in either economic or social matters. We may well attribute to Henry VII especially the characteristics that have been attributed to the Tudor monarchs generally – perhaps too generally. Of him we may well believe that 'economic problems were always secondary, and that economic measures often served non-economic ends'.[2] The paramount aims were peace and security. His policies always remained primarily political, not economic, and any

[1] G. R. Elton, 'State planning in early Tudor England', *Econ.H.R.*, 2nd ser. XIII (1961), 433–9, esp. 439.

[2] P. Ramsey, *Tudor economic problems* (1963), 177.

economic aims that he may have cherished (other than the strengthening of his own economic position) were subordinated to his political and
diplomatic objectives.[1] As for social policy, it is difficult indeed to see
that he had any other than those of the conventional late mediaeval
type, i.e. broadly speaking, those tending to the support and fulfilment
of the existing social structures.

If we first review generally the measures taken by Henry VII's
government in these spheres, we can then examine in more detail those
which appear to be of some importance for our present theme. The
proclamations need not detain us, for, apart from a number concerned
with coinage matters,[2] only six proclamations dealt with the regulation
of trade; all were devoted to regulating exports, mostly consequential
upon treaties with other countries.[3]

Approximately fifty statutes of the reign may be said to impinge in
some way upon the economic and social spheres, but only about a third
of these at most appear to have been initiated by the government. The
great bulk therefore originated either in the petitions of interested
parties presented, usually to the commons, or in the petitions or prayers
of the commons themselves. These included some enactments of importance which have often been spoken of as though they represented
government initiative;[4] many of them dealt with somewhat trivial
matters, some of which were of little more than sectional interest.

Nearly all the statutes relating to shipping, alien merchants, trade
regulations, weights and measures, prices, and usury were based upon
petitions in or by the commons, and are a tribute to the vigilance and
activity of the interested parties or the commons rather than of the
government, and call for a brief survey.

The oft-quoted but narrow 'navigation act' of 1486 was the result
of a petition by the commons asking the king to enact that no person
should buy or sell wines from Gascony but such as 'be aventured and
brought' in English, Irish, or Welsh ships, with mariners of the same
complexion or men of Calais, on pain of forfeiture, half to the king and
half to the finder. But this act was to endure only until the next parliament, and saving always the king's prerogative.[5] The act apparently
lapsed until re-enacted with some additional points in 1489.[6]

---

[1] cf. R. B. Wernham, *Before the Armada* (1966), 62.
[2] *See* below, p. 224.   [3] *See* below, p. 232 ff.
[4] e.g. Busch, op. cit. ch. VII; and followers thereof.
[5] 1 Henry VII, c. 8; *S.R.*, II, 502.
[6] 4 Henry VII, c. 10; *S.R.*, II, 534. Toulouse wood was added to the imports
specified, and the employment of foreign ships was forbidden if English ships were
available.

A petition to the commons sought to prohibit protection in actions between merchants of the Staple before the mayor of the Staple or some other court at Calais.[1] A petition of the commons obtained a recital of statute 17 Edward IV, c. 1, and a perpetuation of its provision that alien merchants were to employ within the realm[2] the money they obtained by the sale of their goods. The commons prayed that corporate companies should not make ordinances without the approval of the chancellor, treasurer, and chief justice of either bench or of both justices of Assize on circuit, and no such ordinances in restraint of suits in the king's courts were to be made.[3] The Merchant Adventurers successfully petitioned the commons that Englishmen should have free passage to Flanders, Holland, Ireland, and Brabant and the adjoining ports under the authority of the archduke, without any exactions by Englishmen.[4] The commons prayed that the freemen of the City of London might go to any fairs or markets in the realm notwithstanding any ordinance of the City.[5] The merchants of Italy petitioned the commons to get statute 1 Richard III, c. 8, repealed as unduly restrictive of their trade.[6] During the trade dispute with Venice the commons prayed the king to extract an additional customs duty on malmsey wine whilst the Venetians maintained the like additional duty on export.[7]

A considerable number, some twenty or so, of the statutes initiated by or through the commons sought to regulate trade or trade practices and few or none appear to warrant special mention here.[8] The most

[1] 1 Henry VII, c. 3; *S.R.*, II, 501.
[2] 3 Henry VII, c. 9; *S.R.*, II, 517.
[3] 19 Henry VII, c. 7; *S.R.*, II, 652.
[4] 12 Henry VII, c. 6; *S.R.*, II, 638.
[5] 3 Henry VII, c. 9; *S.R.*, II, 518.
[6] 1 Henry VII, c. 10; *S.R.*, II, 507.
[7] 7 Henry VII, c. 7; *S.R.*, II, 553.

[8] 1 Henry VII, c. 5; *S.R.*, II, 502, no tanner to be a currier; 1 Henry VII, c. 9; *S.R.*, II, 506, reciting 22 Edward IV, c. 3, and 1 Richard III, c. 10, and confirming for twenty years restrictions on import of certain silk goods by aliens; 3 Henry VII, c. 12, *S.R.*, II, 520, reciting 7 Edward IV, c. 3, and prohibiting export of woollen cloths incompletely finished; 4 Henry VII, c. 2 (possibly initiated by the Crown), *S.R.*, II, 526: regulations for finers and porters of gold and silver, who are to sell to the Mint or goldsmiths; 5 Henry VII, c. 3; *S.R.*, II, 527, butchers not to slay beasts within the City of London or any walled town or in Cambridge; Carlisle and Berwick excepted; 4 Henry VII, c. 11; *S.R.*, II, 535, regulating the seasons for purchase of wool in certain counties; 4 Henry VII, c. 22; *S.R.*, II, 545, regulating the weight and working of gold (threads for embroideries) from Venice, Florence, and Genoa; 11 Henry VII, c. 19; *S.R.*, II, 582, for the proper stuffing of beds; 11 Henry VII, c. 27; *S.R.*, II, 591, against deceitful foreign fustians; 12 Henry VII, c. 1; *S.R.*, II, 636, for apprentices for Norfolk worsted makers; 12 Henry VII, c. 4, reciting 1 Richard III, c. 8, concerning the making of woollen cloth; 12 Henry VII, c. 23; *S.R.*, II, 587, regulating sale of salmon and other fish by aliens; 19 Henry VII, c. 6; *S.R.*, II, 651, restricting sale of pewter to fairs and private houses until the next parliament; 19 Henry VII, c. 17; *S.R.*, II, 662, regulating the craft of worsted sheering;

important of these perhaps was the statute 4 Henry VII, c. 23 (*S.R.*, II, 546) made, at the prayer of the commons, reciting 17 Edward IV, c. 1, which expired after six years, prohibiting the export of gold bullion, money, jewels, and plate without the king's licence, and the payment or delivery of these articles to any alien merchant under penalty of forfeiture of double the value, half to the king and half to the seizor.

The fixing of prices of woollen cloth,[1] and of hats and caps,[2] was probably initiated by the interested parties, and the commons asked for the lifting of customs duties on imported bowstaves until the next parliament because of the shortage of that important commodity.[3] It was likewise the commons who petitioned for the establishment of standard weights and measures of brass in the City of London and other boroughs and that the officers should seal all weights and measures.[4] This act, it was complained four years later, was not being observed, and the unusual expedient was resorted to of providing that standards 'should be sent to every community by the members of parliament themselves and be enforced'.[5] But a year later the Crown appears to have taken a hand on complaints that the standard weights and measures had proved defective, and enacted that a new standard bushel and gallon should be kept in the Treasury, and new measures by these standards should be issued.[6]

It was the commons who prayed for the recital and due execution of 25 Edward III, St. 5, c. 12, and 5 Richard II, St. 1, c. 2, forbidding the establishment of any money exchange without the king's licence and forbidding any unlawful chevisaunce and usury.[7] But later they also called attention to the obscurity of this act and to the difficulty of understanding its intent, procured its repeal and some clarification thereof, reserving the rights of spiritual jurisdiction.[8]

But it was the Crown that initiated measures regarding alien and other merchants, the coinage, wages, 'enclosures', and vagabonds.

It was to the king's interest to enact that aliens made denizens (i.e. citizens) should continue to pay customs at the alien's rate and should

---

19 Henry VII, c. 21; *S.R.*, II, 664, import of certain silk goods prohibited; 19 Henry VII, c. 19; *S.R.*, II, 663, reciting 2 Henry VI, c. 7, and 1 Henry VII, c. 5, regulating the trades of cordwainers, curriers, and tanners.

[1] 4 Henry VII, c. 8; *S.R.*, II, 533.   [2] 4 Henry VII, c. 9; *S.R.*, II, 534.
[3] 19 Henry VII, c. 2; *S.R.*, II, 649.   [4] 7 Henry VII, c. 3; *S.R.*, II, 551.
[5] 11 Henry VII, c. 4; *S.R.*, II, 570.   [6] 12 Henry VII, c. 5; *S.R.*, II, 637.
[7] 3 Henry VII, c. 6; *S.R.*, II, 515. This act had, however, been preceded by a proclamation against unlicensed exchanges. Hughes and Larkin, op. cit. 11–12, No. 10, *c.* June 1486. 'Chevisaunce' means a loan by which profit was obtained.
[8] 11 Henry VII, c. 8; *S.R.*, II, 514.

not allow aliens to operate in their names.[1] No doubt an abuse was obviated by providing that scavage or shewage was to be paid only by aliens, not denizens, except denizens in London.[2] It was policy to declare that no acts relating to merchants or merchandise should prejudice the merchants of the Hanse.[3] The important but customary financial agreement between the king and the merchants of the Staple in 1504 was a fit subject for statutory declaration,[4] as similar agreements had been in the past.

Naturally it was the king who wanted to create a new statutory treason by declaring the counterfeiting of foreign coins to be such,[5] and difficulties arising as to the value of the important new coinage introduced earlier in the reign received definition in 1504.[6]

An attempt to revive the scale of wages for 'servants in husbandry' laid down by statute 23 Henry VI, c. 12, was abandoned by repeal a year later.[7]

The earliest act seeking to curb the growing practice of enclosure, or more precisely engrossing, came in 1489, confined in scope to the Isle of Wight and ostensibly made on grounds of dismay at the depopulation of the island and the threat to defence. Penalties were fixed for the engrosser of holdings exceeding a total value of 10 marks per annum.[8] In the same parliament, however, another act[9] of broader import was passed, foreshadowing the legislative efforts of later periods. Its preamble approached something like a statement of policy. It deplored the decay of villages, the conversion of arable to pasture, unemployment, the decay of tillage, the decay of churches and defences, all 'to the subversion of the policy and good rule of the realm', and laid down that any houses that had been let to farm with twenty acres in tillage or husbandry within three years, must be maintained under penalties. This

---

[1] 1 Henry VII, c. 2; S.R., II, 501.

[2] 19 Henry VII, c. 8; S.R., II, 653. 'Scavage' was a toll leviable by town authorities on merchant strangers on their goods offered for sale within the precincts.

[3] 19 Henry VII, c. 23; S.R., II, 665. See below, p. 235.

[4] 19 Henry VII, c. 27; S.R., II, 667. For the preservation of Calais and the Staple and the payment of the wages of the captain and soldiers of Calais, etc., a grant was to be made to the mayor and fellowship of the Staple of customs duties on wool payable there for sixteen years, in return for which they were to pay £10,000-odd to the treasurer of Calais for these purposes. A convoy for staplers' ships was to be provided by the king. cf. the agreement made by Edward IV, in 1473 (R.P., VI, 55-61). [5] 4 Henry VII, c. 18; S.R., II, 541.

[6] 19 Henry VII, c. 5; S.R., II, 650. On this subject, see below, p. 224.

[7] 11 Henry VII, c. 2, repealed by 12 Henry VII, c. 3.

[8] 4 Henry VII, c. 16; S.R., II, 540. cf. Joan Thirsk, The agrarian history of England and Wales, IV (1967), ch. IV: 'Enclosing and engrossing', 200-55.

[9] 4 Henry VII, c. 19; S.R., II, 542.

may have been 'a muddled act'[1] in the sense that it did not get to the point of mentioning the practice of enclosure, but it does reveal that Henry VII's government was beginning to appreciate the social problems arising and was prepared to make some effort, however tentatively to deal with them.

There can hardly be said to be much enlightenment about the two statutory attempts to deal with the problem of vagabonds and beggars; they were merely punitive and cannot be dignified with a place in the history of the poor law. Statute 11 Henry VII, c. 2,[2] sought to moderate the harsher provisions of 7 Richard II, c. 5, but ordered vagabonds to be set in the stocks for three days and nights, with bread and water only and then to be sent away. Beggars not able to work were to be sent back to the hundred wherein they were best known or were born or had last dwelt. Statute 19 Henry VII, c. 12, did little but reduce the period in the stocks to one day and night for vagabonds and to provide further for dealing with neglect of their duties by officials concerned in these matters.[3]

The creation of new coinage would seem to have been a policy upon which Henry VII reached decisions at a very early date. At any rate as early as 2 November 1485 he granted to Sir Giles Daubeney, and Bartholomew Reed of London, goldsmith, the office of master and worker of Monies and keeper of the Exchange in the Tower, to be held jointly according to certain indentures to be made.[4] These indentures followed two days later, setting out in great detail the various new coins to be made, their value and weight.[5]

The new coins were to be a ryal of gold, worth ten shillings, a half ryal and a quarter ryal, an angel worth six shillings and eightpence, and an anglet worth three shillings and fourpence. In silver, there was to be a groat of fourpence, a half groat, a penny (or 'sterling'), a halfpenny, and a farthing.[6] Later, on 28 October 1489, orders were given also for a gold sovereign, worth twenty shillings. A silver testoon or shilling piece was also introduced, perhaps only for a trial period, but notable as being the first English coin to bear a true portrait of the king.[7]

---

[1] Thirsk, op. cit. 214.   [2] *S.R.*, II, 569. cf. P. Ramsey, op. cit. 156.
[3] *S.R.*, II, 656.

[4] *C.P.R.*, I, 28. The year 1486 at the top of this page is a mistake for 1485. *Materials*, I, 105.

[5] *C.P.R.*, I, 49–53; *Materials*, I, 107.

[6] 45 ryals, 67½ angels, and 135 anglets, were to equal 1 lb of weight of the Tower in gold. Of the silver coins, there were to be 112½ groats, 225 half-groats, 450 pennies, 900 halfpennies, and 1,800 farthings to the pound weight of silver.

[7] *C.P.R.*, I, 319; G. C. Brooke, *English coins* (3rd ed. 1950), 169. *See* pl. 10.

There had been little change in the design of coins in England since Edward III's time, and Henry VII's action in this field has been regarded as a 'first step in the transition from mediaeval to modern currency'. Edward IV had modified the type of noble and raised its value to ten shillings without making much change in the design, had introduced the gold angel with a conventional type and style and had retained the silver coinage without appreciable alteration.[1] Henry VII's innovations broke away from conventional forms. New denominations in gold and silver were introduced, an artistic portrait was adopted for the silver coinage, and a new design with the royal shield of arms replaced the type first introduced by Edward I. The sovereign, the heaviest gold coin to that date, half of a pound of the Tower weight, was among the first to show the king wearing the closed or arched crown, following the example set in the *real d'or* coined in the Netherlands by Maximilian as regent for his son Philip in 1487. The closed crown appeared also on the later issues of the new groats and replaced the traditional open crown that appeared on the earlier issues. There can be no doubt that the closed crown had its symbolism, and that its use in Henry VII's coins gave it a wide publicity. It was meant to give an added aura of magnificence to the king's portrayal, but whether it could have much imperial connotation at the time is perhaps less obvious. On the other hand, it did very soon acquire such a connotation, and wittingly or unwittingly Henry VII made his contribution to a line of thought and propaganda that was going to bear much fruit in his successor's time.[2]

Henry VII clearly concerned himself closely not only with these major innovations but also with the perennial problems of what was to be done about clipped coins and the influx of foreign coinage. The statute 19 Henry VII, c. 5, and the quite numerous proclamations issued testify to this interest. The statute of 1504, followed by an elaborate proclamation, pronounced that all the new gold coins were to pass for their nominal value, the silver groats and half-groats were to pass likewise even if cracked, and the silver pennies also unless clipping had

---

[1] G. C. Brooke, op. cit. 162 ff; L. A. Lawrence, 'On the coinage of Henry VII', *Numismatic Chronicle*, 4th ser. XVIII (1918), 205–61; W. J. W. Potter and E. J. Winstanley, 'Coinage of Henry VII', *B.N.J.*, XXX (1960–1), 262 ff.

[2] P. Grierson, 'The origins of the English sovereign and the symbolism of the closed crown', *B.N.J.*, XXXIII (1964), 118–34. The letter from Cuthbert Tunstall to Henry VIII, dated 12 February 1517, cited, ibid. 133, from H. Ellis, *Original letters*, 1st ser. I, 136, contained the striking assertion, 'But the Crown of England is an Empire of hitself, mych bettyr than now the Empire of Rome: for which cause your Grace werith a close crown' (cited, ibid. 124).

gone beyond a specified point, in which case they were to pass as halfpence.[1] On other occasions proclamations were issued, outlawing Irish pence and declaring English pence legal tender;[2] outlawing imperial groats and pence;[3] and declaring 'small, thin and old pence' legal tender provided they were 'silver and whole'.[4] But the problem of clipped coinage, and the difficulty of getting some of the new coins accepted as legal tender, remained until the end, and provoked yet another and very detailed proclamation at a date after 27 April 1507.[5]

It may well be that the economic achievements of Henry VII's reign have been underrated,[6] and certainly overseas trade increased considerably during the course of the reign, but how far Henry VII himself or his government contributed to this result is more doubtful.

Henry VII did not do very much in any direct way to promote shipping. So far as the royal navy was concerned,[7] he left this in a weaker condition than it had been under the Yorkists. The circumstances of their times and needs for war purposes experienced by Henry V, Edward IV, and even Richard III had obliged them to pursue a policy of sustained vigilance at sea. The example of the ways in which Richard, earl of Warwick, had manipulated his private fleet to press his own or other Yorkist political causes in the late years of Henry VI had not been lost on Edward IV, who built up a substantial fleet of sixteen ships by 1481, some of which were used against the Scots, and had resurrected the office of clerk of the King's Ships at Southampton first set up by Henry V, and did much to make the monarchy into a naval power. It was largely the threat of Henry Tudor's invasion that had obliged Richard III to maintain an effective and vigilant naval force, in which he took a personal interest, and he appointed John Howard as the new admiral, and Thomas Rogers as the clerk.

But the very success of Henry's expedition tended to reduce the immediate need for a strong naval force, and the Yorkist fleet declined. He had seven ships in 1485, mostly taken over from Richard III, but

[1] S.R., II, 650; and Hughes and Larkin, op. cit. I, 60–1, No. 54, wherein a facsimile of an impressive contemporary print of the proclamation is provided.

[2] ibid. 26–7, No. 25 (1491); 41–2, No. 38 (1497); 47–8, No. 43 (1499); 48–9, No. 44 (1499).

[3] ibid. 42, No. 39 (1498); and III, 263, No. 207 (1490).

[4] ibid. I, 47, No. 42 (1498).

[5] ibid. 70–4, No. 57.

[6] P. Ramsey, 'Overseas trade in the reign of Henry VII: the evidence of the Customs accounts', Econ.H.R., 2nd ser. VI (1953–4), 178.

[7] For what follows, see C. F. Richmond, 'English naval power in the fifteenth century', History, LII (1967), 1–15. Fuller details are provided by C. S. Goldingham, 'The navy under Henry VII', E.H.R., XXXIII (1918), 472–88.

these fell to five by 1488, and this remained the number at the end of the reign, despite some new building to replace old hulks. One of these was the largest naval vessel built up to that date. He could supplement his small fleet by hiring merchant ships at the rate of one shilling per ton per month, impress seamen, supply the senior officers and armament, and use these ships to supplement his fleet on occasions, and sometimes was able to hire Spanish ships for this purpose, and so reduce demands on English vessels. He also paid for the construction of the first dry dock, at Portsmouth, and thus no doubt contributed to the better mainten-ance of his ships.[1] The office of clerk of the King's Ships remained, but declined in importance and was probably exercised by deputy in the later years. It was hardly the case[2] that Henry VII could not afford to improve his naval strength, at any rate in the years during which his finances were healthy, but rather that his foreign policy was such as not to envisage serious military risks involving naval intervention.

Even though the royal navy can hardly be said to have flourished at this time, there is plenty of evidence that English shipping generally prospered during at least the last ten years of the reign, especially in the eastern ports.[3] But this was primarily a matter of private enterprise, even though encouraged by the offer of a bounty to private subjects who built large ships[4] and by the acts of 1486 and 1489,[5] and even though affected, either for better or for worse, by the fluctuations in the eco-nomic consequences of his foreign policies.[6]

It has been shown that although cloth exports increased over the years (from an annual average of 50,878 cloths in the first six years to 81,875 in the last six years – an increase of sixty-one per cent), the export of wool declined by about thirty per cent, 'gradually killed by heavy taxation and the demands of the home cloth industry'.[7] Imports also rose. The value of goods paying the petty customs rose by sixty-eight

[1] Richmond, op. cit. 14–15; Goldingham, op. cit. 475, 480. Valuable documen-tation in *Naval accounts and inventories of the reign of Henry VII*, ed. M. Oppenheim, Navy Records Soc., VIII (1896).

[2] Wernham, op. cit. 62

[3] D. Burwash, *English merchant shipping, 1460–1540* (1947, repr. 1969), 155; S. V. Scammell, 'Ship owning in England, c. 1450–1550', *T.R.H.S.*, 5th ser. 12 (1962), 105–22.

[4] There were precedents for such royal bounties from 1449. The scale was 5s a ton but only for large ships; the required tonnage was not specified, but vessels over 80 tons would be deemed in that category. Bounties were also given for the purchase of foreign ships. Goldingham, op. cit. 475–6.

[5] *See* above, p. 220.   [6] *See* below, p. 232.

[7] P. Ramsey, loc. cit. 178–9, and tables, 181. 53 per cent of the exports were by denizens, 24 per cent by Hansards, and 23 per cent by other aliens.

per cent, those paying poundage by eighty per cent, and imports of non-sweet wine by forty-seven per cent.[1]

The most recent and detailed research,[2] however, has shown the extraordinary degree of fluctuations in the amount of export trade, both in wool and in cloth, which can only be explained in terms of the economic repercussions of Henry VII's international diplomacy.

In another sphere, not unconnected with foreign policy, Henry VII showed himself capable of unwonted imaginative enterprise, tempered by his more usual caution. In all the circumstances, his patronage and support for John Cabot's and later Sebastian Cabot's voyages of exploration created the first period in the history of English participation in overseas discovery.[3] He was not, of course, himself the inspirer of the enterprise, nor did the initiative come from him. But he showed sympathy to the proposals put before him, was prepared to make oceanic discovery an element in his foreign policy, and was statesmanlike enough to perceive that the advantages which might be gained outweighed the risks that might ensue from antagonizing Spain and Portugal.[4]

The first prize for enterprise and initiative, however, must be awarded to those nameless Bristol merchants who from about 1480 onwards undertook voyages for the discovery of lands westward. Their discovery of the Isle of Brazil (Newfoundland?) and their opening up of a fishing ground in that region were remarkable achievements even though they were not widely known, except among the Bristol men and their associates.[5] They must have been known to Henry VII (who visited Bristol in 1486 and 1496), and undoubtedly some knowledge of these developments brought John Cabot, a Genoese of Venetian citizenship by 1495, to enlist support for a project of reaching the wealthy parts of Asia by a westward voyage. He got that support, and by 5 March 1496 had succeeded in eliciting from Henry VII himself letters patent, very carefully and precisely worded, authorizing him to undertake a voyage of discovery.[6] Cabot and his three sons were given

---

[1] P. Ramsey, ibid. The value of alien goods paying petty customs rose from £50,849 in 1485–6 to £108,109 in 1508–9, of those paying poundage from £116,780 to, £252,967, and the tunnage of non-sweet wine imported rose from £5,151 to £10,259.

[2] E. M. Carus-Wilson and Olive Coleman, *England's export trade 1275–1547* (1963); graphs, (wool) 123, (cloth) 139; tables 68–70, and 109–13.

[3] J. A. Williamson, *The Cabot voyages and Bristol discovery under Henry VII*, Hakluyt Soc., 2nd ser. CXX (1962), recounts the story very thoroughly, with full documentation. Brief allusions are made in J. H. Parry, *The age of reconnaissance* (1963); and B. Penrose, *Travel and discovery in the Renaissance, 1420–1620* (1963).

[4] Williamson, op. cit. 170.

[5] ibid. 19–43.   [6] ibid. 49–50; printed in full, 203–5.

authority to use five ships of any tonnage to sail to all parts of the 'eastern, western and northern sea' to discover and investigate 'whatsoever islands, countries, regions or provinces of heathens, and infidels ... which before this time were unknown to all Christians'. Cabot, in short, was given practically *carte blanche* for his voyage, so long as he kept away from the Christians in Hispaniola. Henry VII would respect Spanish rights to what Spain had already discovered, but was willing enough for enterprises under his patronage to stake a claim in any lands westward newly discovered: nor did he attempt to conceal these plans.

Any lands discovered were to be occupied in the king's name and the grantees were to become his vassals to hold the lands of him. One fifth of any net profits were to go to him. No other subjects were to intrude without the grantees' licence, under pain of forfeiture of ships and goods.[1]

An expedition set out in 1496 but was turned back by bad weather. One small ship, the *Matthew*, with eighteen men, set out in late May 1497 and made landfall on 24 June. What exactly was the location of the *Prima Terra Vista* on the American mainland is still a matter of debate, but wherever it was there the banners of Henry VII, of the pope, and of St Mark of Venice were duly planted. But there were signs of inhabitants at the spot, and Cabot 'being in doubt returned to his ship and returned eastwards'. By about 6 August he was back and was with the king before the 10th. Henry VII's reaction was to give Cabot an immediate present of £10 – a modest reward for one who was now generally thought to have reached the mainland of Asia and who was now to be treated triumphantly and with much honour, and viewed by foreign envoys with jealous respect.[2]

Doubtless the political crises of 1497 distracted the king from Cabot's affairs for some time, but by 13 December 1497 he granted him an annual pension of £20,[3] and soon turned with enthusiasm to new plans for a further voyage. Henry VII it is said at this time 'achieved a brilliant diplomatic coup by securing the Spanish marriage without having to fight for Spain whilst retaining a free hand to probe the oceans'.[4] At any rate, he would not listen to any Spanish objections, agreed that Cabot should work westwards and southwards down the mainland, and gave him full authority in new letters patent dated 3 February 1498

---

[1] Imports brought back were to go to Bristol only, and the grantees were to be exempt from customs (in practice, for foreigners 3*d* in the £1) but the subsidy of tunnage and poundage was not remitted, ibid. 53.

[2] ibid. 54–64; and doc. No. 26.

[3] ibid. 86; and doc. No. 27.   ibid. 85–6.

which supplemented but did not supersede the earlier ones. Authority was given to impress six English ships not exceeding 200 tons, to be paid for at king's rates (3*d* per ton per week), with a general passport for volunteers to go to the land and isles of late found by John Cabot. Henry's enthusiasm was now sufficient to induce him to equip one of the ships himself and the other four were provided by London and Bristol merchants.[1]

By early May this second expedition set out. But, although he may have put into Ireland because of climatic conditions, John Cabot then disappeared entirely from the annals of maritime discovery, and of his fate nothing is known.[2] It is, however, highly probable that other of the ships did make the voyage, to bring back eventually the disconcerting intelligence that the 'land and isles of late discovered by John Cabot' were not Asia.

Further letters patent were issued to other men in 1501 and 1502, with elaborate regulations for colonies, monopolies, and privileges. A company of Adventurers to the New Found lands could somehow come into existence by 1506. But all these efforts were the outcome of the discovery that the New Found lands were not the land of 'the Great Khan'.[3] When therefore John Cabot's son Sebastian had attracted Henry VII's attention and goodwill and made his voyage of 1508–9, he went as an explorer for an economic prize – the short way to Asia by a north-west passage. He may indeed have found Hudson Strait and part of Hudson Bay, but when he returned to England Henry VII was dead, and the new court was as yet unresponsive to such enterprises.[4]

We are not here concerned to trace the struggle between the two great merchant companies of the Staplers and the Adventurers.[5] This struggle and the defeat of the former was, we are told, largely decided during the reign of Henry VII.[6] It was not perhaps exactly a question of the defeat of the Staplers, but rather of decline consequential upon the diminution in the export of wool and rise of the importance of export of cloth that gave to the Merchant Adventurers their growing prosperity and their penetration into the markets of the Netherlands. It can hardly be suggested that Henry VII had any policy of demoting the Staplers and promoting the Adventurers, but circumstances of politics and diplomacy did induce him to encourage, when it suited him, the

---

[1] Williamson, 88–91; and doc. No. 35.   [2] ibid. 101–3.
[3] ibid. 116–44; and docs. 43, 45, 46, 47, 49.   [4] ibid. 145–72.
[5] For details of this story, *see* G. Schanz, op. cit. I, 327–51.
[6] G. F. Ward, 'The Early History of the merchants Staplers', *E.H.R.*, XXXIII (1918), 297.

organization of the Adventurers. It was only during the reign of Henry VII that a measure of government approval was given to the trend which was turning the Netherlands trade into the preserve of a monopolistic London company.[1] The organization of exporters of cloth as the Merchant Adventurers was of recent origin as a national body, and their potential value as lenders was only just beginning to attract the attention of the Crown in the days of Edward IV and Henry VII.[2]

Undoubtedly Henry VII was inclined to view with favour the consolidation of the organization of the Merchant Adventurers, and to use it when circumstances suited.[3] As early as 4 February 1486 the Merchant Adventurers of London trading into the ports of Holland, Zeeland, Brabant, and Flanders united together successfully to present a petition, as they had to Richard III, for pardon from all subsidies on goods landed before the first day of the first parliament of the new reign, and it was during these early years of the reign that they secured official recognition by the mayor and Corporation of London. Henry VII's desire to encourage them was shown by his willingness on occasion to allow his ships to convoy their ships, but did so cautiously; he was glad enough to have their cooperation with his council when their special knowledge might be useful, but quite ruthlessly ignored their interests when the decision was taken to prohibit commercial intercourse with the Netherlands. He might rebuke them if they acted without his licence, but was prepared to admonish the archduke if he thought they were being unfairly treated. After the so-called *Intercursus Magnus* of 1495 had been negotiated the advantages of promoting a unified trade as a potential diplomatic weapon became more manifest, and the king appointed a governor for the company. The statute 12 Henry VII, c. 6, tacitly admitted the right of the fellowship to compel others to join whilst explicitly limiting the fine that might be imposed to 10 marks, and requiring entrance fees to be raised only by act of parliament.[4] In November 1504 king and council in Star Chamber gave judgment upon certain disputes between the Merchant Adventurers and the merchants of the Staple at Calais, to the effect that either body making use of the privileges of the other should be subject to all the regulations and penalties by which the other was bound, and at the request of the 'society of merchant adventurers'

[1] *Cambridge economic history of Europe*, III (1963), ch. VI, E. Miller, 'Economic policies of governments', 337.

[2] ibid. 471.

[3] *See* generally, E. M. Carus-Wilson, 'The origins and early development of the Merchant Adventurers' organization', *Econ.H.R.*, IV (1933), repr., *Mediaeval Merchant Venturers* (1954, 2nd ed. 1967), 143–82.

[4] *See* above, p. 221.

this judgment was exemplified on the patent roll.[1] Subsequent letters patent[2] gave authority to the governor to call courts in London of twenty-four or at least thirteen of the company to inflict penalties for disobedience.

The most recent survey of Henry VII's diplomacy assures us that in regard to trade matters it hardly looks as if the system was any more foreseen and foredesigned than the rest of his foreign policy; although 'we can see a system of policy developing, a general pattern emerging'.[3] It is perhaps possible that this 'system and pattern' are somewhat illusory, but there can be no doubt that Henry's encouragement of trade was repeatedly subordinated and sometimes sacrificed to more pressing dynastic and strategic interests. 'It was in fact seldom more than a subsidiary purpose in his policy.'[4]

This subordination of trade to diplomacy is most prominently shown in relations with the Netherlands. In this sphere 'English merchants were the instruments, even the victims rather than the beneficiaries of Henry VII's policy'.[5] Trading prospects in that region were seriously affected by the growth of Antwerp as the principal market, a growth fostered by Maximilian, who wished to encourage a removal of trade from the turbulent centres of Ghent and Bruges. In 1488 he required a transfer of foreign traders from Bruges to Antwerp, which rapidly became the great *entrepôt* for the Portuguese spice trade and the centre where English goods could most profitably be marketed. English traders were reluctant to lose their contacts with smaller market centres in the Netherlands, but found themselves increasingly obliged to concentrate on Antwerp.

But by late 1493 Henry VII's patience with Maximilian's and Burgundian countenance of Perkin Warbeck came to an end, and he decided on a policy of economic sanctions. He forbade English merchants or any merchants from England to trade at all with Antwerp and the Low Countries, and obliged them to make the best they could of sharing in the trade of the Staplers at Calais, except by special licence under the Great Seal.[6] This drastic prohibition remained in force for more than two and a half years, until 24 February 1496,[7] and any hope of being

[1] *C.P.R.*, II, 388–9. An impressive list of the councillors present is given.
[2] ibid. 445.
[3] Wernham, op. cit. 62. What follows is much indebted to ch. 5, 'Sea Power and Trade 1485–1509', 62–76.
[4] ibid. 62.
[5] ibid. 67.
[6] Proclamation dated 18 September 1493, Hughes and Larkin, op. cit. 35, No. 31.
[7] ibid. 37, No. 33. Proclamation dated 28 February 1496.

able to trade under such licence was quashed by a counter-embargo imposed by the Netherlands government in May 1494.

In time, however, it was the Netherlands government that gave way and came to terms, and to that extent Henry VII's policy may be described as successful. But whether Maximilian and Philip were moved more by economic considerations or by political ones springing from the failure of Perkin Warbeck to make much headway and their desire by then to secure Henry VII's support against France must remain speculative. But judging from their subsequent actions in the commercial sphere, it was not primarily economic motives that induced them to agree to the treaty which Bacon conveniently immortalized, following, so he said, Flemish usage, as the *Intercursus Magnus*.[1]

The commercial aspects of this treaty appeared to give traders from England good prospects for the renewal of trade. They were allowed to sell freely in any part of Archduke Philip's dominions, except Flanders (included in 1502), without the payment of any tolls or customs in excess of the rates prevailing in the last fifty years; they were to get fair and speedy justice in the local courts, and a number of precise rules regarding commercial procedures were agreed.[2]

But before long Philip thought fit to impose a new import duty on cloth, so that by 21 June 1496 Henry VII was obliged to write a dignified but firm and candid letter of expostulation to the archduke's council, hinting that he knew how he should conduct himself if the treaty were not respected.[3] In the absence of redress the English merchants reverted again to Calais.[4] In June 1497 after much negotiation the new duty was withdrawn.[5] Philip still tried to confine English traders to Antwerp and Bergen, but they declined to leave Calais until the autumn of 1498, and it was not until May 1499 that a new agreement was reached confirming the treaty of 1496.[6]

Further dissatisfaction with renewed imposts imposed by the Netherlands government led, according to Henry VII's own account, to a

---

[1] *Henry VII*, ed. Lumby, 146. 'This is that treaty which the Flemings call at this day *intercursus magnus*; both because it is more complete than the precedent treaties of the third and fourth year of the king; and chiefly to give it a difference from the treaty which followed in the one and twentieth year of the king, which they call *intercursus malus*.' The two earlier agreements referred to are presumably those resulting in the proclamations of 4 April 1489, and 17 November 1489; Hughes and Larkin, op. cit. 24–6, No. 24. But a treaty with the Netherlands, prolonging the treaty of 1478, had been made in January 1487. *Foedera*, XII, 320, repr., Pollard, *Henry VII*, II, 282–5.

[2] *Foedera*, XII, 578–88; repr. with some corrections in Pollard, op. cit. 285–309.
[3] *L. & P.*, II, 69–72; Pollard, op. cit. 309–11.
[4] ibid. 309.   [5] *Foedera*, XII, 654–7.   [6] ibid. 713–20.

request by the English merchants that they might be allowed to revert to Calais once again, but this permission was countermanded when in 1502 Margaret of Savoy, then the regent, agreed to renew the treaty of 1496.[1] Continued disputes over customs duties and the desire of Henry VII to secure the surrender of the 'White Rose', Edward, earl of Suffolk, brought about another suspension of trade.[2] Negotiations for a fresh treaty were not begun until 1504,[3] but these dragged on until brought to a climax by Duke Philip's involuntary visit to England in 1506. Philip did not empower his commissioners until after he had reached Falmouth and was soon to embark, and the treaty was not concluded until 30 April, four days after he left Falmouth. It was to be confirmed within three months, and Henry VII duly confirmed it on 15 May: but it had not been confirmed by Philip before he died at Bruges on 25 September.

This treaty of 1506, which according to Bacon the Flemings called the *Intercursus Malus*, thus never became effective in the Netherlands, but according to the draft treaty English cloth was to be imported and transported and be saleable in Philip's and his heir's dominions in the Netherlands, free of any duties or imports, and numerous clauses clearly shifted the scales to the advantage of the English merchants, while the Netherlands merchants got little if anything beyond the treaty of 1496.[4] It is not surprising therefore that after Philip's death his sister Margaret (who in the meantime had rejected proposals for marriage with Henry VII) as regent during the minority of Archduke Charles firmly insisted that any effective agreement must do no more than confirm the treaty of 1496.[5] This was the essence of the further treaty of 5 June 1507,[6] which remained the basis of commercial relations between England and the Netherlands for the rest of Henry VII's reign and the early years of Henry VIII.[7]

Henry's concession did not cause Margaret to change her mind on the matrimonial project; he had used economic sanctions to dispel the threat of Perkin Warbeck, and had secured the surrender of the 'White

[1] *L. & P.*, I, 327–36, letter of Henry VII to Margaret of Savoy, May 1502.
[2] ibid.
[3] *Foedera*, XIII, 105; *Venetian Calendar*, I, No. 846.
[4] *Foedera*, XIII, 132–42, summarized in Pollard, op. cit. 322–3. I cannot see myself that the *Intercursus Magnus* conceded freedom of wholesale trade, whilst the *Intercursus Malus* included retail trade as well. Wernham, op. cit. 68–70. The distinction is hard to identify in either text.
[5] *L. & P.*, I, 327–31.
[6] *Foedera*, XIII, 168, summarized in Pollard, op. cit. 324.
[7] Busch, op. cit. 197–8.

Rose', but in the end he had obtained little economic advantage except a favourable position as regards customs duties for English merchants. He had indeed ensured a prosperous market in the Netherlands, and so opened up prospects for the future in what was to be the greatest European *entrepôt*, but in the process of trying to get more he had overreached himself and had suffered a diplomatic defeat.

Henry VII's policy towards the powerful Hanseatic League of German merchants in the Baltic ports was conditioned much more by commercial than political motives, and was primarily directed to reducing the privileged position of the Hanse in England and to furthering the trading prospects of the English merchants in the Baltic and Scandinavian regions. Something was achieved in these directions, but the achievements were limited by the practical possibilities, and in the long run were distorted by political considerations.[1]

Edward IV had left behind him serious problems for any successor who might wish to grapple with the Hanse. He had been much indebted to the Hanseatic League for their help in 1471 and had granted them extraordinary privileges by the Treaty of Utrecht of 1474,[2] including less heavy taxation than the English had to pay, full liberty of trade, and the right of judgment by special judges. Their headquarters in London, the Steelyard, was recognized as their free property. But the promises of reciprocal freedom of trade for English merchants were not kept, and the problem for Henry VII was how to force the Hanse to carry out their commitments. At the start he could not risk antagonizing the powerful League, and felt obliged to grant a charter, on 9 March 1486, which confirmed the Utrecht treaty, and another on 26 June ratifying the compensation for damages clauses in that treaty. The fact that the Hansards were not exempted from the provisions of the acts of 1486 and 1489,[3] forbidding aliens from exporting undressed cloth, or bullion, and the 'navigation act', hardly amounted to whittling away their privileges. He need do little to compensate the Hanseatics when mobs attacked the Steelyard as protest against their attempting to profit from the suspension of English trade with the Netherlands in 1493 and could oblige them to desposit £20,000 as security that they also would suspend trade from England to the Netherlands whilst the suspension lasted. He could apply some restrictive interpretation on their privilege of importing their goods at preferential rates by constructing this phrase to mean only goods produced or grown in their own territories and

---

[1] ibid. 71–4, 152–6; Wernham, op. cit. 64, 71–3.
[2] *Foedera*, XI, 793–803.
[3] *Materials*, I, 115–16. *See* Busch, op. cit. 73.

towns. Conferences at Antwerp in 1491 and Bruges in 1498–9 to try to reach amicable settlements on all these questions failed to find a settlement.

But a settlement was reached, in the long run, by Henry VII's giving way entirely to the Hanseatic desires. By the act of 1504,[1] all previous acts, statutes, or ordinances which prejudiced the 'ancient liberties and privileges' of the merchants of the Hanse were nullified, provided that nothing should prejudice the mayor, sheriffs, citizens, and commonalty of the City of London. This measure thus restored to the Hanse their position under the treaty of Utrecht of 1474, notwithstanding the effect of any statute made since. This extraordinary acknowledgement of total defeat against the Hansards was clearly not dictated by economic considerations, and must therefore have been accepted for very strong political reasons. No political explanation has so far been offered other than Henry VII's fears of Edward, earl of Suffolk's, the 'White Rose's', machinations on the continent, and Henry's desire to prevent the Hanseatic League from giving him any support, as once they had to Suffolk's grandfather Edward IV.[2] If this is the true explanation it must raise doubts as to the validity of Henry VII's political judgment by that date, for the sacrifice of English trading interests involved appears to be out of all proportion to the political risks, and is better considered under the heading of diplomacy.

In the course of his endeavours to improve English trading prospects in the Baltic and north German markets, Henry sought and obtained an agreement with the king of Denmark in 1489, extended in 1490, which procured promises of freedom of trade on favourable terms in Denmark and Norway, the reopening of a trade depot at Bergen, and the right to fish in Icelandic waters.[3] It was this sort of pressure that did induce

[1] 19 Henry VII, c. 23; *S.R.*, II, 665; extract in Pollard, op. cit. 272–3.

[2] Busch, op. cit. 179–80; Wernham, op. cit. 73. Henry's subsequent unscrupulous use of the proviso in the act of 1504 to re-exact the higher duties from the Hansards on the grounds that preferential rates were prejudicial to the privileges of London, and his seizure in 1508 of the £20,000 pledge by the Hansards not to trade with the Netherlands during the suspension of trade in 1493, on the ground that they did so trade during the suspension of 1505, were no more than acts of chicanery. For details, *see* Busch, op. cit. 180, and 367, n. 8.

[3] Wernham, op. cit. 72–3, proclamation 15 April 1490; Hughes and Larkin, op. cit. I, 22–3, No. 21. The thrusting commercial enterprise of the English fishermen in Iceland, however, evoked complaint from the king of Denmark, and Henry VII was obliged to forbid them from carrying to Iceland more goods than they required for their own use. *Paston letters*, ed. Gairdner, III, 367–9, No. 922, Henry VII to the earl of Oxford, admiral of England, 6 April 1491, cited (with incorrect reference), E. M. Carus-Wilson, *Mediaeval Merchant Venturers*, 127.

the Hanse to consent at the conference of 1491 to English trade direct to Danzig, but as Danzig refused to allow it, the gesture was useless. When later Riga fell out of the League, Henry VII speedily came to a trade treaty with that town in 1499, but this proved likewise to be in vain, as Riga soon returned to the League and the treaty lapsed.[1] Henry's very protracted and tortuous negotiations with George, duke of Saxony and of Friesland, almost wholly undertaken to frustrate any hopes that the ubiquitous 'White Rose' might have to get support from him, led to a treaty at the end of 1505 which envisaged amicable commercial relations, but appears to have had little practical results in the economic sphere, whatever may have been achieved in the field of Henry's dynastic diplomacy.[2]

The regions in which Henry met the least friction in negotiating trade agreements were those nearest home; Brittany and France. In 1486 he rapidly came to a commercial agreement with the duke of Brittany,[3] and another with Charles VIII of France which removed the obstacles in Franco-British trade set up in the time of Edward IV.[4] The ensuing stresses and strains arising from French designs on Brittany resulted in French impositions on English merchants, but these were modified by the Treaty of Étaples in 1492[5] and removed in 1495. A new Anglo-French commercial treaty in 1498[6] settled matters for the rest of the reign. There had been no difficulty in 1489 in renewing the 1378 treaty with Portugal.[7]

Henry VII's diplomatic dealings with Spain were so much conditioned by broader questions of policy and the project for the matrimonial alliance that the commercial aspect was subordinate, but by no means insignificant. In December 1485 Henry VII could do no more than confirm the privileges granted to the Spanish merchants by Edward IV in 1486,[8] which exempted them from the duties payable by other aliens (except the Hansards) on the export of English goods, and under these conditions the Spanish share of Anglo-Spanish trade prospered, even if restricted somewhat by the 'navigation acts' of 1486 to 1489. But the political pressures which resulted in the earliest

---

[1] *Foedera*, XII, 700; extract in Pollard, op. cit. II, 311–13.
[2] *Foedera*, XIII, 120; extract in Pollard, op. cit. II, 315–22; cf. Busch, op. cit. 181, 185, 370, n. 12.
[3] *Foedera*, XII, 303–12, 315–16.   [4] ibid. 277, 278–9, 281–2.
[5] *Foedera*, XII, 505, proclamation, 12 December 1492; Hughes and Larkin, op. cit. 31, No. 29.
[6] Proclamation, 23 August 1498; ibid. 43–5, No. 40; *Foedera*, XII, 683 ff.
[7] *Foedera*, XII, 351, 378–9.
[8] ibid. XI, 569–72 (Castile), 3; 1486, 633–5 (Aragon).

major diplomatic success of the reign, the Treaty of Medina del Campo, 27 March 1489,[1] brought commercial clauses highly favourable to the English. The English in Spain and the Spaniards in England were to be in the same position, but customs duties were to be fixed on both sides at the rates prevailing thirty years before. This meant for the Spaniards that they were deprived of the favourable rates granted by Edward IV in 1466. Subsequent efforts by the Spaniards to amend these clauses failed. The later treaty of 1499,[2] couched in very amicable terms and intended to bring the marriage proposals to a conclusion, confirmed the reciprocity of commerce, but said nothing about the rate of customs duties. The Spaniards had lost their privileged position and some of their share of Anglo-Spanish trade, but Castile in 1494 had introduced a 'navigation' act of its own which forbade the export of goods in foreign ships when Spanish ships were available, and in so far as it enforced this law it reduced the dispatch of English ships to Spanish ports.

Henry VII's other efforts at promoting trading opportunities elsewhere in the Mediterranean met with no more than very partial success. The great difficulty here was to make inroads on the virtual monopoly of Venice in English trading with the eastern Mediterranean. The spices and luxury trade with the Orient, the wines of Greece and Crete, and the dried fruits of the Levant largely came to England in Venetian galleys putting in to Southampton, while the wool and woollen cloth of England returned in the same galleys to Venice, and northern Italy.[3] Any attempt of English traders to encroach on the trade was apt to be confronted by a Venetian imposition of extra tax. The chief hope of making headway depended upon the manipulation of Venetian-Florentine rivalries. In December 1490 Henry made a treaty with Florence, whereby the Florentine port of Pisa was recognized as the Italian Staple for English wool. The export of English wool to Venice was restricted and its transport confined to English ships. Venetian reprisals provoked in 1492 an English act of Parliament[4] imposing a heavy duty on wines brought to England in Venetian ships. But in the meantime the treaty with the Florentines, who had themselves initiated the proposals as a means of securing a monopoly of the English wool trade for Pisa, did something to promote English trade in the region, and to raise Henry VII's diplomatic prestige, but the treaty was probably never fully effective, and in any event the revolt of Pisa against Florence in

[1] *Cal. S.P. Spanish*, I, 21; text of execution of the treaty, *Foedera*, XII, 420–8.
[2] *Cal. S.P. Spanish*, I, 244; summary in Pollard, op. cit. II, 313–15.
[3] Wernham, op. cit. 64–5, 74–6.
[4] 7 Henry VII, c. 7; *S.R.*, I, 553.

1494 upset the local commercial system, and the prospects of any considerable English trade there were disappointed.[1]

[1] For full details, *see* M. E. Mullet, 'Anglo-Florentine commercial relations, 1465–1491', *Econ.H.R.*, 2nd ser. XV (1962), 250–65.

Chapter 13

RELATIONS WITH THE CHURCH

Henry VII's relations with the papacy and the Church were in no way remarkable. He was himself conventionally orthodox and pious in his religious observances and he made many notable contributions to the building of churches and religious houses.[1] His policy towards the Church followed closely precedents that had been set in the time of Edward IV. There were no new departures of much significance in his attitudes. He allowed occasional influence to his mother Margaret Beaufort in making a few of his many appointments to the episcopate;[2] he appointed several foreigners, for diplomatic reasons;[3] he assented to a few acts of parliament which, in a very modest way, further defined and slightly curtailed one or two ecclesiastical privileges.[4] But he kept a firm control over episcopal appointments, and at the same time remained on amicable terms with the papacy, with which he normally acted in agreement. He was glad of papal support, especially in the earlier years of his reign. The three successive popes, Innocent VIII (1484–92), Alexander VI (1492–1503), and Julius II (1503–13), with whom he had to deal, had no desire to antagonize the English king, whose neutrality or support they sooner or later wanted to cultivate in their efforts to resist French or Spanish aggressions in Italy. Henry VII was therefore, whilst accepting marks of papal favour and support, able to get his own way without overt friction; and being orthodox and at least outwardly pious, he acquiesced in the persecution of heretics in accordance with the existing law.[5] About seventy-three persons are known to have been put on trial for heresy during the reign. Nearly all these abjured, but probably three were burnt. The king did not, of course, have any option in such acquiescence and doubtless had no wish but to acquiesce. He is said to have gained great honour by his successful exhortation to a priest condemned as a heretic at Canterbury in 1498, whom he converted from his erroneous opinions so that 'he died as a Christian'. There were no religious innovations whilst he remained on the throne. 'The advent of the Tudor dynasty formed no landmark;

---

[1] See below, p. 305.   [2] R. J. Knecht (see below, p. 242, n.1), 129.
[3] See below, p. 242.   [4] See below, p. 243.   [5] J. A. F. Thomson, *The later Lollards, 1414–1520* (1965), 237–8; Kingsford, *Chronicles of London*, 222, 327.

11a. King James IV of Scotland. Artist and date unknown (*private collection*)

11b. Margaret Tudor, Queen of Scots, by Daniel Mytens, early seventeenth century, from an original portrait *c*.1515–1516, now lost (*Palace of Holyrood House*)

11c. Perkin Warbeck, by Jacques Le Boucq, mid-sixteenth century. Source unknown (*Library of Arras, MS. 266*)

12a. Prince Arthur, *c.* 1499–1502 (*Great Malvern Priory Church, transept window*)

12b. Henry VIII in early manhood. Date and artist unknown, but perhaps *c.* 1520 (*National Portrait Gallery*)

12c. Mary Tudor, duchess of Suffolk. Artist and date unknown but early sixteenth century. Identity uncertain but supported by the only authentic pictures made of her when Queen of France, 1514–15 (*Woburn Abbey*)

12d. Catherine of Aragon. Artist unknown, *c.* 1530 (*National Portrait Gallery*)

the reign of Henry VII was far from presaging major crises in Anglo-papal or Church-State relations.'[1] Professor Dickens also assures us, 'the advent of the first Tudor sovereign marked no epoch in the history of the religious orders in England', and that 'neither the policy of the king nor the external events of his reign affected in any direct way the fortunes of the monasteries'.

No dispute between the king and the papacy arose. After Bosworth, Henry was prudent enough to declare his obedience, and Innocent VIII quickly reciprocated by providing the necessary dispensation for Henry's marriage with Elizabeth of York and pronouncing that their children would be legitimate, and at the same time obliged by declaring that rebels, including those in Ireland, were *ipso facto* excommunicate.[2] No difficulties were made about Morton's promotion to the archbishopric nor eventual cardinalate. The alliance between Henry and Morton in Church matters was supported by the Curia; papal assistance was forthcoming in various minor matters; privileges were given to the chapels royal at Windsor and Westminster. Henry could allow the pope's jubilee indulgence to be preached in 1501 and permit £4,000 to be contributed to a crusading levy. He could take over the English Hospice in Rome, hitherto an independant lodging for pilgrims, which for a time became a part of the royal administration, accommodating men of rank. In time the papacy could present honours to Henry three times in the form of the Cap and Sword and the Golden Rose.[3] Above all, mutual agreement between the king and the papacy eliminated the cathedral chapters from any active part in the election of bishops throughout the reign. So sure was he of getting his nominees appointed that it became common practice to grant the temporalities before translation or consecration.

Only three of the bishops in post at the time of Bosworth were sufficiently identified with Richard III's regime to be excluded from summons to Henry VII's first parliament, but two of these were soon received back into favour, and of these one, Thomas Langton, was advanced very highly in due course.[4] According to Richard III, Henry

[1] A. G. Dickens, *The English Reformation* (1964), 88–9.

[2] *See* above, p. 66. These texts (pp. 1–2, 14–26) and many documents, mostly of a routine nature, are available up to 1492 in *Cal. Papal Reg., 1484–1492*.

[3] F. R. H. Du Boulay, 'The fifteenth century', *The English Church and the papacy in the Middle Ages*, ed. C. H. Lawrence (1965), 195–242, esp. 220–7. Morton's visit to the Hospice in 1484 (*see* above, p. 106) may have had something to do with Henry's take-over.

[4] A. Hamilton Thompson, *The English clergy and their organization in the later Middle Ages* (1949), 24, 31.

had started promising preferment to some of his followers long before his expedition set out,[1] and certainly he determined both to control and manipulate elections to the episcopal bench primarily in the interests of himself and his government. Circumstances placed many opportunities in his hands for making such appointments. By April 1509 all the bishops elected before 1485 were dead or had resigned, except one.[2] Thirty-six bishops died during the reign, but Henry's manipulations frequently produced one or two vacancies in addition to the see vacated by death or resignation. Thus when Archbishop Bourchier died in 1485, Morton was translated from Ely to Canterbury, Alcock from Worcester to Ely, and Robert Morton (John's nephew) to Worcester. When John Morton died in 1500, similar situations occurred; Deane was translated from Salisbury to Canterbury, Audley from Hereford to Salisbury, and Castello appointed to Hereford. Such manipulations had not occurred to Edward IV, but Henry VII doubtless saw the financial advantages of multiplying vacancies for short periods, whilst promoting several faithful civil servants or supporters at a time.[3]

Otherwise his policy was fundamentally the same as Edward IV's. A high proportion of the bishops at the time of Henry's death in April 1509 had been legally trained civil servants.[4] Nine others were lawyers by training, and only four can be described as theologians. Two Italians had been successively appointed to Worcester,[5] on the strength of their

---

[1] *See* generally, R. J. Knecht, 'The episcopate and the Wars of the Roses', *Birmingham H.J.*, VI (1957–8), 108–31, esp. 126–31. Langton had served Edward IV in a variety of capacities and had, for example, been appointed to St David's in 1483 and translated to Salisbury in May 1485; he was temporarily deprived of his temporalities after Bosworth and put into Courtenay's custody. Before long, however, he was summoned to parliament and convocations, and promoted to Winchester in succession to Courtenay in 1493. Only his death in 1501 prevented him from moving to Canterbury. Richard Redman had been at St Asaph since 1471, and excluded from the first parliament because of his Yorkist associations, but was pardoned in February 1486, and secured translation to Exeter in 1495 and to Ely in 1501. Robert Stillington, bishop of Bath and Wells since 1466, had been keeper of the Privy Seal in 1460 and chancellor on occasions, 1467–75. Edward IV, however, had imprisoned him at one time, but Richard III favoured him, and he was arrested after Bosworth. His pardon by Henry VII did not prevent him from dabbling in treason in connection with the Simnel conspiracy, so that he was arrested again and imprisoned at Windsor, though released shortly before his death in 1491. John Shirwood, appointed to Durham in 1485 by Richard III, was not summoned to the first parliament, not because of disgrace, but because he was absent on Henry VII's business at the Curia (loc. cit. 127–8).
[2] H. Ellis, *Original letters*, 2nd ser. I, 146.

[3] Edmund Audley, of Rochester (1480), Hereford (1492), and Salisbury (1502), survived until 1524.
[4] Knecht, loc. cit.

[5] Giovanne de' Gigli (1497), followed in 1499 by his brother Silvester. cf. A. Hamilton Thompson, op. cit. 25; Du Boulay, op. cit. 222.

services as diplomatic agents at the Curia, and another, Adrian de Castello, who had been appointed to Hereford in 1502 and then translated to Bath and Wells in 1504. A fourth foreigner, Michael Deacon, a native of Normandy, whose main recommendation apparently was that he had made acquaintance with Henry when he was in exile, was appointed to St Asaph. In Wales only three Welshmen were nominated to sees, and of these nominations one took effect only after Henry's death.[1] Henry VII could therefore rely very thoroughly on the loyalty of the bishops, all the more, no doubt, because a number of them were required to enter into recognizances with him.[2] It was not to be expected that any strong resistance would come from the bench when later on Henry VIII adopted different ecclesiastical policies. By then the tradition of close alliance between the episcopate and the Crown was firmly entrenched.

The legislation of Henry VII's reign relating to ecclésiastical matters was of rather minor importance.[3] The first parliament passed a statute authorizing bishops and their ordinaries to punish by imprisonment or otherwise at discretion priests, clerks, and religious convicted by canon law of adultery, fornication, incest, or any other fleshly incontinency.[4] A statute of the fourth year declared void letters patent granted in the past to abbots, priors, and certain other ecclesiastical officials to be quit of collecting tenths,[5] whilst an act of the seventh year limited letters patent exempting abbots and priors from contributions to tenths and fifteenths to the beginning of the reign of Edward IV.[6] The most important act sought to curtail abuse of benefit of clergy. Benefit of ecclesiastical rather than secular penalties was to be allowable once only to persons not actually in orders. Clerics convicted of murder were to be branded with an 'M' on their left thumb, or with a 'T' for any other felony, before being delivered to the ordinary. Any person brought to trial a second time was not to have benefit of clergy if he failed to bring certification of his orders on the appointed day.[7]

The outstanding example of Henry VII's personal interest in these

---

[1] On Henry VII and the Welsh bishoprics, see Glanmor Williams, *The Welsh church from Conquest to Reformation* (1962), 299–304.

[2] A. G. Dickens, op. cit. 88. The precise nature of these recognizances needs proper investigation, but there may have been an element of simony involved.

[3] cf. Pickthorn, op. cit. 175–81; A. G. Dickens, op. cit. 88–9.

[4] 1 Henry VII, c. 4; *S.R.*, II, 500.   [5] 4 Henry VII, c. 5; *S.R.*, II, 530.

[6] 7 Henry VII, c. 5; *S.R.*, II, 552.

[7] 4 Henry VII, c. 13; *S.R.*, II, 538. cf. above, p. 179. St. 7 Henry VII, c. 1, withdrew the benefit from military deserters, and 12 Henry VII, c. 7, withdrew it from laymen in cases of petty treason.

matters, however, was his intervention in the case of the trial of the Staffords for treason in 1486, which resulted in the judicial decision that the right of sanctuary should not henceforth be pleadable in treason.[1]

None of these modest measures met with any opposition from the papacy. The attitude of the common law courts was clearly enough not to allow any encroachments on the law of the land by papal action, but no issues were raised such as to provoke manifest conflict or even friction. Nothing that occurred in the relation between State and Church in Henry VII's time can be regarded as foreshadowing the shape of things to come under Henry VIII. But – and it is perhaps a fundamental point – the very full measure of control over the episcopate attained by Henry VII may have constituted a condition precedent without which his son might well have been confronted with a far greater degree of opposition from the Church than in fact he experienced when it came to the crisis. To many clergy and others it must have seemed that papal power in practice was no great thing,[2] and that its abolition was not so significant as the theorists made out.

[1] *See* above, pp. 161 and 71, for references.

[2] These attitudes are well illustrated by the discussion by the justices in the parliament chamber in the well-known 'alum' case in 1486. *Y.B. 1 Henry VII, Hil.*, pl. 10. *See* Pickthorn, op. cit. 181; Chrimes, op. cit. 379–80; Pollard, *Henry VII*, III, 154–5.

Chapter 14

POLICY TOWARDS WALES
AND IRELAND

(A) Wales

Henry VII had, of course, succeeded to the throne of England without having been prince of Wales, and the princely office had suffered grievous vicissitudes since Edward I had invested his son Edward of Caernarvon in February 1301. True, the 'Black Prince', eldest son of Edward III, had held it for thirty-three years before his death in 1376. But the prince's second son Richard held it only for seven months before he became king. Henry of Monmouth held it from 1399, when he was about twelve years of age, until his accession in 1413. Henry VI was never prince, though his ill-fated son Edward was so created at the age of about six months in 1454. The displacement of his father in 1461 nullified the effectiveness of this creation. Edward IV sought to rectify the position by creating his son Edward prince in 1471 at a similar age. His survival until 1483 offered Edward IV a few years of opportunity to give to the princely office some functions in the governmental sphere other than those envisaged in 1301. But the decease of Edward V early in the reign of Richard III and of his successor as prince by April 1484 brought another hiatus in the history of the office. Not until 29 November 1489 was Henry VII able to create his three-year-old son Arthur prince of Wales, and whatever hopes may have been founded on this revival of the office were dashed by Arthur's death on 2 April 1502. Nearly two years elapsed before the second son Henry was elevated to the position of prince (18 February 1504), and after his accession on 22 April 1509 there was to be no subsequent prince for a century.[1] Apart, therefore, from the vestment of the lands of the principality in the hands of the Crown (or prince) and the introduction into the principality of many features of the English administrative and legal system as decreed by Edward I, the governmental arrangements in Wales persisted with little change until the late fifteenth century. The

---

[1] Henry, son of James I, was created prince in 1610 but died in 1612. His second son Charles was so created in 1616. After Charles's succession to the throne, there was no prince of Wales until 1727.

principality and the marcher lordships (with many of these in the king's hands either as king or as duke of Lancaster) remained side by side to complicate and confuse governmental questions throughout the period.

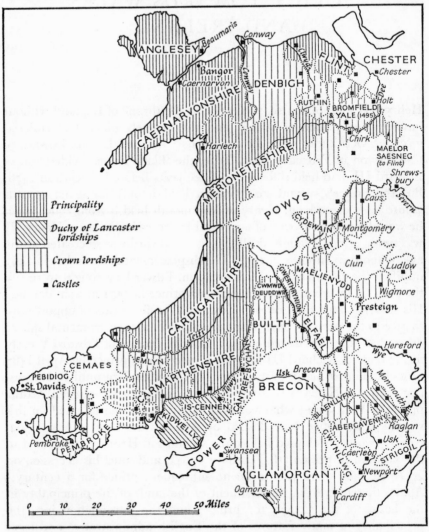

Map 4 Lands of the Crown in Wales in the reign of Henry VII

The fundamental nature of Edward I's provisions for the principality of Wales, as set out in the so-called 'statute' of Rhuddlan or Wales of 1284, has not until recently been as clearly understood as it should. But the union of the principality with the Crown of England did not occur, as often assumed, in consequence of the act of 1536. It was achieved in fact by the 'statute' of 1284. Sir Goronwy Edwards in a recent study[1] not as yet widely known, has made this conclusion irresistible. The words of the decree of 1284 are perfectly plain on the point. Edward I declared without ambiguity that 'Divine providence hath now wholly and entirely transferred under our proper dominion the land of Wales with its inhabitants, heretofore subject unto us in feudal right . . . and hath annexed and united the same unto our Crown of the realm [of England] as a member of the same body'.[2] The act of 1536, misleadingly called by twentieth-century historians the 'Act of Union', could not have created a union that had occurred in 1284, nor does the actual wording of the act, taken in its context, purport to create the union of England and Wales. 'The unions which the Act did purport to create, and actually created, were those which merged the principality of Wales and the March of Wales to form the twelve shires of Wales.' The purport and effect of the act of 1536 was to unify Wales politically within itself.[3]

The position in Wales when Henry VII acquired the Crown in 1485 was that the lands of the principality, with certain marcher lordships regarded as legally held thereof in chief, rested, pending the creation of a prince of Wales, in the hands of the Crown; also in the king's hands were other lands coming to him as parts of the duchy of Lancaster and some marcher lordships which were his either by inheritance, forfeiture, or by wardship. In addition a large number of marcher lordships quite distinct from the principality remained vested in the hands of the individual lords themselves, holding as in chief their lands and rights, not of the principality or prince except in one or two instances, but of the king himself. The possibilities of improving the government of Wales that confronted Henry VII were not very great. The principality would provide a patrimony for his first-born son, and might, following Yorkist precedent, offer opportunities for administrative improvement; fortuitous circumstances might combine to make the king himself the greatest marcher lord. But the possibilities of interfering in the affairs of the other marcher lords remained slight; at best it might be feasible to try to induce the marcher lords to carry out the governmental duties, especially in the matter of enforcing law and order, which legally rested

[1] Sir G. Edwards, *The Principality of Wales, 1267–1967* (Caernarvonshire Historical Society, 1969), esp. App. C, 35–9.

[2] *S.R.*, I, 55–70. cf. some observations by S. B. Chrimes, *King Edward I's policy for Wales* (National Museum of Wales, 1969).

[3] Edwards, op. cit. 39.

upon them. If steps in the right direction were taken, the necessary conditions precedent to the merger of the principality and the March of Wales by the Act of Union of 1536 might be established, even though such a merger can hardly have been consciously envisaged by Henry VII himself.

At the time of Henry VII's accession, the principality consisted of Anglesey, Caernarvonshire, Flintshire, and Merioneth in the north, plus Cardiganshire and Carmarthenshire in the south. In these domains the administration, following Edward I's arrangements, was similar to that in England, with sheriffs, coroners, county and hundred courts, and in addition a justice of North Wales for Anglesey, Caernarvonshire, and Merioneth, and a justice of South Wales for the two southern shires. Flint had been brought under the county palatine of Chester, which had been in the king's or earl's hands for a long time, but retained its own courts of law, with a justice of Chester for Crown and Common Pleas, without justices of the peace, but with a chamberlain and other officials of its own. Glamorgan and Pembrokeshire had become Crown lordships in which the administration was on the lines of English counties, and the same general arrangements prevailed in the border shires of Gloucester, Hereford, Worcester, and Shropshire. But the king's writ did not run in the numerous marcher lordships, probably exceeding one hundred and thirty in number, which were substantially autonomous and wherein the lord was sovereign and alone responsible for the maintenance of justice and order. But twenty-two of these marcher lordships comprised the earldom of March, which had come into the hands of the Crown with the accession of the Yorkists, the heirs of the Mortimers. The earldom of Pembroke and several lordships were restored to Jasper Tudor and after his death passed to Prince Henry. The lordships of Brecon, Caurs, and Newport, all part of the Stafford family estates, had been forfeited by the attainder of Henry, duke of Buckingham, in 1483, and remained in the Crown's hands during the minority of his heir Edward. The attainder of Sir William Stanley in 1495 brought Holt, Bromfield, Yale, and Chirk into the king's hands. Altogether, it is calculated that some fifty marcher lordships were in Henry VII's hands at one time or another. He was therefore in a powerful position to influence affairs not only in the principality, but also to some extent in the Marches.[1]

[1] Penry Williams, *The council in the Marches of Wales* (1958), which largely supersedes C. A. J. Skeel's work of the same title published in 1904, pp. 3–6. *See* also the list of lordships in the latter work, App. IV, 290–3, based on the list in the act of 1536 (27 Henry VIII, c. 26).

In the principality, Henry's first care was to appoint to the chief offices men whom he could trust or thought he could trust. Sir William Stanley, one of the most powerful marcher lords in his own right, had been appointed chief justice of North Wales by Richard III in November 1483,[1] and continued in office until his own downfall in 1495. Jasper Tudor was appointed chief justice of South Wales, 13 December 1485,[2] and so remained until his death also in 1495. Both of these influential men served, along with a number of others, on a commission appointed on 18 February 1486 to restore order in the earldom of March.[3]

But little time was lost in resurrecting the princely office once a son was born to the king. Arthur, born 19 September 1486, was created prince of Wales and earl of Chester on 29 November 1489.[4] With a titular prince, no matter how tender in age, in existence, it was possible to follow the precedents that Edward IV had set, and to establish a Prince's Council that could exercise some degree of supervision over the principality as a whole and over the contiguous border shires. It is certain that the Prince's Council was established shortly after his creation as prince, and that this council was functioning under the aegis of Jasper Tudor by March 1490, some ten or eleven years before Prince Arthur himself came to reside at Ludlow.[5] The rapidity with which a Prince's Council was established could hardly have been achieved without precedent, and this had been firmly set by Edward IV in 1471.[6]

His son Edward had been created prince on 26 June 1471,[7] when he was about eight months old, and a council enlarged to twenty-five members in February 1473[8] was set up to manage his domains. By November 1473 John Alcock, then bishop of Rochester, was recognized as president of this council;[9] and he was associated with Anthony, Earl Rivers, in the care and upbringing of the prince. The primary task of the council was the management of the territories appertaining to the principality and of the prince's Household, but its scope became extended rather further as time went on.[10]

As early as 1474 a commission was issued to Earl Rivers and others to take steps to arrest certain persons who had failed to appear before

---

[1] *C.P.R., 1476–1485*, 368.
[2] ibid. *Henry VII*, I, 47.
[3] ibid. 85–6.
[4] *Materials*, II, 541–2.
[5] T. B. Pugh, *The marcher lordships of South Wales, 1415–1536* (1963), 257–8, and App. 3; which corrects Penry Williams, op. cit. 10; and G. R. Elton, *England under the Tudors* (1955), 66, on this point.
[6] Penry Williams, op. cit. 6–9.
[7] *C.P.R., 1467–1477*, 283.
[8] ibid. 283, 365, 366.
[9] ibid. 401.
[10] Penry Williams, op. cit. 7–8.

the King's Council, and to give assistance in the matter when required
by the Prince's Council.[1] Further important steps to extend the influence of the Prince's Council into the Marches were taken in 1476.
A general commission of *oyer et terminer* was issued to the prince in
the border counties and the Marches of Wales.[2] In February another
commission was issued to the prince and council to be at Ludlow in
March to confer with the marcher lords (summoned separately by the
king) on ways and means of doing justice in the many cases of murder
and other felonies committed in Wales and the Marches, pending the
arrival of the king in person later on.[3] Further commissions were issued
during the year which in effect extended the influence of the council
into the Marches. Within a few years the Prince's Council had become
an established instrument for the supervision of justice in the Marches
of Wales as well as the principality itself. After 1478, however, little is
known of the activities of the council, and it may have ceased to exist
with the death of Edward IV in 1483.[4]

Soon after the creation of Henry VII's son Arthur as prince of Wales
and earl of Chester (29 November 1489), the Prince's Council had been
re-established, and by 1490 was functioning. By 1501 the prince himself
became resident at Ludlow.

A surviving indenture made in March 1490 between the king and
Ralph Hakluyt, steward of the lordships of Clifford, Winforton, and
Glasbury reveals the responsibilities which it was intended the Prince's
Council should undertake.[5] The officers of the royal lordship in Wales
were to be bound by indentures to suppress felonies, and the council was
to ensure that these contracts were observed. All persons from the royal
lordships seeking redress of grievances were to address themselves to the
prince or in his absence to Jasper Tudor, or to the Prince's Council.[6]
By 1493 the prince was given judicial powers similar to those which
Edward IV had given to his son, with power to appoint commissions of
oyer et terminer in the March shires and in the principality, powers of
array, of inquiry into liberties and into the flights of criminals.[7] A large
number of the Crown's marcher lordships, including the earldom of
March, were transferred to the prince,[8] who became in consequence
'the greatest lord of the whole region and in a strong position to
supervise justice'.[9]

After the prince's marriage in November 1501, his council was recon-

---

[1] *C.P.R., 1467–1477*, 429.   [2] ibid. 574.   [3] ibid. 574, 603.
[4] Penry Williams, op. cit. 9.   [5] Pugh, op. cit. App. 3.
[6] ibid. 257.   [7] *C.P.R., Henry VII*, I, 438, 441.
[8] ibid. 453.   [9] Penry Williams, op. cit. 10.

stituted with William Smyth, bishop of Lincoln since 1495, already a prominent figure in the council's work, as president.[1] But the death of Arthur on 2 April 1502 left the council to function as best it might without a prince until the creation of the king's son Henry as prince on 18 February 1504.[2] A precedent had now been set for the existence of a council without a prince of Wales for a period of nearly two years, and it became manifest that a council for Wales might be more than a Prince's Council, and the time would come when there was such a thing as the Council in the Marches of Wales. In the meantime the whole patrimony of the heir to the throne passed to Prince Henry in 1504 (who therefore surrendered the lands of the duchy of York and the lands in Wales granted to him on the death of Jasper Tudor in 1495), but the issues from the new prince's domains continued to be paid into the chamber for the king's use.[3]

Some progress had thus been made in making the Prince's Council an instrument of government in the principality, the Marches, and the Crown lordships. But none of these developments in itself affected the most intractable problem of ensuring justice within the marcher lordships. It was not possible for the king or the prince to attempt direct interference in the internal administration of justice by the lords marcher. But it was possible for the king to enter into indentures with individual marcher lords binding them to observe certain principles in the exercise of their jurisdictions. It is probable that Edward IV had had to resort to this method of attempting to oblige the lords to improve their performance of duty. An 'Indenture for the Marches' was made on 1 March 1490 between Henry VII and Jasper, duke of Bedford, in his capacity of marcher lord of Pembroke, Glamorgan, Newport, Abergavenny, Caldicot, and Magor, whereby Jasper was bound to oblige his officers to exact from his men in the lordships surety for good behaviour and due appearance in court. About the same time a similar indenture was made with William Herbert, earl of Huntingdon, as lord of Chepstow, Gower, Tretower, and Crickhowell. After Prince Arthur's death in April 1502, the council in the Marches advised the king that all lords marcher should be bound by indentures in similar fashion and presumably this was done, although only a few such indentures are

---

[1] *C.P.R.*, II, 295.

[2] *R.P.*, VI, 522, 532. *See* generally, T. B. Pugh (ed.), ch. XI, *Glamorgan county history*, III (1971); *Tudor Wales, 1485–1536: select documents*, ed. T. B. Pugh and W. R. B. Robertson (1972); and R. A. Griffiths, *The principality of Wales in the later Middle Ages: the structure and personnel of its government*, I, *South Wales, 1277–1536* (1972)

[3] B. P. Wolffe, *The Crown lands*, 46.

known to have survived.[1] He did not attempt to encroach upon the
jurisdiction of the lords over felonies within their lordships, but he did
seek to prevent the notorious abuse whereby criminals could escape
justice by fleeing from the jurisdiction of one lord into the territory of
another wherein he had not committed an offence. The agreements
aimed at making such persons 'extraditable' as between lordships and
generally to cause a lord's official to implement properly the jurisdictional rights vested in their lords. But to make agreements was one thing;
it remained another and far more difficult matter to ensure that these
agreements were kept. In practice they could not be enforced, Henry
VII's attempts proved to be inadequate, and their failure contributed
to the more radical changes envisaged in Henry VIII's act of 1536.[2]

All that has been described so far are measures that the king took to
provide for the due functioning of the principality, the adjacent Marches
or borders, the Crown lordships, the doing of justice or the oversight
thereof as behoved the king or prince whether of Welsh descent or not,
and a willingness to see in the Yorkist precedents for a Prince's Council
an instrument that should be revived and strengthened. An awareness
of the weakness and ineffectiveness of judicature, at least in the criminal
sphere, within the marcher lordships, has also been manifested. But for
anything that might be deemed a pro-Welsh policy in the more senti-
mental sense inspired by Henry's ancestry and his upbringing in Wales,
we must consider the several charters of privileges that Henry VII
granted to certain communities in North Wales.

The effect of some at least of these charters was in part to exempt the
inhabitants of the communities specified from the operation of portions
of the 'penal legislation' against the Welsh which had been enacted by
Henry IV a century or so earlier. The most important of these measures
disabled Welsh people from acquiring certain property or status or
offices in specified locations. Thus by an act of 1401 Welsh people were
forbidden to purchase lands or tenements in the towns of Shrewsbury,
Bridgenorth, Ludlow, Leominster, Hereford, Gloucester, Worcester,
and other towns in the Marches; none was to be eligible to be a citizen
or burgess in any city, borough, or merchant town, nor bear arms in

[1] T. B. Pugh, *The marcher lordships of South Wales, 1415–1536* (1963), 29–30; and
'The indenture for the Marches' (between Henry VII and Edward Stafford (1477–
1521), duke of Buckingham), *E.H.R.*, LXXI (1956), 436–41. I am indebted to my
former pupil, Mr David H. Thomas, for providing me with a transcript of part of the
ndenture with William Herbert, earl of Huntingdon, from 'Herbertorum Prosapia',
Cardiff Public Library MS. 5.7, 78–9.

[2] Pugh, ibid. 438–9. The duke of Buckingham's failure to observe parts of the
agreement brought a severe rebuke from Henry VIII in 1518.

any such.[1] A further act of the same year extended the prohibition to the purchase of lands and acquisition of burgess status by Welsh people to England generally and English boroughs in Wales.[2] By other acts made two years later, Welshmen were forbidden to hold castles or defensible houses 'otherwise than was used in the time of Edward I, conqueror of Wales', except by bishops and temporal lords.[3] No Welshman was to be made a justice, chamberlain, chancellor, treasurer, sheriff, steward, constable of a castle, receiver, escheator, coroner, chief forester, nor keeper of records in any part of Wales, nor be of the council of any English lands, except bishops.[4] Nor should an Englishman married to a Welshwoman have privileges in any English boroughs or bear office in Wales.[5] No Englishman was to be convicted at the suit of a Welshman except by judgment of English justices or of English burgesses.[6] A statute of 1447 confirmed all the statutes against the Welsh not already repealed.[7] None in fact appears to have been repealed until 1624.[8]

The letters patent issued by Henry VII which purported to suspend the operation of some parts of these statutes in favour of the inhabitants of certain communities in North Wales were seven in number and all dated between 1504 and 1507, all that is to say were issued after the creation of the future Henry VIII as prince of Wales.

The earliest, dated 28 October 1504, appears to have been ignored by modern historians until very recently, and is known only in a confirmatory charter of the first year of Henry VIII.[9] If this *Inspeximus* is to be believed Henry VII granted by his own mere notion and the advice of his council in 1504 that notwithstanding the legislation of the fourth year of Henry IV, the inhabitants of the counties of Caernarvon and Merioneth were to be allowed in future to acquire lands, tenements or any hereditaments in England and English boroughs in Wales in fee simple or fee tail or by any tenure, to hold any office if chosen in England or English boroughs and towns in Wales, and to become burgesses

---

[1] 2 Henry IV, c. 12; *S.R.*, II, 124.   [2] 2 Henry IV, c. 20; *S.R.*, II, 124.
[3] 4 Henry IV, c. 31; *S.R.*, II, 140.   [4] 4 Henry IV, c. 32; *S.R.*, II, 140.
[5] 4 Henry IV, c. 26, 34; *S.R.*, II, 140.
[6] 2 Henry IV, c. 19; 4 Henry IV, c. 26; *S.R.*, II, 124, 110.
[7] 25 Henry VI.   [8] 21 James I, c. 28.

[9] The charter does not appear on any patent roll, but is printed in full in *Arch. Camb.* (1847), 202–6. Mr J. Beverley Smith has called attention to this document in his article 'Crown and community in the principality of North Wales in the reign of Henry Tudor', *W.H.R.*, 3 (1966), 145–71, esp. 157–8. Confusion has no doubt arisen because the heading given to the article in *Arch. Camb.* implies that the *Inspeximus* merely recites and confirms the charter to bondmen granted in 1507, whereas in fact it confirms also this charter of 1504.

therein. The charter further abrogated the custom of gavelkind or 'Welsh tenure' (i.e. the equal partition of land among a man's sons) and prescribed descent of land by English common law and abrogated a large number of customary financial and other exactions.

The next grant, dated 8 August 1505, gave to the tenants and inhabitants of the lordship of Bromfield and Yale in North Wales the power to acquire lands and tenements in fee in England and English boroughs in Wales and the office of sheriff and municipal offices therein, notwithstanding the act of the second year of Henry IV, and abrogated gavelkind and a variety of Welsh customary exactions.[1] Very similar concessions were made on 20 July 1506 to the inhabitants of the lordships of Chirk and Chirkland in the Marches of Wales.[2] On the same date similar licence was given to the inhabitants of the lordship of Denbigh and the commote (administrative district) of Cynmeirch.[3]

On 3 March 1507 a charter was granted to the inhabitants of Anglesey, Caernarvon, and Merioneth. Apart from the inclusion of Anglesey and the additional provision in favour of bondmen, it is difficult to see how the substance of this grant differed from that of 1504.[4] Notwithstanding the acts of the second and fourth years of Henry IV, the king granted with the advice of his council that the inhabitants of the counties specified should have, use, and enjoy all their land and tenements, hold them in fee or otherwise, and might alienate them all without fine to him or molestation from anyone.

The most important fresh provision was that the king's bondmen and those of the bishop of Bangor were granted a general emancipation and liberty, and should henceforth hold their lands by a free tenure, paying an annual rent in lieu of every service and custom; and should be free also from service as *rhingyll* (or beadle) and the dues hitherto payable to that officer. A variety of customary exactions were also abolished or reabolished. Some new concessions in the judicial sphere, however, were made. Any of the persons specified who were released on bail on condition of good behaviour or of keeping the peace should not be required to appear before the justice of North Wales more than once a year, immediately after Michaelmas; all the inhabitants should also be free to enquire or cause enquiry to be made in all cases which concerned Englishmen, just as Englishmen could regarding Welshmen.[5]

---

[1] *C.P.R., Henry VII*, II, 434. [2] ibid. 464–5. [3] ibid. 471.

[4] ibid. 434–5; printed in full in *Arch. Camb.* (1847), 215–22, from the Bangor register. cf. J. Beverley Smith, loc. cit. 157.

[5] The letters patent were witnessed by the king himself at Westminster, 3 March in the twenty-second year of his reign. The significance of the additional sentence

Also in 1507, on 2 July, came a confirmation of two charters granted to the inhabitants of Ceri and Cedewain by Richard, duke of York, in the twenty-fifth year of Henry VI releasing those of Ceri of certain financial exactions and emancipating the bondmen of Cedewain.[1]

In June 1508 licence was granted by advice of the council to the inhabitants of the lordship of Ruthin to hold lands and offices notwithstanding the act of the second year of Henry IV, and freed them from the custom of gavelkind and various financial exactions, and making the town of Ruthin a free borough.[2]

Of the regions brought within the scope of these concessions by Henry VII, Anglesey, Caernarvon, and Merioneth of course comprised the principality in North Wales. All the others were lordships that had come into the hands of the Crown. Bromfield, Yale, and Chirk fell into the king's hands in consequence of the forfeiture of Sir William Stanley's lands in 1495; Denbigh, Ceri, and Cedewain were part of the earldom of March. Ruthin was sold to the king by Richard, earl of Kent. All these lordships other than Ceri and Cedewain were contiguous with the principality and intervening between the three northern counties and Flint, and the grant of these concessions to this block of territory meant a grant to an area corresponding roughly to the ancient region of Gwynedd. No doubt if concessions were to be made it was logical to extend them, in part at any rate to the whole region. The reason for confirming similar concessions to Ceri and Cedewain, not contiguous with the principality in the north, is not apparent, except for the fact that Richard, duke of York, had previously made them. But why such concessions were not made to the principality in the south or to the numerous other Crown lordships (so far as we know) remains a matter of conjecture. How far Henry VII expected to get or did get money payments for these concessions is a matter needing closer investigation, and the answer to it is likely to be complicated.[3]

But how far were Henry's grants (or licences) purporting to be made

---

printed in *Arch. Camb.*, loc. cit. 222, 'Per ipsum regem et de data praedicta auctoritate Parliamente' (by the king himself and given by the aforesaid authority of parliament), is a mystery at present. There was of course no parliament of Henry VII's after 1504 and there is apparently no reference to any such grant in that or any other parliament. The assertion cannot be taken at its face value as in J. Beverley Smith, loc. cit. 157, fn. 52.

[1] *C.P.R.*, II, 523–4. [2] ibid. 586–7.

[3] For example, the charter of 28 October 1504 specifically stated that it was given without payment of fee or fine, but in fact the communities concerned agreed to pay substantial sums, and the same applied to the charter of 1507. J. Beverley Smith, loc. cit. 158–9.

despite the statutes of Henry IV's parliaments legally valid? It was received doctrine at this time that the king could by his letters patent grant exemption from the provisions of statutes, but he could not by any exercise of prerogative, repeal or revoke any statute.[1] There could not therefore be any question of his abrogating these statutes *in toto*, even though he might perhaps exempt from their operation a large proportion of the people to whom the statutes were to apply. There was no doubt that acts of the English parliament applied to Wales.[2]

The validity of these licences might therefore be difficult to uphold should any parties contest them, and the burgesses of the English walled towns (in particular Conway, Caernarvon, and Beaumaris) raised objections to the concessions which affected their interests. In response the King's Council on 20 February 1509[3] issued ordinances ordering that the Welsh should not 'use, occupy, exercise, nor enjoy any manner of liberties nor franchises within the principality of North Wales but such as they of old times have used, and occupied before any charters were granted to them'. Representatives of the parties were summoned to appear before the king at a date fixed, when the matter was to be discussed and finally determined according to law. But before the day arrived, Henry VII was dead and apparently no final decision was reached. Uncertainty as to the legal validity remained, however, to confuse the issues far into the Tudor period, though it may be supposed that the act of 1536 side-tracked the problem.

It is possible therefore that Henry VII may have over-reached himself in granting concessions by letters patent to these communities, at any rate so far as exemptions from statute law were concerned. But if it be a pro-Welsh policy to try to give to the Welsh of these regions the benefits of English land law and to permit them to take offices, and to abolish some archaic Welsh customary exactions, then it can be said that Henry VII did, within such limits, cherish such a policy. None the less, whatever his precise motives in this matter may have been, there is nothing to suggest that he was influenced in this attempt by any sentiments springing from his birth or ancestry. On the contrary, there is good reason to suppose that the policy was dictated by the economic and administrative enquiries and advice of the officials primarily concerned with the management of affairs in the principality of North Wales over a term of years preceding the grant of the earliest of the

[1] *See* S. B. Chrimes, *English constitutional ideas*, 58, 268, 279, 283.

[2] ibid. 267–8.

[3] *See* references in Skeel, 'Wales under Henry VII', op. cit. 13; J. Beverley Smith, loc. cit. 170–1.

charters.[1] But in any event, though he did get as far as the Crown lordships of Holt and Montgomery, he did not, so far as we know, ever visit the principality throughout his reign.[2]

(B) Ireland

The lordship of Ireland, which had been conferred by Henry II on his youngest son John in 1177 and which from John's accession had been incorporated in the royal style, was an inheritance more nominal than real when Henry VII succeeded to it in 1485. The authority of the English king had seldom effectively extended beyond a region about sixty miles north and forty miles west of Dublin, called the Pale, even though his lieutenants had been able to exert some degree of influence over the Irish as distinct from the Anglo-Irish chiefs and magnates at different times. But the political circumstances of the thirty or forty years before 1485 had reduced that authority to a shadow. As it turned out, Henry VI's appointment of Richard, duke of York, to be king's lieutenant in Ireland in 1447 proved to be a source of grave embarrassment for many decades to the English Crown, both Lancastrian and Yorkist, especially the Lancastrian as resurrected by the Tudor.[3]

The circumstances and consequences of Richard, duke of York's lieutenancy made Ireland the happy hunting ground for Yorkist plots and imposters when the Yorkist regime in England had run its course.[4] Edward IV had been able to do little to subdue the 'Home Rule' lords of Ireland, and Richard III even less. Nothing had impeded the rise to dominance of the Fitzgerald earls of Kildare; from 1478, of Gerald, eighth earl, who remained throughout the reign of Henry VII the most powerful man in Ireland, whether in office or out of it, the man whom Henry himself could not subdue and therefore after years of contention in the long run found he could not do without as his lieutenant's deputy. When Henry VII succeeded to the throne, the eighth earl of Kildare had been deputy continuously since 1479, at first to two boy

[1] This matter is discussed by J. Beverley Smith, loc. cit. 159–69.

[2] Skeel, 'Wales under Henry VII', loc. cit. 7. Queen Elizabeth, however, got so far as Monmouth, Raglan, and Chepstow in 1502.

[3] The chief studies of Anglo-Irish relations in this period are to be found in E. Curtis, *Mediaeval Ireland* (1923); Agnes Conway, *Henry VII's relations with Scotland and Ireland* (1932); H. G. Richardson and G. O. Sayles, *The Irish parliament in the Middle Ages* (1952); and A. J. Otway-Ruthven, *A history of mediaeval Ireland* (1968). A useful short collection of documents is contained in A. F. Pollard, *The reign of Henry VII* (1914, repr. 1967), III, iii, 259–313.

[4] *See* above, p. 74 ff.

princes successively, and then from 21 August 1484 to John de la Pole, earl of Lincoln. Not until 11 March 1486 did Henry VII appoint as Lincoln's successor the nearest substitute for a royal prince that was available to him for the titular office, namely his veteran and ubiquitous uncle, Jasper, duke of Bedford.[1]

But about this time Kildare had already been in communication with the king and Henry had responded privately to his advances, through the intermediation of John Estrete.[2] Only the king's instructions to Estrete survive and these cannot be dated with certainty, but they probably belong to the year 1486, well before 1 August, by when the king required Kildare to come to him personally wherever he might be at that time.[3] Kildare had petitioned to hold his office of deputy lieutenant for nine or ten years, to which the king replied that he would better arrange for Ireland to be brought into full obedience and prosperity if he were to have the advice of the earl, considering the long rule that he had borne and that no other man could better counsel the king. Henry therefore sent him letters of protection under the Signet and sign manual and requested him to come to England, bringing with him in writing a statement of the revenues of Ireland, whereupon his office of deputy would be granted as he desired.

But Kildare did not respond to these overtures and the absenteeism of Jasper Tudor left the deputy full scope and made possible the extraordinary events which included Kildare's succumbing to the allurements of the 'White Rose', his embracing the cause of Lambert Simnel, his connivance at the latter's coronation in Dublin as Edward VI, and his acceptance of the lieutenancy itself at the hands of the new 'Yorkist' king, in May to October 1487. The battle of Stoke on 11 June, however,

---

[1] C.P.R., I, 84. Jasper was to hold the office in as ample manner as the duke of Clarence held it for two years and then at pleasure. Appointments of archbishops, bishops, the chancellor, treasurer, and of chief justices were, however, reserved to the king.

[2] John Estrete had been king's serjeant-at-law in Ireland in Richard III's time (Richardson and Sayles, op. cit. 330, citing P.R.O., Dublin, transcript of statute roll, 2 Richard III), but by 26 March 1487 was described as king's councillor and servant (also his description in the king's instructions attributed to 1486), when he was granted the office of master of the coinage in Ireland (C.P.R., I, 158, 169). Bayne and Dunham, op. cit. xx, assume that this meant that Estrete was a king's councillor in England; but the reference must surely be to the council in Ireland.

[3] L. & P., I, 91–3. Gairdner assigned the document to 1486? Some Irish historians, including Professor Otway-Ruthven (op. cit. 401), attribute it to Richard III; and J. D. Mackie, The early Tudors (1952), thought that such an attribution might be justified. Richardson and Sayles, however, give very strong arguments in favour of Gairdner's date (op. cit. 328, fn. 19).

Map 5 Ireland

put an end to this fantasy, and within a year Henry VII took steps to make his first direct intervention into Irish affairs by commissioning Sir Richard Edgecombe to go to Ireland to reassert the formal authority of the Crown.[1]

---

[1] *C.P.R.*, I, 225, 25 May 1488. £300 was allowed to him for his reward and expenses, and 100s to Robert Bolman, one of the clerks of the Privy Seal, who was to accompany him (*Materials*, II, 321, 318). Edgecombe, at this time a king's councillor

Edgecombe was empowered to give safe-conducts to those Irish wishing to go to England to treat on matters concerning the sound rule of peace in Ireland, to grant pardons to those wishing to submit themselves, to administer to them oaths of fealty and allegiance, and to imprison rebels and traitors. The form of the oaths to be taken were specifically set out in English in the letters patent,[1] as follows.

I become feithful and true ligeman unto kyng Henry the vijth kyng of England and of Fraunce and lord of Irland of lif and lym and erthly worship and feyth and trouth. I shall beer unto hym as my soveraigne liege lord to lyve and dye agenst all maner creatours so god help me and his seyntes.

I shall from this day forthward duryng my lyf be true feithful and obeysaunt ligemen and subjet unto my soveraigne lord kyng Henry the vijth, kyng of England and of Fraunce and lord of Irland and to his heyres kynges and lords of the same, aswell in thynges concernyng the suertie and well of his most noble persone, his hygh estate preemynence, dignite and prerogative royall as in thynges concerning the well and defence of the realme of England and land of Irland. And yf I may be knowe at eny tyme hereafter any persone of what estate degree or condition he be of that woll presume to attempt eny thyng contrary to thes premisses or of eny of theym, I shall lette it after my power, and yf I may not let it I shall disclose it to such of the kynges councell which I knowe for certen woll showe it to the kyng withoute delay or feyntyse and the kynges councell and the councell of the said realme and land of Irland I shall not disclose in prejudice of the same so helpe me God and his seyntes.

Edgecombe, landing at Kinsale on 27 June, with at most perhaps five hundred men behind him, could not, of course, make much show of military force. But he had behind him also the force of recent events which even Kildare and other Anglo-Irish magnates could not ignore: his master's victory at Stoke, the death of John, earl of Lincoln, and the capture and relegation to the royal kitchens of the erstwhile 'King Edward VI', Lambert Simnel. Kildare might snub the royal commis-

---

and controller of the Household, had taken part in Buckingham's rebellion and had escaped to join Henry in Brittany, and was knighted at Bosworth. He became a chamberlain of the Exchequer and sheriff of Devon. He had been employed on a diplomatic mission to Scotland in 1487 (Conway, op. cit. 10). More might have been heard of him later, but he died in 1489 whilst on a mission to Brittany. It is worth noting that on 13 May, a meeting of the King's Council decided that 'the messenger of Ireland should put all his requests which he made in the name of the lords of Ireland in writing and that all things shall be accomplished accordingly', but nothing further appears to be known of these requests (Bayne and Dunham, op. cit. 18).

[1] *C.P.R.*, I, 225.

sioner and keep him waiting in Dublin for some days before entering into negotiations, but negotiate he did; indeed he could do no other if he wanted to remain in the office of deputy lieutenant. There was room for manœuvre, for Henry VII apparently had instructed Edgecombe to extract bonds from Kildare and other pro-Yorkist lords by which their lands would be automatically forfeited if they should ever again rebel against him. This they refused to do and gave Edgecombe to understand that they would rather all become Irish, that is repudiate the English Crown. Edgecombe did not persist in face of this threat, all the more no doubt because of the news that James III of Scotland had been murdered on 11 June, an event likely to weaken Henry VII's political position. But the taking of the oath of fealty and allegiance on 25 July by Kildare and the other spiritual and temporal lords substantially in the form prescribed meant that Henry VII could retain the well-nigh indispensable Kildare in office without loss of face. By 30 July Edgecombe was able to leave Ireland, his official mission accomplished. Kildare and the Irish 'Home Rule' lords had been obliged to admit publicly that they had a new king and a new lord of Ireland. The recognition of the fact was fundamental, but much or little might be made of it thereafter, according to the ebb and flow of political circumstance.[1]

It was not until June 1492 that Kildare was superseded by Walter FitzSimons, archbishop of Dublin, in the office of deputy, and four years were to elapse before he was restored to that office. Many vicissitudes in Anglo-Irish relations occurred during the eight years that passed between Edgecombe's departure in 1488 and Kildare's restoration at Henry VII's hands to the office he was to retain until 1513.

Henry VII's renewed demand for Kildare to come and see him in England, Kildare's excuses and the excuses made by others, probably belong to the period intervening between Edgecombe's departure in 1488 and the arrival in Ireland of Perkin Warbeck in November 1491.[2] How far Kildare may have been tempted by the spectacle of another Yorkist pretender on Irish shores must remain a matter of speculation, but at least he refrained from overt connivance, and subsequently denied that he lent 'the French lad' any countenance at this stage, as some of the Irish lords had. Not enough of them did so, however, to

---

[1] Curtis, op. cit. 396–7; Richardson and Sayles, op. cit. 270; Otway-Ruthven, op. cit. 405–6.

[2] *See* the letters from the lords of Ireland, Kildare, Desmond, and others to Henry VII, printed in *L. & P.*, I, 377–82; also, letter of Kildare to Ormond, 11 February 1493, denying he had supported Warbeck, ibid. II, 56.

encourage Warbeck to stay very long, and his early departure to France eased the tensions in Ireland for the time being.

Henry VII, however, clearly saw the dangers of another Yorkist conspiracy across the Irish Sea. By 6 December 1491 he had issued a commission to James Ormond and Thomas Garth to lead an army to suppress rebellion in Kilkenny and Tipperary, to array men, to make statutes and proclamations for the government there, and to arrest and imprison delinquents. All persons were commanded to obey them and were absolved from obedience to the lieutenant of Ireland for the time being.[1] Kildare was thus suspended from office, but a successor was not appointed for another six months, when a clean sweep was made of the government in Ireland. On 11 June 1492 Walter FitzSimons, archbishop of Dublin, was appointed deputy, James Ormond[2] treasurer, and Alexander Plunket chancellor.[3] But the bitter struggles that ensued mainly between the Kildare[4] and the Ormond factions proved to be more than the archbishop could handle, and he was replaced on 6 September 1493 by Sir Robert Preston, Viscount Gormanston. The new deputy speedily called a council at Trim and a parliament at Drogheda to try to ensure the keeping of the peace. He succeeded at least in getting Kildare and other magnates to attend, and with the assistance of the king's special commissioners,[5] Henry Wyatt[6] and Thomas Garth, brought Kildare and other lords to give sufficient pledges and to enter into the recognizances that had been sought in vain in 1488. After this measure of pacification Kildare at long last agreed to go to England, along with the archbishop, Gormanston (whose son William was left as deputy in Ireland for the time being), and Sir James Ormond. Kildare was to make his peace with Henry VII and remained in England until late 1494. During these months the king could take his measure of Kildare, consult with all concerned, and formulate his policy and decide on his next steps. The outcome was the appointment on 12 September 1494 of his son Prince Henry as king's

[1] *C.P.R.*, I, 367.

[2] James Ormond was the illegitimate son of John Butler, sixth earl of Ormond. The complications of the Ormond family are too involved to be unravelled here.

[3] ibid. 376.

[4] A general pardon and for all infringements against livery and retinues had been granted to Kildare, 29 July 1490, on condition that he came into the king's presence in England within ten months (ibid. 316). A further general pardon was issued, 30 March 1493, on condition that he should send his son and heir to the king (ibid. 423); this condition appears to have been waived on 22 June, when Kildare sued for a pardon, supported by many lords spiritual and temporal of Ireland (ibid. 429).

[5] *See*, generally, refs on p. 257, n. 3, above.

[6] Conway, op. cit. 55–6.

lieutenant, and on 13 September of Sir Edward Poynings as deputy, of Henry, bishop elect of Bangor, as chancellor, and Sir Hugh Conway as treasurer.[1] Poynings soon set out on his famous mission, accompanied by Kildare, and landed at Howith with a modest force of some seven hundred men on 13 October. By the time Poynings left Ireland fifteen months later in December 1495, the course of Anglo-Irish history had been changed; Perkin Warbeck had come and gone again; Kildare had been attainted of treason and sent to England as a prisoner but soon pardoned and restored to office as deputy. Poynings had unconsciously immortalized his name in the annals of Ireland and of Anglo-Irish relations.[2]

Edward Poynings, like Richard Edgecombe, had participated in the rebellion of 1483, was prominent in the uprising in Kent, and had escaped to Brittany to join Henry there, and returned with him to Milford Haven and Bosworth, where he was knighted. He had taken part in a military expedition to assist Maximilian in Flanders in 1492 and became governor of Calais in 1493.[3] He was already a councillor and a knight of the Garter.[4]

The powers given to the new king's lieutenant and in his absence to his deputy were extensive. He was to keep the king's peace and the laws and customs of Ireland and to punish offenders, whether English or Irish; to admit rebels to fine and pardon; to go with the king's power against those who would not submit; to confer ecclesiastical benefices other than cathedral or collegiate churches; to receive fealties and homages, etc.; to summon a parliament; to call all officers other than the treasurer to account, and to do all other things pertaining to his office. All with the proviso that should Prince Henry or in his absence his deputy do anything contrary to the king's law he should be corrected by the King's Council.[5]

It is perhaps an exaggeration to say that Poynings's 'first object was the military conquest of Ireland'.[6] The military forces at his disposal were at no time large enough for such a hazardous enterprise. After having summoned a parliament to meet on 1 December at Drogheda, he set out on an expedition into Ulster, which had been overrun by the 'savage Irish', the purposes of which became frustrated by a rising by

[1] C.P.R., II, 12, 15.

[2] For the history of Poynings's mission, see especially the wealth of documentation in Conway, op. cit., including the chapter (118–43) by E. Curtis on the acts of the Drogheda parliament, 1494–5; Richardson and Sayles, op. cit. 269–81. On financial matters, see also L. & P., II, 64–8, 297–333.

[3] Conway, op. cit. 63; D.N.B.

[4] C.P.R., II, 12.   [5] ibid. 1.   [6] Conway, op. cit. 78.

O'Hanlon of Orior in Armagh against him, the hostility of the powerful Hugh O'Donnell of Tyrconnell, and the involvement in these events in some obscure way of Kildare himself, apparently from 10 November, from which date his eventual forfeiture was fixed, although he was not arrested until 27 February 1495. In the meantime Poynings returned in time for the opening of the parliament at Drogheda on 1 December, one of the last acts of which was to attaint Kildare, whose dispatch on 5 March to England and the Tower kept him out of the way during Warbeck's reappearance, at Cork and Waterford, in July 1495.

With Poynings's preoccupations during the last few months of his mission to Ireland, the repercussions of Warbeck's incursion and departure, the involvement in these treasonable activities of the earl of Desmond and a small number of the Irish lords, the efforts of the under-treasurer, William Hatcliffe, to instil some order into the financial accounts of the government in Ireland, we are not here concerned. Poynings's rule, we are told with justification, 'had achieved its main object – the rout of the Yorkist faction, and the year 1495 ended with Ireland calmed and Henry's reputation considerably higher upon the continent'. On 1 January Henry Deane, bishop of Bangor, the chancellor, was appointed deputy.[1] Before then Poynings had departed from Ireland, but unwittingly had left his name behind permanently.

Historians' propensity to affix and cherish labels has indelibly stamped 'Poynings's Law' on the pages of all text-books, but the law so identified was only one of forty-nine acts passed in the Drogheda parliament of 1 December 1494 to March/April 1495. These were the context in which the famous law was enacted.[2]

Of these forty-nine enactments[3] three were formal and traditional,[4] and eleven were of a miscellaneous minor character,[5] and none of these needs further considerations here. The pardon for Kildare set out in one of the earlier acts[6] was more than outweighed by his attainder in a

[1] *C.P.R.*, II, 65.

[2] The fullest analysis is in E. Curtis's chapter in Conway, op. cit. 118–43.

[3] Less than half of these acts have been officially printed. Twenty-three out of the forty-nine are in printed editions, of which the most accessible is *Statutes at large (Ireland)*, I (1786). The others are to be found in P.R.O. E. 30 1548; and Lambeth, Carew MSS 608 fos 113–16. *See* list in Conway, op. cit. App. xx, 201–2, who also printed versions of all the MS. texts otherwise unprinted in Apps XXI–XXXVI, 202–19.

[4] These are the only acts in Norman French, not English, and merely confirm to the Church, the land of Ireland, and the towns, their ancient liberties and franchises.

[5] Acts Nos 15–18, 43–9.

[6] Act No. 24; Conway, op. cit. App. xxvi.

later one.[1] The rest fell into roughly five categories. Two dealt with financial matters; six with legal questions; seven with problems of law and order; five with defence; twelve with constitutional or governmental or parliamentary arrangements – some of which were relatively insignificant.

In the matter of finance, an attempt was made by the eighth act to raise revenue for the king by the grant of twelve pence on every pound of merchandise of imports and exports payable by all merchants other than the freemen of Dublin, Waterford, and Drogheda, for five years from the beginning of the parliament.[2] The eleventh act sought to resume into the king's hands all Crown properties alienated since the last day of Edward II's reign, but whatever effect the act might have had was substantially reduced by a large number of exemptions.[3]

The six acts of general legal significance re-enacted and confirmed the statutes against papal provisions that had previously been made in England and Ireland;[4] cancelled and revoked all the records, processes, and pardons made in the name of the pretended king lately crowned in Ireland (Lambert Simnel);[5] confirmed the statutes of Kilkenny (1366)[6] and all other acts made in Ireland for the common weal;[7] and declared murder by 'malice prepensed' to be high treason.[8] Other acts sought to confirm 'the act against the Lollards and other heretics',[9] and to abolish the provision made by a parliament in the time of Richard, duke of York's lieutenancy, declaring it to be treason for any person to bring in from England any writs to arrest any person in Ireland.[10] The seven acts dealing with law and order referred to a variety of problems and abuses. One act sought to prohibit abuses in the extortion of the customs imposition of 'coign, livery and pay',[11]

---

[1] Acts Nos 41, 42 (attainted James fitz Thomas Gerald and many others); ibid. App. xxxi.

[2] Act No. 8; ibid. App. xxii.   [3] Act No. 11; ibid. App. xxiii.

[4] Act No. 10; St. L, cap. v.   [5] Act No. 14: Conway, op. cit. App. xxiv.

[6] The statutes of Kilkenny sought to codify enactments which aimed at preserving the English language, dress, and other habits of the English in Ireland and to perpetuate the differentiations between the English and the Irish. *See* Otway-Ruthven, op. cit. 291–4; and G. J. Hand, 'The forgotten statutes of Kilkenny: a brief survey', *The Irish Jurist*, n.s. I (1966), 299–312.

[7] Act No. 19; St. L, cap. viii.   [8] Act No. 38; St. L, cap. xviii.

[9] Act No. 31: Conway, op. cit. App. xxix. Only the heading of this act is given in the MSS.

[10] Act No. 7; St. L, cap. iii. The act was said to be 'for annulling a prescription which traitors and rebels claimed within this land'.

[11] Act No. 4; Conway, op. cit. App. xxi. 'Coign', repeatedly forbidden by previous statutes, was the custom used by soldiers to exact payments in kind or money from the countryside where they were quartered. 'Livery' (or purveyance) was the

whilst another act later in the parliament tried to reinforce these intentions.[1] Captains in the Marches were required to certify the names of their retainers and regulations for the defence of these districts made,[2] and special prohibitions put upon the extortion of coign and livery therein.[3] No one henceforth was to keep ordinance or artillery in his house or garrison without licence.[4] A doubtless futile effort was made by another act to substitute the cries of 'St George' or the name of the sovereign lord the king for the Irish war cries of 'Cromabo' or 'Butlerabo'.[5] More practicable was the attempt to re-enforce the statute of Winchester for the preservation of order.[6]

The act providing for the payment of Poynings's army might be considered as both a financial and a military measure.[7] For the future no one not English-born was to be constable of one of the seven chief castles belonging to the king.[8] No peace or war should be made without the licence of the governor of Ireland for the time being.[9] For better defence, ditches were to be dug around the English Pale.[10] Every subject of Ireland was to have arms suitable to his status.[11]

Of the acts relating to governmental or parliamentary matters one defined, the duties of the treasurer of Ireland;[12] another declared that the chancellor, treasurer, judges of the two benches, the chief second barons of the Exchequer, the master of the Rolls, and all accountant officers should hold their offices solely at the king's pleasure.[13] Another act specifically declared that anyone who stirred up the Irishry or Englishry to make war against the king's lieutenant or his deputy or should procure the Irish to make war on the English should be deemed a traitor attainted of high treason.[14] In the absence of the deputy, the treasurer was to be governor,[15] and the chancellor was given authority to continue, adjourn, prorogue or dissolve the present parliament in the absence of the deputy and to perform therein all the duties of the deputy.[16]

Two acts were passed which sought to avoid misgovernance in the cities and towns. No citizen, burgess, or freeman of a town was to

requisitioning of supplies, the payment for which often took the form of tallies or bills. cf. Richardson and Sayles, op. cit. 232–3.

[1] Act No. 35; St. L, cap. xviii.　　　　[2] Act No. 22; ibid. cap. x.
[3] Act No. 27; Conway, op. cit. App. xxviii.　　[4] Act No. 23; St. L, cap. xii.
[5] Act No. 38; ibid. cap. xx.　　　　[6] Act No. 21; ibid. cap. xi.
[7] Act No. 36; ibid. cap. xix.　　　　[8] Act No. 28; ibid. cap. xiv.
[9] Act No. 32; ibid. cap. xvii.
[10] Act No. 34; Conway, op. cit. App. xxx.　　[11] Act No. 20; St. L, cap. ix.
[12] Act No. 5; ibid. cap. i.　　　　[13] Act No. 6; ibid. cap. ii.
[14] Act No. 25; ibid. cap. xiii.
[15] Act No. 26; Conway, op. cit. App. xxvii.　　[16] Act No. 33; ibid. App. xxix.

receive livery or wages from any lord or gentleman,[1] and no one was to be admitted to be alderman, juror, or freeman in any town unless he had been an apprentice or inhabitant thereof, and any acts made in any city or town contrary to the king's majesty and royal jurisdiction should be revoked.[2] The earldom of March and Ulster and the lordship of Trim and Connaught were declared annexed to the Crown.[3]

If we can pass over the act which directed the lords spiritual and temporal of parliament to wear robes in the same manner as the lords in England, as they had been accustomed to do twenty or twenty-five years previously,[4] and the act which declared void the acts of the parliament held at Drogheda in 1493,[5] we are left with two acts for consideration. The thirty-ninth act declared that all statutes lately made in England for the public good of the same should be deemed good and effective in law and be accepted, used, and executed in Ireland.[6] As this had for long been the legal position, no further comment is necessary. The ninth act is the one which has commonly been called 'Poynings's Law'.

The substantive part of this act reads as follows:

... no parliament be holden hereafter in the said land of Ireland but at such season as the king's lieutenant and council there first do certify to the king, under the Great Seal of that land, the causes and considerations and all such acts as them seemeth should pass in the said parliament, and such causes, considerations, and acts affirmed by the king and his council to be good and expedient for that land and his licence thereupon, as well in affirmation of the said causes and acts as to summon the said parliament, under his Great Seal of England had and obtained, that done, a parliament to be had and holden after the form and effect afore rehearsed; and if any parliament be holden in that land hereafter contrary to the form and provision aforesaid, it be deemed void and of none effect in law.[7]

It can hardly be pretended that this act was phrased with any masterly lucidity, but its intent was that (1) the king's lieutenant (or

---

[1] Act No. 12; St. L, cap. vi. [2] Act No. 13; ibid. cap. vii.

[3] Act No. 29; St. L, cap. xv. Henry VII was in the right of his wife, heir to the houses of De Burgo and Mortimer, titular earl of Ulster, and lord of Connaught, Trim, and Leix. [4] Act No. 30; ibid. cap. xvi.

[5] Act No. 40; ibid. cap. xxiii. This was done on the grounds that Jasper, duke of Bedford, surrendered his patent of office as lieutenant before the parliament was summoned, and his deputy, Viscount Gormanston, had no power to summon parliaments.

[6] Act No. 39; ibid. cap. xxii. This act added nothing to the already accepted theory that English statutes applied to Ireland, but in practice few had been executed there.

[7] Act No. 9; ibid. cap. iv. Text cited from Richardson and Sayles, op. cit. 274. cf. Pollard, op. cit. 298–9.

deputy?) and the council in Ireland should inform the king under the Great Seal of Ireland the reasons for summoning a parliament and the nature of the acts to be passed therein; (2) if the king signified his approval thereof under the Great Seal of England, then the proposed parliament might be summoned; but (3) any parliament in Ireland summoned otherwise than in accordance with this procedure was to be void.[1]

We may well believe that Henry VII and his advisers did not foresee the remoter repercussions of this enactment,[2] or promote it as part of any far-seeing programme of constitutional reform.[3] But because the motive for it, inspired by the recent experiences, was doubtless to ensure that 'there should be no legitimate parliament to give authority to an illegitimate king', this does not justify us in thinking of it as 'an opportunist and transient expedient'.[4] It is an exaggeration, and also an anachronism to suppose that Henry VII wanted to subordinate the parliament of Ireland to himself in any precise or detailed sense, nor is there any contemporary suggestion that this was the effect of the act. For such notions one must wait until the eighteenth century.[5] Henry VII had no 'imperialist' policies. What he was primarily concerned with in Ireland as elsewhere was the security of his crown. His aim was to end the Wars of the Roses in Ireland as in England, and to restore his *dominium Hiberniae*.[6] If Sir Edward Poynings could do that, it was the utmost that he could achieve or aspire to do, and by and large, this is what he did, so far as in him lay. But what Henry VII had the insight to perceive was that the *modus operandi* framed by Poynings's laws would continue to be operative only if he could win over to its support the most powerful of the Irish magnates. Hence the reappointment for the rest of his reign to the office of deputy of the eighth earl of Kildare. Whether or not it be true that Henry actually said of Kildare that if all Ireland cannot rule him, then he should rule Ireland,[7] this was certainly an apt statement of the realities of the situation. Henry VII was above all a realist. With the reappointment of Kildare on 6 August

[1] cf. R. Dudley Edwards and T. W. Moody, 'The history of Poynings's law', Pt. I, 1494–1615, *Irish Hist. S.*, II (1940–1), 415–24; and D. B. Quinn, 'The early interpretation of Poynings's law, 1494–1534', ibid. 241–54.

[2] Richardson and Sayles, op. cit. 279.

[3] ibid.

[4] ibid. The procedural questions particularized, ibid. 276–8, are important, but should not be over-emphasized at the expense of the general importance.

[5] Edwards and Moody, loc. cit. 416–17.

[6] Curtis, in Conway, op. cit. 131, 132.

[7] Book of Howth, 178–80, quoted Pollard, op. cit. III, 281–5.

1496,[1] the cause of Warbeck was lost in Ireland, and being lost there, was lost everywhere.

Kildare's attainder was reversed in the English parliament and the reversal exemplified at his request on 14 February 1496.[2] His sojourn in England resulted in the establishment of amicable terms between himself and Henry VII, who provided him with a wife in the person of his second cousin Elizabeth St John. By 26 August 1496 a general pardon[3] was issued for the former supporters of Warbeck, including Kildare, Desmond, and other lesser figures. On 26 July 1497 Warbeck, ousted from Scotland, reappeared at Cork. But no Irish support was now forthcoming, and before long he set out again on what was to prove his disastrous incursion into Cornwall.[4] Soon after John Topcliffe, chief justice of the Common Bench in Ireland, was on his way to England to seek leave for the deputy to summon a parliament in Ireland and, all in accordance with 'Poynings's Law', submitted legislative proposals for the king's prior approval.[5] On 25 March 1498 approval was given and a commission issued for Kildare to hold such a parliament,[6] the first to be held in Ireland since Poynings had left.

Within its limits, therefore, Henry VII's policy had been vindicated. Kildare indeed was now again the effective master of Ireland, but no longer as a rebel or semi-rebel. He was now in command with Henry VII's full approval and support. The king's lordship of Ireland had been restored, and a firm basis laid for future developments. No king of England had set foot in Ireland since Richard II's fateful expedition in 1399; Henry VIII was to become titular king of Ireland in 1542, but for a visit from a reigning sovereign Ireland had to wait until the time of William III.

But the limits to Henry VII's policy towards Ireland were necessarily somewhat narrow and restricted to the politically possible. He could with impunity largely disregard the 'wild Irish', who together owned more than a third of the land, for they had never yet combined to

[1] Conway, op. cit. 93. His reappointment was preceded by an indenture made in the king's presence and witnessed by members of the King's Council in England, between Kildare on the one part, Walter, archbishop of Dublin, Thomas, earl of Ormond, and Sir James Ormond on the other part, swearing that the old enmity between the Geraldines and Butlers should cease; printed, ibid. App. XL. Kildare also swore to a number of articles broadly committing him to observe the essential points in Poynings's laws; ibid. App. XLII.

[2] *R.P.*, VI, 481–2; *C.P.R.*, II, 64.   [3] *C.P.R.*, II, 76.

[4] *See* above, p. 91.   [5] Richardson and Sayles, op. cit. 275–6.

[6] *C.P.R.*, II, 128. The bills approved included repetitions of several of Poynings's laws. For a further specimen of such a commission in 1507, *see* ibid. 576.

extinguish the English Pale.[1] The mass of Anglo-Irish feudatories, often more Irish than English, likewise had not threatened directly the king's lordship. The menace had come from the very few magnate families, especially the Kildares, Desmonds, and Ormonds, who between them owned a very large part of the land of Ireland.[2] By 1500 the three families, Butlers (Ormond) and two Fitzgeralds (Desmond and Kildare), divided between them all Ireland south of the Upper Boyne and Limerick. The Butler family descended from Theobold Walter (brother of Hubert Walter) who had been butler in John's Household and had accompanied him on his first visit to Ireland, became the leading Anglo-Irish family in the fourteenth and early fifteenth centuries. James Butler became earl of Ormond in 1328. The family estates centred in Tipperary, Ossory, and Kilkenny. The family developed close Lancastrian associations, was the only one of the three great families to do so, and the earls were absentee in England for many years. The earls of Desmond and Kildare were descended from a common ancestor, Maurice Fitzgerald, Strongbow's associate. Two Fitzgerald brothers founded the two branches of the family in the thirteenth century, and the earldoms of Desmond and of Kildare were created in 1329 and 1316 respectively. The earls of Desmond in the fifteenth century attained a most powerful position in Kerry, parts of Cork, Limerick, Waterford, and Tipperary. They had strong Irish leanings and connections, and the somewhat obscure circumstances in which the seventh earl was executed in 1468 by Tiptoft, earl of Worcester, then king's lieutenant, are thought to have been largely because of these associations. At any rate the Desmonds were thereby alienated from the English Crown for a very long time. The earls of Kildare became the feudal lords of half the Pale and held jurisdiction over the Irish chiefs in the southern and western marches. The whole of county Kildare and parts of counties Meath, Dublin, and Carlow were under their domination. The three earldoms by 1500 covered most of Munster and much of Leinster.

Some of these magnates had for their own purposes pursued 'Home Rule' policies in the past and some of them had not been averse to trying to break the connection with the Crown of England altogether. Henry VII's cautious and statesmanlike approach to the problem, perhaps influenced by his knowledge of some analogies in Wales,[3]

[1] The Pale by 1500 is said to have dwindled to a coastal strip fifty miles long by twenty wide, Conway, op. cit. 42.

[2] Curtis, *Mediaeval Ireland*, 416; cf. Conway, op. cit. 42 ff.

[3] This suggestion, made by E. Curtis, in Conway, op. cit. 138, deserves further consideration.

manifested in the enactments of Poynings's parliament and his winning over of the eighth earl of Kildare, removed this threat and terminated the Irish version of 'The Wars of the Roses'. He could scarcely have attempted more.

Chapter 15

FOREIGN POLICIES

The foreign policies pursued by Henry VII have so recently been lucidly expounded that little purpose would be served by attempting here any very fresh or detailed appraisal.[1] The unravelling of the complicated and sometimes puzzling diplomacy of the reign has never been a simple task. Changing fortunes on the continent, the tergiversations, the intrigues, rapid shifts, and turns manifest in the international politics of Europe at this period make more than usually difficult the discernment of any clear principles in the relations between the rulers concerned. It is perhaps an exaggeration to say that 'the foreign policy of Henry VII was the mainspring of his government'.[2] He was no interventionist for intervention's own sake. He did not aspire to any grandiose schemes on the continent; he could not aim at any dominant or even decisive role in European affairs. We may well agree that he was 'compelled to pursue a more active and much more elaborate foreign policy than he had at first attempted or perhaps desired. Yet his aims remained essentially defensive, subordinated always to the overriding domestic purposes of making the monarchy rich and its subjects obedient. As a result his policy developed piecemeal, as the outcome of a series of defensive reactions to external events'.[3] If we add to these domestic purposes the most fundamental one of all, namely the preservation of his crown and dynasty and the establishment of both as things to be reckoned with in international affairs, perhaps we are saying almost as much as we can about his basic motives. Certainly his policy was 'not a carefully planned system', but whether it really 'grew into the likeness of a coherent system' is doubtful. It seems difficult to per-

[1] J. D. Mackie, *The earlier Tudors* (1952), gave much space to a valuable survey of Henry VII's foreign policy; and the subject is given fresh and illuminating treatment in the first five chapters of R. B. Wernham, *Before the Armada* (1966). Busch, op. cit., gave substantial attention to it. G. Mattingley, *Catherine of Aragon* (1942), and *Renaissance diplomacy* (1955), are important contributions. But it is clear that the large amount of evidence available for the subject, in print as well as in manuscript, has still not received the detailed examination which it deserves. It is much to be hoped that in time some expert in the field will give to the theme the entirely fresh scrutiny that it requires.

[2] Mackie, op. cit.

[3] Wernham, op. cit. 38.

13a. Henry VII, by Michel Sittow, 1505, by order of Herman Rinck, agent of Emperor Maximilian I, intended to be sent to Margaret of Savoy (*National Portrait Gallery*)

13b. Queen Elizabeth of York. Artist unknown. Late-sixteenth century version of an unknown original (*National Portrait Gallery*)

13c. Queen Isabella of Castile. Artist and date unknown (*Windsor Castle*)

13d. King Ferdinand of Aragon. Artist and date unknown (*Windsor Castle*)

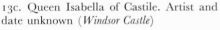

(Both probably of Flemish origin, and part of Henry VIII's collection)

14a. Henry VII, *c.* 1499–1502 (*Great Malvern Priory Church, transept window*)

14b. Henry VII's Chapel, *c.* 1504–12, vaulting (*Westminster Abbey*)

ceive much of a 'system' in Henry's diplomacy, though 'his reactions to external pressures sprang from firm-seated and consistent instincts, or rather from a clear and balanced understanding of the basic interests of the dynasty and the nation'.[1] We may well believe in Henry's consistency, but the external pressures to which he was subjected varied so much, were so fraught with unpredictable elements, including the accidents of the deaths of important participants in affairs, that persistent coherence was a quality perhaps hardly attainable at the time. The mainspring of his government was always dynastic and domestic policy, to which his foreign policy was consistently subordinated.

The measure of his success is not, however, to be found by estimating his consistency or the coherence of his system, or in any particular example of the diplomatic skill of his own, or of his agents, who served him well. Rather it is to be found by comparing the extreme weakness of his international position in 1485 with its unspectacular but substantial strength towards the end of his reign. At the start his position was weak indeed. He became king as the not very impressive protégé of the French government, and as one who owed much also to the duke of Brittany. He began his kingly career as an unknown and insignificant, though for the moment at least, a successful, rebel and quasi-usurper whose potential could hardly have been deemed very fearsome by foreign rulers,[2] who might however hope to use him or to embarrass him for their own ends but who scarcely expected to be cajoled or deflected by him. The potentates with whom Henry VII was principally concerned were those of Burgundy, France, Castile and Aragon, and the four popes of the period. Maximilian I, king of the Romans from 1486, emperor from 1493, son of Emperor Frederick III (of Hapsburg), married in 1477 as his first wife Mary, daughter and heiress of Charles the Bold, duke of Burgundy by his second wife Isabella of Bourbon. Charles subsequently married Edward IV's sister Margaret. Maximilian and Mary's son Philip married Joanna, heiress of Castile; and their son was the future emperor, Charles V; and their daughter Margaret married firstly John, son of Ferdinand and Isabella of Spain, and secondly Philibert II of Savoy. The younger daughter of Ferdinand and Isabella, Catherine, became the bride of Prince Arthur and subsequently of Henry VIII. Louis XI of Valois died in 1483. His elder daughter Anne, who had married Peter II, duke of Bourbon, acted as

[1] ibid.

[2] The popes of the period were Innocent VIII from 1484; Alexander VI, August 1492 to 1503; Pius III, September to October 1503; and Julius II, November 1503 to 1513.

H — K

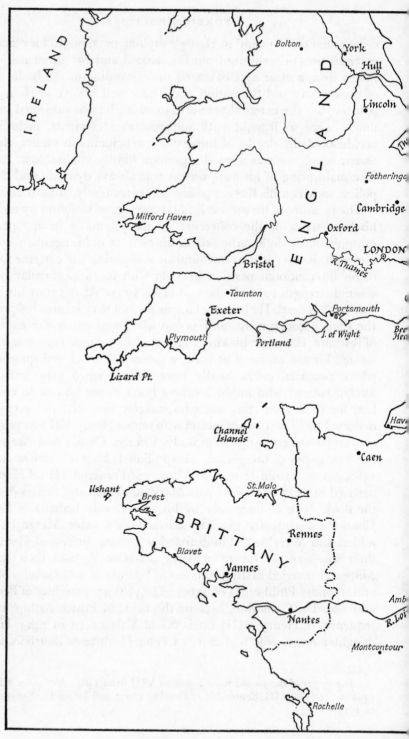

Map 6 Northern Fr...

the Low Countries

regent during the minority of his son Charles VIII, who married Anne, duchess of Brittany, in 1491, who subsequently married as his second wife Louis XII, the husband of Louis XI's youngest daughter Jeanne. Louis XII's third wife was to be Mary, Henry VII's younger daughter.

But as his reign progressed all of these sovereigns and popes had learnt that he was a monarch who could not readily be bent to their wills, and one whose goodwill it was desirable to cultivate. Henry achieved this position, moreover, without sacrificing any essential interests and without engaging in any but minor military activities. He attained his meed of triumph because he negotiated from a position of domestic strength that grew steadily as the years passed. The weakling among sovereigns had become an enviable and eventually unassailable dynast whose sights were pretty firmly set on the attainable, or who at any rate was not disposed to pursue any will-o'-the-wisps into the quicksands of diplomatic disaster.

Circumstances in the nature of things and circumstances that arose as events unfolded themselves determined that certain objectives inevitably presented themselves to Henry. He must try to restrain hostile actions by Scotland and if possible safeguard his northern borders by establishing amicable relations with that dangerously contiguous foreign realm. He could not be unaware of the home-truth contained in Sixtus V's telling phrase, 'England is only half an island'.[1] He could scarcely refrain from rendering some aid, however nominal, to the duchy of Brittany when its hour of reckoning with Charles VIII of France came, but he could not afford to antagonize France unduly, and had to be prepared to accept failure to defend Brittany's independence in the long run. Should a confrontation with France come, he must not appear to emerge from it with less than Edward IV had done. He must use all his skill to reduce and if possible eliminate the capacity of Scotland, France, Spain, and Burgundy to profit from Yorkist pretenders and claimants and take all feasible measures to extinguish the threat to his dynasty from the 'White Rose', by whomsoever it might be aided and abetted. He must, so far as he could, play off Spain and France against each other, so as to diminish the capacity of either to do him mischief, and to use Maximilian in the same game as circumstances, including Maximilian's volatile schemes and the interests of trade with the Netherlands, might from time to time dictate. Should opportunity offer, he would need to try to cement truces and alliances, otherwise apt to be short-lived and shifting, with appropriate marriages of his children,

---

[1] Cited, Wernham, op. cit. 19, from *Cal. S.P. Venetian*, VIII, 345.

or even, after he had become a widower, with a second marriage of his own, if only he could make a match that was practicable and profitable. As it turned out he could not so provide for himself, but at the end of his reign he had in fact attained a very high degree of success in the pursuit of these other objectives. By then he had managed to eliminate the 'White Rose' from the arena of serious politics, had staved off the threats or hostilities of all foreign powers, had married his eldest son into the royal house of Spain and when the death of that son terminated the connection, so arranged matters that it was still possible to preserve the connection by the substitution of his second and only surviving son; had married his elder daughter into the royal house of Scotland; had betrothed his younger daughter to the young man destined to become the Emperor Charles V, even if unbeknown to him she became, not the empress, but the queen of France. By 1509, the adventurer of 1485 had put his house firmly alongside the royal dynasties of Europe, and had brought his realm to a position in international affairs such as it had scarcely ever before attained, at any rate since the days when it seemed that Henry V would unite in himself the crowns of England and France. No such aspirations deflected Henry VII from his pursuit of the practicable. But he did much to confirm and consolidate the revival of England's prestige that had been initiated by Edward IV. He largely cast the role that England was to play in European affairs far into the modern period.

The inherent difficulty in expounding diplomatic history lies in the fact that whereas in reality a multitude of motives, moves, and negotiations are activated more or less simultaneously, it is impossible in exposition to unravel the threads at the rate of more than one or two at a time if the exposition is to be intelligible. The selectivity necessarily imposed upon the historian of any theme inevitably results in an over-simplification and artificiality which fail to reflect the complex reality. This defect is perhaps nowhere more apparent than in diplomatic history. As in all historical studies, the historian has an advantage denied to the men who made the history itself. We are in a position to know the outcome of their actions, whereas they could only guess and hope what the upshot would be.

Three fairly clear phases of Henry's foreign policy are discernible. The first of these ran from the first cautious moves in 1485 up to the Treaty of Étaples with France in 1492; in the course of it the Breton question was settled, Anglo-French relations were defined for the time being, the project for an Anglo-Spanish matrimonial alliance was first mooted, and the Treaty of Medina del Campo in 1489 set up a basis for further negotiations with Spain.

The second phase went up to 1503. European affairs in this period were largely conditioned by the freedom which Charles VIII of France had gained during the earlier phase to turn his aggressive attentions in an easterly direction and to invade Italy in 1494, a turning-point in continental history. This fresh orientation of affairs enabled Henry VII to figure as a significant European monarch by bringing him into the Holy League of 1496, designed to restrain Charles VIII's aggrandize-ments, as well as by the conclusion in the same year of the important commercial treaty with the Netherlands; whilst he also initiated pro-posals for a marriage treaty between his daughter Margaret and James IV of Scotland, and made such a proposal possible by the conclusion in 1497 of the Treaty of Ayton, the first treaty of peace with Scotland since 1328; in the same year the negotiations with Spain reached the stage of a marriage treaty and the betrothal of Prince Arthur and Catherine; before this phase was over, the marriage of Arthur and Catherine had taken place and been terminated by the death of the prince in April 1502; the question of her being married to Prince Henry had been mooted; the marriage of James IV and Margaret had occurred in November 1503, four months after Henry's queen, Elizabeth, had died.

The third phase of Henry VII's foreign policy was largely conditioned by the facts that the king was now a widower and could consider the possibilities of a matrimonial alliance on his own account, and of the death in November 1504 of Isabella of Castile, which not only threatened that cohesion of Castile and Aragon which went to make up 'Spain', but reduced Ferdinand of Aragon to a widowerhood similar to Henry's and also raised to the forefront the question of the succession to Castile. The heiress was the eldest daughter of Isabella and Ferdinand, Joanna, married to the Archduke Philip of the Netherlands, with whom Henry VII came into very friendly relations in 1506. But Philip's death before the end of that year entirely changed the prospects. With him died the union of the Netherlands and Castile, leaving Joanna a discon-solate widow, Henry VII's marriage with whom might have substituted some sort of union of Castile and England. This somewhat grandiose project did not materialize, but the next best thing, also destined to frustration, that Henry could devise was the betrothal of his second daughter Mary to Joanna and Philip's son – the Archduke Charles. In the meantime in 1505 Ferdinand had swallowed his antipathies towards France, and solved his widowerhood problem by marrying a niece of Louis XII, king of France since 1498. When, therefore, the time came in December 1508 for Louis XII, Maximilian, the Archduke Charles, Ferdinand, and the pope to arrange among themselves the League of Cambrai, Henry was not invited to join in this plot directed against Venice. Nevertheless, his reign did not end by any means on a note unfavourable to himself. He remained uncommitted to the plans of the European potentates, but at the same time, each of them, for their own purposes, sought his goodwill and cultivated friendly relations with him. He could by that time scarcely have desired much more than that.

Henry VII's first moves in the sphere of foreign affairs were designed to ensure a breathing space before more far-reaching policies could be pursued. Having been assisted by France to make the expedition that had led to Bosworth, naturally he sought to establish relations with that realm. A proclamation of a one-year truce with France was made on 12 October 1485, and this was subsequently extended to last until January 1489.[1] Although James III of Scotland had shown that his sympathies laid with Henry rather than Richard III, and some Scots may have participated at Bosworth,[2] tensions between the two countries continued; attempts at establishing pacific relations got off to a slow start, but were actively pursued by Henry as circumstances permitted.[3] By 3 July 1486 a three-year truce was signed, confirmed, and ratified by October.[4] Negotiations with James III went on almost continuously, and abortive proposals for an alliance in the form of a marriage between James III and Henry VII's mother-in-law, the widow of Edward IV, as well as between his two sons and two of her daughters, were seriously considered.[5] But the political conditions in Scotland were not conducive to such schemes. Soon James III was confronted with the rebellion that was a prelude to his assassination and the accession of his son as James IV, aged fifteen, on 11 June 1488. Any further advance must needs wait on events, and in the meantime Henry maintained his contacts and agents in Scotland and was kept fully informed of Scottish affairs.[6] Before this, in July 1486, amicable relations had been confirmed with his former host, the duke of Brittany, by the conclusion of a commercial treaty.[7]

---

[1] *Foedera*, XII, 277, 281; Pollard, op. cit. III, 1–2.

[2] *See* above, p. 70, fn. 1.

[3] The most detailed account of Anglo-Scottish relations at this time is in Conway, op. cit. 1–41.

[4] *Rot. Scot.*, II, 477; *Materials*, I, 572; *Foedera*, XII, 316. Miss Conway, op. cit. 10, showed that Rymer in *Foedera* post-dated this treaty by two years, to the confusion of much subsequent historical writing.

[5] Conway, op. cit. 11; D. MacGibbon, *Elizabeth Woodville* (1938), 193–4.

[6] Conway, op. cit. 24 ff.   [7] *Foedera*, XII, 303.

Overtures from Maximilian, king of the Romans, however, resulted only in a renewal of Edward IV's treaty as from January 1487 for one year.[1] As early as March 1488 negotiations for a future marriage between the infants Prince Arthur and Catherine of Aragon were begun, which led to a draft treaty by 7 July[2] and paved the way to the Treaty of Medina del Campo, on 28 March 1489. But before that date arrived Breton affairs had grown to crisis point, and Henry VII was faced with the need to consider intervention.

The deterioration in the affairs of Brittany, the prospect of the succession to the duchy of a young heiress in the event of the death of the aged and infirm Duke Francis II, the intrigues resulting from the marriageability of the heiress, Anne, and the overt intentions of Charles VIII of France to intervene and to annex the duchy[3] brought Henry VII reluctantly to the point of agreeing in the Treaty of Redon (14 February 1489) to aid Brittany.[4] He had striven hard to avoid this commitment. He had sent envoys to try to mediate between Brittany and France, had extended his truce with France until January 1490,[5] had connived at the unofficial military intervention by Edward Woodville, Lord Scales, governor of the Isle of Wight, which did nothing to prevent disaster for Brittany at the battle of St Aubin du Cormier on 28 July 1488. But by 20 August Duke Francis capitulated, acknowledged himself to be Charles VIII's vassal, and died three weeks later. The wardship of the twelve-year-old heiress Anne was at once claimed by the king of France. Henry feverishly sent another mission to France, and sought the aid or the countenance of Ferdinand and Isabella, of Maximilian and his son the Archduke Philip. Negotiations with the former resulted in the Treaty of Medina del Campo, and with the latter to a treaty which in effect renewed Edward IV's treaty of 1478.

The Treaty of Medina del Campo,[6] the negotiations for which were

---

[1] *Foedera* XII, 318–21.   [2] *Cal. S.P. Spanish*, I, Nos 13 and 14.

[3] The fullest account in English of these affairs is in J. S. C. Bridge, op. cit.

[4] *Foedera*, XII, 362–72. By its terms Henry VII merely promised to send 6,000 men to serve the duchess, at her own expense, until All Saints' day, for whom two strong places fully equipped were to be provided by her. She agreed to support England if ever that realm sought to obtain its ancient possessions on the continent; to arrange no marriage or treaty of alliance (except with Maximilian or Ferdinand) without Henry's assent, and then only if England were included in such treaties.

[5] ibid. 344, 345.

[6] *Cal. S.P. Spanish*, I, No. 34; *Foedera*, XII, 411–29. A detailed account of the embassy to Spain and Portugal written by Roger Machado, 157–99, 328–68; Richmond Herald and Norroy king of Arms since 1485, and Clarenceux king of Arms from 1494 is printed in *Memorials*. A treaty with Portugal was also made. *Foedera*, XII, 378.

protracted and difficult, was a considerable triumph for Henry VII, who showed himself a tougher diplomat than Ferdinand at first thought him to be. Apart from haggling over the precise terms of dowry and the date for the bride's arrival in England, the important thing was that the Tudors were brought into a definite prospect of marriage with the Spanish royal family. The prospect was of a matrimonial alliance of far greater significance than had befallen the English mon-archy since the far-off days when Henry V had married the daughter of the king of France, Henry VII's grandmother. It was important too that Ferdinand should have been brought to repudiate aid to any of Henry's rebels. The fact that at the same time he was obliged to agree to clauses concerning attitudes towards France that were more ad-vantageous to Ferdinand than to himself, was much less important, as they were more academic than practical.[1]

But in the end, Henry had to 'go it alone'. He could not avoid asking the parliament of 1489–90 for financial aid, and dispatched the six thousand men promised in the Treaty of Redon to go to the defence of Brittany in April 1489. Despite the English aid under Daubeney, which secured a victory for Maximilian's forces at Dixmude on 13 June, all was in vain.[2] Maximilian was soon bought off by Charles VIII, and his attempt at clinching matters by marrying Duchess Anne by proxy in early 1491 proved to be derisory. All the trump cards were in Charles VIII's hands. Nothing could now impede his virtual conquest of the duchy nor indeed of Anne herself, to whom he was married on 6 December 1491. The king of France was now duke of Brittany and the duchess was queen of France.

The dilemma now facing Henry VII was perhaps the most acute of his whole reign. He could scarcely hope to reverse the *fait accompli* but he could not avoid a direct military confrontation with France. He must needs vindicate his pledge to support Brittany, show that his intervention could not be flouted, and display that his part in inter-national affairs was not to be merely supine. But at the same time he could not afford the grave risks that would follow from any major military defeat at the hands of Charles VIII.

Henry made a brave show at penalizing the Valois. He could assert his intention of claiming the crown of France for himself, elaborately

---

[1] These matters are discussed in Mackie, op. cit. 93–7.

[2] Machado's journal of two embassies to Brittany in June and August 1490 is printed in *Memorials*, 200–22, 369–90. For Maximilian's vacillations and Charles VIII's efforts at negotiations, supported by Pope Alexander VI, who desired French help against the king of Naples and the Turks, *see* Mackie, op. cit. 99–102.

prepare for war, and set out himself with a substantial army to Calais and lay siege to Boulogne in October 1492. But it was already very late in the season for serious military campaigns, and by 27 October he was able to consult his councillors on proposals for peace which had been sent to him at Étaples. Within a few days, by 3 November, these proposals were accepted.[1] Charles VIII, being eager and anxious to be freed from English annoyances so that he could set out to pursue his aggressive policies in Italy, was quick enough to be placatory. Henry got what he wanted – Charles's agreement not to assist Henry's rebels and to pay off the arrears of the payments due under the Treaty of Picquigny and a large indemnity for the costs of Henry's interventions in Brittany, amounting in all to 745,000 gold crowns payable at the rate of 50,000 crowns a year.

By his rapid intervention at a crucial moment Henry had scored something of a triumph. He had obliged the king of France to come to terms quickly, had scotched any hopes that Perkin Warbeck entertained of help from Charles VIII, and had secured a useful supplement to his income. These gains were undoubtedly important to him in the circumstances of 1492, but none the less they concealed the harsh fact that his endeavour to save Brittany had entirely failed. The independence of the duchy had gone for ever. The farther side of the Channel, except for Calais, was now to be French. The power of the French monarchy and its potentiality for future action inimicable to English interests had become much greater. But there was nothing that Henry VII could effectively do to prevent these results. He had shown that he could not be ignored in continental affairs, but must be placated. He had done what he could and had secured solid concessions. Time alone would show the outcome. His vacillating allies were also placated. By January 1493 Ferdinand of Aragon was appeased by France's cession to him of Rousillon and Cerdagne;[2] by May Maximilian's hostility was deflected by the cession of Artois and Franche-Comté. By September 1494 Charles VIII was free to march towards the Alps.

Perhaps Henry VII's greatest successes fell within the period of the second phase, running from the end of 1492 to the end of 1503. These years saw some of the plans he had initiated during the first phase come to fruition without undue strain and anxiety, and it was not until the last year or so of this second phase that he suffered the shattering blows

[1] *Foedera*, XII, 497 ff; Pollard, op. cit. III, 6–25; the treaty was confirmed by act of parliament, 11 Henry VII, c. 65; *S.R.*, II, 635; *R.P.*, VI, 507.

[2] *Cal. S.P. Spanish*, I, No. 78; Pollard, op. cit. 26–7.

of the death of his eldest son and of his queen, both of which events not only represented grave personal loss but imperilled or distorted the objectives of his diplomacy.

The successes in the early years of this phase, however, were scored not so much by Henry's own moves as by the consequences of Charles VIII's triumphs in Italy. These so alarmed the European powers that by March 1495 the League of Venice was formed by the pope, Ferdinand, Maximilian, Venice, and Milan to restrain him and if possible to oust him from Italy. This objective was realized without any assistance from England, but Ferdinand spared no effort to strengthen his own position by sweetening his relations with both Maximilian and Henry VII. He married his daughter Joanna, the heiress of Castile, to Maximilian's son the Archduke Philip of Burgundy (1496); the following year saw a confirmation of the treaty made in 1496 for the future marriage of his youngest daughter Catherine with Prince Arthur; his agents had been active in promoting negotiations for a treaty between England and Scotland, and the Treaty of Ayton of 1497 marked the success of these protracted efforts.

Both 1496 and 1497 were outstanding years in Henry's diplomacy. His conclusion of the important commercial treaty, known as the *Magnus Intercursus*, in February 1496[1] achieved an economic agreement regardless of what other powers thought of it. By July of that year he figured as an associate of the Holy League reformed to restrain Charles VIII's Italian ambitions,[2] but was able to do so without attracting any serious hostility from France; and was even able to make a commercial treaty with her in the following May,[3] and he refrained from embarrassing Louis XII on his accession in April 1498.

Ferdinand and Isabella's desire to strengthen their relations with England induced them to conclude a fresh treaty for the Anglo-Spanish marriage on 1 October 1496, which, however, was not confirmed by Henry VII until 18 July 1497.[4] After a great deal of argument matters reached the point when on 19 May 1499 Catherine was married by proxy to Prince Arthur.[5]

In the meantime the career of Perkin Warbeck had to run its course before much headway could be made with improvement in Anglo-Scottish relations, however much Ferdinand, the pope, and indeed Henry VII might wish for it. Some progress had been made since 1487, but very slowly. Truces had been made and renewed, but it was not

---

[1] *See* above, p. 233.   [2] *Foedera*, XII, 638–42; Pollard, op. cit. III, 33.
[3] *Foedera*, XII, 592.   [4] *Foedera*, XII, 658–66.
[5] *Cal. S.P. Spanish*, I, 241; Pollard, op. cit. I, 206–8.

until 25 June 1495 that a commission was issued to negotiate a marriage between Princess Margaret and James IV.[1] But by November Perkin Warbeck arrived in Scotland and was taken into the king of Scots's favour.[2] Naturally in these circumstances no headway could be made with such talks, and it was not until after James IV had abandoned Warbeck (July 1496) that any hope of progress could be entertained. At long last in July 1497 fresh instructions could be issued to Henry VII's experienced negotiator Richard Fox, now bishop of Durham, to reopen the negotiations[3] which resulted at first in an indenture of a truce for seven years, later extended for life, and finally in the Truce of Ayton ratified by James IV on 12 February 1498.[4] But it was not until after the defeat, capture, and execution of Warbeck, and the Spanish envoy Pedro de Ayala's mission to Scotland, that a full treaty of peace and a marriage alliance was concluded on 24 January 1502.[5] On 8 August 1503 Margaret Tudor and James IV were married.[6]

But before this date Anglo-Spanish relations had reached their climax. On 10 July 1499 a treaty of alliance between Ferdinand and Isabella and Henry VII had been concluded in London,[7] and confirmed by the Spanish monarchs on 20 January 1500[8] (before which date both Warbeck and the earl of Warwick had been executed). The die was now cast, and Catherine and Arthur were married by proxy for the third time in November 1500.[9] In October 1501 Catherine arrived in England[10] and was married in person to Arthur on 4 November.

[1] *Foedera*, XII, 572–3, 635–6. [2] *See* above, p. 88.
[3] *L. & P.*, I, 104–9; Pollard, op. cit. III, 37–44.
[4] *Foedera*, XII, 673, 721–8, 729. [5] ibid. 787, 793, 803.
[6] cf. S. Anglo, *Spectacle, pageantry, and early Tudor policy* (1969), 106. It is worth remembering that Margaret by her marriage with James IV became the grandmother of Mary, queen of Scots; and by her second marriage to Archibald, sixth earl of Angus, the grandmother also of Henry, Lord Darnley, Mary's second husband. Margaret married thirdly Henry, Lord Methven.
[7] *Foedera*, XII, 741–9; Pollard, op. cit. III, 44–59.
[8] Ratified by Henry VII, 5 May 1500, *Foedera*, XII, 751. The Spanish ambassador's dispatch to Ferdinand and Isabella, in which he asserted that 'not a doubtful drop of royal blood remains in this kingdom except the true blood of the king and queen and above all that of the lord prince Arthur', was dated 11 January 1500 (*L. & P.*, I, 113–19). He said also that he had previously informed their majesties of the execution of Warbeck and the earl of Warwick. But as Busch conclusively pointed out (op. cit. 354), the contract of marriage was concluded before the executions occurred.
[9] Busch, op. cit. 137, and refs fn. 1. Letters dated June and July from Henry VII to Ferdinand and Isabella on the subject of Catherine's future arrival are printed in *L. & P.*, I, 119, 121.
[10] Elaborate plans had been made for her reception, *L. & P.*, I, 404 ff; II, 103 ff. King Henry was unable to meet her on arrival because of bad weather, but sent her

Jubilation and pageantry at these events was great and lavish, and the designers of public spectacle excelled themselves.[1] Henry VII's long-drawn-out negotiations and haggling over terms and conditions had justified themselves, and had brought to conclusion the remarkable and seemingly unlikely marriage alliance between the Tudors and the Spanish monarchs. Much indeed was to spring from this event, all of it quite unpredictable at the time. But the more immediate rejoicings were to be terminated abruptly five months later by the death of Prince Arthur at Ludlow on 2 April 1502.[2] Ten months later, on 2 February 1503, Queen Elizabeth, then lodged in the Tower of London, was delivered of a baby daughter, who was christened Catherine and lived for a few days. But in the early morning of 11 February the queen herself died.[3]

The cup of Henry's domestic sorrows had been filled very nearly to the brim, but something might be saved from the wreck of his dynastic hopes. Within five weeks of the death of Prince Arthur, Ferdinand and Isabella instructed an ambassador to reclaim from Henry the hundred thousand scudi that had been paid as the first instalment of the marriage portion for the princess of Wales, to demand that he should deliver to her the lands that had been assigned as her dowry, amounting to one third of the revenues of Wales, Cornwall, and Chester, and to return the princess to Spain as soon as possible and in proper manner. But at the same time they also instructed the ambassador to conclude a marriage between the princess and Henry, the king's son and heir, and to settle the amount and other terms of the marriage portion and dowry.[4] Little time was lost in negotiating a treaty for the marriage. An English draft treaty dated 24 September 1502[5] led to a formal treaty on 23 June 1503,[6] confirmed by Ferdinand and Isabella on 30 September.[7] But the treaty itself declared that a full papal dispensation would be needed because Catherine by marrying Arthur had become related to Henry in the first degree of affinity and because their marriage had

---

a charming letter in French drafted in his own hand (ibid. I, 126–8). The next day both he and Prince Arthur visited her with great ceremony; Leland, *Collecteana*, IV, 352 ff.

[1] *See* Anglo, op. cit. 56–97; Busch, op. cit. 139–40, and refs 353, n. 5.

[2] *Chronicles of London*, ed. C. L. Kingsford, 255; Pollard, op. cit. I, 223.

[3] Kingsford, op. cit. 258; Pollard, op. cit. 231. Wernham, op. cit. 51, wrongly attributes the queen's death to April.

[4] *Cal. S.P. Spanish*, I, 317, 318; Pollard, op. cit. III, 59–60.

[5] *Cal. S.P. Spanish*, I, 351.

[6] *Foedera*, XIII, 76–86; Pollard, op. cit. III, 75–8.

[7] *Foedera*, XIII, 76.

been solemnized by the rites of the Catholic Church and had afterwards been consummated.[1] The marriage was to be solemnized as soon
as Prince Henry completed his fourteenth year. If the dispensation were
obtained, a marriage by proxy was to be contracted within two months
of the ratification of the treaty by both the parties. Agreements about
the marriage portion and dowry were made part of the treaty.[2] But long
delays were to be experienced in obtaining the needful dispensation.
The death of Alexander VI – in August 1503 – would have caused
delay in any event, but the new pope, Julius II, hesitated to grant it.
The precise date when valid bulls of dispensation arrived is uncertain
but it was not until some date after March 1505.[3]

But before that time arrived, other events occurred which were destined
to set in train circumstances that postponed the marriage until after

[1] This assertion, agreed to by both contracting parties in the treaty without protest
by Catherine, cannot but throw grave doubts on any denials of its truth either earlier
or later. Why the testimony of Doña Elvira (whatever validity it may have had) was
set aside when it came to the point of agreeing a fresh treaty remains obscure. But
apart altogether from the truth of the matter (which will never be known) and from
the canonical questions arising, it needs to be remembered that important financial
questions were also involved, and these may well have decided the issue for the time
being. If the marriage had been consummated, the outstanding half (100,000 crowns)
of the dowry promised by Spain would be payable before Henry VII need put
Catherine in possession of her dower revenues. Both Henry and Ferdinand therefore
would have seen advantages in the affirmative assertion. Moreover, to obtain a
papal dispensation on grounds of less than the first degree of affinity might prove
to be dangerous in the future. The Spanish ambassador, De Puebla, whose services
over some twenty years, ill-requited or recognized by the parties at the time (except
by Henry VII), were of great importance to Anglo-Spanish relations, had advocated
the affirmative from the start. On the question generally, see Mattingley, *Catherine of
Aragon*, 48–52; J. J. Scarisbrick, *Henry VIII*, 191–2; Wernham, op. cit. 52. On
De Puebla, see Mattingley, *Renaissance diplomacy*, 141–2.

[2] The 100,000 scudi already received as half of the marriage portion paid on
Catherine's first marriage were to be reckoned as half of her new marriage portion;
the same dower as Prince Arthur had settled was to be arranged. Part of the agreement was that solemnization of the marriage should not occur until after the whole
marriage portion should arrive in London ready for delivery. The scudo was to be
reckoned as worth 4s 2d.

[3] The difficulties of establishing with certainty the dates in question arise from
doubts as to the nature of a papal brief sent by the pope to comfort Isabella of Castile
on her deathbed in November 1504, some version of which appears to have reached
England at some date – presumably the bull referred to in Ferdinand's letter to
Henry VII dated 24 November 1504, which he said he had sent to De Puebla (*L. &
P.*, I, 241–3). As late as 17 March 1505, the bishop of Worcester wrote to Henry VII
saying that the pope desired him to bring to England the original bull of dispensation
and regretted that a copy of some kind had been transmitted to England previously
(*L. & P.*, I, 243–5). All these and cognate documents later came under close scrutiny

the death of Henry VII himself. On 26 November 1504,[1] Queen Isabella died, and the prospect for Anglo-Spanish relations changed at once. The heiress of Castile, Joanna, became queen, but the question soon was to be whether Ferdinand would be governor of that realm, as Isabella had willed, or would Joanna's husband the Archduke Philip of the Netherlands seek to be recognized as more than titular king of Castile? The Castilian problem thus arose to bedevil Henry VII's foreign policies for the rest of his reign, and to conjure up in his mind visions of possible aggrandizements that would not otherwise have arisen.

Both Henry VII and Ferdinand were now in a position to enter into negotiations for new matrimonial alliances on their own accounts. Both watched each other's moves with close attention; both were most anxious to keep on as outwardly friendly terms with each other as was compatible with the pursuit of their own interests; both were keen enough to steal a march on the other and secure a profitable match for themselves if they could. As things turned out, Ferdinand was able to do this, but Henry VII could not, and in the end, after much fruitless negotiation, he was obliged to content himself with arranging what he thought were the most promising matches for his son and his unmarried daughter. All these negotiations were, of course, conditioned by the underlying motive of trying to maintain the balance of power between England, Spain, France, and Burgundy.

We can safely acquit Henry VII of having formed any intention to marry his daughter-in-law Catherine, as this improbable allegation has never been based upon any valid evidence.[2] His first choice for serious consideration was apparently Ferdinand's niece, the recently widowed Queen Joan of Naples. At any rate he sent three envoys to Valencia to interview her and her mother the Dowager Queen, Ferdinand's sister, and to find out all they could about her potential as a bride for him. His instructions to them were astonishingly detailed and comprehensive, in the form of twenty-four questions, including very specific enquiries as to her physical as well as her financial assets. The envoys arrived at Valencia on 22 June 1505, and made a very full report as

---

and controversy in the course of Henry VIII's divorce proceedings. *See* Scarisbrick, op. cit. 216–19.

[1] Ferdinand wrote on the same day to inform Henry VII of the event, *Cal. S.P. Spanish*, I, 409; Pollard, op. cit. I, 240.

[2] It was unfortunate that James Gairdner (who held somewhat unnecessarily jaundiced views of Henry VII's endeavours to find a second wife) should have lent his authority to what he called this 'monstrous proposal' (*L. & P.*, II, xxvii). The flimsy nature of the allegation was exposed by Busch, op. cit. 378, n. 4.

soon as practicable.[1] They were unable to obtain the portrait of Joan that the king desired, but whilst their report on the lady's physical charms was not unfavourable, her financial position and prospects were much more doubtful. The same envoys moved on to interview Ferdinand himself at Segovia on 17 July, again furnished with full instructions and twenty-two specific questions, including close enquiries as to the political conditions in Aragon and the probable impact of the expected arrival in Spain of Philip and Joanna of Castile.[2] In this regard Henry VII was clearly trying to find out what the most profitable line would be for him to take in the Castilian question. The whole document is a remarkable manifestation of Henry's care and foresight in getting reliable information before showing his hand in diplomacy. As regards the project of Henry's marriage with Joan of Naples, Ferdinand showed himself all in favour of it. But this attitude was of doubtful sincerity, and nothing came of it. Henry VII himself appears to have abandoned the project after it was known that Ferdinand had made an alliance (Treaty of Blois) with France in October 1505 and married Louis XII's niece Germaine de Foix on 18 March 1506. Information of this intention had reached Henry VII's envoys in Aragon in July and been included in their report to him.[3]

But before this date, other matrimonial plans for Henry VII were being mooted. Before March 1505, it would seem, Maximilian had offered his daughter Margaret, widow of Philibert II of Savoy, and the effective governor of the Netherlands.[4] Henry VII in March 1505 instructed his envoy Anthony Savage, sent on a mission to De Ayala, the former Spanish ambassador in England, then in Flanders, to make some searching enquiries into the potentialities of this, to investigate the sincerity of Maximilian's offer, to find out about Margaret's likely financial assets, to enquire closely into the intentions of Philip and Joanna of Castile, and, not least, to discover Maximilian's attitude towards Edmund de la Pole, earl of Suffolk.[5]

In the meantime the attractions of a marriage alliance with Henry VII had not been overlooked by Louis XII of France, who before July 1505 gave to Sir Charles Somerset, Henry VII's envoy, full instructions about his views on a number of questions, including the proposal that

---

[1] The instructions and report of the envoys (Francis Marsin, James Braybrooke, and John Stile) are printed in *Memorials*, 223–39.

[2] ibid. 240–81.

[3] ibid. 278.

[4] *Cal. S.P. Spanish*, I, 429 ff.; Pollard, op. cit. I, 253.

[5] ibid. 253–7.

Henry VII might marry his niece, Margaret of Angoulême, daughter of Charles, duke of Angoulême, on certain conditions; and even offered a dowry comparable to that which Henry informed him Ferdinand had offered for Joan of Naples. He also promised to help Henry VII to secure Edmund de la Pole, expressed his desire to meet Henry personally when circumstances permitted, and allayed any fears that Henry might have about the continuance of the pension payable under the terms of the Treaty of Étaples.[1]

These plans were known in diplomatic circles by the autumn, together with other real or imaginary projects,[2] but with whatever degree of sincerity Henry VII entertained the project, little more was to be heard of it. He was, it seems, much more serious about the prospect of marrying Margaret of Savoy, which, if it should materialize, would go far to change the balance of power in his favour and in that of Maximilian's family connections. The possibility of such a marriage dragged on until 1508,[3] until Margaret herself finally declined the suit. If Henry's heart went where his money went, he set great store on his relations with Maximilian and Philip of Castile, for he 'lent' both of them large sums of money to further their political aims,[4] and events in early 1506 brought him into still closer relations with Philip and Joanna.

On 7 January King Philip, as he was now called, and his wife Joanna, now queen of Castile, set out from Zeeland to voyage to Spain, but violent storms on 16 January in the Channel drove them to seek refuge off Weymouth and to land the next day at Melcombe. Some of his ships were lost and most of them scattered for the time being. When he heard of this Henry VII sent help and invitations. The outcome was the exercise by Henry of zealous and prolonged hospitality, cordially extended with great ceremony and lavish entertainments, with exchanges of the Garter and the Golden Fleece, continued for so long that it was not until 23 April[5] that Philip finally set sail again.

But naturally these three months saw a great deal of negotiation, and

---

[1] *L. & P.*, II, 125–46, esp. 133, 143.

[2] cf. letter of Thomas Lopez to Emmanuel, king of Portugal, 10 October 1505, ibid. 146–50.

[3] *See* below, p. 290.

[4] Henry had lent £108,000 to Philip 'for his next voyage to Spain' on 25 April 1505, and another £30,000 on 27 September. Bentley, *Excerpta*, 132, 133, cited Pollard, op. cit. I, 257, fn. 2. £10,000 in silver had been lent to Maximilian in October 1502 (Bentley, op. cit. 129). It is reckoned that some £342,000 was provided in cash or plate and jewels for the use of Maximilian, Philip, or his son Charles during the years 1505–9. B. P. Wolffe, *E.H.R.*, LXXIX (1964), 253, fn. 2, 254, fn. 1.

[5] A detailed account of the social side of the visit up to 12 February written by an unknown contemporary is printed in *Memorials*, 282–303.

Henry was now in a very strong position to drive bargains with Philip. As early as 9 February 1506 in the secret Treaty of Windsor, Henry VII went far to commit himself to the cause of the Hapsburgs in Spain, recognized Philip as king of Castile, and pledged himself (within limits) to assist him with military aid should any person invade his dominions which he was then possessed of or which he or his heirs and successors in future should have right to possess. In effect Henry promised to assist Philip in the Netherlands, in the Narrow Seas, or in Castile. It is true that the promise was limited to 'such an army as he might be able to spare and as the circumstances may demand', with the king of Castile paying the expenses, but the importance of the commitment must not therefore be underrated. 'The Treaty of Windsor countered the Treaty of Blois (which Ferdinand had made with Louis XII), and the realignment of Europe was completed.'[1] Henry VII now aligned himself with the Hapsburgs in Spain against the schemes of Ferdinand of Aragon. He had perceived that if Ferdinand's position in Castile could be undermined, Aragon would sink to a third-class power. The two princes promised mutual assistance and refusal to countenance the other's rebels. Philip concluded the treaty in his own name and in that of his father Maximilian, but it was to remain valid even if Maximilian failed to ratify it within four months. By 20 March Philip concluded with Henry a treaty of marriage between Henry and Philip's sister Margaret of Savoy, with full details as to dowry, rights of succession, etc., and all backed by the previously-given authority of Maximilian.[2] So far as Henry was concerned, this treaty was ratified on 15 May 1506. Long before then he had had the satisfaction of the fulfilment of what to him was a highly important practical point – the surrender at long last of the 'White Rose' in the person of Edmund de la Pole, earl of Suffolk. Edmund was by Philip's orders brought to Calais on 16 March, handed over and escorted to Dover and the Tower of London, where he remained for the rest of his life.[3] A few days before Philip embarked

[1] Mattingley, *Catherine of Aragon*, 67–8; Treaty of Windsor, *Foedera*, XIII, 123 ff., epitome in Pollard, op. cit. III, 83–96. Mackie, op. cit. 184–5; and Wernham, op. cit. 56, appear to underestimate the significance of this treaty.

[2] *Feodera*, XIII, 127–32; and ibid. III, 96–100. Some of the delay is accounted for by Philip's illness at Reading, which was kept as secret as possible, and by the reluctance of the council at Mechlin to surrender Edmund de la Pole when ordered to do so (*Venetian Cal*, I, No. 869; Pollard, op. cit. I, 277).

[3] *See* above, p. 93. The extraordinary attitudes adopted by Suffolk, and the ramifications of his intrigues on the continent are too complicated to be unravelled here, but are well documented in Pollard, op. cit. I, 220, 222, 232, 252–7, 267–74; and *L. & P.*, I, 134–51, 177–89, 225–9, 253–85; II, 381–5.

from Falmouth on 23 April he authorized his agents to conclude the commercial treaty to be known as the *Intercursus Malus*, to be confirmed within three months. Henry duly confirmed it on 15 May, but the confirmation from the other party was never to be forthcoming.[1]

Whilst King Philip and Queen Joanna were pursuing their claims and policies in Spain, Maximilian and Henry VII continued the somewhat inconclusive correspondence on the subject of the marriage proposed and at least nominally agreed upon between Henry and Margaret of Savoy.[2] By mid-September, however, Maximilian began proposing that a marriage should be arranged between his grandson Charles, Philip's son, and Henry's daughter Mary, and at much the same time was obliged to admit that he had not yet been able to persuade Margaret of Savoy to agree to a match with Henry himself, though he promised to continue to try.[3] But on 25 September Philip died, and the prospects for the important parts of Henry's diplomacy died with him, as well as any prospect of an early union between Philip's possessions in the Netherlands with Castile.

The death of Philip opened up the possibility that his widow might marry again, and that Henry might be her second husband. There was nothing shocking about such a proposal at this time. Profoundly shaken by her bereavement as she was, there was not as yet any reason to suppose that she was deranged. Henry had seen a good deal of her during the visit to England, and apparently had been favourably impressed by her.[4] It was all the more likely that his thoughts would turn towards her after Maximilian had informed him that despite prolonged personal argument with his daughter, Margaret of Savoy had turned down the prospect of marrying Henry and had decided to remain a widow.[5] All that Henry could do by May 1507 was to write amiable letters to Margaret, now regent of the Netherlands for her nephew the young Archduke Charles, seeking to placate her on the commercial questions, and hoping for a confirmation of the treaties that Philip had agreed upon, without, presumably, the clauses relating to the marriage project or the more objectionable parts of the *Intercursus Malus*.[6] It was still possible, however, to envisage a future marriage

[1] *See* above, p. 234.

[2] *L. & P.*, II, 153–64.

[3] ibid. I, 301–4, 305–6.

[4] According to Catherine of Aragon's letter to her sister, *see* below, p. 292.

[5] *L. & P.*, I, 323–7; Pollard, op. cit. III, 124–8. Gairdner dated this document 1507, but Pollard, on not very conclusive grounds, thought that 1508 was the more likely year.

[6] *L. & P.*, I, 327–36; Pollard, op. cit. III, 119–24.

between Henry's daughter Mary, and Philip and Joanna's son the Archduke Charles. A treaty including that proposal, as well as a treaty of alliance between Henry and Charles, was concluded on 21 December 1507, and finally confirmed by Margaret as regent on 1 October 1508.[1] The future prospects for a powerful alliance seemed assured.

But nothing was to come of the project for a marriage between Henry and the widowed Joanna. Catherine of Aragon could inform her father Ferdinand of Henry's aspiration before March 1507,[2] and could herself write to her sister on 25 October commending the match in glowing terms[3] (perhaps at Henry's behest); Ferdinand could dissemble and assert several times that if Joanna married anyone it should be Henry VII,[4] but time passed without any outcome, and the project faded away, not surprisingly because in fact Joanna was being kept in close confinement, first by Ferdinand and then by the archduke, later the Emperor Charles V, in harsh and at times brutal conditions, and the story of her 'madness' was never, until perhaps towards the end of her long life, more than very successful propaganda put out by her ruthless and unscrupulous father and son. It is probable that Henry VII knew or suspected the truth, which oddly enough appears largely to have evaded the serious consideration of modern historians.[5]

In the few months that remained for Henry, he was not able to carry any of his own matrimonial schemes to fruition. No further alliances were to be concluded. He had woven his complicated webs of diplo-

[1] *Foedera*, XIII, 171, 189, 200, 212, 220, 229–33, 259–61; Pollard, op. cit. III, 128–33. It was in connection with these negotiations that Henry VII's chaplain, Thomas Wolsey, was first employed on a continental diplomatic mission, though he had previously been sent to the court of James IV of Scotland. The voluminous letters between Henry VII and Wolsey are printed in *L. & P.*, I, 426–52. It is evident from the letters that Henry VII had come to appreciate Wolsey's abilities.

[2] *Cal. S.P. Spanish*, I, 502; Pollard, op. cit. I, 290.

[3] *Cal. S.P. Spanish*, I, 553; Pollard, op. cit. I, 300–2.

[4] *See* above, fn. 2.

[5] The overwhelming weight of the evidence which compels such conclusions was printed from the Spanish archives and commented on by G. A. Bergenroth as long ago as 1868 in *The supplement to volumes I and II of letters, despatches, and state papers (Spanish)*, 47–430, respectively, and xxiv–lxxx. This volume was published seven and five years, respectively, after the publication of Gairdner's two volumes of *Letters and papers*, and is not mentioned at all in Busch's list of authorities. Inadequate consideration to this evidence was given in Garrett Mattingley's allusions in *Catherine of Aragon* (1942), who, however, pp. 82–3, was well aware that Henry VII was highly suspicious about the allegations. Joanna did not die until 1555, and then in dreadful circumstances at her place of confinement at Tordesillas. Pollard, op. cit. cites the first part of Bergenroth's volume, relating to Catherine of Aragon, but apparently not the second part relating to Joanna.

macy; his agents had probed here and there; his indefatigable and ill-rewarded resident ambassador in Spain, John Stile, could send him an immense amount of news, rumour, and gossip from Spain on 26 April 1509[1] – but that was to be too late for his master ever to receive it. Henry remained on friendly even if wary terms with the chief powers of Europe, who all seem to have held him in respect, even though perhaps by 1508 they had begun to discount somewhat his capacity to intervene effectively in their affairs. He seems, indeed, to have lost some of his grasp of international affairs towards the end of 1508; he fell ill for a time and was unaware of the realities underlying the conference of the powers summoned to meet at Cambrai in December of that year. He assumed that the meeting would be between Burgundy and France, and that Ferdinand would not be invited.[2] In fact it was Henry who was not invited, and the League of Cambrai that resulted was a league aimed against Venice formed by Maximilian, the Arch-duke Charles, Louis XII, the pope, and Ferdinand. All these rulers in one way or another, however, continued to display moderate goodwill towards Henry; and did nothing to thwart his plans for the prospective marriages of his son and daughter. No vital interests of his were threatened by the League, and indeed the preoccupation of its members with Italy diverted any pressures they might otherwise have been inclined to exert towards England. When the end came for Henry on 21 April 1509, he had no reason to feel unduly apprehensive about England's international position. He had brought her to a point at which her friendship had been courted by all the chief powers, who, even though they could scarcely by then have feared any active military intervention on his part, had learned to respect his financial power, his knowledge of foreign affairs, and his diplomatic skill, his shrewd judg-ment, and up to a point his reliability. He had attempted no grandiose schemes, no aggrandizement by military threats; he cherished no illu-sions that he could or should emulate the glories of Henry V, but he achieved a solidity of position beyond the reach of the victor of Agin-court. What his son and heir might be able to build on this position, if anything, remained to be seen.

But there was unfinished business when Henry died, and the most

---

[1] *Memorials*, 431–48; printed in full in Pollard, op. cit. III, 133–50. For John Stile, *see* Gairdner's introduction to *Memorials*, liii–lv, and Mattingley, *Renaissance diplomacy*, 159.

[2] Henry VII to Margaret of Savoy, 7 November 1508, *L. & P.*, II, 365–7; Pollard, op. cit. 131–3: cf. Sir Edward Wingfield to Margaret of Savoy, *Cal. S.P. Spanish*, I, No. 600; Pollard, op. cit. I, 307–10.

important items were the prospective marriages of his daughter Mary and his son Prince Henry.

A treaty of marriage between Mary and the Archduke Charles had been concluded in December 1507, and ratified by Margaret as regent of the Netherlands on 1 October 1508.[1] But when Henry VII died, Mary was still only eleven years old; there could at that time have been no expectation of the marriage's taking place for several years, and in fact it never took place. The story of how it was that five years later Henry VIII's desire to snub the Hapsburgs and to make alliance with France induced him, to the chagrin of the Archduchess Margaret, to arrange a hasty marriage in 1504 between Mary and the elderly Louis XII is a story that belongs to the new reign, where we must leave it.[2]

But the fact that the marriage proposed and agreed between Prince Henry and Catherine of Aragon so soon after the death of Prince Arthur in 1502 did not occur until 11 June 1509 needs further consideration; all the more because it involves the problem of Catherine's treatment by Henry VII during her widowhood.

The long delay in completing the marriage is at first sight all the more surprising since it seems evident that the Spanish monarchs were most anxious to secure its completion. The initiative came from them very soon after the death of Arthur.[3] Isabella's instructions to Hernan Duque de Estrada, then ambassador, in July 1502, clearly reveal the great importance she attached to the plan, especially as a means of preventing any alternative alliance that the king of France desired to make with Henry VII. She apparently accepted Catherine's lady-in-waiting's (Doña Elvira's) assertion that the marriage with Arthur had not been consummated, believed that delay might be dangerous, and declared that the rest of the dowry would be paid when the second marriage was consummated but not before that.[4] In September Ferdinand himself stressed to Estrada the need to hinder Louis XII's schemes.[5]

But long delays there were to be. Prince Henry did not, indeed, reach the stipulated age by completing his fourteenth year until

[1] See above, p. 235.

[2] See J. J. Scarisbrick, *Henry VIII*, esp. 54–7.

[3] See above, p. 285.

[4] *Cal. S.P. Spanish*, I, No. 327; Pollard, op. cit. I, 225–8. 'It is clearly known for a certainty,' Isabella wrote, 'that the said princess of Wales our daughter, remains as she was here (for so Doña Elvira has written to us).' Hernan Duque was *not* the duke of Estrada, *see* Mattingley, *Catherine of Aragon*, 328.

[5] *Cal. S.P. Spanish*, I, 287–8: and Pollard, op. cit. 228–31.

28 June 1505. On the day before that the prince made a declaration protesting against recognition of the marriage treaty that had been made when he was under age.[1] Before that date and after it, until perhaps nearly up to the time of his death, Henry VII became reluctant to allow the completion of the marriage treaty. Until he could be sure of getting on to terms of firm alliance with the Hapsburgs, he had been willing enough to contemplate the renewal of the matrimonial alliance with Spain, on the understanding that a valid marriage with Arthur had been completed – at which Catherine had not at the time protested. Pending the settlement of outstanding dowry questions he had granted her the not inconsiderable allowance of £100 a month to maintain her in her largely Spanish household at Durham House.[2]

But the death of Queen Isabella on 26 November 1504, and the sudden emergence of the question of the succession to Castile, fundamentally changed the position and gave to Henry VII quite different thoughts. The opportunity now came for him to undermine Ferdinand of Aragon's position by supporting the Hapsburg's ambitions in Castile, and his eventual alliance with King Philip and his schemes for matrimonial alliances for himself and Prince Henry with the Hapsburgs were hardly compatible with the furtherance of the earlier plan for the marriage of the prince with Catherine of Aragon. Ferdinand's *rapprochement* with France signalized in the Treaty of Blois of 1504 and his subsequent marriage to Germaine de Foix, together with the hostility shown by the council of Castile towards English merchants, and the abandonment of his project for his own marriage to Joan of Naples, all tended to swing Henry's mind away from furthering the Spanish marriage. Inevitably his wooing of the Hapsburgs, culminating as it had in the agreements with Philip in 1506, received a severe blow by the subsequent death of Philip, whilst the frustration of his plan to remedy the situation by himself marrying Joanna seemed to destroy his objective of scoring off Ferdinand. Not unnaturally in these circumstances Henry

---

[1] The text of the declaration made by Prince Henry to Bishop Fox, witnessed by Daubeney, Somerset, Thomas Ruthall, and others, is printed in G. Burnet, *History of the Reformation*, ed. N. Pocock, IV, *Collection of records* (1865), 17–18; cf. Scarisbrick, op. cit. 9, 182. Henry was said by Sir Edward Wingfield in November 1508 not to be eager to pursue the secret project of Prince Henry's marrying Margaret of Angoulême except as a means of dissolving the alliance between France and Ferdinand. *Cal. S.P. Spanish*, I, No. 600; Pollard, op. cit. 307–10.

[2] The only full account, which is largely followed here, of Catherine's life as widow is in G. Mattingley, *Catherine of Aragon*, based for the later years on the little used but invaluable *Correspondence de Gutierre Gomez de Fuensalida*, ed. duke of Berwick and Alba (Madrid, 1907).

developed a feeling of acute hostility towards Ferdinand and a distaste for the Spanish marriage.[1]

But it is difficult to see how Henry can be acquitted of meanness and harsh spite towards the unfortunate victim of these twists and turns in high politics – Catherine of Aragon. In order to show his disapprobation of Ferdinand's activities, it was not necessary to stop his allowance to her, to oblige her to give up her household at Durham House and to live in straitened circumstances and poor accommodation at one or other of his royal houses, and generally to treat her not as a widowed daughter-in-law and prospective wife for his heir, but as an insignificant pawn in his diplomatic game. Catherine, at least in the earlier years of her widowhood, was admittedly a difficult and querulous person to deal with, full of complaints about her health and the efforts of the Spanish resident ambassador, De Puebla, dominated as she was by Doña Elvira for some years and later by her confessor Fray Diego Fernandez.[2] But she learnt much from her privations, became more discreet after at her own request she was given by her father credentials as an ambassadress, and became adept in the arts of dissimulation.[3] She remained steadfast in her aim of achieving marriage with Prince Henry, thereby furthering, she believed, her own and the Spanish interest.

The time came when Ferdinand, fearing the threats to Spain on the continent, sought to improve the prospects by agreeing to terms acceptable to Henry on the dowry question, made Catherine at long last a grant of some money with which to pay part of her mounting debts, and sent, in response to Catherine's request for an ambassador more acceptable than De Puebla, an additional envoy in the person of Don Gutierro Gomez de Fuensalida,[4] to try to further the completion of the marriage. The extraordinary bunglings of Fuensalida and his inept and disastrous interviews with Henry VII did nothing to enhance the king's enthusiasm for the marriage but confirmed him in his delaying tactics. The time came, however, when what Henry wanted most was Ferdinand's consent to the marriage of Henry's daughter Mary to Ferdi-

---

[1] It should be remembered that Henry VII was justifiably doubtful about the allegation as to Joanna's madness, and Philip died somewhat suspiciously some three months after his meeting with Ferdinand at Villa Fafilla in April to May, at which an unexpected agreement on plans was reached.

[2] Pt I of Bergenroth's supplementary volume prints some more of the relevant Spanish correspondence, 1501–15, pp. 1–47, and commentary, xiii–xxiii, additional to the large amount of material in his *Calendar*, I.

[3] Her capacity in this respect is well revealed in her letter to Ferdinand dated 4 October 1507 (*Cal. S.P. Spanish*, I, No. 551).

[4] Not a grandee, but of high social standing and knight commander of Membrilla.

nand's grandson the Archduke Charles. Henry's anger, both at
Fuensalida's refusal to convey such an assent and his extreme tactless-
ness, was immense, all the more alarming in Henry's state of declining
health.

Henry decided in the end to do without Ferdinand's assent, and proceeded to a public bethrothal of Mary and Charles, which Fuensalida
refused to attend and forbade Catherine to attend. But by this time
(17 December 1508) Catherine had learnt to appreciate the experienced
wisdom of De Puebla and the inept pomposity of Fuensalida, and
herself decided to attend the ceremony, whilst Fuensalida was turned
away from court. The partisans of the Hapsburgs now seemed
triumphant and the eventual marriage of Prince Henry with Eleanor,
the Archduke Charles's sister, also seemed very likely, but it may be
that Catherine's sensible action softened Henry's attitude towards her
cause.

It is possible that when King Henry reached his deathbed he did
desire his son to carry out the old-standing treaty obligations and marry
Catherine. At any rate this was Henry VIII's explanation to Margaret
of Savoy of his own decision taken shortly after his father's death on
21 April 1509. On 11 June 1509 Catherine became queen of England.

Catherine had indeed experienced troubles since at the age of sixteen
she had become princess of Wales, most of them not of her own making.
She did perhaps little to endear herself to many people in England
before 1509, but the far greater troubles that were eventually to engulf
her during the second half of her life she was to endure with a nobler
dignity and a still greater fortitude.

Epilogue

THE KING'S GRACE

To form an appraisal of Henry VII as a man and monarch is not an easy task. He died too early for Holbein to paint him from the life. Genuine portraits of him are hard to find, and his death mask, striking as it is, suffers from the obvious defect that it has no life and moreover is partly false.[1] If we wish to get as near as we can to the real man, we must avoid being mesmerized by seductive Baconian phrases and beautifully rounded sentences. The imaginative power of Francis Bacon, splendid as it was, must not be allowed to get between us and the contemporary evidence.[2] That evidence, on the personal side, is not very extensive. Very rarely, so far as we know, did Henry VII reveal himself in record, as distinct from his policies and actions. We are, therefore, largely dependent upon the comments made about him by other people in his own lifetime or soon after, and these may, of course, differ in veracity and reliability. There is, however, a substantial degree of consensus of opinion among his contemporaries as to his appearance, demeanour, and general characteristics.

The fullest and on the whole probably most reliable description of Henry is provided by Polydore Vergil, who, although writing several years after his death – doubtless all the more candid for that reason – had certainly seen and talked with him in the flesh. Polydore wrote of him:[3]

[1] *See* below, Appendix F.

[2] As Busch (op. cit. App. II, 421) observed, 'we must, therefore, regard every statement of Bacon's for which no special original authority can be referred to, with a distrust which is only too well justified'. I am indebted to the kindness of Dr D. S. T. Clark, of University College, Swansea, for allowing me to see and use his at present unpublished Ph.D. thesis, 'Francis Bacon: the study of history and the science of man' (Cambridge, 1970). In this thesis Dr Clark includes a substantial critique of Bacon's *Henry VII*, not so much from the point of view of the validity of Bacon's account of Henry VII's reign as in relation to his general philosophical and scientific principles and outlook. It is much to be hoped that this important study will become available in print.

[3] *Anglica historia*, ed. Hay, 145–7. Henry VII invited Vergil in 1506 to compose a history of England, and the text for Henry VII's reign was probably composed 1512–13 (ibid. xx). He recorded that when he first came to England, as deputy for Adriano Castelli as papal collector, he was most courteously received by the king, and was ever after treated kindly by him (ibid. 133). It is hardly sufficient to dismiss

His body was slender but well built and strong; his height above the average. His appearance was remarkably attractive and his face was cheerful, especially when speaking; his eyes were small and blue, his teeth few, poor and blackish; his hair was thin and white; his complexion sallow.[1] His spirit was distinguished, wise and prudent; his mind was brave and resolute and never, even at moments of the greatest danger, deserted him. He had a most pertinacious memory. Withal he was not devoid of scholarship. In government he was shrewd and prudent, so that no one dared to get the better of him through deceit or guile. He was gracious and kind and was as attentive to his visitors as he was easy of access. His hospitality was splendidly generous; he was fond of having foreigners at his court and he freely conferred favours on them. But those of his subjects who were indebted to him and who did not pay him due honour or who were generous only with promises, he treated with harsh severity. He well knew how to maintain his royal majesty and all which appertains to kingship at every time and in every place. He was most fortunate in war, although he was constitutionally more inclined to peace than to war. He cherished justice above all things; as a result he vigorously punished violence, manslaughter and every other kind of wickedness whatsoever. Consequently he was greatly regretted on that account by all his subjects, who had been able to conduct their lives peaceably, far removed from the assaults and evil doing of scoundrels. He was the most ardent supporter of our faith, and daily participated with great piety in religious services. To those whom he considered to be worthy priests, he often secretly gave alms so that they should pray for his salvation. He was particularly fond of those Franciscan friars whom they call observants, for whom he founded many convents, so that with his help their rule should continually flourish in his kingdom. But all these virtues were obscured latterly by avarice, from which he suffered. This avarice is surely a bad enough vice in a private individual, whom it forever torments; in a monarch indeed it may be considered the worst vice since it is harmful to everyone, and distorts those qualities of trustfulness, justice and integrity by which the State must be governed.

It may be that there are worse vices than avarice, even in a monarch, but Polydore was not alone in ascribing this characteristic, and it is one

---

Vergil's picture of Henry VII as 'highly idealized', as does M. McKisack, *Mediaeval history in the Tudor age* (1971), 103. Nor does it follow that because the attribution of avariciousness to princes was common form among the biographers of (deceased) princes of the period, therefore Henry VII was *not* avaricious.

[1] The contemporary ballad, 'The song of the Lady Bessy', described Henry, when still in exile, as having a long pale face, with a wart a little above his chin; 'His face is white, the wart is red', Kingsford, *English historical literature*, 251. The vivacity of his expression and the liveliness of his eyes were often remarked; *Cal. S.P. Spanish*, I, xlviii.

to which we must return later. John Fisher, bishop of Rochester, naturally did not think it fit to refer to vice of any kind when in 1509 he made the funeral oration[1] for Henry, but in other respects Fisher made observations that support Polydore Vergil's remarks.

His politic wisdom in governance was singular, his wit always quick and ready, his reason pithy and substantial, his memory fresh and holding, his experience notable, his counsels fortunate and taken by wise deliberation, his speech gracious in diverse languages, his person goodly and amiable, his natural complexion of the purest mixture, his issue fair and in good number; leagues and confederacies he had with all Christian princes, his mighty power was dreaded everywhere, not only within his realm but without also; his people were to him in as humble subjection as ever they were to king; his land many a day in peace and tranquility; his prosperity in battle against his enemies was marvellous; his dealing in time of perils and dangers was cold and sober with great hardiness. If any treason was conspired against him it came out wonderfully; his treasure and riches incomparable; his buildings most goodly and after the newest cast of all pleasure.

The comments of foreign ambassadors writing home to their masters sometimes provide an insight into a monarch's character supplementary to the remarks of natives and subjects, even though ambassadorial comments might, of course, be jaundiced, prejudiced, biased, or mistaken.

It is evident from many sources that Henry was at great pains to cultivate the ambassadors at his court and to obtain information on foreign affairs from them and his own envoys and agents. The Milanese ambassador warned the duke of Milan that Henry was admirably well informed of affairs in Italy and elsewhere.[2] The several Spanish envoys certainly had Henry under close observation and were addicted to sending their comments home.

In 1498 Pedro de Ayala informed Ferdinand and Isabella that:

... his crown is, nevertheless, undisputed, and his government strong in all respects. He is disliked, but the queen is beloved, because she is powerless. ... The king looks old for his years but young for the sorrowful life he has led. One of the reasons why he leads a good life is that he has been brought up abroad. He would like to govern England in the French fashion, but he cannot. He is subject to his council, but has already shaken off some, and got rid of some part of this subjection. Those who have received the great

---

[1] *The English works of John Fisher*, ed. J. E. B. Mayor, E.E.T.S., extra ser. XXVII (1886, repr. 1935), Pt I, 269).

[2] *Cal. S.P. Venetian*, I, 751; Pollard, op. cit. 158-9.

est favours from him are the most discontented. He knows all that. The king has the greatest desire to employ foreigners in his service. He cannot do so; for the envy of the English is diabolical, and, I think, without equal. He likes to be much spoken of, and to be highly appreciated by the whole world. He fails in this because he is not a great man. He spends all the time he is not in public or in his council, in writing the accounts of his expenses with his own hand. . . . He is much influenced by his mother and his followers in affairs of personal interest and in others. The queen, as is generally the case, does not like it. . . .[1]

De Ayala appears to have suffered from a good many delusions in writing these remarks. Hernan Duque de Estrada, writing in 1504, had something more complimentary to say. Speaking of Henry's devotion to his son Prince Henry, and his desire to 'improve him', he commented, 'certainly there could be no better school in the world than the society of such a father as Henry VII. He is so wise and attentive to everything; nothing escapes his attention.'[2]

De Puebla in 1507 thought that 'the king of England has no confidential advisers'.[3] When it was all over in 1509 the Venetian envoy characterized Henry as having been 'a very great miser but a man of vast ability'.[4]

This somewhat brusque and over-terse summary would certainly not have satisfied Margaret Beaufort, Henry's mother. To her he was 'my own sweet and most dear king and all my worldly joy'.[5] She could write to him from Calais town, on St Agnes's day, the day on which 'I did bring into this world my good and gracious prince, king, and only beloved son'.[6] Not many letters from Henry to Margaret survive, but the long letter which he wrote in his own hand to her in July, probably in 1501, is very revealing. It serves to remind us that by that date his burdens had begun to tell on him.

[Having agreed to dispense her from the statute of Mortmain to enable her to proceed with one of her foundations at Cambridge] all of which things according to your desire and pleasure, I have, with all my heart and good will given and granted unto you; and my dame, not only in this but in all other things that I know should be to your honour and pleasure, and weal of your soul, I shall be glad to please you as your heart can desire

[1] Cal. S.P. Spanish, I, 177–8; Pollard, op. cit. II, 4.
[2] Cal. S.P. Spanish, I, 238; and Pollard, op. cit. I, 238–9.
[3] Cal. S.P. Spanish, I, 439; and Pollard, op. cit. I, 298.
[4] Cal. S.P. Venetian, I, No. 942; Pollard, op. cit. I, 331.
[5] H. Ellis, Original letters, 1st ser. I (1825), 46; and Pollard, op. cit. I, 217.
[6] ibid. 218.

it, and I know well, that I am as much bounden so to do, as any creature living for the great and singular motherly love and affection that it hath pleased you at all times to bear me. Wherefore, mine own most loving mother, in my most hearty manner I thank you, beseeching you of your good continuance in the same.

These are more than conventional phrases, but it was in the post-script that he lifted the veil rather more.

Madame, I have encumbered you now with this my long writing, but me-thinks that I can do no less, considering that it is so seldom that I do write, wherefore I beseech you to pardon me, for verily, madame, my sight is nothing so perfect as it has been, and I know well it will appear daily wherefore I trust that you will not be displeased, though I write not so often with mine own hand, for on my faith I have been three days ere I could make an end of this letter.[1]

Little precision can be given to any estimate of Henry's relations with his queen, for lack of appropriate material. He appears to have been a devoted and faithful husband and father, and Bacon's facile phrase that 'towards his queen he was nothing uxorious'[2] has no justification, unless it was meant to convey that he did not indulge her desire (if she had any such) to interfere in matters of political decision. Queen Elizabeth is described by contemporaries as a very handsome woman and of great ability,[3] as beloved,[4] as a woman of the greatest charity and humanity.[5] There seems, indeed, good reason to suppose that she was an admirable and wholly acceptable spouse in the king's eyes. Certainly they shared fully in the social life of the court, both formal and informal, gave each other little presents, and generally gave the impression of a happy married life. Very few evidences survive of displays of affection by the couple, but it is not to be expected that there would be. This dearth, however, is more than compensated for by the following anecdote of what happened when news of the death of Prince Arthur was brought to court. Its vividness demands quotation in full.

In the yeare of our Lord God 1502, the seconde daye of Aprill, in the Castle of Ludlowe deceased Prince Arthur first begotten Son of our Soveraigne Lord King Henry the VIIth and in the XVII yeare of his

---

[1] H. Ellis, *Original letters*, 1st ser. I (1825), 53; Pollard, op. cit. III, 187–9.

[2] *Henry VII*, 217.

[3] *Cal. S.P. Venetian*, I, 754, 833; Pollard, op. cit. I, 162, 231.

[4] *See* above, p. 301, fn. 1.

[5] *Annals of Ulster*, III, 465; Pollard, op. cit. III, 289. She is said to have been somewhat dominated by Lady Margaret Beaufort (*Cal. S.P. Spanish*, I, xlix).

Raigne. Immediately after his death Sir Richard Poole[1] his Chamberlaine, with other of his Councell, wrote and sente letters to the King and Councell to Greenwich, where his Grace and the Queene's laye, and certified them of the Prince's Departure. The which Councell discreetly sent for the Kings ghostly Father a fryer observant, to whom they shewed this most sorrowful and heavye Tydings, and desired him in his best manner to shewe it to the Kinge. He in the morning of the Tuesday following, somewhat before the tyme accustomed, knocked at King's Chamber dore, and when the Kinge understood it was his confessor, he commanded to lett him in. The Confessor then commanded all those present to avoide, and after due salutation began to saie, *Si bona de manu dei suscipimus, mala autem quare non sustineamus*? [if we have received good things by the hand of God, wherefore should we not also sustain misfortunes?] and so showed his Grace that his dearest sonne was departed to God. When his Grace understood that sorrowful heavy tydings, he sent for the Queene, saying that he and his Queene would take the painful sorrows together. After that she was come and sawe the Kyng her Lord, and that naturall and paineful sorrowe, as I have heard saye, she with full great and constant comfortable words besought his Grace that he would first after God remember the weale of his own noble person, the comfort of his realme and of her. She then saied that my Ladye his mother had never no more children but him only, and that God by his Grace had ever preserved him, and brought him where he was. Over that, howe that God had left him yet a fayre Prince, two fayre Princesses and that God is where he was, and we are both young ynoughe. And that the prudence and wisdome of his Grace spronge over all Christendome, so that it should please him to take this accordingly thereunto. Then the King thannked her of her good comfort. After that she departed and came to her owne Chamber, naturall and motherly remembraunce of that great losse smote her so sorrowful to the hart that those about her were faine to send for the King to comfort her. Then his Grace of true gentle and faithful love, in good hast came and relieved her, and showed her howe wise counsell she had given him before, and he for his parte would thanke God for his sonn, and would she should doe in like wise.[2]

There is no reason to doubt the authenticity of this story, and to dismiss it, as Busch did,[3] with the remark that 'on the occasion of

[1] Sir Richard Pole (K.G., 23 April 1499; G.E.C., II, App. II), together with other members of the Prince's Council, had been appointed to the commission to enquire into the lands of Sir William Stanley in 1495. *C.P.R.*, I, 29.

[2] Printed in John Leland, *De rebus Brittanicis collectanea*, V, 373–4; and F. Grose and T. Astle, *Antiquarian repertory*, II (1808), 322–3, from College of Arms MS. 1st m.13. cf. S. Anglo, *Journal of the Warburg and Courtauld Institute*, XXVI (1963), 54, n. 7; and *Spectacle, pageantry, and early Tudor policy*, 57–8. On Leland's work, *see* M. McKisack, op. cit. c. 1.　　　　　　　　　　　　　[3] op. cit. 307.

Arthur's death, husband and wife displayed a certain warmth of affection' seems to be a gross understatement. When a year later Queen Elizabeth herself died, Henry, it is said, 'privily departed to a solitary place, and would no man should resort unto him'.[1]

Henry shared the conventional religious beliefs and superstitions of his era. He was meticulous in his religious observances, his alms-giving, his patronage of churches and religious orders, his respect for saints and relics, and endowed prayers for his soul. All of these characteristics, together with his tactful and respectful relations with the papacy, gave him a generally recognized reputation as a sound churchman. But how far this reputation was based upon any genuine religious feeling remains a matter for conjecture. It is difficult to see how Professor David Knowles's verdict can be improved upon. 'Henry VII,' he writes, 'was not personally interested in religion in its theological or devotional aspects, still less in its spiritual depth, but neither was he a critic or libertine. His actions and policies, as we see them, were earthbound.'[2]

It is clear enough that mundane considerations weighed most with him in making appointments to the episcopal bench,[3] and also in his dealings with the papacy. Whilst he was glad enough to receive the advantage of papal support for his accession and throne, his diplomatic endeavours, his position as a European monarch, his desire to make a second marriage, and to receive symbols of papal favour and goodwill, he could resist papal blandishments to participate in a sort of Crusade against the encroachments of the Turks, with diplomatic skill. He could carry on a voluminous correspondence with the popes on this subject, spread over the years, pay eloquent lip-service to the excellence of the cause, and even contribute to it substantial 'financial aid out of his own funds, but when it came to the question of his personal participation in such a war, his evasion was masterly.

> If [he wrote] neither of the kings of France and Spain will take upon him the charge to give in proper person assistance to the Pope's Holiness, the king for great care, zeal, and good mind that he beareth to the religion of Christ's faith ... albeit that he is farther from those parts than other princes be, and also that his costs by reason of such farness, should be greater than the other princes should, yet, having a sufficient space to prepare himself to so long a journey, is contented in his own proper person and with army according, to take upon him the said charge, to come

---

[1] Cited by R. L. Storey, op. cit. 62.
[2] *The religious orders in England*, III (1959), 3.
[3] *See* above, p. 241.

enricus Dei gra Rex anglie et franc̄ ac dn̄s hibn̄e/ Ill.me ac potetissime dn̄e archiduc̄isse austrie burgundie z c̄
c̄onsanguinee nr̄e char.me Salute et prosperitatis icremētiz · Binas antehac ad ur̄as Cel.nes lr̄as dedimus mutua nostr̄
Ill.mi dn̄i archiducis negocia tangētes/ quaz postremas sectario nr̄o i ligua gallica/quem paulo atte Oratore nostrū
uc misimus ur̄e Subl.ti reddendas dedimus Cui istuc p̄ficisc̄ti specialiter iniuximus ut ad ur̄as Cel.nes deriuaret: ostd̄
et q̄ qntop̄e illi afficemur q̄ntaq̄ et quas p̄cipua dilection̄e eam p̄sequeremur declararet is̄up nos nō aliter n̄ minore
ffection̄e ur̄as Subl.tem estimare quas ȳpsam nr̄a infilia q̄ndoq̄d̄m mutua nr̄a c̄onsanguinitas qua Sere.nis paretibz ur̄is/
striginur id maiop̄e deposc̄it · st̄e; et rogaret ur̄as Cel.nes ut sicuti nos eam ȳ filia nr̄a ȳp̄a hēmus · Ita et ip̄a nos ȳ patre p̄p̄o
no estimare uelit Demū eidz nr̄o sectario Oratori p̄dicto mād̄auamus ut circa ea qūe ad mutua nr̄a negocia p̄tinerent
otissimū ageret cū ur̄a cel.ne et c̄onsilio ductu atq̄ industria eidz oino uteretur : Qūe quidz oia licet i suis istructionibz essen
ngulatim exp̄ssa isdem orator noster p̄rsus omisit · qd̄ c̄te nō satis equo aīo fūimus Putamus autez i causa fuisse q̄
r̄a mādata fuerit ab eo p̄missa/ quoniaz ip̄e secretarius noster tam ligua latina quaz hispana careret/ quibz sibi desti
ntibz que exponen̄ fuerat expone nō potuit Ita ut absq̄ ulla uera negocior̄ nr̄or̄ c̄oclusione ad nos rediuerit Nuper
ero immediate post pascha applicuerut ad nos Oratores Ill.mi dn̄i archiduc̄/ a quibz lr̄as ur̄as libēter accepissem̄
eru ubi nullas e̅e ad nos datas cognouimus Illico de totius negoc̄ī et cause statu eam c̄oiectura fecimus quam rei cue
is c̄opbauit/ nulla sc̄ilicet bona c̄oclusione aduenisse Qūe nempe oia si s̄oditis nr̄is magis e̅ent cognita quaz sint ma
res p̄culdubio querelas p̄enaret/ p̄ptea q̄ nusq̄ atea s̄o alis alio rege p̄dec̄ssore nr̄o p̄siti talem et ta diutur̄a iniur̄az
nt passi · Hihilo tn̄ minus i h̄is oibz ad p̄cipua dn̄i Oratoris Sere.mor̄ regis et regine parētu ur̄or̄ hic penes nos c̄omo
ātis requisition̄e et istatiaz supsedn̄du adhuc duximus/ don̄e q̄uisq̄ ur̄as Cel.nes huiusmoi negocior̄ redderemus
tiore̅ Quod sane egimus preter et c̄otra totī nr̄i ȳpsi̅us dispositionez et uolutatem/ sicuti Orator ip̄e satis nouit/ as q̄
ur̄a Cel.do tam itima nr̄az erga se dilection̄e/ quaz etia metem circa h̄ec oia, mutua nr̄a negocia c̄oenc̄tia latius
ntelliget/ que felix ualeat ad uota · Ex Castello nr̄o de Shena die viij aprilis · M.o c c c c l x x x x vij ·/

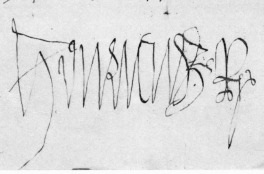

15. Letter from Henry VII, in the handwriting of Peter Carmeliano, Latin Secretary, signed by the king at Sheen, to Joanna (of Castile), archduchess of Austria and Burgundy, wife of the archduke Philip, 8 April 1497 (*Hofmann and Freeman's Catalogue, No. 32*). The letter refers to the difficulties experienced in the implementation of the treaty of February 1496 (known as the *Magnus Intercursus*), and speaks in terms of great affection for Joanna, whom the king loves as his own daughter. Her sister, Catherine of Aragon, had been betrothed to Prince Arthur on 1 January 1497.

16a and b. Death mask of Henry VII and funeral effigy of Queen Elizabeth.
See Appendix F below (*Westminster Abbey*)

16c. Tomb effigies of Henry VII and Queen Elizabeth by Pietro Torrigiano,
c. 1512–19 (*Westminster Abbey, Henry VII Chapel*)

personally and join with the Pope's said holiness, *if the same Pope will personally go against the said Turk.*[1]

It is not surprising that Henry never did set out on such an impractical project. His patronage of ecclesiastical buildings and foundations provides more tangible manifestations of his contribution to the religious life of his time.[2]

That he especially favoured the Spiritual or Observant branch of the Franciscan order may well be taken as an indication of his religious discrimination. At any rate he founded three houses for them, at Canterbury, Newcastle, and Southampton. But he did likewise for the conventuals at Richmond, Greenwich, and Newark. He built the Savoy Hospital in London to succour a hundred poor people, and planned another at Bath. Part of the cost of these foundations, however, he met by the appropriation and diversion of the revenues of sundry decayed ecclesiastical institutions, and he was willing enough to encourage others, including his mother, to found important and enduring educational bodies.

The destruction by fire of his favourite residence at Sheen in 1497 gave him the opportunity to lavish care and money on the erection of a new palace at the same site, renamed Richmond. He spent money also on rebuilding Baynard's Castle and the palace at Greenwich. Above all, he conceived and carried through nearly to completion, partly with financial assistance from decayed priories and other benefices, the superb project now known as the Chapel of Henry VII at the east end of Westminster Abbey. This was to be the last resting place of himself and his only queen, the monument and symbol of his life's work.

Neither this nor any of his architectural creations was such as one would ascribe to a monarch who was a miser. These were not the products of a niggardly mind. Whether he was avaricious or rapacious is quite another question, but that in fact he was a liberal spender of his gains is demonstrated beyond doubt not only by these products but also by the magnificence of his court and expenditure upon a great diversity of interests, pastimes, and causes.

It would be a great mistake to suppose that the court life[3] maintained by Henry VII was drab, glum, or dreary. On the contrary, there was

[1] J. O. Halliwell, *Letters of the kings of England* (1896-8), I, 185–94; Pollard, op. cit. III, 165–72.

[2] For the subject generally, *see* Busch, op. cit. 311–13, and refs therein. On Sheen, *see* R. Allen Brown, H. M. Colvin, A. J. Taylor, *History of the king's works* (1963), II, 994–100.

[3] *See* the account of Catherine of Aragon's reception and entertainment in 1501, in Leland, *Collectanea*, IV, 352–73; cf. generally, S. Anglo, op. cit. 8–108.

magnificence, impressive ceremonial, lavish display of costly clothing, decorations, jewels and plate, festivity on appropriate occasions, pageantry, banqueting, jousting, music, dancing, disguisings, revels, play-acting, and the like. All these displays and elaborate entertainment marked the great Church festivals, St George's day, the outstanding family events, such as the christening, and knighting of Arthur, the reception of Catherine of Aragon, and their wedding; not to mention family funerals. By such displays of wealth, taste, and ingenuity, Henry could and did impress his courtiers, his subjects, and the ambassadors of foreign potentates. It was all part of Henry's idea of kingship. But it was also an expression of his personality. It is evident that Henry knew how to enjoy himself in a great variety of ways, and was quite capable of participating in many recreations, pastimes, jollifications, and drolleries that one would not at first sight associate with the somewhat grim portrayals we have of him. The notion that his chief leisure occupation was initialling accounts of his income becomes an absurdity when it is seen how he spent substantial portions of that income.[1] The care he lavished on his income accounts may well be deemed a fitting prudence for a monarch in his position, but the man himself can be better known by what he spent his money on.

It is no surprise that he was addicted to the country life and was passionately devoted to hunting and hawking, and that he travelled about the country a very great deal, as indeed mediaeval kings commonly did. More revealing of his domestic occupations are the comparatively small but very frequent expenditures on a great variety of interests. Prominent is the frequency with which he lost money, sometimes considerable sums, in playing at cards, dice, tennis, and archery; at these he was often a loser; whether he ever won is not recorded. He often rewarded musicians and minstrels, singers, dancers, and sometimes bought musical instruments. Lords of Misrule, revellers, joculars, jesters,[2] and dancers,[3] frequently received bounty. Those that brought

---

[1] The great bulk of the accounts of Henry VII's expenditure remains in manuscript, in P.R.O., or B.M. collections, and has never been given the detailed study and analysis that it deserves. *See* the list in W. C. Richardson, op. cit. App. III. Craven Ord's incomplete transcripts from the King's Book of Payments 1491–1505 are in B.M. MSS Add. 7099. Selections from these were published as an appendix to Robert Henry's *History of Great Britain* (1824). Excerpts from Ord's volume were printed by S. Bentley, *Excerpta historica* (1831), 85–133, which are largely relied upon here. Detailed references to items of expenditure appear to be otiose for the present purpose. *See* below, Appendix E.

[2] One of his jesters was called 'the foolish duke of Lancaster'.

[3] 'To the young damsel that daunceth £30; to a little mayden that daunceth £12.'

him rare animals, a lion, or a leopard, wild cats, or indeed some human freak, could expect tangible appreciation. Some, but not very much money was spent on the purchase of books or book-binding. That he collected some books, for which a librarian and a 'keeper' were provided,[1] and that he could speak and read Latin, as well as speak French, is evident, but that much in the way of humanistic influences were at work in his court is far from clear. The fact that he instituted a Latin secretaryship and appointed the Italian scholar Peter Carmeliano to it before July 1495 is of no great significance in this connection, and may have been occasioned by a growing ignorance of Latin at court.[2] The record of Erasmus's visit in the company of Thomas More to court in 1499 is a tribute to the domestic bliss and musical pleasures of Henry VII and the precocity of Prince Henry rather than to any particular intellectual interests, however impressed he may have been by the progress of humanism elsewhere in the realm.[3] Printers, poets, and rhymsters got rewards, as well as physicians, spies, and informers. Very large sums indeed went to the jewellers and goldsmiths who sold him his favourite forms of treasure.

Some of these disbursements were only what would be expected from a monarch of the time. Others, especially casual gifts and alms, some clearly made on the spur of the moment, whether to the queen, to ambassadors, or to humble unfortunate subjects, show him capable of the impulsive gesture. When it came to the question of paying the costs of burials, it was doubtless inevitable that very large payments were made in respect of Prince Arthur and Queen Elizabeth, but he need not have defrayed the cost of the burial of Edward, earl of Warwick, nor of Sir William Stanley, nor of a tomb for Richard III.

It has been alleged (by Bacon) that Henry was 'full of apprehensions and suspicions'. This may well have been so. Certainly the circumstances of most of his reign were such as to give him good cause. The long sequence of plots, conspiracies, and rebellions were quite enough to

---

[1] Quintin Paulet, from Lille, was keeper of the king's library before 30 March 1500 (C.P.R., II, 208). The king's humble servant, John Porth, keeper of certain books of the king, was rewarded in 1508 (ibid. 564). As early as December 1485 Peter Actoris was granted the office of king's stationer with licence to import printed and unprinted books free of customs (ibid. I, 45). It is known that Henry VII gave Caxton the French text of The Book of Fayttes of Armes and of Chivalrye (published in London in 1490) for translation and printing (S. Anglo, Machiavelli (1969), 154).

[2] J. Otway-Ruthven, The king's secretary (1939), App. F. For further on Carmeliano and humanism in general, see R. Weiss, Humanism in England during the fifteenth century, 2nd ed. (1957).

[3] Opus epistolarum, ed. P. S. Allen, etc., cited Scarisbrick, op. cit. 13–14.

make any monarch apprehensive and suspicious. An unusually revealing document, which we have not yet had occasion to cite, discloses not
only the basic fear that he had to contend with – that his dynasty might
be displaced – but also a surprising reluctance on his part to credit tales
of treasonable conduct.

The document[1] is a report sent to the king by one John Flamank (or
Fleming) of a confidential conversation (at which Flamank was present)
between Sir Richard Nanfan, deputy governor of Calais, Sir Hugh
Conway, treasurer, Sir Sampson Norton, the master porter, and William
Nanfan.

In the course of the conversation, touching the security of the king
and of Calais, Sir Hugh asserted that they must think of the future as
well as the present, 'for the king's grace is but a weak and sickly man,
not likely to be a long-lived man'. Not long since, he was sick and lay
at his manor of Wanstead. At that time a number of great personages
discussed among themselves the shape of things that might come should
his grace depart this life. Some spoke of Buckingham, some of Edmund
de la Pole, but none of them spoke of the prince of Wales. Sir Hugh,
since coming to Calais, had mentioned this episode to Sir Nicholas
Vaux, lieutenant of Guisnes and to Sir Anthony Brown, lieutenant of
Calais Castle, and both had replied that they had 'good holds to resort
to', by which they were sure to make their peace, 'howsoever the world
might turn'.

Both Sir Richard and Sir Sampson urged that these matters should
be reported to the king, but Sir Hugh repudiated the suggestion. 'If,' he
said, 'you knew King Harry our master as I do, you would be wary
how you broke to him any such matters, for he would take it that
anything you said came out of envy, ill-will, and malice, and you would
have only blame and no thanks.' In a previous experience, he said, he
had incurred the king's displeasure at the time when Lord Lovel was at
Colchester, when a trusty friend of Sir Hugh's had revealed Lovel's

---

[1] L. & P., I, 231–40; Pollard, op. cit. I, 240–50. The date of this document is
uncertain. As Pollard noted (ibid. 240), it is probably later than Gairdner's suggestion of 1503. It must be between 1502 when Sir Nicholas Vaux was appointed
lieutenant of Guisnes and such date early in 1506, when it became no longer feasible
that Sir Anthony Brown's wife Lucy (niece of Warwick the Kingmaker and daughter
of John Neville, Marquis Montagu), who 'loveth not the king's grace', might let in
through a postern of the castle her kinsman Edmund de la Pole, as Sir Hugh Conway
feared. Who Flamank was is not clear, but he might conceivably be the John Flem-
ming who was mayor of Southampton in 1505, probably the same person who was
granted the office of controller of customs and subsidies in that port in 1507 (C.P.R.,
II, 437, 532).

plans under a pledge of secrecy. Nevertheless, because of his allegiance he had hurried to Sir Reginald Bray and informed him of the plot. Bray told the king, who sent for Conway and reasoned with him always contrary to his report and insisted that it could not be so. When Conway refused to reveal who the informer was, the king became angry and displeased. Conway now asserted that he would never again 'tempt the king' in such matters.

Sir Richard Nanfan affirmed that the king had been very reluctant to believe any ill of Sir James Tyrell or Sir Robert Clifford. All the officials expressed grave concern for what would happen should the king die, and apprehension for the safety of Calais, in which there were a number of enemies both of the king and of them.

What happened to Flamank's report we do not at present know. What is significant in it is its revelation of the kind of grounds Henry had for apprehensions and suspicions, but at the time his reluctance to accept allegations of treason.

Nevertheless, apprehension or suspicions of one kind or another, real or feigned, were doubtless in part at the root of those actions of his which in the long run earned him a reputation for avarice or rapacity. Such a reputation could not have come from his fiscal impositions, which were not remarkable, nor, as we have seen, from his unwillingness to spend money. But it could indeed arise from the extraordinary lengths to which he resorted in imposing bonds for monetary payments from a large number of his subjects, including many of the peers, bishops, and other men of substance, and lesser persons. The existence of this practice, not original to Henry VII, has, of course, been known for many years, but the extent and nature of it as operated by him, has only recently come to be realized.[1]

Some years ago lengthy discussions were published[2] mainly on the theme of whether Henry VII's reputation for rapacity and extortion in his later years and the suggestion that he showed remorse during his last days were justified. These articles, running to over seventy pages of detailed argumentation and contention, were the most substantial contributions to an appraisal of Henry VII's actions in certain spheres that have ever appeared. Professor Elton, in the first of these articles, sought to acquit Henry VII of both rapacity and remorse and perhaps adopted

---

[1] *See* above, p. 213.

[2] G. R. Elton, 'Henry VII: rapacity and remorse', *H.J.*, I (1958), 21–39; J. P. Cooper, 'Henry VII's last years reconsidered', ibid. II (1959), 103–29; G. R. Elton, 'Henry VII: a restatement', ibid. IV (1961), 1–29. Elton's two articles are hereafter referred to as (1) or (2).

a somewhat roseate view of some of his financial activities whilst possibly underestimating his pious aspirations at the end. Mr J. P. Cooper indicated some of the weaknesses in Elton's arguments, and this provoked a rejoinder which clarified matters in some particulars but left the general conclusions to be drawn somewhat in the air, except that Elton continued to maintain that it is 'a false view which speaks of rapacity and oppression'.[1]

It would be tedious and inappropriate to examine this controversy here in detail. Much can be learned from these articles, but the authors did not perhaps at the time they were writing focus sufficient attention on the field of action in which the king, if he were rapacious, had the maximum scope for displaying rapacity and so gave rise to cause for remorse, if he were remorseful. It is surprising that even then, out of the total of seventy-five pages devoted to the debate, barely two were spared to the vital question of the uses that Henry made of recognizances. There was nothing very significant about the king's ordinary fiscal arrangements;[2] he was if anything notably slack in enforcing the penal statutes, except in the sphere of commercial regulations.[3] He was zealous in exercising his feudal prerogatives, which although basically lawful were undoubtedly stretched as far, if not indeed farther, than the older interpretation of the law would have countenanced, and it is hard not to conclude that these rights were applied with a rigour that was harsh enough to border on rapacity, whether by the king or by his agents.[4]

But it was in the almost limitless possibilities of exacting bonds that the greatest scope for rapacity naturally existed, and the evidence has accumulated since 1958 that the king fell a victim to avarice which did manifest itself more markedly in 1502 onwards, and that this activity may have induced some remorse at the end. The exaction of recognizances from the nobility is now known[5] to have gone much further than used to be imagined, and even though there might be a justifiable policy behind many of these exactions, and the actual cash exacted was much less than the totals bonded for, these totals themselves were often outrageously high and bespeak a distinctly rapacious mind, and a mind perhaps rather over-sensitive to fear and suspicion. These fears and suspicions as to the preservation of their allegiance by the peerage were certainly magnified by the deaths of Prince Arthur in 1502 and Queen Elizabeth in 1503 and the continued freedom of Edmund de la Pole and

---

[1] Elton (2), 28.   [2] See above, ch. 11.
[3] See above, ch. 10.   [4] See above, p. 211.
[5] See above, p. 215.

some of his brothers. All this no doubt comes under the heading of 'policy' whatever the pyschological motivations may have been. But the discovery in an unlikely place of a hitherto unknown document cannot fail to throw fresh and a distinctly baleful light on Henry VII's zeal for exacting bonds or cash from many persons whose standing and potential were hardly such as to justify fears as to their future actions, political or otherwise.

This document[1] is nothing less than a confession by Edmund Dudley of eighty-four cases of unjust exactions for which he considered the executors of Henry VII's will ought to make restitution or allowance. Dudley, who was arrested a few days after the death of Henry VII, indicted on a charge of constructive treason on 12 July 1509, found guilty and sentenced, was returned to the Tower to await execution, and wrote his confession and petition within the next four weeks.

He addressed his document to Fox and Lovell, whom he wanted to be the instruments of 'help and relief for the dead king's soul', and of justice. His plea for mercy was not for himself but for others. He had attempted to discuss the cases with Fox, whose failure to respond induced him to write the document. The document was kept secret, but Fox, Lovell, and Young were all three among the executors of Henry VII's will and were also appointed to assess reparations to be made to those wronged by him. It was not Dudley's purpose to accuse or malign his late master, but to press for his will to be carried out in the matter of reparation. But it is clear from a number of items in the petition that Henry was responsible for the decisions taken in many of these cases, and Dudley expressly states that the king's purpose was 'to have many persons in his danger at his pleasure'.

In as much as Henry's 'mind and last will was especially that restitution should be made to all persons by his grace wronged contrary to the order of his laws', Dudley had perused his books touching all such matters as he had been privy to, and set down the persons whom he thought were hardly treated 'and much sorer than the causes required'.

1 I am greatly indebted to the good offices of Dr C. F. Richmond, and the kindness and generosity of Mr C. J. Harrison, of the University of Keele, for allowing me to see and use his article and transcript of the document, which he discovered among the papers of the marquis of Anglesey at Plas Newydd, under the title of 'The petition of Edmund Dudley', now published in E.H.R., LXXXVII (1972), 82–99. The petition was addressed to Bishop Fox, keeper of the Privy Seal and Sir Thomas Lovell, chancellor of the Exchequer and constable of the Tower; it was handed to John Young, master of the Rolls, who had it copied into his book, and on 20 August 1509 a copy of this was made. The surviving copy appears to have been a copy of that, made later in the sixteenth century.

Many persons were bound to the king's grace in sums of money, some by recognizance, others by obligation without any condition, but as a simple and absolute bond, payable at a certain day, 'for his grace would have them so made'. 'It were against reason and good conscience, these manner of Bondes should be reputed as perfect debtes: for I think verily his inward mind was never to use them, of these there are very many.'

A few examples may be quoted here:

Item the abbot of Furness had a hard end for his pardon for he paid and is deemed to pay 500 marks for a little matter.

Item one Hawkyns of London, draper, upon surmise of a lewd fellow, paid 100 marks for a light matter.

Item the earl of Northumberland was bound to the king in many great sums, howbeit the king's mind was to have payment of £2,000 and no more, as his grace showed me, yet that was too much for ought that was known.

Item the Lord Abegeny had a very sore end, or any proof that was against him to my knowledge.

Item Sir Nicholas Vaux and Sir Thomas Parr paid 9,000 marks upon a very light ground.

Item Peter Centurion a Genenois was evil intreated and paid much money and upon malicious ground in my conscience.

Item one Catesby of Northampton was in a manner undone upon a light surmise.

Item the king had the substance of Nicholas Nivesgoods, by reason of another man's obligation given unto his grace for his wife and creditors had nothing.

Item one Haslewood was kept long in prison and paid a great sum of money upon a light ground.

Item one Windial a poor man in Devonshire lay long in prison and paid £100 upon a very small cause.

Item Heronden lay in prison and paid much money only upon a surmise.

Item a poor gentleman of Kent called Roger Appleton paid 100 marks upon an untrue matter.

Item doctor Horsey was long in prison and paid £100 in my mind contrary to conscience.

Item Sir John Pennington paid 200 marks upon an obligation of 300 marks wherein he was bound not to depart without the king's licence, and yet for truth I was by when the king took him by the hand at his departure.

Item one Simmes a haberdasher without Ludgate paid and must pay £500 for light matters only upon a surmise of a lewd quean.

Item the king's grace dealt hardly with young Clifton in his bond contrary to my will.

If these cases and the others like them do not reveal a rapacious spirit on the part of the king it is difficult to think of what could constitute such evidence. Dudley, in the circumstances in which he wrote and for the purpose he had in mind, could have had no motive for mendacity. If, then, Henry VII did not show remorse at the end, he certainly should have done so. In point of fact he did, at the last, if not exactly express remorse, reveal in his will awareness that he might have gone too far in some of his demands. His will set up a committee to investigate 'the circumstances if any person of what degree so ever he be, show by any complaint to our executors any wrong to have been done to him, by us, by our commandment, occasion or mean, or that we held any goods or lands which of right ought to appertain to him'. Such complaints were to be effective if grounded in conscience 'other than matter done by the course and order of our laws, or if it were thought that his soul ought to stand charged with the said matter and complaints'.[1] This was precisely the kind of case that Dudley clearly sought in his confession and petition to get the executors (of whom he himself had been named one) to remedy. Henry did at the last experience twinges of conscience, and all argumentation to the contrary appears to be beside the essential point. Certainly what Henry VIII may or may not have done in these matters belongs to the biography of that monarch, not to his father's.

Henry VII's health had been failing for several years before the end came. As early as 1501 he was complaining to his mother that his eyesight was giving him serious trouble,[2] and in the secret conversations at Calais as reported by Flamank it is revealed that at an uncertain date 'not long since' Henry was very ill at his manor of Wanstead and apprehensions that he might not live long were entertained.[3] In the spring of 1507 he was very seriously ill of a 'quinsy', and his life was despaired of.[4] In February 1508 he was again seriously ill[5] and by July was reported to be in the last stage of consumption and in *extremis*.[6] According to Polydore Vergil he was greatly incapacitated round about

[1] *The will of Henry VII*, ed. T. Astle (1775), 11 ff., cited G. R. Elton, loc. cit. 37–8. Elton concedes that Henry's remorse was real enough, but sought to enter into questions of his motives and the practical results of his gesture which are irrelevant to the point.

[2] *See* above, p. 302.

[3] *See* above, p. 308.

[4] *Cal. S.P. Spanish*, I, No. 811.

[5] Bernard André, *Annales*, 108, 109, 113, says that Henry had an attack of gout in February to March 1508.

[6] *Cal. S.P. Venetian*, I, No. 906; *Cal. S.P. Spanish*, I, 460.

springtime in three successive years, his bodily strength declining by
degrees, accompanied by a mental decline.[1] By 24 March 1509 he was
again very ill and 'utterly without hope of recovery'.[2]

What the nature of his fatal illness was remains imprecise.[3] But the
end was not sudden. For the space of twenty-seven hours, we are told,[4]
he lay 'abiding the sharp assaults of death', at his palace of Richmond,
where his release came on 21 April. His body was conveyed in state to
St Paul's Cathedral, where on 10 May, John Fisher, bishop of Rochester,
preached the funeral sermon which was afterwards printed at the
special request of Lady Margaret Beaufort.[5] Fisher was assuredly not
wrong to interject into his pious and long rambling discourse what
seems a genuine *cri de cœur*:

'Ah king Henry king Henry, if thou were alive again, many a one that
is here present now would pretend a full great pity and tenderness upon
thee.'

What could Bishop Fisher have meant by these words spoken less than
three weeks after Henry's death? He must surely have been making a
covert allusion to persons who, if the king had been still alive would
have curried favour with him, but who had taken a different line since
he had died.

It is clear enough that soon after Henry VII's removal from the
scene, many persons sought and obtained opportunity to air their
grievances and lodge complaints. Unfortunately it seems virtually
impossible, at present at least, to disentangle in these moves much
reliable information about Henry VII's and his agent's activities, from
the inevitable desire of the young and dashing new king and his councillors to emphasize the change of regime and to win popularity and public
acclaim for themselves and especially to win over a cowed peerage.
What was now done belongs essentially to the new reign and only
indirectly and not very clearly can it be used to illuminate the realities of
Henry VII's government. Neither Henry VIII nor his officials, of

[1] P.V., 142–3.

[2] *Cal. S.P. Venetian*, No. 939. cf. Nos 941, 945; *Cal. S.P. Spanish*, I, 408, 439, 457,
460.

[3] J. Gairdner in *Henry VII* (1889), 208, stated that the king 'had also pains in the
chest and difficulty of respiration', but I have not seen any authority for this assertion.
John Fisher, loc. cit. 278, infers that Henry was unwilling to eat his food, however
delicately prepared, long before his death.

[4] ibid. 277.

[5] His body was thereafter interred alongside that of his queen in the chapel he
had begun to build in Westminster Abbey, which was completed in Henry VIII's
time. Busch, op. cit. 315–17, gives a short account of the funeral ceremonies, mainly
from Leland, *Collectanea*, IV, 303–9.

course, could openly impugn the conduct of his father 'of blessid memory' and at best they could offer to hear complaints, remedy any of these that might seem justified, identify and punish any suitable scapegoats, and perhaps attempt, at any rate nominally, to amend by statute a few general points of grievance which appeared to be capable of amendment by legislative process.[1]

According to the proclamation authorized by Henry VIII on 23 April 1509,[2] Henry VII himself had thought fit to proclaim a general pardon covering a wide range of mostly criminal offences committed before 16 April. How Henry VII himself could have much personal knowledge of this proclamation made shortly before his actual death, or Henry VIII could have taken much personal initiative in the proclamation dated two days after his father's death is a matter for speculation. The assent of both monarchs was necessarily obtained, but it could only have been the council who could have had much to do with either proclamation. Nor, as Professor Elton has argued,[3] can it be supposed that the earlier proclamation had much to do with the question of Henry VII's remorse, nor the later one with Henry VII's generosity. There were precedents for general pardons in the past, and in any case an amnesty for criminal offences has little to do with the fundamental question of extortion by recognizances. Certain recognizances were, however, brought within the scope of the general pardon. Whether in consequence of this, or of the actions of Henry VII's executors, or of Henry VIII and his councillors, it was significant that at least forty-five recognizances were cancelled during the first year of the new reign, and another one hundred and thirty during the next five years. Fifty-one of these cancellations specifically stated that the recognizances had been unjustly extorted.[4] However optimistic Lord Mountjoy's letter to Erasmus may have been,[5] his assertion that 'avarice has fled the country' was, it would seem, by no means entirely pointless.

The appointment in July 1509 of commissions of *oyer et terminer* has

[1] Thomas More made a covert attack on Henry VII's policies in his epigram on Henry VIII's coronation (*The latin epigrams of Thomas More*, ed. L. Bradner and C. A. Lynch (Chicago, 1953), 16–21). Edmund Dudley also made implied criticisms of Henry VII's regime, especially in the matter of interference with justice by Privy Seal and other letters, in his *Tree of the commonwealth*, ed. Brodie (1948), 35–6.

[2] Hughes and Larkin, op. cit. 79–81. Henry VIII also issued an accession pardon of his own, dated 25 April, covering a far wider range of matters (ibid. 81–3).

[3] loc. cit. (1), 36–7.

[4] J. R. Lander, loc. cit. 352.

[5] *Opus epistolarum Desiderii Erasmi Roterodami*, ed. P. S. Allen, etc. (1906–58), I, No. 215, cited ibid. 351; and Scarisbrick, *Henry VIII*, 12.

little or nothing to do with questions of Henry VII's remorse or conscience.[1] The result may have been 'a nation-wide enquiry to redress grievances'.[2] But there was nothing new in this kind of investigation. Henry himself had issued similar commissions many years before his death, and others were to be issued later in the Tudor period. Whether the flood of grievances was too great or too many of them on investigation proved to be unsustainable, the council terminated the proceedings of these commissions as early as 26 November 1509.[3] What had been revealed, in general terms, was little more than the perennial difficulties of law enforcement in the localities and the difficulties of getting the common-law courts to operate effectively and expeditiously.

It was not until 17 October 1509 that writs were issued for the first parliament of the new reign to meet on 21 January 1510. It was almost six years since a parliament had met, but it was not thought necessary to keep the new assembly in being for much more than a month, until 23 February. No doubt the Great Council of magnates which had met in June 1509 had prepared the ground by influencing Henry VIII's mind to the extent of making him realize that there were features in his father's regime that required some amendment, and it may be that the peers' bid to regain recognition of their traditional claim to political consideration met with initial success',[4] that is, if their claim had ever been ignored by Henry VII. But the legislative achievements of the parliament were not very striking and it is perhaps going too far to say that 'in this parliament Henry VII's rule received a slap in the face'.[5] Its enactments did little but amend some manifest abuses in legal procedure and the precise effect of these measures is open to some doubt.[6]

Nor did the parliament assist very materially in providing the new regime with the needful scapegoats. The bills for the attainder of Richard Empson and Edmund Dudley had not been passed before the parliament ended. Just why Empson and Dudley were singled out from other similar agents of Henry VII's government we shall probably never know with any assurance. They were both arrested, presumably by Henry VIII's or the council's orders, and confined in the Tower. Indicted at the Guildhall on charges of constructive treason, Dudley on 16 July was found guilty and sentenced, and was returned to the Tower to await execution, which was to be delayed until 17 August 1510, when Empson, tried and sentenced at Northampton, was also executed. The charge of treason was palpably fictitious, and great

---

[1] Elton, loc. cit. (2), 20–1. [2] J. C. Cooper, loc. cit. 177 ff.
[3] Elton, ibid. (1), 23. [4] R. L. Storey, op. cit. 210.
[5] Elton, loc. cit. (2), 26. [6] ibid. 24–6.

difficulty must have been experienced in finding justification for execution, which may have been the reason for the long delay. The possibilities of an act of attainder were explored but faded in the parliament. That both were guilty of harsh acts, some of them corrupt, and that both were efficient and ruthless agents of Henry VII's policies and behests need not be doubted. Both therefore were unpopular. They were, indeed, singularly well suited for the role of scapegoats, on whom 'were to be focused all the popular discontent with the old regime'. The reputation of the old king had to be preserved, the reputation of the new king had to be enhanced.[1] The two victims had been influential agents but not otherwise powerful. Their removal would not alienate any sections of the public.[2] Their fall was 'deliberately contrived by the Crown'. The episode was, in short, an example of 'the new policies of prestige'.[3] 'The young Henry made what was to be a characteristic response of his to certain sorts of political difficulties when he had the two ex-ministers executed.'[4] It was, indeed, the first item in that long series of judicial murders for which the reign of Henry VIII was to become unique in English history. Any avarice that Henry VII mingled with his practice of 'government by recognizances' was a mild failing compared with his son's addiction to more savage methods of solving his problems.

If we ask ourselves what manner of man Henry VII was, there is no simple or assured answer. When all the available evidence is surveyed we are still obliged to rely a good deal upon conjecture. Notwithstanding the substantial materials that survive for the history of the reign and of the king's activities, there is astonishingly little of an intimate nature, little unequivocal revelation of his personality.

As to his appearance, we have to think of a man impressive and outstanding – tall, rather slender, dignified, of sallow complexion, and rather aquiline features, whose most striking characteristic was the

[1] Harrison, op. cit.

[2] On Dudley's career, see D. M. Brodie, 'Edmund Dudley, minister of Henry VII', *T.R.H.S.*, 4th ser. XV (1932), 133–61; and her edition of his *The tree of the commonwealth* (1948). Little modern work has been done on Empson, but the careers of both were very similar. Both were common lawyers by profession, both had been members of parliament and speakers of the commons, both rose to influence by Henry VII's employment of them as very active members of the Council Learned in the Law. Neither appears to have had powerful relatives or friends.

[3] T. F. T. Plucknett, Taswell-Langmead's *English constitutional history*, 11th ed. (1960), 251. Elton makes a similar point in *England under the Tudors* (1955), 71

[4] Harrison, loc. cit.

vivacity of his expression and the brilliance of his small blue eyes, especially animated in conversation.

He was a man of high qualities and great ability and he devoted himself to his duties as king with a degree of devotion and a professionalism unwonted in most of his predecessors. He displayed a far-reaching comprehension of affairs of State and remained always the essential pivot upon which government turned. No minister of his at any time overshadowed the throne. His talent for choosing the right man for ministerial posts was remarkable. Their loyalty and service to him were matched by his loyalty and trust in them. Only one of his high-ranking adherents was eliminated; he did not hesitate to strike down the man (Sir William Stanley) to whose intervention at Bosworth he owed his victory.

He was astute, cautious, prudent, patient. He attempted nothing rash or ill-considered, avoided impetuosity, and generally manifested a well-informed and well-balanced mind.

He was neither bloodthirsty nor militant. Generally conciliatory, he could be drastic, ruthless, and firm when occasion demanded. He was markedly decisive in thought and action. He was never dilatory when crises demanded fast response. His political wisdom came to be universally acknowledged. His relations with his parliaments were tactful and sensible, generally constructive, and he avoided any acute friction by his recognition that there were limits to what was practicable. He did not regard himself as a great legislator, but assented to numerous measures of a practical, unspectacular nature which he, his ministers, or other persons initiated. There was nothing theoretical about his attitudes or his policies. He followed the art of the possible in a calm and sober manner, eschewing bombast, vainglory, and over-inflated ambition.

He may have been a more colourful personality than our generally opaque materials reveal, perhaps more human, warmer, and more capable of humour than our evidence shows. That he could occupy himself in a variety of pastimes, and encourage music, dancing, poetry, and literature, is clear enough, but the impression remains of a degree of austerity and aloofness which always stood between him and popularity. His subjects learnt to respect him and his achievements, or most of them, but it is hard to find evidence that they loved him. He was capable of liberality, of compassion, and of unpredictable gestures of consideration for unfortunates. He may indeed have been thought of as the English Solomon, but this tribute is not one which in itself inspires affection.

He had a reputation for honesty and reliability and was generally

candid and forthright, but capable of sustained dissimulation and prolonged diplomatic manœuvring, whilst as a rule keeping steadily to his
own targets. He attained too a measure of diplomatic skill that was not
unequal to coping with the arch-intriguers of his day, Ferdinand and
Isabella of Spain, and the more powerful even though less tortuous
Charles VIII and Louis XII of France, and was far superior to Maximilian and his family. He knew how to get substantially his own
objectives without excessive commitment and without stooping to the
unscrupulousness of his rivals.

He was unwavering in the pursuit of his political ends. These were
fundamentally: security, wealth, as good law and order as was practicable, but subjected to interference at times in his own self-interest; the
maintenance of peace, the supremacy of the Crown, the firm establishment of his dynasty at home and abroad; the furtherance of his realm's
position among the European powers. He did not fail in these basic
objectives.

But it will not do to say with Bacon that 'what he minded he com-
passed'. True, it is not perhaps possible to be sure what exactly he did
'mind'. It is however clear that he was by no means always successful
in compassing what he appears to have minded. He did not, for
example, succeed in obliging the landed interest to accept his aims in
the matter of uses; he did not attain more than a limited success in
curtailing the practice of retainer or the enforcement of law and order,
except perhaps in so far as his personal interests were concerned. Nor
could he obtain the kind of financial aid he sought in 1504. He could
overreach himself in the field of commercial negotiations and could
suffer diplomatic defeats. Try as he did, he could not succeed in making
a second marriage for himself and had to do without the advantages
that might have ensued from success in this objective. He did, indeed,
have to cope with more frustrations than perhaps we realize. He did
mind and did encompass the laying of the ghost of the 'White Rose' and
the cowing of the turbulent and recalcitrant magnates, but he was not
able to do either without some sullying of his own reputation at the time,
and forever.

His was not an original mind; he was no great innovator. He was
rather a highly skilful builder on existing foundations, an eclectic
adopter and adapter. He could bring an essentially mediaeval spirit and
practice of government to its highest point of effectiveness without in
any important way changing its character. A lover of power he certainly
was, but to wield power was his vocation and his destiny.

His first twenty-eight years were spent devoid of power or influence.

The twenty-four years that remained to him were consumed in intensive application to business, to warding off dangers, to overcoming crises, and to taking thought for the future. He met all his trials with courage and resolution, but it would not be surprising if his judgment towards the end deteriorated along with his health. The loss of his wife, his first and third sons, and several other children left him a very lonely and much aged man, with no one close enough and old enough to fill the gaps in his domestic circle. The frustration of his matrimonial hopes and schemes in the last years, his inability to find a consort both to his liking and conducive to what he conceived to be his material and political interests, cannot have failed to exacerbate his frustrations and to some extent to have warped his judgment. Apart from the grandiose political accompaniments of his plan to marry Joanna of Castile, his affection for her was real, and the circumvention of his aspirations by Ferdinand embittered and infuriated him to a degree that induced him to subject Ferdinand's daughter Catherine to unbecoming privations, to conduct out of character and damaging to his reputation.

If the penury of his earlier years contributed, along with reasons of State, to his becoming sufficiently over-zealous in the accumulation of wealth as to incur a reputation for avariciousness, even miserliness, in his later years, this was a fault which gave an unwonted strength to a Crown weakened for generations by improvident kings. If over-preoccupation in his later years with the problem of security which had inevitably loomed large during the earlier years became something of an obsession and led him into arbitrary and unjust actions, at least he left a Crown more secure than it had been since the best days of Edward III. It was unfortunate perhaps that his fears for security should have taken on the colour of additional avarice. Yet to seek to control his subjects by getting at their purse-strings was better than the more violent forms of terrorism that had been not uncommon in the past and were to reappear in magnified form in the times of his successors. It may be that Henry VII's reputation would have been less ambiguous if his life had ended a few years sooner. But it would hardly have been conducive to either the security of the dynasty or the welfare of the realm if his heir had succeeded to the throne at any earlier age than he did. Providence does, after all, move in mysterious ways (it would not be Providence otherwise), and the humble historian can hardly expect to assess the swings and the roundabouts with any precision.

His reign was unspectacular and though full of surprising and striking events, not at any point sensational, glamorous, or dramatic. But his services to the realm were immeasurable, far greater than he himself could have imagined or predicted. His regime produced a pacification, an orderliness, a cohesion, a viability in the forms and machinery of government, a sustained effectiveness without which stability and consolidation could not have been obtained, and provided an indispensable standpoint for subsequent growth and flowering. It vindicated the achievements of the past, and provided potential for the fluorescence of the later Tudor period. It brought England on towards its 'manifest destiny' as Great Britain. He himself and his policies introduced a Welsh element that could make more meaningful and fruitful the further integration of the next reign. He brought pacification, albeit temporary, into relations with Scotland, the matrimonial alliance with which was to usher in the formation of the greater kingdom. With Ireland he could at least create a *modus vivendi*, whilst maintaining in principle the ultimate sovereignty of the Crown.

He made a fresh appraisal of the problems of European international relations. He jettisoned the chimera of the old Angevin empire and the Plantagenet day-dreams of expansion. He recognized *faits accomplis* without too much useless protest. Mediation and the encouragement and preservation of a balance of power, not aggression or conquests, were his objectives, as befitted a realist who realized the limitations of his power. The influence he sought to wield was financial rather than military. In any event, the force of circumstances prevented him from making any disastrous interventions that he may have entertained, as indeed he did as regards Castile in his last years. On the whole, he maintained a substantial measure of non-commitment. When he did commit himself, he avoided committing himself too far, and continued to enjoy a large measure of freedom of manœuvre. The *parvenu* Tudor diplomatized himself into a position in which at one time or another Aragon and Castile, the Valois, and the Hapsburgs all sought his goodwill, and achieved or contemplated marriage alliances with his family. All of them learnt to forgo attempts to subvert him; all learnt to respect his strength; all preferred his goodwill to his hostility.

If it be true that England showed a greatness and a marked flowering of her spirit and genius in the course of the sixteenth century, such a development would have been inconceivable without the intermediation of Henry of Richmond's regime. Not for him were the vast egoisms of his son Henry nor the gloriations of his grand-daughter Elizabeth. But without his unspectacular statecraft their creative achievements would have had no roots. His steady purposefulness saved England from mediocrity. It was not the union of the Roses that mattered, symbolic enough though that was. What mattered most in the long run was the spadework without which the springs of national genius would not be freed. In the ultimate analysis, the quality of Henry VII was not that of a creator, but rather of a stabilizer, for lack of whom the ships of State are apt to founder. For that quality, he stands out pre-eminent among British monarchs.

APPENDICES

Appendix A

OWEN TUDOR AND
THE PRIVY COUNCIL
1437

The documents are printed in *Proceedings and ordinances of the Privy Council* (1834–7), V, 46–50, from B.M. MS. Cott. Cleopatra F. IV, fos 103b–105b. They are in English, not in Norman French as T. Artemus Jones (loc. cit. 103) unaccountably stated, and the 'translations' he provided were simply extended transcriptions, and the source is not pp. 6–19 of the *Proceedings*, but as above. What Jones called Nicolas's 'long footnote' is in fact a passage in the latter's Preface, xvi–xix.

The more important of the two documents is specifically dated 15 July in the fifteenth year of Henry VI, i.e. 1437, and is written in not very lucid style, with a good many lacunae and uncertain phrases, even though collated by Nicolas with another extant version (contained in the same MS. as above, loc. cit.).

A paraphrase of the contents of the two documents is needed in order to make sense of them. On 15 July 1437, the council met in the Chapel Chamber at Kennington. The king himself was not present, but those attending were Humphrey, duke of Gloucester, John, bishop of Bath and Wells, chancellor, John Kemp, archbishop of York, William Alnwick, bishop of Lincoln, Humphrey, earl of Stafford, Henry, earl of Northumberland, William de la Pole, earl of Suffolk, Walter, Lord Hungerford, John, Lord Tiptoft, Ralph, Lord Cromwell, treasurer, William Lyndwood, keeper of the Privy Seal, and William Philip. It was recalled that not long ago, soon after the death (i.e. 3 January) of Queen Catherine, the king's mother, with whom 'Oweyn Tidir dwelt', the king had desired Owen to come into his presence. Owen, however, had refused to do this unless on the king's behalf it were promised that he should 'freely come and freely go'. Henry VI had promised this, and had instructed the duke of Gloucester to inform Owen accordingly. The question was whether the arrest 'now late made' by the king's command was lawful and not derogatory to either the king or the duke. The conclusion reached was that the act was lawful, for the following reasons.

When the king's promise had been conveyed to Owen, then at Daventry, by Gloucester's emissary, one Miles Sculle, he refused to accept it because it was not in writing and declined to come to the king. He did, none the less, come to London and went straight into sanctuary at Westminster, where he remained for many days. Some people, however, out of 'friendship and fellowship', induced him to go to a tavern at Westminster Gate, and some time after that, he did come into the king's presence. He had told Henry VI that he understood that he, the king, had been 'heavily informed' about him and allegations made that he had offended and displeased the king. Owen had declared his innocence and affirmed that he had given no occasion for offence or displeasure, offered to answer anything that could be laid against him, and so submitted himself. Thereafter he had 'returned to Wales'.

In short, he had freely come and freely gone. But subsequently an arrest had been made, *at the suit of the party*, in prejudice of whose rights common law and statute the king's grant could not take effect unless the circumstances were covered by statutory exception, which was not so in the case. Owen could not have the advantages of the safe-conduct twice. The council, therefore, advised the king that the arrest was lawful, and Gloucester asked for and was granted a declaration under the Great Seal to that effect.

The second document takes us a little further, but not much. At the time when Owen returned to Wales, neither the king nor Gloucester, it is asserted, were aware of the malicious purpose and imagination of Owen that subsequently came to light. He was now 'in ward', and the lords would have much to answer for 'if they now advised the king to release him, and any rebellion, murmur, or inconvenience should arise'. Further, the 'disposition of Wales' should be declared to the king.

For what reason, then, Owen was arrested shortly before 15 July 1437, is not revealed. There is no clear evidence that his arrest was directly connected with his marriage to Queen Catherine, although knowledge of that event must have made him a marked man, and obviously had made the council very sensitive and nervous about his treatment. The only positive information we are given is that the arrest made was 'at the suit of the party'. This assertion strongly suggests that Owen was involved in private litigation, which would help to explain why it was that he was committed to Newgate. But who the 'party' was remains a mystery at present. If we knew the source of the £89 found on the priest captured with Owen after the escape from Newgate, we might obtain more light on the point. Doubtless Henry VI had summoned Owen into his presence because he wished to see his deceased mother's husband, whom he had most probably never met, but there is no evidence at all that the subsequent arrest was made because of the mere fact of the marriage. Nor is it hard to understand why the documents are evasive in referring specifically to any offence committed, and display such caution. Even the council would have been wary of recording allegations against the king's step-father.

HENRY OF RICHMOND'S COMPANIONS IN EXILE
1483–5

It does not appear to be possible to identify any of Henry's companions in exile before the autumn rising of 1483, except his uncle Jasper. After the rising, however, Polydore Vergil (op. cit. 200) specifically states that the following reached Brittany:

*Peter Courtenay, bishop of Exeter
Edward Courtenay, earl of Devonshire
*Thomas Grey, marquis of Dorset, and Thomas his son, a child
*John Bourchier
John Wells
*Edward Woodville
Robert Willoughby
Giles Daubeney
Thomas Arundel
John Cheyney and his two brothers (including *Humphrey)
William Barclay
William Brandon and his brother *Thomas
Richard Edgecombe
Evan Morgan (*Camb. Reg.*, 96)

Some of those who fled to Flanders at this time may well have reached Brittany in due course. Among these was John Morton, bishop of Ely (who apparently did not do so), and Christopher Urswick (who did do so, at least for a time).

*Those names marked with an asterisk are specifically mentioned as having been with Henry in Brittany or France, 1484–5, and in addition the following are mentioned:

Edward Poynings
John de Vere, earl of Oxford
James Blunt
Sir John Fortescue
Richard Fox

Appendix C

THE ATTAINDERS
OF JANUARY TO FEBRUARY
1484

The four acts of attainder passed in Richard III's parliament of January to February 1484 taken together attainted 104 named persons, convicted them of high treason, and forfeited their estates, including estates held by others to their use. The total included one duke, one marquis, two 'so-called' earls, one countess, three bishops, one baron, eighteen knights, twenty-six esquires, fifteen gentlemen, two merchants, one necromancer, six yeomen of the Crown, fourteen yeomen, and three persons not specifically designated, but apparently of the esquire or gentleman class. Of the 104 names one is repeated exactly and may be merely a repetitionary mistake, in which case the total is 103.

The first of the acts attainted all but five of the total; the second dealt with the three bishops; the third with Margaret Beaufort, countess of Richmond; the fourth with Walter Roberd.

The lists of names, of their places of habitation, and other descriptions, and the identification of the region with which their treason was associated, are of considerable interest and may be studied in more detail as follows: –

1 The first act (*R.P.*, VI, c. 3, 244–9)

   (a) The Rising at Brecon, 18 October. Six persons, including Henry, late duke of Buckingham, Henry, calling himself earl of Richmond, and Jasper, calling himself earl of Pembroke.

   (b) The Rising in Kent and Surrey, at Maidstone,[1] 18 October, Rochester, 20 October, Gravesend, 22 October, Guildford, 25 October, and elsewhere. Twenty-eight persons.

   (c) The Rising at Newbury, Berks., and elsewhere, 18 October. Fourteen persons.

   (d) The Rising at Salisbury and elsewhere, 18 October. Thirty-three persons.

   (e) The Rising at Exeter and elsewhere, 18 October. Eighteen persons.

2 The second act (ibid. c. 5, 250). Attainder of John Morton, bishop of Ely, Lionel Woodville, bishop of Salisbury, and Peter Courtenay, bishop of Exeter. Penalty restricted to forfeiture of all possessions temporal and feudal as from 18 October.

[1] Agnes Conway, 'The Maidstone sector of Buckingham's rebellion', *Arch. Cantiana*, XXXVII (1925), 97–119, gives some particulars of these risings and of the men attainted.

3 The third act (ibid. c. 6, 150–1). Margaret, countess of Richmond.

Margaret, countess of Richmond, mother to the king's great rebel and traitor, Henry, earl of Richmond, has conspired and committed high treason, especially by sending messages, writings and tokens to Henry, stirring him to come into the realm to make war; and has made *chevisancez* of great sums of money in the City of London and elsewhere to be employed in treason; and has conspired and imagined the destruction of the king and was asserting and assisting Henry, duke of Buckingham, in treason.

But the king, of his especial grace, remembering the good and faithful services that Thomas, Lord Stanley has done and intends to do to him, and for the good love and trust that the king has in him, and for his sake, remits and forbears the great punishment of attainder of the said countess that she deserves.

It is ordained and enacted that she shall be disabled in the law from having or inheriting any lands or name of estate or dignity, and shall forfeit all estates whatsoever, which shall be to Thomas Lord Stanley for the term of his life and thereafter to the king and his heirs. Any estates she has or are held to her use, of the inheritance of Thomas Lord Stanley, shall be void.

4 The fourth act (ibid. c. 7, 251).

Walter Roberd of Cranbrooke, Kent, having levied war at Maidstone, 18 October, and having harboured Sir John Guildford and other traitors on 10 February.

THE PAPAL DISPENSATION
FOR THE MARRIAGE OF
HENRY VII AND ELIZABETH
1486

The publication of the *Calendar of entries in the papal registers relating to Great Britain and Ireland*, XIV, 1484–92 (1960) has made accessible documents of considerable interest. The papal bull of dispensation from Innocent VIII, dated 2 March 1486 addressed to Henry and Elizabeth, rehearsed their recent petition, read before him and the cardinals in consistory, which had stated that, in order to end the dissensions which had prevailed between their ancestors of their respective houses and families of Lancaster and York, they desired to contract marriage, and have been entreated by the prelates, nobles, magnates, and people of the realm to do so, but inasmuch as they were related in the fourth and fifth degrees of kindred, and perhaps also in the fourth degree of affinity, they cannot do so without apostolic dispensation which was now granted.

On 27 March, a further bull was issued, confirming the dispensation for the marriage to be contracted or already contracted in virtue of any other dispensation obtained from the apostolic see or legates having the requisite faculty, confirming the legitimacy of any children of the marriage, and also the declaration of parliament concerning the king's title and of his heirs. Further, the pope now inhibited all the inhabitants of the realm from stirring up fresh disturbances in the matter of the right of succession, under pain of *ipso facto* excommunication and the greater anathema. In addition, it was decreed that should Elizabeth predecease the king without offspring by him surviving, then his offspring by any other lawful wife should succeed (loc. cit. 1–2).

On 23 July 1486 a decree was issued setting out, at King Henry's and Queen Elizabeth's petition, a notarial copy of the process before James, bishop of Imola, apostolic nuncio with power of a legate *de latere*, in regard to the dispensation granted. The lengthy instructions included in this exemplification disclose that on 16 January Robert Morton, archdeacon of Winchester, keeper of the Rolls of Chancery, later bishop of Worcester, and John de Giglis, doctor of both laws, appeared before Bishop James, as proctors for King Henry, and Richard Hill, dean of the Chapel Royal, and David William, doctor of decrees, for Elizabeth, who laid before the bishop the petition of the parties.

The bishop-legate having received the petition, judicially sitting, at once committed to John, bishop of Worcester, and Thomas, bishop of London, power to examine the witnesses specified by the petitioners, which was done in the presence of the notaries public, who published their depositions and gave copies to the parties. Each of the witnesses was required to state his age, how long he had known either of the parties, what he knew of their intentions to marry, and to outline their respective pedigrees, so far as they were acquainted with them. The witnesses chosen and some of their testimony offer points of interest. The witnesses were Thomas, earl of Derby, William, earl of Nottingham, John Weston, prior of St John of Jerusalem, Sir Richard Croft, Christopher Urswick, archdeacon of North Wiltshire, Sir Richard Edgecombe, Sir William Knyvet, and Sir William Tyler.

After consideration of the testimonies, and rehearsal of the powers vested in him, Bishop John of Imola duly pronounced a decree of dispensation, which was later confirmed by Innocent VIII as above mentioned.

How much credence is to be attached to some of these testimonies as to length of acquaintance with the parties is a matter for speculation. Why did Thomas, earl of Derby, and Prior Weston state precisely that they had known Henry VII only since 24 August (*citra* . . . in the case of Lord Derby, *a* . . . in the case of Weston, *Vicesimum quartum diem Augusti*), a date two days *after* the battle of Bosworth? Not sufficient is known of Prior Weston's movements to be able to judge of the accuracy of his assertion, but Lord Derby's assertion is remarkable, and caused the late K. B. McFarlane (*E.H.R.*, LXXVIII (1963), 771–2) to raise doubts about Stanley's part in the events of 20–2 August. But it is impossible to believe, on this evidence, that Stanley's part at Atherstone and Bosworth was any different from that ascribed to him by Polydore Vergil and other chroniclers. He must certainly have met Henry VII on 22 August, and almost certainly two days earlier. He could therefore have testified to an earlier date. He may, it is true, have thought it prudent not to have revealed a date earlier than 22 August, but everyone concerned must have known that he met Henry on 22 August. In his testimony, therefore, he either deliberately chose a date two days later, or as the editor of the Papal Register surmises, a scribal error was made in the record, and 'quartum' written instead of 'secundum' (ibid. 17, fn.).

The other periods of alleged acquaintance with Henry VII, if not also with Elizabeth, can hardly be taken with precision, and cannot be used as exact calculations. One can hardly, for example, argue, as K. B. McFarlane suggested (ibid.), that because Sir Richard Edgecombe in January 1486 said he had known Henry for three years, therefore he visited Henry in Brittany before he fled there in November 1483. It seems reasonably clear that the witnesses were thinking (as after all they were bound to do) in terms, not of exact numbers of years, but of whether they knew him before the Readeption (1470–1), during the Readeption, and before his flight to Brittany, perhaps, whether in Brittany or France, and testified in general terms accordingly.

An English version of the dispensation was printed and published at an early date, perhaps by Caxton, and later by Walter de Machlinea; further editions were printed in 1494, 1495 and 1497, and its propaganda value was considerable. A text is edited by J. Payne Collier, in *Camden Misc.*, I (1847). See A. W. Pollard and G. R. Redgrave, *Short-title catalogue of books printed in England 1475–1640* (1926); cf. Anglo, loc. cit. 10.

Appendix E

HENRY VII'S BOOKS OF PAYMENTS

Five original books of payments drawn up by John Heron, treasurer of the Chamber, survive. The accounting years run from 1 October.

1. 1495–7, P.R.O. E 101/414/6, fos 1–91
2. 1497–9, P.R.O. E 101/414/16, fos 1–78
3. 1499–1502, P.R.O. E 101/415/3, fos 1–104
4. 1499–1505, B.M. Add. MS. 21480, fos 2–32
5. 1505–9, P.R.O. E 36/214, fos 7–351

All the books contain very large numbers of detailed items of expenditure, in great variety, totalled week by week, and usually quarterly, annually, and biennially. Each of these totals was initialled by Henry VII himself, except for the years 1505 to 1509, when none were so initialled. The reason why no such initialling occurs in the last book can only be conjectured, but obviously the omission may well have been connected with the king's decline in health.

Each volume contains several hundred folios, a number of which were left blank. But each, after the statements of payments, contains lists of landed revenues, recognizances, obligations, often an index of personal names, lists of acquittances, debts, the king's wards, liveries of lands, and miscellaneous memoranda. Many items in these lists were deleted or cancelled, and it seems that they were compiled for the king's personal information.

Craven Ord (1756–1832), the antiquary and at one time in the office of the king's remembrancer of the Exchequer, made extensive extracts from all these books, and others dating from 1491, not now known to exist. His extracts, very neatly and carefully done, showing all sums in Arabic numerals, are most valuable, and are now in B.M. Add. MS. 7099, wherein the payments occupy fos 1–96. The only substantial printing of these extracts from these accounts are mentioned in p. 306, fn. 1 above. Detailed investigation and analysis of the original books of payments, and more publication of the materials, are desirable objectives.

It is noticeable that in the only surviving book of payments of Henry VII's queen (P.R.O. E 36/210, now displayed in the P.R.O. museum), for the years 1502 to 1503, she habitually signed each page with her name 'Elizabeth' in full.

Appendix F

PORTRAITURE OF HENRY VII AND QUEEN ELIZABETH

HENRY VII

The only portrait known to exist of Henry VII painted in his lifetime is the one now in the National Portrait Gallery, London. This was painted in oil on panel in 1505 by Master Michel Sittow, by order of Herman Rinck, the agent of Maximilian I, to be sent to Margaret of Savoy (Plate 13a).[1]

At least one other portrait of Henry VII was, it seems certain, painted in his lifetime, c. 1500. The original of this, presumably the one listed in the inventory of Henry VIII, is not now known, but it was copied a number of times during the sixteenth century, and these showed the head turned either to the right or the left.[2] Holbein followed the former type in his 1537 Privy Chamber fresco.[3]

The only other full representation of Henry VII from the life is the polychrome bust of him made by Torrigiano, c. 1508–9,[4] now in the Victoria and Albert Museum, London (frontispiece). There can be little doubt that this bust is, in fact, the best depicture that now exists of Henry VII as he was towards the end of his life. It has a realism about it that seems to bring us as near as we shall ever get to Henry's appearance. The head of the tomb effigy in Westminster Abbey, also by Torrigiano, was not done until between 1512 and 1519, and resembles the bust but in a more glorified and less realistic style. (Plate 16c.)

Three other depictures of Henry VII are known to have been made during his lifetime. One is contained in a votive altar piece at Windsor showing Henry VII and Queen Elizabeth and their children adoring St George, made c. 1505–9, but too formalized to be of value as a portrait.[5] The second is contained in the painted glass transept window in Great Malvern Priory Church (Plate 14a). This remarkable window deserves careful study, but the depicture of the king therein appears to be too conventional to be regarded as portraiture.[6]

There is less doubt about the image of Henry VII which appeared on the silver testoon and groat included in his new coinage. The image of the king's

---

[1] Roy Strong, *Tudor and Jacobean portraits*, 2 vols (1969), I, 149–52; and II, Plates 290, 291; N.P.G. 416.

[2] At least six of the first type and three of the second are known, ibid. I, 151.

[3] ibid. I, 151, 154; II, Plates 305, 307.

[4] ibid. I, 151; II, Plate 292; J. Pope-Hennessy, *Italian Renaissance sculpture* (1958), 320–1.

[5] ibid. I, 151; II, Plate 297.   [6] *See* below, p. 335 ff.

profile to the right (Plate 10d) is clearly an attempt at genuine portraiture, and bears a marked resemblance to the Torrigiano representations. These profile types belong to the period 1500–9, but who was responsible for the portrayal of the king's profile is not known.[1]

Another representation of Henry VII, not made from the life, but of great interest both for its provenance and for its depicture of Henry VII at a markedly younger age than any of the above is the sketch by Jacques Leboucq de Valenciennes, Hainault Herald, now in the Library of Arras (Plate 5). This impressive sketch is believed to have been done in 1559–60, but from what source is unknown. We cannot therefore draw any conclusions as to its evidential value.[2]

Apart from depictures of the king from the life, the next nearest representation of his features one might have hoped to get is the death mask made of his head very shortly after his death. Unfortunately the well known wax death mask[3] attached to his funeral effigy in Westminster Abbey cannot, as it now is, be regarded as a true likeness (Plate 16a). Of the ten or more royal effigies in the Abbey collection, only two, those of Edward III and Henry VII, in fact have actual wax death masks instead of carved wooden heads, and but for the ravages of the centuries we should doubtless have had a fine and accurate presentation of Henry VII's head and face. The head that survives, apart from the crude plaster ears, is clearly a masterly piece of work by a craftsman of high calibre. But, most regrettably, the nose of the mask has been missing for a very long time and there is no record of what it looked like. It was not, as has sometimes been said, lost during the disastrous flooding of the Abbey Undercroft during an air raid in May 1941. It was certainly missing long before, as is obvious from the photograph of it published in 1907.[4] When it was lost no one can say, but when after the war the late R. P. Howgrave-Graham, then the assistant keeper of the Muniments, undertook with remarkable success the most formidable task of restoring the saturated, partly disintegrated effigies, he was confronted with the problem of what was to be done about supplying the mask of Henry VII with a nasal organ. Mr Howgrave-Graham himself has told us in detail[5] the technical difficulties he encountered and the meticulous care with which he sought to reproduce as nearly as possible the noses of Torrigiano's bust and tomb effigy of Henry. These two noses do indeed differ somewhat. The tomb bronze one is rather longer and slenderer than the bust. For technical

[1] For references, see p. 225 above.

[2] Strong, op. cit. I, 151; II, Plate 294; H. Bouchot, Les portraits aux crayons des 16e et 17e siècles (Paris, 1884).

[3] Strong, op. cit. I, 151; II, Plate 296.

[4] W. H. St John, 'On the funeral effigies of the kings and queens of England, with special reference to those in the Abbey Church of Westminster', Archaeologia, LX (1907), 517–70, and plates LXI and LXII. For the cost of the various items required for the interment, see ibid. 539–40. The cost of the 'pictour' or effigy was £6 12s 8d.

[5] R. P. Howgrave-Graham, 'The earlier royal funeral effigies: new light on portraiture in Westminster Abbey', prepared for publication by Martin Holmes, ibid. XCVIII (1961), 159–69, esp. 166–7, and plates LI and LII.

reasons Mr Howgrave-Graham could not exactly reproduce either example. But it is clear that the nose he was able to make is markedly different in character from that shown either in Sittow's portrait, or the pictures derived from the presumed original portrait, or the bust and tomb effigy, or the profile of the silver coinage. All these (except the tomb effigy) were done in Henry's lifetime, and all are markedly similar. We are bound to conclude that in fact Henry VII's nose was rather long and slender, not broad at the base nor rather bulbous and slightly snub as in the restored death mask. Whether or not the restoration of it resulted in a 'Welsh' face is entirely beside the point, for there is no reason at all why Henry VII should have 'looked like a Welshman'. His genetics were too variegated to justify any such assumption, even if one could be sure what 'Welsh face' looks like.[1]

QUEEN ELIZABETH

No original portrait of Queen Elizabeth (of York) survives. All extant portraits derive from an original which has not been located but which was probably the one listed in the 1542 and 1547 inventories of Henry VIII and Edward VI. This was the one used by Holbein for the 1537 Privy Chamber fresco-group. The National Portrait Gallery picture (No. 311) is a version by an unknown artist of this original, probably late sixteenth century in date[2] (Plate 13b).

Queen Elizabeth also had her funeral effigy (Plate 16b), the arrangements for which are documented more fully than usual. The head carved in wood also needed partial nasal restoration, for which less technical difficulty was experienced. The hair now attached is however entirely modern and cannot be regarded as characteristic of Elizabeth as she actually was.[3] It is assumed, without any particular evidence, that Torrigiano may have used the original effigy for his bronze tomb effigy of her (Plate 16c).

THE TRANSEPT WINDOW OF GREAT MALVERN PRIORY CHURCH

This magnificent window, depicting with a splendid wealth of colour and detail the Joys of Mary, contained at the bottom in the place usually reserved for the commemoration of the donors pictures of Sir Thomas Lovell (now very fragmentary), Sir John Savage (now lost except for a tabard bearing his arms), Sir Reginald Bray, Prince Arthur, Queen Elizabeth (now very fragmentary), and Henry VII. The pictures of the king, the prince, and Bray are

---

[1] The fine hair – bright red and grey – which was attached to the mask, Mr Howgrave-Graham thought might perhaps be Henry's own. But this is unlikely, since Polydore Vergil (ed. Hay, 144–5) describes his hair as 'thin and white'. Vergil also describes his eyes as small and blue (*ceruleos*) or alternatively, bluish-grey (*glaucis*) (ibid. 144). Strong (op. cit. 149) describes the N.P.G. portrait by Sittow as showing dark grey eyes with brown hair streaked with grey.

[2] Strong, op. cit. I, 98; II, Plate 182.

[3] St John Hope and Howgrave-Graham, loc. cit., respectively, 546, 550, and Plate LX; and 164–5 and Plates XLIX (d) and (e), and L.

in excellent (restored) condition.[1] Underneath these pictures runs the legend (partially restored): *Orate pro bono statu nobillissimi Et: excellentissimi regis Henrici septimi Et: Elisabethe regine ac domini Arturis: principis filii eorundem nec non: Predilectissime consortis sue: Et suorum trium militum predictorum.*[2]

The picture of Henry VII, as restored in 1917, shows him 'kneeling at a carved desk covered with a white cloth and hung with red, on which is an open book with a gold sceptre lying on it. Behind it is a handsome gold, jewelled, and crested canopy.'[3]

No evidence has so far come to light to prove that Henry VII himself was the donor of this window. We are dependent at present upon the fact that there is the row of six pictures in the line usually reserved for 'donors'. All or some or one of these might in theory have been responsible. But if the Sir John Savage depicted is the person greatly favoured by Henry VII, as is almost certain, he was killed at the siege of Boulogne in 1492. He at any rate can hardly himself have been a donor.[4] It is furthermore unlikely that the king himself would have thought it proper to commemorate Lovell and Bray, important councillors and officials as they were, along with his queen and son in a church window. Far more likely that Lovell and Bray initiated

[1] G. McN. Rushforth, *Medieval Christian imagery as illustrated by the painted windows of Great Malvern Priory Church* (1936), has a most exhaustive and scholarly account, esp. 373 ff. L. A. Hamand, *The ancient windows of Great Malvern Priory Church* (1947), offers a useful short survey, esp. 69–81.

[2] 'Pray for the good estate of the most noble and most excellent King Henry the seventh and of Elizabeth Queen and of the lord Prince Arthur their son and also of his most well-beloved consort and of their three knights aforesaid.'

[3] Hamand, op. cit. 80 (Plate 14a).

[4] Confusion arises, as in Rushforth (op. cit. 373), because this Sir John's father, also Sir John Savage, of Clifton, Cheshire, lived until 1495 and it was he who married Katherine Stanley, sister of Thomas Lord Stanley, earl of Derby, Henry VII's stepfather. Their nine sons included the Sir John who presumably was the subject of the picture. This Sir John, who also had a son John (eventually knighted but not much before 1504), climbed in the service of Edward IV and Richard III. He was made a knight of the Bath in 1465, appointed king's carver, and among other preferments was granted in 1478 £40 a year from lands known as the 'Salisbury' lands, during the minority of Edward, earl of Warwick. In 1482 he was appointed to survey lands, including the chace of Malvern, which were the inheritance of Warwick from his mother Isobel Neville. Further grants were given him by Richard III. But he deserted the Yorkists, joined Henry of Richmond in Wales and fought at Bosworth, reputedly commanding the left wing. Henry VII took him into great favour. No time was lost in making major grants to him 'in consideration of his services with a multitude of his brothers, kinsmen, servants, and friends at great costs in the conflict and battle against the king's great adversary Richard III, eminent in arms as in character and counsel' (*C.P.R.*, I, 101–2). He had already been granted for life the office of master of the game of Malvern Chace (ibid. 9), and soon among many of the appointments he and his son John were granted in survivorship was the office of sheriff of Worcester (ibid. I, 204). He became one of the king's more intimate councillors and was made K.G. in 1488. His widow's name was Margaret (ibid. II, 178). Among his brothers was Thomas Savage who became eventually archbishop of York and a very influential councillor.

the project, doubtless with the king's permission and approval, as Rushforth suggested. Of the two, Sir Reginald Bray, with his well known interest in architecture, his part in the design of St George's chapel, Windsor, and Henry VII's chapel in Westminster Abbey, and his close connections with Malvern and his other benefactions to the priory church, is by far the most likely instigator, though not necessarily the sole donor. Lovell also had his connections with Malvern.[1]

We can be certain that the window was completed before the death of Prince Arthur on 2 April 1502 – he was buried in Worcester Cathedral – and therefore also before the death of Queen Elizabeth on 11 February 1503. But we cannot be so confident of the date of its initiation. We cannot jump to the conclusion that because the bidding prayer refers to the prince's consort therefore it was not initiated before their wedding on 14 November 1501, though it might have been completed after that date. It is surely inconceivable that the great window could possibly have been made between 14 November 1501 and 2 April 1502. Nor is there any need for such an improbable supposition. In fact the couple were married by proxy three times before the final wedding, for the first time on 19 May 1499, and for the third time in November 1500. At any time after 19 May 1499 the window might have been started and the legend completed in its present form, or the legend itself added at any time before the prince's death. The date of the window may therefore be put at any time between 19 May 1499 and 2 April 1502, but hardly so far back as before the death of Sir John Savage in October 1492.

Indeed late 1499 or early 1500 is a highly likely date for other reasons. The manor of Malvern Chace had been part of the Neville family estates which formed part of the inheritance of Edward, earl of Warwick. During the minority of the earl his lands had been in the hands of the Crown. As a consequence of the attainder and execution of Warwick on 28 November 1499, Henry VII found himself lord of the manor of Malvern Chace. But Richard, duke of Gloucester, had married Ann Neville, Warwick's mother's sister, and therefore he had an interest in part of the Neville lands.

The great west window of the priory church had been donated by Richard. His arms and those of his wife, as well as those of Edward IV's son and heir Edward, the future Edward V, appear on windows within the church. A powerful motive, therefore, for the provision of a splendid piece of Tudor commemorative piety was manifest from late 1499, whether or not Henry VII personally instigated it or contributed to it.

[1] Bray was born near Worcester and both he and Lovell in their official capacities had business with the lands of which Malvern formed a part. He too is reputed to have built the north transept itself. Rushforth, op. cit. 373 ff; cf. *D.N.B.*; and Wedgwood, *History of parliament*, Register, 104–5, 555–6. This work lists Sir John Savage, junior (d. 1527) as being the brother of the Sir John (d. 1492), whereas he was his son (*C.P.R.*, I, 204, 454; II, 62; *Materials*, II, 245).

H — M

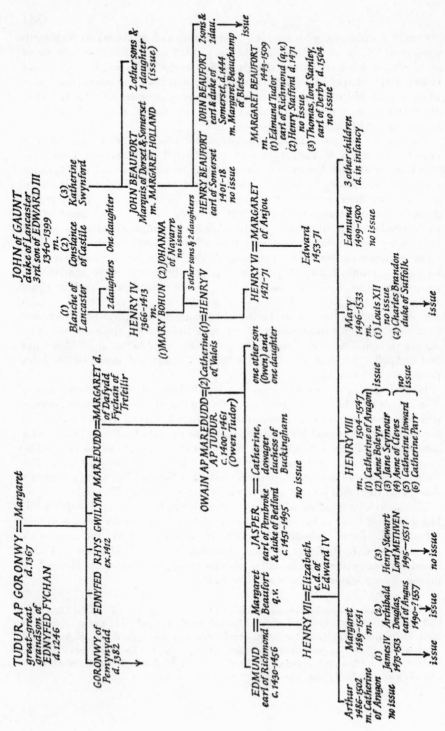

Select Pedigrees: I The Descent and Descendants of Henry VII

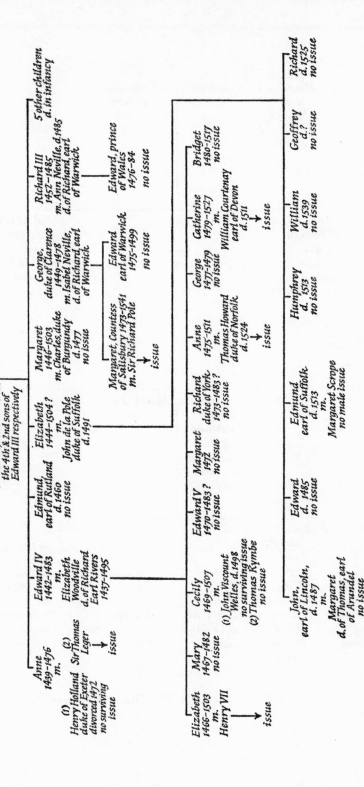

Select Pedigrees: II The House of York

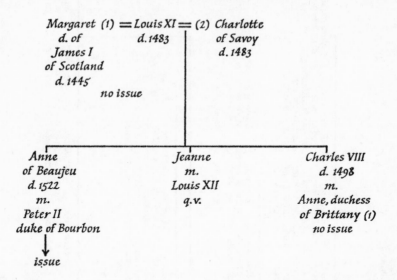

Margaret (1) ═ Louis XI ═ (2) Charlotte
d. of   d. 1483   of Savoy
James I   d. 1483
of Scotland
d. 1445
                    no issue

Anne   Jeanne   Charles VIII
of Beaujeu   m.   d. 1498
d. 1522   Louis XII   m.
m.   q.v.   Anne, duchess
Peter II   of Brittany (1)
duke of Bourbon   no issue

issue

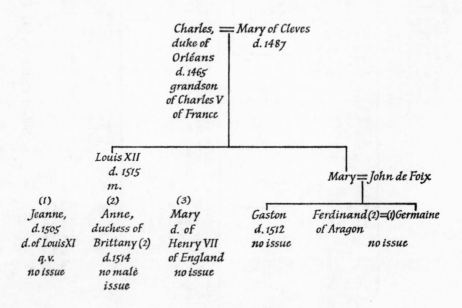

Charles, ═ Mary of Cleves
duke of   d. 1487
Orléans
d. 1465
grandson
of Charles V
of France

                    Louis XII
                    d. 1515
                    m.
(1)   (2)   (3)   Mary ═ John de Foix
Jeanne,   Anne,   Mary
d. 1505   duchess of   d. of   Gaston   Ferdinand (2)═(1) Germaine
d. of Louis XI   Brittany (2)   Henry VII   d. 1512   of Aragon
q.v.   d. 1514   of England   no issue   no issue
no issue   no male   no issue
                    issue

Select Pedigrees: III The House of Valois

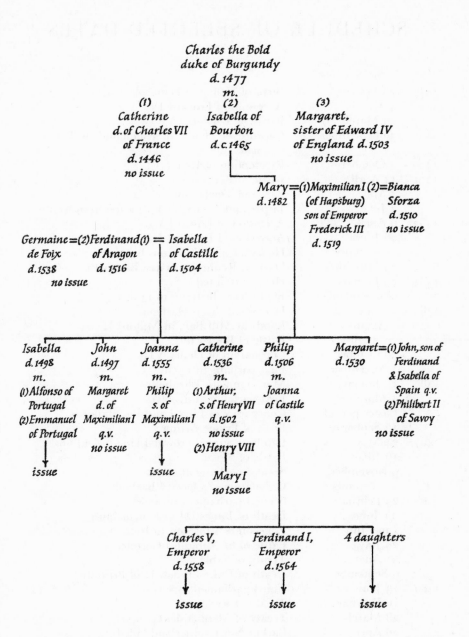

**Charles the Bold
duke of Burgundy
d. 1477**
m.

(1)
Catherine
d. of Charles VII
of France
d. 1446
no issue

(2)
Isabella of
Bourbon
d. c. 1465

(3)
Margaret,
sister of Edward IV
of England d. 1503
no issue

Mary = (1) Maximilian I (2) = Bianca
d. 1482   (of Hapsburg)   Sforza
  son of Emperor   d. 1510
  Frederick III   no issue
  d. 1519

Germaine = (2) Ferdinand (1) = Isabella
de Foix   of Aragon   of Castille
d. 1538   d. 1516   d. 1504
   no issue

Isabella
d. 1498
m.
(1) Alfonso of
Portugal
(2) Emmanuel
of Portugal

↓
issue

John
d. 1497
m.
Margaret
d. of
Maximilian I
q.v.
no issue

Joanna
d. 1555
m.
Philip
s. of
Maximilian I
q.v.

↓
issue

Catherine
d. 1536
m.
(1) Arthur,
s. of Henry VII
d. 1502
no issue
(2) Henry VIII

Mary I
no issue

Philip
d. 1506
m.
Joanna
of Castile
q.v.

Margaret = (1) John, son of
d. 1530   Ferdinand
  & Isabella of
  Spain q.v.
  (2) Philibert II
  of Savoy
  no issue

Charles V,
Emperor
d. 1558

↓
issue

Ferdinand I,
Emperor
d. 1564

↓
issue

4 daughters

↓
issue

Select Pedigrees: IV The Houses of Burgundy, Hapsburg, and Spain

SCHEDULE OF SELECTED DATES

1457	28 January	Birth of Henry in Pembroke Castle
1461	4 March	Accession of Edward IV
	29 March	Battle of Towton
	30 September	Capture of Henry of Richmond at Pembroke Castle
1470	3 October	Readeption of Henry VI
1471	14 April	Battle of Barnet
	4 May	Battle of Tewkesbury
	2 June	Jasper and Henry Tudor escape from Tenby
1483	9 April	Accession of Edward V
	26 June	Accession of Richard III
	12 October	Henry's expedition from Brittany
	25 December	Oath at Rennes to marry Elizabeth
1484	25 January	Henry attainted
	late September	Flight from Brittany to France
1485	1 August	Henry sails from Harfleur
	7 August	Lands at Mill Bay, in Milford Haven
	22 August	Battle of Bosworth
	30 October	Coronation of Henry VII
	7 November	First parliament opens
1486	18 January	Marriage with Elizabeth
	4 March	First parliament dissolves
	Easter period	Conspiracy of Lovell and the Staffords
	19 September	Birth of Prince Arthur
1487	24 May	Lambert Simnel crowned king in Dublin
	16 June	Battle of Stoke
	9 November	Second parliament opens
	25 November	Coronation of Queen Elizabeth
1488	23 February	Second parliament dissolves
	11 June	Death of James III at Sauchieburn
	June–July	Edgecombe's mission to Ireland
	28 July	Battle of St Aubin du Cormier
	31 August	Treaty of Sablé
	9 September	Death of Duke Francis II of Brittany
1489	13 January	Third parliament opens
	10 February	Treaty of Redon
	28 March	Treaty of Medina del Campo
	28 April	Earl of Northumberland killed
	13 June	Battle of Dixmude
	29 November	Birth of Princess Margaret
1490	27 February	Third parliament dissolves

1491	17 October	Fourth parliament opens
	November	Warbeck appears in Ireland
	6 December	Marriage of Charles VIII and Anne of Brittany
1492	5 March	Fourth parliament dissolves
	October	Henry VII invades France
	18 October	Siege of Boulogne
	3 November	Treaty of Étaples
		Warbeck in France and Burgundy
1493	November	Warbeck with Maximilian in Vienna
1494	September	Charles VIII invades Italy
	13 October	Sir Edward Poynings lands in Ireland
	1 December	Parliament at Drogheda
1495	16 February	Execution of Sir William Stanley
	27 February	Arrest of the earl of Kildare
	20 March	League of Venice
	July	Charles VIII flees from Italy
	23 July–3 August	Warbeck's failure in Kent
	14 October	Fifth parliament opens
	November	Warbeck arrives in Scotland
1496	January	Sir Edward Poynings leaves Ireland
	February	The *Magnus Intercursus* with the Netherlands
	5 March	Letters patent to John Cabot
	March	Birth of Princess Mary
	6 August	Earl of Kildare reappointed deputy
	September	Invasion by the Scots
	1 October	Treaty for marriage of Prince Arthur and Catherine of Aragon
	21 December	Fifth parliament dissolves
1497	16 January	Sixth parliament opens
	?13 March	Sixth parliament dissolves
	May	Cornish rebellion
	17 June	Battle of Blackheath
	July	Warbeck leaves Scotland
	7 September	Warbeck lands in Cornwall
	30 September	Treaty of Ayton
	5 October	Surrender and confession of Warbeck
1498	3 February	Second letter patent to John Cabot
1499	May	First proxy marriage of Prince Arthur and Catherine of Aragon
		Edmund, earl of Suffolk flees to Calais
	September	Louis XII invades Italy
	16 November	Execution of Warbeck
	29 November	Execution of Warwick
1500	9 June	Meeting of Henry VII and the Archduke Philip at Calais
	19 June	Death of Prince Edmund
	15 September	Death of Cardinal Morton

1501	July	Second flight of Edmund, earl of Suffolk
	14 November	Marriage of Prince Arthur and Catherine of Aragon
1502	2 April	Death of Prince Arthur
	6 May	Execution of Sir John Tyrell
1503	11 February	Death of Queen Elizabeth
	23 June	Betrothal of Prince Henry and Catherine of Aragon
	8 August	Marriage of Princess Margaret and James IV
1504	25 January	Seventh parliament opens
	30 March	Seventh parliament dissolves
	26 November	Death of Isabella of Castile
1505	October	Treaty of Blois
1506	12 January	Landing of Archduke Philip at Melcombe Regis
	9 February	Treaty of Windsor
	18 March	Marriage of Ferdinand of Aragon and Germaine de Foix
	23 April	Archduke Philip departs
	24 April	Edmund, earl of Suffolk imprisoned in the Tower of London
	30 April	*Intercursus Malus*
	25 September	Death of the Archduke Philip
1507	21 December	Betrothal of Princess Mary and Archduke Charles
1508	10 December	League of Cambrai
1509	21 April	Death of Henry VII

SELECT BIBLIOGRAPHY

The following list includes only printed works cited or mentioned in the text, footnotes, or appendices of this book. For more extensive bibliographies, see *Bibliography of British history, Tudor period, 1485–1603*, ed. Conyers Read, 2nd ed. (1959); *Tudor England, 1485–1603*, ed. Mortimer Levine (1968); and *A bibliography of the history of Wales*, 2nd ed. (1962). Some of the standard histories listed below, e.g. those of J. D. Mackie and Wilhelm Busch, contain substantial bibliographical sections; for specialized bibliographies, see the more important monographs. Unless otherwise stated the works below were published in Great Britain.

A. ORIGINAL SOURCES

André, Bernard, *Vita Henrici VII*
——, *Annales Henrici VII*
——, *Les douze triomphes de Henry VII*, see *Memorials*, below
Bentley, S. (ed.), *Excerpta historica* (1831)
Bernier, A. (ed.), *Procès-verbaux des séances du Conseil de Régence du roi Charles VIII* (Paris, 1836)
Calendar of Charter Rolls, VI, *1427–1516* (1927)
Calendar of Close Rolls, Henry VI, III, *1435–41* (1937)
——, *Edward IV–Richard III, 1476–85* (1954)
——, *Henry VII*, I, *1485–1500* (1954); II, *1500–9* (1963)
Calendar of papal registers relating to Great Britain and Ireland, XIV, *1484–92* (1960)
Calendar of Patent Rolls, Henry VI, III, *1436–41* (1907)
——, *Edward IV, 1461–7* (1897)
——, *Edward IV–Richard III, 1476–85* (1901)
——, *Henry VII*, I (1956); II (1963)
Calendar of state papers, Milan, I, *1385–1618*, ed. A. B. Hinds (1913)
——, *Spanish*, I, *Henry VII, 1485–1559*, ed. G. A. Bergenroth (1862); Supplement to I and II, ed. G. A. Bergenroth (1868)
——, *Venetian*, I, *1202–1509*, ed. R. Brown (1864)
Cambrian register (1796)
Chrimes, S. B., and Brown, A. L. (eds), *Select documents of English constitutional history, 1307–1485* (1961)
Chronicles of London, ed. C. L. Kingsford (1905)
Collier, J. Payne (ed.), *Bull of Pope Innocent VIII on the marriage of Henry VII with Elizabeth of York, Camden Misc.* I (1847)
Commynes, Philip de, *Mémoires*, ed. B. de Mandrot, 2 vols (Paris, 1901–3)
Cotton, Sir Robert (ed.), *An exact abridgement of (parliamentary) records in the Tower of London* (1657)

Croyland chronicle, continuations of, ed. Fulman, Gale's collection, *Rerum Anglicorum scriptores* (1684)

——, ed. H. T. Riley, *Ingulph's chronicle* (1854)

Dudley, E., *The tree of the commonwealth*, ed. D. M. Brodie (1948)

Egidi, Pietro (ed.), *Fonti per la Storia d'Italia*, Inst. Storia Italiana, 45 (1914)

Ellis, Sir H. (ed.), *Original letters illustrative of English history, etc.*, 11 vols (1824–46)

——, *The pilgrimage of Sir R. Guylforde to the Holy Land*, Cam. Soc. LI (1851)

Erasmus of Rotterdam, Desiderius, *Opus epistolarum*, ed. P. S. Allen, etc., 12 vols (1906–58)

Fisher, John, *English works*, ed. J. E. B. Mayor, E.E.T.S., ext. ser. XXVII (1886), repr. (1935)

Fortescue, Sir John, *De laudibus legum Anglie*, ed. S. B. Chrimes (1942)

——, *The governance of England*, ed. C. Plummer (1885)

Fuensalida, Gutierre Gomez de, *Correspondencia de*, ed. duke of Berwick and Alba (Madrid, 1907)

Gairdner, J. (ed.), *The historical collections of a London citizen in the fifteenth century*, Camden Soc., n.s. XVII (1876)

Giles, J. A. (ed.), *Incerti scriptoris chronicon de regnis . . . Henrici IV, Henrici V, et Henrici VI* (1848)

Gregory's chronicle, *see* Gairdner, J., *Historical collections*

Grose, F., and Astle, T., *Antiquarian repertory* (1808)

Hall, E., *Chronicle*, ed. H. Ellis (1809)

Halliwell-Phillips, J. O. (ed.), *Letters of the kings of England*, 2 vols (1846–8)

Harrison, C. J. (ed.), 'The petition of Edmund Dudley', *E.H.R.*, LXXXVII (1972).

Henry VII, *The will of*, ed. T. Astle (1775)

Howth, Book of, ed. J. S. Brewer and W. Bullen, *Calendar of the Carew MSS*, 6 vols (1867–73), V

Leland, John, *De rebus Brittanicus collectanea*, ed. T. Hearne, 6 vols (1715)

——, *Itinerary*, ed. L. T. Smith, 5 vols (1906–8)

Letters and papers illustrative of the reigns of Richard III and Henry VII, ed. J. Gairdner, 2 vols (Rolls Series, 1861–3)

London, The Great Chronicle of, ed. A. H. Thomas and I. D. Thornley (1938)

Mancini, Dominic, *De occupatione regni Anglie per Ricardum Tercium libellus*, ed. C. A. J. Armstrong (1936), 2nd ed. (1969)

Materials for a history of the reign of Henry VII, ed. William Campbell, 2 vols (Rolls Series, 1873–7)

Memorials of King Henry VII, ed. J. Gairdner (Rolls Series, 1858)

Morice, Dom Hyacinthe (ed.), *Mémoires pour servir de preuves à l'histoire ecclesiastique et civile de Bretagne* (Paris, 1746)

Myers, A. R. (ed.), *English historical documents*, IV, *1327–1485* (1969)

Nicolas, Sir H., and Tyrrell, E. (eds), *Chronicle of London* (1827)

Paston Letters, ed. J. Gairdner, 3 vols (1874–5)

Plumpton correspondence, ed. T. Stapleton, Cam. Soc., 4 (1839)

Pollard, A. F. (ed.), *The reign of Henry VII from contemporary sources*, 3 vols (1913), repr. (New York, 1967)

Proceedings and ordinances of the Privy Council, ed. Sir H. Nicolas, 7 vols (Record Comm., 1834–7)

Pugh, T. B., and Robinson, W. R. B. (eds), *Tudor Wales 1485–1536: select documents* (1972)

Raine, Angelo (ed.), *York civic records*, II, Yorks. Arch. Soc., Record Series, CIII (1941)

Red Paper Book of Colchester, ed. W. Gurney Benham (1902)

Register of the Great Seal of Scotland, 9 vols (1882–1912)

Registrum Thome Bourgchier, ed. F. R. H. du Boulay, Cant. and York Soc LIV (1957)

Rotuli parliamentorum, 7 vols (Record Comm., 1767–1832)

Rotuli scaccarii regum Scotorum, 23 vols (1878–1908)

Rymer, T. (ed.), *Foedera, conventiones, etc.*, 20 vols (1704–35)

Select cases in Chancery, 1364–1471, ed. W. P. Baildon, S.S., X (1896)

Select cases in the council of Henry VII, ed. C. G. Bayne and W. H. Dunham, S.S., 75 (1964)

Select cases in the court of Requests, 1497–1569, ed. I. S. Leadam, S.S., 12 (1898)

Select cases in the Exchequer Chamber before all the justices of England, ed. M. Hemmant, 2 vols, S.S., 51 (1933); 64 (1943)

Select cases before the King's Council in the Star Chamber, ed. I. S. Leadam, S.S., XVI (1963)

Statutes of the realm, 11 vols (Record Comm., 1810–28)

Statutes at large (Ireland), I (1786)

Treasurer's accounts (Compota thesauriorum regum Scotorum), 11 vols (1877–1916)

Ulster, annals of, ed. W. M. Hennesey and B. MacCarthy, 4 vols (1888–1901)

Vergil, Polydore, *Three books of English history*, ed. Sir Henry Ellis, Camden Soc., o.s. XXIX (1844)

——, *Anglica historia*, ed. D. Hay (ibid., n.s., LXXIV (1950)

Wickham Legg, L. G. (ed.), *English coronation records* (1901)

Williams, C. H. (ed.), *English historical documents*, V, *1485–1588* (1967)

Year books or *Les reports des cases*, 10 vols (1679)

B. SECONDARY AUTHORITIES

Anglo, S., 'The foundation of the Tudor dynasty', *Guildhall Miscellanea*, II (1960)

——, 'The British history in early Tudor propaganda', *B.J.R.L.*, 44 (1961)

——, *Spectacle, pageantry, and early Tudor policy* (1969)

——, *Machiavelli: a dissection* (1969)

Archbold, W. A. J., 'Sir William Stanley and Perkin Warbeck', *E.H.R.*, XIV (1899)

Avery, Margaret E., 'The history of the equitable jurisdiction of Chancery before 1460', *B.I.H.R.*, XLII (1969)

Bacon, Sir Francis, Viscount St Alban, *History of the reign of Henry VII* (1622); ed. Spedding, etc., *Works*, VI, new ed. (1878); ed. J. R. Lumby (1885); ed. R. Lockyer (1971)

Baldwin, J. F., *The King's Council in England during the Middle Ages* (1913)

Barbour, W. T., *The history of contract in early English equity* (1914)

Barton, J. L., 'The medieval use', *L.Q.R.*, 81 (1965)

Bean, J. M. W., *The decline of English feudalism, 1215–1540* (1968)

Blatcher, Marjorie, 'The working of the court of King's Bench in the fifteenth century', unpublished Ph.D. thesis (London, 1936); summary thereof, in *B.I.H.R.*, XIV (1937)

Bouchot, H., *Les portraits aux crayons des 16iéme et 17iéme siécles* (Paris, 1884)

Bridge, J. S. C., *A history of France from the death of Louis XI*, 5 vols (1921–36)

Brodie, D. M., 'Edmund Dudley, minister of Henry VII', *T.R.H.S.*, 4th ser., XV (1932)

Brooke, G. C., *English coins*, 3rd ed. (1950)

Brooke, R., *Visits to fields of battles in England in the fifteenth century* (1857)

Brooks, F. W., *The Council of the North* (1953), rev. ed. (1966)

Brown, R. Allen, Colvin, H. M., and Taylor, A. J., *History of the King's Works*, 3 vols (1963)

Burnet, G., *History of the reformation of the Church of England*, ed. N. Pocock, 7 vols (1865)

Burwash, D., *English merchant shipping, 1460–1540* (1947), repr. (1969)

Busch, Wilhelm, *England unter den Tudors*, I, *König Heinrich VII* (Stuttgart, 1892), Eng. trans. A. M. Todd, *England under the Tudors*, I, *Henry VII* (London, 1895), repr. (New York, 1965)

Carr, A. D., 'Welshmen and the Hundred Years War', *W.H.R.*, 4 (1961)

Carus-Wilson, E. M., 'The origins and early development of the Merchant Adventurers' organization', *Econ.H.R.*, IV (1933), repr. in *Mediaeval Merchant Venturers*, 2nd ed. (1967)

——, and Coleman, Olive, *England's export trade, 1275–1547* (1963)

Chrimes, S. B., *English constitutional ideas in the fifteenth century* (1936), repr. (New York, 1965)

——, 'The landing place of Henry of Richmond, 1485', *W.H.R.*, 2 (1964)

——, *An introduction to the administrative history of mediaeval England*, 3rd ed. (1966)

——, *Lancastrians, Yorkists, and Henry VII*, 2nd ed. (1966)

——, 'Sir Roland de Veleville', *W.H.R.*, 3 (1967)

——, *Edward I's policy for Wales* (Nat. Museum of Wales, 1969)

Clark, D. S. T., 'Francis Bacon: the study of history and the science of man', unpublished Ph.D. thesis (Cambridge, 1970)

Cokayne, G. E. (ed.), *Complete peerage of England, etc.*, 12 vols, rev. V. Gibbs, etc. (1910–59)

Coke, Sir Edward, *Institutes of the laws of England* (1628–44)

Conway, Agnes, 'The Maidstone sector of Buckingham's rebellion', *Arch. Cantiana*, XXXVII (1925)

——, *Henry VII's relations with Scotland and Ireland, 1485–98* (1932)

Cooper, J. P., 'Henry VII's last years reconsidered', *H.J.*, II (1959)

Cosgrove, Art, 'The Gaelic resurgence and the Geraldine supremacy', *The Course of Irish History*, ed. T. W. Moody and F. X. Marten (Cork, 1967)

Curtis, E., *A history of mediaeval Ireland* (1923)

Cust, L., 'Note on effigy of Sir Thomas Lovell', *Procs. Soc. of Antiquaries*, 2nd ser. XVIII, ii (1901)

Dickens, A. G., *The English Reformation* (1964)

Dietz, F. G., *English government finance, 1485–1558* (Illinois, 1920), 2nd ed. (1964)

Du Boulay, F. R. H., 'The fifteenth century', *The English church and the papacy in the Middle Ages*, ed. C. H. Lawrence (1965)

Dunham, W. H., 'The Ellesmere extracts from the "Acta Consilii" of Henry VIII', *E.H.R.*, LVIII (1943)

——, 'Members of Henry VIII's whole council', ibid. LIX (1944)

——, *Lord Hastings's indentured retainers, 1461–83* (Yale, 1955)

Dupuy, A., *Histoire de la réunion de la Bretagne à la France* (Paris, 1880)

Edwards, Sir J. G., *The principality of Wales, 1267–1967* (Caernarvonshire Hist. Soc., 1969)

Edwards, R. Dudley, and Moody, T. W., 'The history of Poynings's Law', Pt I, 1494–1615, *Irish Hist. Soc.*, II (1940–1)

Elton, G. R., *The Tudor revolution in government* (1953)

——, *England under the Tudors* (1955)

——, 'Henry VII: rapacity and remorse', *H.J.*, I (1958)

——, *The Tudor constitution* (1960)

——, 'State planning in early Tudor England', *Econ. H.R.*, 2nd ser. XIII (1961)

——, 'Henry VII: a restatement', *H.J.*, IV (1961)

——, 'Why the history of the early Tudor council remains unwritten', *Annali della Fondazione italiana per la storia amministrativa*, I (Milan, 1964)

——, 'The problems and significance of administrative history in the Tudor period', *Journal of British Studies*, IV (1965)

——, *The sources of history, England, 1200–1640* (1969)

Emden, A. B., *Biographical register of the University of Oxford to 1500*, 3 vols (1957–9)

——, *Biographical register of the University of Cambridge to 1500* (1963)

Evans, F. M. G., *The Principal Secretary of State* (1932)

Evans, H. T., *Wales and the Wars of the Roses* (1915)

Foss, E., *The judges of England*, 9 vols (1848–69)

Gairdner, J., *Henry VII* (1889)

——, 'The battle of Bosworth', *Archaeologia*, 2nd ser. V (1897)

——, *History of the life and reign of Richard III*, rev. ed. (1898)

Goldingham, C. S., 'The navy under Henry VII', *E.H.R.*, XXXIII (1918)

Gras, N. S. B., *The early English customs system* (Harvard, 1918)

Gray, H. L., *The influence of the commons on early legislation* (Harvard, 1932)

Grierson, P., 'The origins of the English sovereign and the symbolism of the closed crown', *Brit. Num. J.*, XXXIII (1969)

Griffiths, R. A., *The principality of Wales in the later Middle Ages: the structure and personnel of its government*, I, *South Wales 1277–1538* (1972)

Guth, de Lloyd John, 'Exchequer penal law enforcement, 1485–1509', unpublished Ph.D. thesis (Pittsburgh, 1967)

Halstead, Caroline A., *Richard III*, 2 vols (1844)

Hamand, L. A., *The ancient windows of Great Malvern Priory Church* (1947)

Hanbury, H. G., 'The legislation of Richard III', *American J. of Legal Hist.*, 6 (1962)

Hand, G. J., 'The forgotten statutes of Kilkenny: a brief survey', *The Irish Jurist*, n.s. I (1966)

Harriss, G. L., 'Aids, loans, and benevolences', *H.J.*, VI (1963)

Hastings, Margaret, *The court of Common Pleas in fifteenth-century England* (New York, 1947)

Henry, R., *History of Great Britain* (1824)

Holdsworth, Sir William S., *History of English law*, 15 vols (1903–65), I, 7th ed. rev. S. B. Chrimes (1956)

Hooker, J. R., 'Some cautionary notes on Henry VII's Household and Chamber system', *Speculum*, XXIII (1958)

Hope, W. H. St John, 'On the funeral effigies of the kings and queens of England, with special reference to those in the Abbey Church of Westminister', *Archaeologia*, LX (1907)

Howgrave-Graham, R. P., 'The earlier royal funeral effigies: new light on portraiture in Westminster Abbey', *Archaeologia*, XCVIII (1961)

Hughes, P. L., and Larkin, J. F. (eds), *Tudor royal proclamations*, 3 vols (1964–9)

Hurstfield, J. B., 'The revival of feudalism in early Tudor England', *History*, XXXVII (1952)

Hutton, W., *The battle of Bosworth field* (1788), 2nd ed., ed. J. Nichols (1813)

Ives, E. W., 'Promotion in the legal profession of Yorkist and early Tudor England', *L.Q.R.*, 75 (1959)

——, 'The reputation of the common lawyers in English society, 1450–1550', *B.H.J.*, VII (1959–60)

Ives, J., *Select papers, chiefly related to English antiquities* (1773)

Jarman, H. N., 'A map of the routes of Henry Tudor and Rhys ap Thomas through Wales in 1485', *Arch. Camb.*, XCII (1937)

Jay, Winifred, 'List of members of the fourth parliament of Henry VII', *B.H.R.*, III (1925–6)

Jenkins, C., 'Cardinal Morton's register', *Tudor studies*, ed. R. W. Seton-Watson (1924)

Jones, J. Gwynfor, 'The supposed prohibition of intermarriage in 1401' (forthcoming, *Flintshire Hist. Soc. Trans.*)

Jones, T. Artemus, 'Owen Tudor's marriage', *Bull. Bd. Celtic Studies*, XI (1943)

Jones, W. J., *The Elizabethan court of Chancery* (1967)

Kaye, J. M., 'The early history of the legal concept of murder and manslaughter', *L.Q.R.*, 83 (1967)

Kendall, P. M., *Richard III* (1955)

Kingsford, C. L., *English historical literature in the fifteenth century* (1913)

Knecht, R. J., 'The episcopate and the Wars of the Roses', *Birmingham H.J.*, VI (1957–8)

Knowles, M. D., *The religious orders in England*, III, *The Tudor Age* (1959)

Lander, J. R., 'The Yorkist council and administration, 1461–85', *E.H.R.*, LXXII (1958)

——, 'Council, administration and councillors, 1461–85', *B.I.H.R.*, XXXII (1959)

——, 'Attainder and forfeiture, 1553–1609', *H.J.*, IV (1961)

——, *The Wars of the Roses* (1965)

——, *Conflict and stability in fifteenth-century England* (1969)

——, 'Bonds, coercion and fear: Henry VII and the peerage', *Florelegium Historiale: essays presented to Wallace K. Ferguson* (Toronto, 1971)

Lawrence, L. A., 'On the coinage of Henry VII', *Numismatic Chronicle*, 4th ser. XVIII (1918)

Laws, E., and Edwards, E. H., *Church book of St Mary the Virgin, Tenby* (1907)

Lloyd, J. M., 'The rise and fall of the house of Dinefwr (the Rhys family), 1430–1530', unpublished M.A. thesis (Cardiff, 1963)

MacGibbon, D., *Elizabeth Woodville* (1938)

Mackie, J. D., *The early Tudors* (1952)

McKisack, M., *Medieval history in the Tudor age* (1971)

Madden, F., 'Documents relating to Perkin Warbeck', *Archaeologia*, XXVII (1838)

Makinson, A., 'The road to Bosworth field, August 1485', *History Today*, XIII (1963)

Mattingley, G., *Catherine of Aragon* (1942)

——, *Renaissance diplomacy* (1955)

Miller, E., 'Economic policies of governments', *Cambridge economic history of Europe*, III (1963)

Milsom, S. F. C., *Historical foundations of the common law* (1969)

More, Sir Thomas, *Utopia*, ed. A. W. Reed (1931)

——, *The history of King Richard III*, vol. 2, *The complete works*, ed. R. S. Sylvester (New Haven and London, 1963)

Mullet, M. E., 'Anglo-Florentine commercial relations, 1465–1491', *Econ.H.R.*, 2nd ser. XV (1962)

Newton, A. P., 'The King's Chamber under the early Tudors', *E.H.R.*, XXXII (1917)

Nicolas, Sir H., and Courthope, W. (eds), *The historic peerage* (1857)

Oppenheim, M., *Naval accounts and inventories of the reign of Henry VII*, Navy Records Soc., VIII (1896)

Otway-Ruthven, J., *The King's Secretary and Signet office in the fifteenth century* (1939)

——, *A history of mediaeval Ireland* (1968)

Owen, E., 'The decline of the Tudors of Penmynydd, Môn', *Trans. Anglesey Antiquarian Soc.* (1934)

Parry, J. H., *The age of reconnaisance* (1963)

Pauli, R., *Geschichte von England*, V (Gotha, 1858)

Pelicier, P., *Essai sur le gouvernemat de la Dame de Beaujeu, 1483–91* (Chartres, 1882)

Penrose, B., *Travel and discovery in the Renaissance, 1420–1620* (1963)

Pickthorn, K. W. M., *Early Tudor government*, I, *Henry VII* (1934)

Pocquet du Haut-Jussé, B. A., *François II, duc de Bretagne et l'Angleterre, 1458–88* (Paris, 1929)

Pollard, A. F., 'The "de facto" act of Henry VII', *B.I.H.R.*, VII (1929)

——, 'Council, Star Chamber, and Privy Council under the Tudors', *E.H.R.*, XXXVII (1922)

Pollard, A. W., and Redgrave, G. R., *Short-title catalogue of books printed in England, 1475–1640* (1926)

Pope-Hennessy, J., *Italian Renaissance sculpture* (1958)

Powell, J. Enoch, and Wallis, Keith, *The house of lords in the Middle Ages* (1965)

Power, E., and Postan, M. M., *Studies in English trade in the fifteenth century* (1933)

Prall, S. E., 'The development of equity in Tudor England', *American J. Legal Hist.*, 8 (1964)

Pugh, T. B., 'The indentures for the Marches between Henry VII and Edward Stafford, duke of Buckingham, 1477–1521', *E.H.R.*, LXXI (1956)

——, *The marcher lordships of South Wales, 1415–1536* (1963)

—— (ed.), *Glamorgan county history*, III, *The Middle Ages* (1971)

Pulling, A., *The order of the Coif* (1884)

Putnam, B. H. (ed.), *Early treatises on the practice of the Justices of the Peace in the fifteenth and sixteenth centuries* (1924)

—— (ed.), *Proceedings before the Justices of the Peace in the fourteenth and fifteenth centuries* (1938)

Quinn, D. B., 'The early interpretation of Poynings's Law, 1494–1534', *Irish Hist. Soc.*, II (1940–1)

Ramsay, Sir James H., *Lancaster and York*, 2 vols (1892)

Ramsey, P., 'Overseas trade in the reign of Henry VII: the evidence of the Customs accounts', *Econ.H.R.*, 2nd ser. VI (1953–4)

——, *Tudor economic problems* (1963)

Rees, William, *An historical atlas of Wales* (1951)

Reid, R. R., *The King's Council in the north* (1924)

Richardson, H. G., and Sayles, G. O., *The Irish parliament in the Middle Ages* (1952)

Richardson, W. C., 'The surveyor of the King's Prerogative', *E.H.R.*, LVI (1941)

——, *Tudor chamber administration, 1485–1547* (1952)

Richmond, C. F., 'English naval power in the fifteenth century', *History*, LII (1967)

Roberts, Glyn, 'Wyrion Eden', *Trans. Anglesey Antiquarian Soc.* (1951)

Roper, W., *Life of Sir Thomas More* (1626), ed. of 1907

Roskell, J. S., 'The problem of the attendance of the lords in mediaeval parliaments', *B.I.H.R.*, XXIX (1956)

——, *The commons and their speakers in English parliaments, 1376–1523* (1965)

Roth, C., 'Perkin Warbeck and his Jewish master', *Trans. Jewish Hist. Soc. of England*, IX (1922)

Rowse, A. L., *Bosworth field and the Wars of the Roses* (1966)

Rushforth, G. McN., *Mediaeval Christian imagery as illustrated by the painted windows of Great Malvern Priory Church* (1936)

Russell, W. Dane, 'The Lady Margaret Beaufort and Henry VII', *Arch. Camb.*, XVI, 6th ser. (1916)

Ryland, R. H., *History of Waterford* (Dublin, 1824)

Scammell, S. V., 'Ship-owning in England, c. 1450–1550', *T.R.H.S.*, 5th ser. 12 (1962)

Scarisbrick, J. J., 'Clerical taxation in England, 1485–1547', *J. Eccles. Hist.*, II (1960)

——, *Henry VIII* (1968)

Schanz, G., *Englische Handelspolitik gegen ende des mittelalters*, 2 vols (Leipzig, 1881)

Schofield, R. S., 'Parliamentary lay taxation, 1485–1547', unpublished Ph.D. thesis (Cambridge, 1964)

Schramm, P. E., *A history of the English coronation* (1937)

Scofield, Cora L., *The life and reign of Edward IV*, 2 vols (1923)

Skeel, C. A. J., *The council in the Marches of Wales* (1904)

——, 'Wales under Henry VII', *Tudor studies*, ed. R. W. Seton-Watson (1924)

Smith, J. Beverley, 'Crown and community, in the principality of North Wales in the reign of Henry Tudor', *W.H.R.*, 3 (1966)

Somerville, R., 'Henry VII's "Council Learned in the Law" ', *E.H.R.*, LIV (1939)

——, *History of the duchy of Lancaster* (1953)

Steele, R. (ed.), *A bibliography of royal proclamations of the Tudor and Stuart sovereigns, 1485–1714* (Bib. Lindesiana, V), I, *England and Wales* (1910)

Storey, R. L., 'The wardens of the Marches of England towards Scotland, 1377–1489', *E.H.R.*, LXXII (1957)

——, *The reign of Henry VII* (1968)

Strickland, Agnes, *Lives of the queens of England*, 2nd ed. (1841)

Strong, Roy, *Tudor and Jacobean portraits*, 2 vols (1969)

Stubbs, W., *The constitutional history of England*, 3 vols, 5th ed. (1903)

Tanner, J. R. (ed.), *Tudor constitutional documents* (1930)

Taswell-Langmead, T. P., *English constitutional history*, 11th ed. by T. F. T. Plucknett (1960)

Thirsk, Joan (ed. and cont.), *The agrarian history of England and Wales*, IV (1967)

Thomas, D. H., 'The Herberts of Raglan as supporters of the house of York in the second half of the fifteenth century', unpublished M.A. thesis (Cardiff, 1968)

Thomas, Roger S., 'The political career, estates, and "connection" of Jasper Tudor, earl of Pembroke and duke of Bedford (d. 1495)', unpublished Ph.D. thesis (Swansea, 1971)

Thompson, A. Hamilton, *The English clergy and their organization in the later Middle Ages* (1949)

Thomson, Gladys Scott, *The lords lieutenant in the sixteenth century* (1923)

Thomson, J. F., *The later Lollards, 1414–1510* (1965)

Thorne, S. (ed.), *Prerogativa regis* (Yale, 1949)

——, *Readings and moots at the inns of court in the fifteenth century*, S.S., 71 (1954)

Thornley, Isobel D., 'The destruction of sanctuary', *Tudor Studies*, ed. R. W. Seton-Watson (1924)

Vickers, K., *Humphrey, duke of Gloucester* (1907)

Ward, G. F., 'The early history of the Merchant Staplers', *E.H.R.*, XXXIII (1918)

Wedgwood, J. C. (ed.), *History of parliament, 1439–1509*, 2 vols (1936)

Wernham, R. B., *Before the Armada* (1966)

Williams, C. H., 'The rebellion of Humphrey Stafford in 1486', *E.H.R.*, XLIII (1928)

Williams, D., 'The family of Henry VII', *History Today*, IV (1954)

Williams, Glanmor, *The Welsh church from the Conquest to the Reformation* (1962)

Williams, Penry, *The council in the Marches of Wales* (1958)

Williams, W. Tom, 'Henry of Richmond's itinerary through Wales', *Y Cymmrodor*, XXIX (1919)

Williamson, J. A., 'The Cabot voyages and Bristol Discovery under Henry VII', *Hakluyt Soc.*, 2nd ser. CXX (1962)

Winfield, P. H., *The chief sources of English legal history* (1925)

Winstanley, E. J., 'Coinage of Henry VII', *Brit. Num. J.*, XXX (1960–1)

Wolffe, B. P., 'The management of English royal estates under the Yorkist kings', *E.H.R.*, LXXI (1956)

——, 'Henry VII's land revenues and Chamber finance', ibid. LXXIX (1964)

——, *The Crown lands, 1461–1536* (1970)

——, *The royal demesne in English history* (1971)

Yale, D. E. C. (ed.), *Epieikia* (Yale, 1953)

INDEX

Abingdon, abbot of, conspirator, 88, n. 2
Actoris, Peter, king's stationer, 307, n. 1
Acts of parliament, conception of repeal,
179
  assemblies, riots, etc., 189–90
  attainder, 177, 207 and n., 328–9
  benefit of clergy, 243 and n.
  'de facto', 178–9
  ecclesiastical matters, 243
  enclosure, 222, 223–4
  justices of the peace, 169–70, 176, n.
  14, 178
  Hanseatic League, 236 and n. 2
  Navigation, 220, 235, 237
  pro camera stellata, 78, 100 and n. 1,
  148, 154 and n. 3, 155, 156 and
  n. 4, 178, 179, 186
  resumption, 120, 123–4, 206
  retaining unlawfully, 188–9
  statuta de Praerogativa regis, 210
  treason, 186
  Union of Wales and Crown of England, 246–7, 248, 252.
  See also under Legislation
Administration, financial, overlap and
  development of Yorkist expertise,
  119, 124; reorganization of the
  Household, 127; keepership of Jewel
  House, 127; uses of money received,
  128; investment of surplus, 128;
  future of Exchequer, 129; profits of
  wardships and marriages, 129;
  audit process, 131, 208; unsophisti-
  cated presentation of accounts, 132;
  confusion of officer and office, 132;
  position of Council Learned, 133;
  payment of debts, 133 and n. 2;
  collection of feudal incidents, 182;
  management of landed revenues,
  208; and State's increasing needs,
  211; nature of bonds (obligations
  and recognizances), 212–14
Adrian de Castello, bp. of Bath and
  Wells, 242, 243, 298, n. 3
Adventurers to the New Found Lands, 230
Albert, duke of Saxony, and Warbeck, 83
Alcock, John, bp. of Worcester, 242;
  opens parliament, 61; interim chancellor, 105; president of Prince's
  Council, 249

Alexander VI, Pope, 85, 273, n. 2, 281,
  n. 2, 283, Henry VII and, 240; death,
  286
Alleyn, John, baron of the Exchequer, 158
Alnwick, William, bp. of Lincoln, 325
Andreas Scotus, tutor to Henry VII, 16,
  n. 5
Anglesey, 4, 248; charter of privilege,
  254, 255
Ann Neville, queen of Richard III, 337;
  death in 1485, 35, 38, 205
Anne of Beaujeu, sister of Charles VIII,
  31–2, 79, 273
Anne, duchess of Brittany, 80, 83, 204,
  280; marriage to Charles VIII, 80,
  273, 281; wardship, 280
Antwerp, removal of the Staple, 83;
  trading centre, 232; economic sanctions, 232–3; conference on Hanse,
  235–6, 237
Arthur, Prince of Wales, 245, 249, 250;
  birth, 66–7, 78; marriage to Catherine
  of Aragon, 81, 89, 92, 93, 116, 250,
  273, 278, 280, 284–5; death, 91, 93,
  216, 251, 278, 280, 284–5, 302–4;
  warden-general, 98; knighting, 200;
  financial provisions, 206; earl of
  Chester, 249, 250; guardianship, 249;
  residence at Ludlow, 249, 250; judicial
  powers, 250; marcher lordships, 250;
  depicture, 335; burial place, 337
Arundel, Sir Thomas, 327
Ashton, Christoper, 91, n. 2
Ashwell, Robert (*alias* Lancaster), 11
Assheton, Ralph, vice-chamberlain, 24,
  n. 4
Atherstone, 41; meeting between Henry
  VII and Lord Stanley, 45 and n. 1,
  331; compensation, 54, n. 1
Attainder and forfeiture, effect of, 63,
  n. 2, 328; need for parliamentary
  assent, 135 and n. 5, 161; and land
  forfeiture, 207; numbers affected, 207,
  328; proceeds from, 207 and n. 3; the
  peerage and, 215; four acts, 328–9
Audley, Edmund, bishoprics, 242 and n. 3
Ayala, Pedro, Spanish ambassador, in
  Scotland, 284; despatch to Ferdinand,
  284 and n. 8; in Flanders, 288; on
  Henry VII, 300–1